The Mighty
Warrior Kings

To Joyce
Out of the bleakness of the cold and dark winter days
That sweeps across the barren garden
You bring the first rose of spring to me
Now walk with me through fields of golden flowers
And be my love in joy and tranquillity

The Mighty Warrior Kings

From the Ashes of the Roman Empire to the New Ruling Order

Philip J Potter

PEN & SWORD
HISTORY

First published in Great Britain in 2020 by
Pen & Sword History
An imprint of
Pen & Sword Books Ltd
Yorkshire – Philadelphia

ISBN 978 1 52675 626 8

Printed and bound in the UK by TJ International Ltd,
Padstow, Cornwall.

Pen & Sword Books Limited incorporates the imprints of Atlas,
Archaeology, Aviation, Discovery, Family History, Fiction, History,
Maritime, Military, Military Classics, Politics, Select, Transport,
True Crime, Air World, Frontline Publishing, Leo Cooper, Remember
When, Seaforth Publishing, The Praetorian Press, Wharncliffe
Local History, Wharncliffe Transport, Wharncliffe True Crime
and White Owl.

For a complete list of Pen & Sword titles please contact

PEN & SWORD BOOKS LIMITED
47 Church Street, Barnsley, South Yorkshire, S70 2AS, England
E-mail: enquiries@pen-and-sword.co.uk
Website: www.pen-and-sword.co.uk

Or

PEN AND SWORD BOOKS
1950 Lawrence Rd, Havertown, PA 19083, USA
E-mail: Uspen-and-sword@casematepublishers.com
Website: www.penandswordbooks.com

Contents

Prelude

D uring the era of *Pax Romana*, the Roman Empire brought 200 years of order, stability and prosperity to a large region of Europe, whose boundaries stretched from Britain in the north to the Danube in the east, south to Egypt and along the coast of northern Africa to Spain in the west. The assassination of Julius Caesar in 44 BC was the stimulus for the creation of the *Pax Romana*. Following Caesar's death, a period of civil war erupted for control of Rome. From this ruthless turmoil the Second Triumvirate emerged, with Marius Lepidus, Mark Antony and Octavian ruling jointly in the name of the people. The new triumvirate governed for ten years before internal dissent again broke out in civil war. After Lepidus was forced out of the government, Octavian moved against Antony, defeating him at the Battle of Actium on 2 September 31 BC. He was now acknowledged as master of the Roman world and his reign marked the beginning of the *Pax Romana*.

The Roman Empire reached its peak of power in AD 180 under the reign of Emperor Marcus Aurelius. Thereafter, its western lands began a gradual deterioration militarily, politically and economically. The decline and eventual collapse of the Empire took place over a period of years before reaching its climax in the middle of the fifth century. The final phase of Rome's demise began in the mid-fourth century as the Huns stormed out of central Asia, driving the local Germanic tribes westward into a collision with the Romans. In 376 the pagan Visigoths crossed the Danube, which had served as the boundary of the Roman Empire in the east, driving back the imperial troops. In the following years the 'barbarians' swept through the Empire, with the Visigoths seizing control of Spain, the Franks occupying Gaul and the Burgundians settling in south-eastern France, while the Angles and Saxons crossed the Channel to take possession of current-day England, beating back the native Britons to establish their independent rule. In the aftermath of the sack of Rome by the Vandals in 455, Italy was ruled by a succession of pagan generals and the Roman emperor served only as a figurehead. In 476 the Germanic mercenary soldiers, who made up the majority of the imperial army, rebelled and proclaimed their chieftain, Odoacer, as king. After defeating the imperial forces at the Battle of Pavia, the last emperor, Romulus Augustus, was deposed, thus ending the Roman Empire's rule across Europe. The year 476 marked the final breakdown of the centuries-old Roman political system and the dawn of the so-called Dark Ages that swept across the defenceless European lands.

In the vacuum created by the collapse of the Roman Empire, pagan chieftains seized power by force of arms, creating new kingdoms that would battle for supremacy across Europe. The Germanic tribes across the eastern bank of the Danube continued to rule their lands, while to the west in modern-day France, the Franks began to consolidate their power. The invading Angles, Saxons and Jutes established their independent monarchies in Britain. In current-day England, the small kingdom of Kent developed in the fifth century after the immigration of the barbarian Jutes. Located on the south-eastern coast of England, between Wessex and Mercia, the kings of Kent struggled to maintain their independence against their larger, stronger neighbours. The monarchy of East Anglia, situated north of Kent, was settled in the fifth century. During the 700s, the Kent regime fell under Mercian control and was later incorporated into Wessex. To the north, Northumbria was established from the small Deira and Bernicia monarchies and united by King Aethelfrith in the early seventh century. Northumbria suffered severely from frequent Viking raids and pillaging attacks across the North Sea. Mercia developed into one of the most powerful Anglo-Saxon realms. In the seventh and eighth centuries, Mercian might and influence was at its summit, but its dominance later passed to Wessex. Wessex was the last Anglo-Saxon demesne to be settled, later developing into the nucleus for a united kingdom of England. It was founded in the sixth century with the migration of Germanic immigrants and Jutes from Kent. Wessex gained greatly from the damage inflicted on its rivals – East Anglia, Northumbria and Mercia – by the unrelenting Viking forays. Beginning in 802 under the rule of King Egbert, the monarchy of Wessex expanded its lands to reign over most of modern-day England, with only Mercia and Northumbria retaining their independence. However, the political system of England began to crumble in the 850s as the Vikings from Scandinavia overran the Anglo-Saxon kingdoms and created a new ruling order.

While the Angles, Saxons and Jutes established their kingdoms in Britain, across the English Channel in Gaul – modern-day France – the Franks had become the dominant tribe, first settling in the north-west of the region. By the middle of the fifth century, northern Gaul had been brought under the Franks' control by the first Merovingian king, Childeric. He unified the north-west Salian tribes and in 481 bequeathed to his son, Clovis, the beginnings of a united France. After safeguarding his sovereignty over the northern tribes, in 500 Clovis began the conquest of southern Gaul, which was completed seven years later following his victory over the Visigoths at Poitiers. In the aftermath of Clovis' death in 511, the Merovingian realm was thrown into 250 years of internal turmoil under the reigns of weak, ineffectual kings, resulting in the break-up of the kingdom into sub-monarchies and ongoing civil wars. There were twenty recognized Merovingian monarchs, who reigned primarily in only Austrasia in north central Gaul and Neustria in the north-west. The southern areas of Aquitaine, Septimania and Burgundy were largely lost to local kings, who were dominant enough to establish their own regimes.

The later Merovingian sovereigns became known as the 'do-nothing kings' and were under the authority of controlling barons and high churchmen. The real power now rested with the court official known as the Mayor of the Palace, who governed the realm in the name of the monarch. In 687 Pippin II, ruling as Mayor of the Palace in Austrasia, invaded Neustria and defeated King Theuderic III's army at the Battle of Tertry, seizing his kingdom. Pippin II did not claim the monarchy as king, but ruled the united northern Frankish Kingdom as Mayor of the Palace with separate figurehead monarchs in Austrasia and Neustria.

After Pippin II's death in 714, his son, Charles Martel, was acknowledged as Mayor of the Palace in Austrasia, but the nobles and ecclesiastic magnates in Neustria rebelled, challenging his rule. By 723 the uprising had been crushed and Charles reigned over the untied Frankish realm in the north. With his government secure in Austrasia and Neustria, Charles expanded his supremacy into the southern princedoms, and by his death in 741 had established control throughout most of Gaul, passing a unified kingdom to his sons, Pippin III and Carloman, who continued to solidify and enlarge their sphere of power in Gaul.

Chapter One

Charlemagne

Forefather of the Holy Roman Empire

By 771 Charlemagne, or Charles the Great, was the acknowledged king of the Frankish realm, and spent the next thirty years establishing his kingdom with the sword and cross into the Holy Roman Empire. His vast empire extended through modern-day France, the Netherlands and Belgium into Switzerland and large regions of Germany, Spain and Austria. As ruler over most of Europe, Charlemagne was recognized by the papacy as the defender of the Christian Church and promoter of the religion. When the governing pontiff, Leo III, was accused of perjury and immoral acts, he was forced to flee to the court of Charlemagne in Germany for protection against rioting Roman mobs. The sovereign agreed to intervene to settle the growing rift, sending Leo III back to Rome with an escort of Frankish bishops and noblemen. Before the pope departed from Paderborn, the Francian king agreed to follow him to the Holy City and convene a conclave to settle the crisis. In late autumn 800 the monarch travelled to Rome and soon assembled his council of Frankish and Roman priests and nobles. At the synod on 23 December, in the presence of Charlemagne, the pontiff swore an oath of his innocence with his hand on the Holy Scriptures, and was exonerated of the charges. Two days later at St Peter's Basilica, as Charlemagne ended his prayers following High Mass, Leo III came forward, placing a jewelled crown of gold on his head and announcing to the worshipers: 'Long life and victory to Charles, the most pious Augustus, the great emperor and peacemaker, anointed by God.' The coronation signalled to the courts of Europe and Asia the restoration of the Western Roman Empire, with Emperor Charlemagne at its head.

Charles was the eldest legitimate son of the Frankish ruler, Pippin III, and Queen Bertrada, and was born on 2 April 742 near Liege in present-day Belgium. At the time of his birth, Charles' father served the last figurehead Merovingian king, Childeric III, as Mayor of the Palace. As mayor he ruled the kingdom in the name of the monarch, administering his government and fighting his wars. Charles spent his first years under the care of his mother in the Merovingian court. Pippin was frequently away from the palace and Charles developed a close relationship with Bertrada, who remained an influence on him throughout her life. Around the age of seven he began his education at the palace school with the sons of other government officials and nobles, with the Abbot of St Denis, Fulrad, as his principal tutor. He was taught to read and write to a level above a prince of his time. Attending classes at the school, the future emperor's education also included the study of mathematics, geometry, music and astronomy, along with the languages of Latin and Greek. Through the influence of Bertrada and Fulrad, Charles acquired a deep devotion to the Christian Church and the teachings of Jesus, which greatly affected his future policies in the governing of the imperial empire.

While Charles was acquiring his academic education, he began martial training as a feudal warlord. When Pippin III became King of Frankland, he commanded an army comprised of freemen from all parts of his realm, who were required to serve when summoned with their own weapons, armour, provisions and equipment. The size of the army varied, but for a major war against the Saxons or Lombards it likely approached 100,000 soldiers, with a cavalry force of over 30,000. The troops were usually mustered in the spring and the campaigning season lasted until late in the autumn. The men received no pay but shared in the plunder of a successful battle, and were occasionally allowed to pillage the enemy's towns and countryside. As a son of the sovereign, Charles was expected to lead soldiers in the regime's battles against its enemies, and was associated with the Carolingian army at a young age.

Under the tutelage of experienced warriors, Charles was taught to fight with the weapons of a Frankish soldier. He spent long hours practicing with the short sword, battle axe and spear of an infantryman. The foot soldiers in the Frankish army also carried a bow with a quiver of arrows, and the young lord developed into a skilled archer under the guidance of veteran instructors. Charles also trained as a mounted soldier, learning to ride a warhorse and charge into an enemy formation with the long sword and spear of a cavalryman. As a horseman, he was dressed in a protective leather jacket with iron plates and wore an armoured helmet. The area around the royal palace was heavily forested, and Charles honed his battle skills by hunting deer and wild boar in the dense woodlands. In preparation for his future assumption of the throne, Charles frequently took part in his father's wars against rebellious nobles, experiencing the hardships of campaigning while gaining experience in the leadership skills and war tactics of a Carolingian warlord.

As a son of the king and member of his court, Charles was exposed to the daily administration of the kingdom, attending council meetings with noblemen and priests while listening to his father's discussions with visiting foreign envoys. He regularly attended the annual assembly of Frankish nobles and prelates, where he personally experienced the political and diplomatic skills required to govern the expanding kingdom of Pippin, while learning court etiquette. As a Frankish nobleman, Charles was always attired in the national dress, refusing to wear the garments of foreign kingdoms. In the warm weather he dressed in a tunic over a linen shirt, with cotton trousers and long hose wrapped in bands of cloth. For greater warmth during the winter months, Charles wore an otterskin jacket and long blue cloak around his shoulders. During feast days the Carolingian prince was attired in apparel of gold cloth, golden crown on his head and jewelled shoes on his feet.

While Charles continued his education and participated in his father's military campaigns, Pippin made preparations to overthrow the ruling Merovingian monarchy. In 741, following the death of his father, Charles Martel, Pippin assumed the office of Mayor of the Palace for the Kingdom of Neustria, while his older brother, Carloman, ruled Austrasia and Aquitaine as Mayor. Six years later Pippin usurped the government of his brother to now rule the unified Merovingian realm in the name of the king. The prior reigns by the weak Merovingian monarchs and rebellions of their warring vassals had created disarray in the kingdom. There was no functioning central government and the laws were ignored, while the warlords, who held the power, battled each other for supremacy.

By 750 the Mayor had solidified his rule over the nobles and Church and felt secure in his power to seize the Merovingian throne from King Childeric III. Before deposing the monarch, he needed to establish a legal claim to the crown, sending the Abbot of St Denis, Fulrad, with the Bishop of Wurzburg, Burcard, to Rome to petition for Pope Zacharias' approval. When the two envoys were brought before the pontiff in St Peter's, on behalf of Pippin they asked: 'Should a ruler who was without kingly power continue to be called king?' They added that the Frankish people felt abandoned without the authority of a real king and longed to be protected by a powerful ruler. The papacy-ruled duchy in the north-east had been under attack by the Lombards and Zacharias urgently needed military aid to defend his lands, looking to Pippin to intervene on his behalf. To gain the favour of the palace Mayor, the pontiff sent word to Pippin, telling him: 'He who has the power should be recognized as king.' The pontiff ended his response by ordering the coronation of Pippin. Zacharias' message gave the Mayor a legal basis to act against the monarch, and with a united political base supporting him, Pippin III was elected sovereign by the nobles and prelates in 751. Before a large assembly of Carolingian noblemen, priests and peasants in November at the town of Soissons in modern-day France, sixty miles north-east of Paris, Pippin III and Bertrada were anointed with holy oil by the Archbishop of Mainz, Boniface, and crowned king and queen. The new monarch swore an oath pledging to rule as a Christian and defend the Church. As the eldest legitimate heir of Pippin III, the nine-year-old Charles likely attended the coronation ceremony, and he and his recently born brother Carloman were recognized as successors to what became the Carolingian Empire.

In the aftermath of his usurpation of the Merovingian kingdom, Pippin quickly solidified his rule and increasingly included Charles in his military campaigns and governmental council meetings. The papacy had agreed to sanction Pippin's seizure of Childeric III's realm to gain influence at the Frankish court, and now, following the capture of northern Italy by the King of Lombardy, Aistulf, and facing the threat of the sack of Rome by the Lombard tribes, the pope turned to the new king for military support. In early 753, in great secrecy, the new pope, Stephen II, sent an urgent message to Pippin requesting a private meeting with him. When the king received the pope's letter, he agreed to the conference, sending Frankish dignitaries to escort the pontiff from Rome to his court near Paris.

Pope Stephen II departed from the Holy City in October 753, slowly making his way north with an escort party of nobles, priests and soldiers. The papal assemblage crossed the snow-covered Alps into current-day France in the bitterly cold closing days of the year, and as the delegation continued to travel toward Paris it was met by a welcoming party of nobles and prelates from Pippin. To honour the pope, the sovereign appointed his eleven-year-old son, Charles, as head of the retinue. The Frankish embassy rode south-east, and finally, after many weeks of travelling, saw the pontiff in the distance. Charles ordered the noblemen and prelates to dismount, and as Stephen II neared, walked forward to greet him, falling to his knees to receive the papal blessing. With Charles leading the way, the Franks and Romans resumed their journey, meeting Pippin near his palace at Ponthion north of Paris. The monarch dismounted and prostrated himself in front of the pontiff before leading him to the warmth and comfort of his palace after his arduous mission to reclaim his lost northern papal lands.

Seeking the intervention of the Frankish regime against the marauding Lombards, Stephen II remained at the palace for several weeks discussing the plight of the Holy City. The pontiff asked that Rome and its lands be freed of the alien menace posed by Aistulf. During the talks, Stephen II requested military assistance from the Franks against the Lombards, citing the Constantine Donation, which ceded to the pope spiritual and secular authority over the Western Roman Empire, and compelled Pippin to intervene in defence of the papacy. As the negotiations continued at the royal palace, Charles frequently attended the meetings, learning the skills of diplomacy first-hand from his father. The Frankish king had earlier signed a treaty of peace with the Lombards, and needed to first receive the approval of his nobles and chieftains at the annual assembly in early March before agreeing to intervene in Italy. The Italian region usurped by Aistulf was also claimed by the Eastern Roman Empire, and the Carolingian monarch was reluctant to incur the anger of Emperor Constantine V. While the pontiff waited for the meeting of the warlords, he relocated to the Abbey of St Denis to rest and recover from the long journey from Rome.

As the king remained at Ponthion, on the advice of his leading noblemen he opened negotiations with Aistulf to find a peaceful resolution. Pippin

III was unwilling to intervene in Italy without the full support of his nobles, and was hopeful the talks would succeed. The Lombard king had little interest in abandoning his recent Italian conquests, sending Pippin's brother, Carloman, to defend his occupation of the territory. Carloman had earlier renounced his properties and had withdrawn to the monastery at Monte Cassino, south-east of Rome, following his brother's seizure of his realm. When the Frankish monarch met Carloman, he quickly ordered his arrest and imprisonment to guard against his attempted usurpation of the Carolingian regime. In March 754 the Frankish nobles assembled at Quierzy to offer advice to their overlord. During the grand assembly, Pippin convinced his vassals of the need for the Italian campaign and sent a message to the pope promising to restore the seized papal lands. In return for his protection, Stephen II agreed to crown Pippin as King of the Franks. On 28 July 754 at the Abbey of St Denis, before a large assemblage of nobles, prelates and peasants, the pope anointed Pippin III, Bertrada and the two sons with holy oil to legitimize the assumption of the throne by the Carolingians. Following the anointment, Pippin swore an oath to rule as a Christian king and protect the Holy See against all enemies.

During the winter of 755 the Franks began preparations for the campaign in support of the papacy, under the watchful eye of the king and Charles, who was increasingly assuming a larger role in the governing of the regime. In March Pippin III led his army south through the Alps into the plains of Italy, marching his troops to Pavia in south-western Lombardy to attack King Aistulf. At the approach of the Carolingians, the King of the Lombards refused to deploy his men into battle formation, withdrawing into the defensive works of the city and forcing Pippin to begin siege operations. After a brief investment, the Lombard king agreed to negotiate a settlement. Under the terms of the treaty, Aistulf pledged to restore the seized Italian cities and lands claimed by the pope and pay a sizeable tribute to Pippin. The incursion was over quickly, and with the promise of the Lombards to abandon the papal territory, the Frankish king and Charles returned north through the Alps with their army to their kingdom, with chests of gold and silver.

Pippin and Charles returned to their court, but soon received a message from Stephen II that Aistulf had broken his promises and was now advancing his army south against Rome. Pippin, occupied with ruling his large kingdom and defending his overlordship against mutinous vassals, was reluctant to again travel into Italy in defence of the papacy. Stephen II sent additional envoys to the Carolingian court, telling the king and his son they risked eternal damnation if they refused to rescue the Holy City of God. Fearful of being denied the Kingdom of God, Pippin assembled his army and again advanced over the mountains in the spring of 756. As he moved against the rebellious Lombards, Aistulf lifted his siege against Rome, proceeding north to confront the Franks. However, when the Lombard king saw the size of the enemy forces, he surrendered without a fight. Aistulf was forced to relinquish his seized territory to the Franks and provide hostages to guarantee his compliance with the agreed terms. Shortly after the submission of the Lombards, an embassy arrived at the Frankish encampment from Constantine V of the Eastern Roman Empire, demanding the immediate return of his cities and lands taken by King Aistulf. Despite the offers of numerous gifts, Pippin refused to comply. He sent the Abbot of St Denis to Pope Stephen II with a document transferring his conquest to the papacy, which became known as the Donation of Pippin III. With the ceding of the northern Italian territories to the pontiff and his successors, the Papal States were created.

By 756 Pippin III ruled a kingdom that reached from the Atlantic Ocean in the west to the Danube in the east and south to the Mediterranean. When Charles reached the age of fifteen in 757, his father appointed him ruler of his Austrasian lands, in present-day Normandy, to give him experience in governing the frequently rebellious local warlords. While the Carolingian prince intervened frequently in his Austrasian duchies to maintain obedience from the local nobles, the Duke of Aquitaine, Waifer, rebelled against the overlordship of Charles by force of arms. With part of the Carolingian kingdom now in revolt, Pippin and Charles began preparations for a spring attack against the Aquitainian duke, reinforcing the Frankish army and demanding additional troops from their vassals, while also expanding the strength of the cavalry forces.

As the weather improved, the Frankish forces advanced south into Aquitaine to begin a lengthy campaign to subdue Duke Waifer. Charles spent the next nine years in the duchy, slowly regaining control of the region. The Aquitainians withdrew to their fortified towns, forcing Pippin and Charles to deploy their troops around the defensive works and begin time-consuming siege operations. The Franks gradually moved across the duchy, seizing the areas of Auvergne, Berry and Quercy. By 768 the king, with Charles at his side, was at the southern end of Aquitaine, defeating the local Basques and forcing their submission to complete the subjugation of the rebellious duchy.

While the Franks continued the subjugation of Aquitaine, Charles was also involved with uprisings in Bavaria led by Duke Tassilo and military expeditions along the eastern border against marauding barbarian incursions. During the periods when the Frankish army was not in the field, the king and his two sons remained at court governing the kingdom. In 757 Pope Stephen II died and was succeeded by Paul I. The new pontiff followed his predecessor's policy of friendship with the Frankish crown, sending frequent letters to Pippin reminding him of his obligations to defend the papacy. When the new King of Lombardy, Desiderius, delayed surrendering the northern Italian towns of Bologna, Imola and Ancona to the papacy, as previously pledged by Aistulf, Paul I sent urgent messages to his Frankish protectors imploring their intervention, but Pippin was too involved with his campaigns against rebellious vassals to travel into Italy.

As the two Carolingian heirs to the throne continued to lead the army and rule the realm, Charles was married according to Frankish law to Himiltrude, who bore him a deformed male child. The prince named the boy after his father, and he became known as Pippin the Hunchback. The marriage to Himiltrude was outside the Church, and the question of Pippin's legitimacy led to the future dissidence between him and his three younger half-brothers.

During the final months of the subjugation campaign against Aquitaine, Pippin became increasingly ill. After the peace treaty with the Aquitainians was settled, he began the long journey to his palace at Ponthion, but after reaching St Denis Abbey was forced to stop and rest. As the king remained at St Denis, he grew weaker daily, dying on 24 September 768, and was buried at the abbey before an assemblage of nobles, prelates and peasants. On the eve of his death, in the presence of his magnates and chieftains, the king partitioned his kingdom between Charles and Carloman, in accordance with the old Frankish custom.

The relationship between Charles and his younger brother had grown increasing antagonistic during the several years prior to the king's death, and Pippin's division of the kingdom reinforced their hostile feelings. According to Pippin's orders, Charles was assigned the lands along the Atlantic coast and eastward toward the Rhine, while his brother received the central region of the kingdom. Charles established the capital of his Austrasian realm at Noyon in current-day northern France, sixty miles from Paris. After his affirmation by an assembly of nobles and vassals as King of Frankland, Charles was crowned overlord of the Carolingian Kingdom at the cathedral in Noyon on 9 October. Soon after the Austrasian king's coronation, the Duchy of Aquitaine again revolted, attempting to take advantage of the uncertainty during the transitional period following the death of Pippin. Charles assembled his army, marching southward to unite with the forces of Carloman for a combined attack against the duchy. A dispute quickly erupted between the two brothers when they met in northern Aquitaine, Carloman withdrawing his troops from the war. The Frankish king had campaigned extensively in the duchy with his father, and now moved alone against the Aquitainians, who were under the command of their new duke, Hunald. The Aquitainians were defeated in a lightning two-month offensive, compelling Duke Hunald to surrender. Following the suppression of the uprising, Charles built a strong fortification by the Dordogne River at the current-day south-western French city of Fronsac to keep a close vigil on the recalcitrant Aquitainians. After his defeat, Duke Hunald fled from his duchy to avoid capture, seeking refuge at the court of the Duke of Gascony, Lupo II. Charles ordered the pursuit of Hunald, and he was soon taken prisoner in Gascony after Lupo II refused to provide sanctuary. While the king remained in Aquitaine, the Duke of Gascony appeared before him offering homage for his lands, ensuring his continued loyalty. Before leaving for his palace in the north, the Austrasian king established a new local government, issuing a set of laws and regulations for the administration of the duchy. The Aquitainians were allowed to govern themselves under the king's rule, but were required to recognize Charles as their overlord and provide him with soldiers in times of war. The once-rebellious duchy thereafter remained loyal to Charles and his successors.

Carloman's refusal to participate in the campaign against Aquitaine intensified the ongoing animosity between the two brothers. Charles' successful intervention against the Aquitainians heightened his renown and prestige among his vassals and clerics, solidifying his power over the Austrasia region of the Frankish realm. The Abbot of St Denis, a close advisor to Pippin III, interceded on several occasions in an attempt to settle the dispute between the brothers, but was unable to resolve the controversy. When the new Pope Stephen III learned of the hostile feelings between the co-Frankish rulers, he sent letters to the Austrasian king and Carloman, reminding them of the importance of their united responsibility to safeguard the papacy against Lombardy. The messages of the pope were ignored by the brothers, and the dissension continued to escalate toward civil war.

To prevent Carloman from establishing military alliances with his neighboring realms, Charles decided to divorce his wife and marry a daughter of King Desiderius of Lombardy, thereby gaining his friendship. Desiderius' three daughters were directly related to the Duke of Bavaria, and the marriage would strengthen Frankish influence with Duke Tassilo. The Austrasian monarch sent his mother, Queen Bertrada, whose sister was married to Desiderius, to negotiate the Lombardy marriage agreement. After several weeks of discussions, she returned to the Frankish court with Princess Desiderata.

The marital union between Charles and his wife, Himiltrude, had been made outside the Church and their divorce was quickly arranged. The Austrasian king now married Desiderata, but after less than a year sent her back to her father after becoming enamoured with Hildegarde, a young woman from a Frankish noble family. The marriage to Hildegarde lasted for thirteen years until her death in 783 and resulted in nine children, including the future Emperor Louis I.

The rejection of Desiderata threw Charles' plans to build a strong alliance with Lombardy against Carloman into disarray. The king's attempt to separate his brother from possible allies now resulted in his isolation. He was threatened to the east by the Bavarians and in the south by Carloman and Desiderius. Throughout the next two years, relations between the two co-kings bordered on open warfare, and the Frankish kingdom was only saved from a disastrous civil war by the unexpected death of Carloman in early December 771.

Shortly following the death of his brother, Charles gathered his Frankish army and advanced into Carloman's realm to impose his kingship. An assembly of local nobles and clergymen was summoned and they pledged their loyalty to the king. A small faction of magnates refused to accept Charles and fled with Carloman's widow and two sons to the realm of King Desiderius at Pavia. Charles was now recognized as sovereign of the reunited Frankish kingdom, but opposition to him continued in Lombardy with Desiderius supporting the claims of Carloman's two heirs to the crown of Frankland. As king of the Carolingian people, Charles ruled over all the lands from the Main River in the north to the Bay of Biscay in the south, and from the mouth of the River Rhine to the outlet of the Rhone into the Gulf of Lion in the east.

Soon after solidifying his rule over the Frankish realm, King Charles renewed his father's campaign of conquest against the Saxon tribes on his eastern border. The barbarians had crossed the Rhine, unleashing numerous raids with impunity for several years and attacking Carolingian villages, farms and churches. To bring peace to his eastern border, Charles led his soldiers across the river to compel the tribal chieftains to end their pillaging forays; it was also a means to further unite his two kingdoms by campaigning against a common enemy. In 772 the regime sent its men into Saxony, but the enemy warriors refused to fight, slipping away into the safety of the dense forests, from where the barbarians launched hit-and-run sorties, attacking the monarch's lines of communications and reconnaissance patrols. Despite the harassing strikes of the pagans, the foot soldiers and cavalrymen pushed deep into German territory, encountering little opposition and fighting only minor skirmishes. Charles' forces razed settlements and destroyed the pagan religious shrine at Irminsul. The pagan German tribes were tree worshippers and the site at Irminsul was the centre of their religion. Under the king's orders, the Frankish army spent three days demolishing Irminsul, signalling to the barbarians that he intended to forcibly promote Christianity in their lands. The continued presence of the Franks in Saxony finally forced the pagans to seek peace terms, the tribal leaders agreeing to give their pledges of fealty and remain on the eastern side of the River Rhine.

In the wake of his successful expedition into Saxony, Charles recrossed the river, riding to his small palace at Thionville near the Moselle River in current-day north-eastern France. While he remained at his residence, messengers arrived from Pope Hadrian I with reports that King Desiderius had broken the peace and was proceeding to Rome with his army to force the papacy to declare the eldest son of Carloman as the rightful ruler of the Carolingian Kingdom. With the legitimacy of his throne now challenged, Charles was compelled to muster his troops and march into northern Italy to defend his succession. He divided his army into two forces, ordering his uncle, Bernard, to advance south through the Alps by the St Bernard Pass, while he led his soldiers over the Mont Cenis route into Italy. Desiderius had fortified the access avenues in the mountains that reached into his lands, with strong defensive positions at the gorges of Ivrea and Susa, but the Frankish sovereign sent a large detachment of men over the mountains to assail the Lombards from the flank. Confronted with two advancing armies, in October 773 the Lombard monarch was compelled to withdraw to the protective works of Pavia. Charles followed the Italians, and as Desiderius entered the safety of the fortified city he moved his troops forward to besiege Pavia.

As the siege at Pavia continued, Charles learned that Carloman's wife, Gerberga, and his two nephews had earlier left the city and made their way to Verona. Leaving most of his army to press the siege against Desiderius, Charles took a small force of soldiers and hastened eastward to Verona. When the Franks approached Verona, the king was met by a delegation of city officials who surrendered without a fight to avoid the horrors of a siege. The Frankish overlord marched his troops into the city, demanding possession of Gerberga and her sons. To prevent future claims against his monarchy in support of the two boys, Charles had them tonsured and sent to a monastery, while his sister-in-law was forced into a nunnery. After establishing his rule over the city, Charles rode back to Pavia.

Despite being surrounded by the Francian army and struggling with starvation and disease, Desiderius continued to resist the Frankish siege behind the formidable walls of Pavia, giving no sign of surrender. With his army surrounding the besieged city, Charles took the opportunity to celebrate the coming Easter season in Rome. In the spring of 774 he travelled south to the Holy City of Christendom with many of his nobles, high prelates and his wife and children, who had joined him during the prolonged siege. On 2 April the Franks arrived at Rome and were greeted by men from the local militia, who escorted them into the city. As Charles rode through the streets, a large crowd cheered and waved palm and olive branches to welcome the protector of the Holy City. He dismounted from his horse and walked up the steps to St Peter's Basilica, where he was met by Pope Hadrian I and conducted to the tomb of St Peter to worship.

Following the Easter celebrations, the Frankish king met with Hadrian I to discuss the threat of Lombardy against the papacy. The pope reminded Charles of Pippin III's Donation and pressed him to honour his father's pledge of protection. The king had a copy of the Donation prepared, and after signing it placed the document on the altar of St Peter, pledging to observe the terms, while adding the duchies of Spoleto and Benevento to the papal lands, which became known as the Donation of Charlemagne.

In the aftermath of his talks with Pope Hadrian I, Charles along with his wife, children and delegation of nobles and prelates returned to the ongoing siege at Pavia. The Lombard king's troops and inhabitants managed to hold out for two additional months, but the investment had lasted over nine months and, weakened by rampant disease and food shortages, the residents rose up in revolt, overthrowing Desiderius and opening the gates to the Franks. Charles entered the city and took charge of Desiderius, sending him to a monastery. On 5 June 774 Charles assumed the Iron Crown of Lombardy, crowning himself king, and was acknowledged by the nobles, clerics and people as ruler of two kingdoms. The Frankish king's seizure of Lombardy ended over 200 years of independence for the kingdom. Before returning north, Charles appointed local Lombard nobles to his new administration after they swore allegiance to him, permitting them to govern themselves as part of the enlarged Carolingian kingdom. The conquest of the northern Italian realm was the sovereign's first major acquisition of territory.

Charles' punitive foray into Saxony in 768 had resulted in the German chieftains' pledges of peace along his eastern border. Despite their oaths of fealty, the barbarians had repeatedly broken their word, resuming their pillaging raids into Frankish lands and ravaging settlements and farmlands. The king's border troops retaliated, crossing the Rhine to plunder German villages and farms, but failed to subdue the Saxons. In

775 the pagan German tribes rallied around Chief Widukind, intensifying their attacks against the Franks. Widukind, from a wealthy noble family, became allied with the peasants and serfs to escalate the ongoing conflict against King Charles.

At the annual assembly of the Frankish army in 775, Charles told his magnates, churchmen and soldiers: 'Our policy is to wage war upon the oath-breaking Saxon people until they are conquered and converted to Christianity or wholly destroyed.' The infantry and cavalry were mustered in the early summer of 775 at Duren, between current-day Aachen and Cologne, and marched northeast to the Rhine. The Frankish troops crossed the broad river in rafts and small boats, and after landing on the eastern bank Charles led his men into Saxony, determined to subdue the barbarian warriors and occupy their territory, a challenge the Romans had been unwilling to pursue. As the Franks moved into Saxony, Widukind withdrew his soldiers, abandoning large areas to the invaders. During the first days of the campaign, the Saxon fortress of Sigeburg was captured after only token resistance. The Carolingian forces now swept eastward, encountering little opposition. When Charles neared the fortification at Eresburg, Widukind abandoned it, withdrawing his garrison. The king took possession of the two forts, leaving garrisons to protect his newly claimed territory, while taking hostages from the surrounding area to guarantee the peace of the local Germanic barbarians. The Saxons continued their strategy of refusing to engage the invaders in a large-scale battle, only unleashing small attacks against Charles' flanks and lines of communications. As the Frankish monarch advanced his army deeper into Saxony, he built fortified outposts at strategic locations and continued his policy of taking hostages. The strongholds were usually erected on hilltops, with palisades surrounded by deep wide trenches. During the Saxon campaign he laid waste to a wide region, burning crops, destroying villages and slaughtering livestock. After meeting little resistance from the Saxons, Charles reached the Weser River, where his army was confronted by a force of local soldiers under the command of Chief Hessi. The king attacked the Saxons, quickly defeating them and compelling Hessi to agree to terms recognizing Charles as his overlord and abandoning his pagan gods to accept Christianity.

While Charles pressed his campaign against the Saxons, he received messengers from Pope Hadrian I telling him that the Lombards had again broken their treaty and were threatening the papacy. With his newly acquired Italian realm in revolt, Charles left part of his army in Saxony to resume the war and during the frigid winter hastened with the remainder of his troops over the snow-covered Alps into Lombardy. He struck the rebels with the full might of his veteran army, forcing the chieftains to surrender and honouring his pledge to protect the papacy.

Following his rapid victory over the Lombards, the king returned to Saxony and his subjugation of the barbarians. As he continued to press forward into tribal lands, sweeping across large areas and building fortified strongholds to control his newly occupied lands, he received reports that the Saxons had overrun one of his rearguard outposts and slaughtered the garrison. Charles assembled a force of soldiers and set out in pursuit of the Saxons. His men quickly overtook the Germans, killing and capturing many of them. To enforce his authority over the barbarian tribes, the king ordered the execution of the prisoners. The chieftains from the local tribes soon arrived at the fortified Frankish campsite, pledging peace with the Franks and agreeing to convert to Christianity.

By the end of 776 Charles believed his campaign had pacified the Saxons, and after leaving troops to enforce his kingship he led his army back to Frankland. While the king remained at his palace with his wife and growing family, he received letters from Pope Hadrian I warning him of an impending revolt in northern Italy. At first Charles ignored the pontiff's pleas, but as Hadrian I became increasingly desperate he agreed to intervene to once more honour his vow to defend the papacy. He mustered a small veteran force and set out in midwinter over the Alps into Italy.

When the Franks reached Lombardy after struggling through the icy passes of the mountains, the king learned that the people of the kingdom had risen up against the local government now dominated by members from Desiderius' former administration. Under the rule of the Lombardy noblemen, the realm had been thrown into economic depression and the inhabitants had been reduced to poverty. Charles quickly replaced the ruling council with pro-Frankish officials, visiting many towns to reassure the people that under his new regime corruption and mismanagement would end. While he stayed in Lombardy, the barbarian warriors in Saxony again broke their vows of fealty, attacking Frankish outposts and returning to their pagan gods.

After receiving reports of the barbarian uprising, Charles assembled his army to return north, and after collecting additional troops in Frankland proceeded east into Saxony. When the Carolingian forces approached the pagans, the Saxons quickly submitted, pledging their loyalty and agreeing to adopt Christianity. The monarch accepted their vows and took additional hostages. He had been deceived before, so now to bind the tribes to his kingdom he divided Saxony into several districts, appointing a cleric to govern each as secular and ecclesiastical ruler. To further enforce his power, he built a new royal palace at Paderborn in current-day north central Germany to more closely monitor the activities of the Saxons. In the spring of 778 the King of the Franks held his annual assemblage of nobles at the new palace, inviting the Saxon chieftains to attend to integrate them further into his realm.

While Charles was attending the annual assembly, he was approached by a delegation of strangely dressed men from Spain. He agreed to meet with them and was introduced to three Muslims who had travelled to Saxony to offer him a martial alliance to overthrow the Emirate of Cordoba. In return for his support, the Muslims agreed to cede numerous cities and lands in northern Spain. Charles accepted the proposal as a means to expand his realm farther to the south and free the local Christians in the region from the persecutions of their Muslim rulers. He issued a summons for soldiers from all areas of his vast kingdom to meet in southern Aquitaine near the city of Bordeaux with their weapons, armour, provisions and equipment. Charles left his court at Paderborn in the early spring with Hildegarde and his children, travelling south-westward into Aquitaine. A large expeditionary force assembled in the south of the duchy, and after Easter set out towards the Pyrenees. As the Franks moved farther south, the king divided his multinational army, sending one force over the Pyrenees into eastern Spain while he led the second contingent over the mountains to the west.

When the Franks arrived at the Christian-held city of Pamplona, Charles expected the inhabitants to throw open the gates and welcome him as their liberator from Muslim rule. To his surprise, the garrison refused to surrender and he was compelled to take the city by storm. The Carolingian forces captured several additional towns, including Barcelona, but the Spanish Christian population refused to join the campaign of liberation and actively fought against them. When the expeditionary force reached Saragossa in central Spain, the Spanish Christians rejected an order to submit, withdrawing behind the city's formidable defensive works. The three Muslim envoys at Paderborn had promised support from the local inhabitants, but they remained loyal to their overlords. Charles was now alone in a foreign land, burdened with long supply lines.

While the Franks remained outside the walls of Saragossa, the Emir of the Cordoba Emirate, Abd al-Rahman I, was assembling a large army to repel the Frankish invaders. Lacking siege towers and engines to batter the walls of Saragossa, and with a formidable relief army gathering to the south, Charles was compelled to abandon his Spanish campaign. As the Carolingians withdrew through the Pyrenees in mid-August 778 over the same route by which they had entered Spain several months earlier, their rearguard, led by Count Roland, was attacked by local Spanish insurgents who charged down a steep mountainside, ploughing into the baggage train. The attackers slammed into the unsuspecting Franks before they could deploy into a defensive line, killing all of them and plundering the baggage. The encounter in the Pyrenees became the source for the epic medieval poem *The Song of Roland* many years later, sung by minstrels throughout Europe to glorify the brave fight of Roland and his soldiers.

In the aftermath of the defeat in the mountains, Charles continued his retreat to Aquitaine, finally rejoining Hildegarde and his six children. After resting his army in southern Aquitaine, the Carolingian king returned to Frankland, spending the winter at his palace. Soon after arriving in his homeland, he received reports that the Saxons under Chief Widukind had again risen in revolt, assailing and overrunning the Frankish outposts and plundering across the border. Widukind's warriors burnt towns, demolished churches and left a wide strip of destruction in their wake. Charles decided to remain in his lands following his exhausting Spanish campaign, but sent a trusted general with a small army to subdue Widukind and his renegade warriors. The punitive force crossed the Rhine, but as the troops proceeded into Saxony the rebels withdrew and the king's sovereignty remained ignored. Forcing the barbarians back under Frankish rule would require a major expeditionary force, but Charles' army was weakened and ill-equipped following the Spanish incursion, compelling him to delay the offensive.

While his small army marched against Widukind, Charles spent the winter months of 779 at his palace with his wife and children, surrounded by his noblemen, churchmen and twelve paladins. The paladins were an elite fighting force dedicated to their king. Charles was occupied governing his vast kingdom, issuing a series of new decrees to encourage economic growth and stabilize his sovereignty. The realm's commerce was conducted with money from over fifty mints, each issuing different-weighted coins. To standardize the payment system, the king ordered the creation of a universal coinage network with the same-weighted coins produced. To aid the merchant class further, he issued a law setting a fixed price for the farmers' grains and fruits, while forbidding landowners from charging excessive tolls on roadways through their properties. By royal decree, members of the clergy were no longer permitted to marry, visit inns or hunt to ensure their uninterrupted devotion to the work of the Church. The Carolingian ruler sent his personal agents to the towns four times a year to certify his laws were obeyed and establish a personal bond between the monarchy and its people. The representatives assembled the people and read the new decrees, while examining the accounts of the churches, monasteries and nobles, looking for irregularities. During their stay at each village, the royal proxies heard appeals from inhabitants who believed they had not received justice from the local magistrate. The king's personal deputies served him well, and during the winter their powers were expanded. The royal agents were now sent out in pairs with representatives from the secular and ecclesiastical sectors.

Charles ruled an extensive kingdom of varied peoples, and to provide for the continuance of Carolingian power he now decided to divide the realm between his three legitimate sons, as recognized by the Church. He named his first-born Charles as the future monarch of the northern section of his domain, while Carloman was ceded Italy and Louis received Aquitaine. The two younger sons would rule as sub-kings in their kingdoms, while Charles held sovereignty over his brothers. Pippin the Hunchback, the monarch's son by his first wife, was disinherited because of his physical deformity.

When King Charles was in Spain, Duke Hildeprand of Spoleto rebelled against Pope Hadrian I's sovereignty, declaring his independence and recognizing the Carolingian ruler as his new overlord, while papal areas in the Tuscia region of central Italy were seized by Duke Reginbard of Chiusi in defiance of the Holy See. Unable to regain possession of his usurped lands, the pontiff sent messages to Charles pleading for his intervention. With his borders and kingdom secure, Charles decided to meet the pope in Rome in response to his request for aid against the rebels and to associate his dynasty closer to the Holy See by having his sons, Carloman and Louis, baptized and crowned by Hadrian I in St Peter's Basilica. The coronation by the Holy See would also serve to eliminate any future hereditary claims against his monarchy and enhance his recognition as supreme European ruler.

In late 780 Charles set out with Hildegard and his two sons for Rome. The Frankish king and his entourage crossed the Alps and celebrated Christmas at Pavia before pushing on to the Holy City, arriving in April 781. After reaching Rome, he met privately with the pontiff, asking him to rechristen Carloman with the name of Pippin to bind his son closer to his popular grandfather. While Charles was talking with Hadrian, the pope agreed to crown the two brothers kings of their new realms. Shortly after Easter, the pope anointed the five-year-old Pippin and three-year-old Louis before the high altar in St Peter's Basilica as King of the Lombards and Aquitainians respectively. Following the ceremony, both brothers were sent to their kingdoms with large retinues and trusted advisors to rule their subjects.

While remaining in the Holy City, the Carolingian king held discussions with the pope to secure his assistance in regaining the fealty of Duke Tassilo of Bavaria. The Bavarian duke had earlier given his pledge to serve as vassal to Pippin III and his successors, but had broken his vow and proclaimed himself king. The pontiff agreed to intercede, sending envoys to Tassilo demanding his appearance at the assembly of the Franks at Worms in August to reaffirm his allegiance to the Carolingian monarchy. During the Frankish king's meetings with the pope, they formally defined the territorial possessions of the Holy See, with the Church retaining ownership of the Roman Duchy, Ravenna Exarchate and several other areas, but the Tuscia and Spoleto regions were lost. While Charles was in Rome, he received emissaries from Byzantium, who had been sent by Empress Irene to negotiate the marriage of the king's young daughter Rotrud to her minor son Constantine VI. The negotiations were quickly settled and the Frankish sovereign began the return journey to his lands. During the advance north, Charles made stops in Florence, Pavia and Milan before crossing the Alps and travelling to his homeland, satisfied that he had gained recognition as the equal of the venerated Emperor of Byzantium and as the supreme ruler of Western Europe.

In the summer of 781 the assembly of paladins, magnates and high church officials at Worms, in present-day south-western Germany, was the first gathering since Charles divided his kingdom among his sons. He was anxious for all of his vassals to attend and give their pledges of fealty to his heirs. Tassilo agreed to attend the meeting, but only if hostages were given to him to guarantee his safety. The king accepted the condition and when the nobles and ecclesiastical magnates gathered in Worms, Tassilo was present, binding his strategic Duchy of Bavaria closer to the Carolingian monarchy and acknowledging the inheritance rights of Charles' sons.

Following the assembly at Worms, Charles returned to his court and was occupied ruling his kingdom, and was personally involved with revamping the Palace School. While the king remained at his palace, in the summer of 782 the Saxons, again led by Widukind, crossed the border to ravage Frankish towns and farms. The king ordered his army to subdue the rebels, but the uprising had gained momentum and his forces were too weak to defeat Widukind. Charles gathered reinforcements, sending them across the Rhine to join the punitive expedition. After uniting with the army in Saxony, the troops marched against the barbarians. As the Franks proceeded east into the interior, Widukind withdrew his warriors to a fortified encampment on the slopes of a mountain. During the advance to the Saxons' position, dissension erupted between the leaders of the Frankish army and when their disorganized attack was made against Widukind's forces, the king's men were easily beaten with heavy losses, with only a few survivors escaping the bloody onslaught.

When Charles received reports of the shattering defeat, he became enraged and vowed to destroy all barbarian resistance to his rule. He assembled a large army, hastening into Saxony to subdue the Saxons, who had repeatedly broken their vows of peace and fealty. As his forces approached the Weser River in current-day north western Germany, Widukind as usual withdrew his troops, disappearing into the dense forest. Charles sent messengers to the Saxon villages, ordering the chieftains to appear before him at Verden to explain their continued disobedience. When the Saxons gathered at the small settlement near current-day Bremen in October 782, the Frankish king demanded the surrender of Widukind and his followers. The chiefs denied any involvement in the attack, but Charles refused to believe their innocence and in a violent fury insisted they turn over the guilty men. Fearing the wrath of Charles, the chieftains turned on each other and their people. Over 4,500 German warriors were seized and brought to Verden, where they were brutally beheaded.

Following the bloody massacre of the rebels at Verden, Charles returned to his court at Thionville in north-eastern France, believing his act of vengeance had finally brought peace to Saxony. While he remained at his palace in Francia, in late April 783 Hildegarde died during the birth of their ninth child. Charles and his wife had been married for thirteen years and had developed a close and loving relationship. The king was deeply distraught by the loss of Hildegarde and the newborn daughter, who died two weeks after her birth. In honour of his wife, he ceded a great estate to the Church with revenue designated for Masses and prayers for her soul. While he was still mourning the loss of his beloved wife, in July his mother Queen Bertrand also died and was buried alongside her husband King Pippin III at the great Abbey of St Denis.

While King Charles continued to mourn the loss of his wife, mother and daughter, the nobles of Saxony were enraged by the massacre of their people at Verden and dissension spread through the land. Widukind, who had fled to safety in Denmark after Charles' invasion of Saxony in 782, returned to lead another rebellion. Charles had spent ten years attempting to subdue the German tribes, but the land remained unconquered and was again in revolt. In the spring of 784 a large Frankish army of infantrymen and horse soldiers under the command of Charles crossed the border into Saxony to unleash a campaign of sword and fury. He first moved his forces to the north to attack the Westphalian Saxons, but after reaching the flooded Weser valley was compelled to divert his army to the south-east. A large contingent of troops led by the king's thirteen-year-old son Charles the Younger was left in the north to monitor and harass the Germans. The main Frankish army, under the king's personal command, hastened to the south-east, and after reaching the Elbe and Saale rivers launched a brutal campaign, ravaging villages and burning crops. Charles remained in the south, and as the colder weather set in abandoned the common practice of withdrawing to winter quarters, continuing to pursue and destroy the enemy. The relentless Frankish attack was maintained throughout the winter months, leaving the region in disarray and ruin.

Despite the ongoing military campaign against the Saxons' defiance of his rule, Charles held his annual assembly of paladins, nobles and high church officials at Paderborn, where decisions were made concerning the reorganization of Saxony and the establishment of Frankish authority. At the conclusion of the assembly, Charles returned to the Elbe River region, where Widukind and his barbarians were reportedly camped. When the Carolingian army reached the river, the king sent envoys to Widukind's encampment offering to end the war and negotiate a settlement to the revolt. He promised the Germans clemency and hostages as a security guarantee. The Saxon chieftains accepted the offer and fighting was suspended.

Following the end of hostilities, Charles returned to his palace at Attigny in the Ardennes region of north central France, and was soon joined by Widukind and other chieftains involved in the Saxon uprising. When the king met with the rebel leaders, they agreed to end their revolt and accept baptism as Christians. Charles stood beside Widukind during his baptism ceremony, serving as his godfather, to create a closer bond of friendship.

In the aftermath of his suppression of the revolt in Saxony, the king issued new laws to enhance the subjugation of the rebel tribes. Saxon warriors and their families were required to abandon their pagan gods and accept Christianity. The penalty for refusing to accept the new religion or to defile it was death. A second decree dictated that rebellious Germans were to be resettled in other distant regions of the kingdom, while loyal Franks were relocated into Saxony. The Frankish crown had previously created sub-kingdoms in newly occupied lands governed by local officials, but the continuous uprisings of the Saxons compelled the king to enact harsh measures to enforce his sovereignty, appointing his Frankish representatives to rule.

The Frankish military offensive into Saxony had ended the ongoing local rebellion, restoring peace to the realm, but in 786 Hardrad, Count of Thuringia in present-day eastern Germany, revolted against the Carolingian king's rule. Charles reacted quickly to subdue the uprising before it gained momentum, sending his soldiers to seize Hardrad, and during the foray many of the count's supporting nobles were taken prisoner or killed. The captured rebels were exiled and their properties confiscated. Soon after the disorder in Thuringia was crushed, the Bretons refused to pay their annual tribute and a second expeditionary force was sent to bring the leaders before the annual assembly for judgment. At the meeting of nobles and high church prelates, the Bretons readily abandoned their independence, pledging to pay their levy and acknowledge Frankish overlordship.

While Charles was subduing the outbreaks of revolt in his kingdom, the government of the Byzantine emperor, Constantine VI, was negotiating a military alliance against the Franks with Arechis II, Prince of Benevento, and Duke Tassilo of Bavaria. The union of the three realms created a serious threat to Charles' monarchy, and he acted quickly, striking the Italians before the alliance launched a combined offensive against him. He assembled his army and set out for Italy, crossing the mountains in the winter, and after reaching Rome he met with Pope Hadrian I to discuss the campaign in southern Italy against Benevento. The pontiff, eager to expand his papal lands to the south, encouraged the king to conquer the principality. After receiving the blessings of the pope, the Carolingian monarch resumed his advance against the rebels. As the Franks proceeded south and besieged the city of Capua, the Benevento prince sent his eldest son to negotiate a settlement. Still facing two formidable enemies, Charles quickly agreed to terms with the prince. Under their agreement, Arechis II promised to pay an annual tribute, while pledging his allegiance and giving a younger son to the Franks as a guarantee for his loyalty.

After gaining the pledge of suzerainty from Prince Arechis II, Charles returned to Rome. While he prepared to advance against Tassilo he asked Hadrian I to condemn the duke and his supporters for breaking their vows of vassalage. Seeking to continue in the favour of the powerful Frankish kingdom, the pope ordered Tassilo and his nobles to submit to their overlord, threatening to excommunicate them if they failed to comply. After securing the pope's approval for the campaign against Bavaria, the sovereign led his army north across the Alps to his palace at Worms. From his court he issued a summons for his paladins, nobles and ecclesiastical magnates to meet in the autumn of 787. As a sworn vassal of the Frankish king, Tassilo was obligated to attend the assembly, but when he failed to appear, Charles prepared his army to march against Bavaria as just cause had been established. When the Bavarian nobles learned their duke had failed to join the assembly and had incurred a decree of excommunication from the papacy, they refused to answer his call to arms, forcing him to surrender. He appeared before his overlord, again swearing his allegiance, and was pardoned by the monarch. However, soon after the Franks returned north, Tassilo revolted again, forming an alliance with the pagan Avars. The Bavarian magnates refused to recognize Tassilo as their duke, appealing to the Franks for their intervention. At the assembly of nobles the following year at Ingelheim, Charles ordered the arrest of the duke, sentencing him to be tonsured and sent to a monastery. Bavaria was annexed into the Frankish kingdom, resulting in the unification of all Germanic peoples under a single ruler. The Frankish realm now rivalled the Byzantine Empire in the east and the Muslim domain to the south in size and power.

During the Carolingian king's visits to Rome, he marvelled at the magnificent architecture of the many palaces, monuments, buildings and cathedrals. As the ruler of a powerful and wealthy kingdom, he decided to construct a new capital for his realm, choosing the small town of Aachen. Aachen was located between present-day Cologne and Liege in western Germany and was in the heartland of the Carolingian kingdom. He relocated his court to the town and prepared plans for the construction of the new capital. After the preparations were completed, building materials were collected and transported to Aachen, while skilled craftsmen were brought from Italy. The king was very enthusiastic about his capital, but was forced to delay its construction to devote his energies to the conquest of the pagan Slavic and Avar tribes on his eastern frontier.

In 789 the Frankish troops and their Saxon and Frisian allies crossed the Elbe into the present-day Czech Republic, and on the eastern side of the river encountered the Slavic tribes. As the Franks expanded their presence in the area, the tribes failed to unite against the invaders and Charles' army quickly seized control of their lands. The king of the Abotrites, Witzin, negotiated a settlement with the Carolingians, offering his homage, agreeing to pay an annual tribute and provide hostages to guarantee his loyalty, while Dragovit of the Wiltzes soon agreed to similar terms. The Slavic kings also pledged to permit Christian missionaries to preach the word of the Christian God to their people. The Carolingian army resumed its attack to the east through dense woodlands and swamplands to the Baltic Sea in Pomerania before returning triumphantly to the Rhine. Following their foray to the sea the Frankish forces continued their campaign, conquering the northern Slavic region for the king. After their submission, the Slavs remained loyal allies to the Frankish sovereign, taking part in the Carolingian offensive against the once again rebellious Saxons.

The conquest of the Slavic region was later resumed when Charles sent his eldest son, Charles the Younger, south to suppress the Czech tribes in Bohemia. He marched his army of veteran infantrymen and cavalry forces into the barbarian lands, unleashing a savage attack against the southern tribesmen. After the king's son ravaged the valleys in the Upper Elbe area, the Czech chieftains submitted to the Carolingians, acknowledging King Charles' suzerainty and pledging to pay a tribute.

As the Franks increasingly expanded their kingdom to the east, they came into contact with the hostile Avars. These tribes had migrated to the west from Central Asia and lived in settlements protected by large circular earthen walls, called rings, with their capital built in the centre. They were skilled and fierce warriors and horsemen who had conquered and settled in current-day Hungary, establishing a formable military presence. The Avars farmed the rich black soil and frequently unleashed ravaging raids against their western neighbours. By 791 the savage Avars had become a threat to the Frankish frontier lands, and Charles was compelled to intervene against them. The occupation of the Avar region would advance the Carolingian realm farther east and result in the Christianization of the local pagan tribes. At the Regensburg assembly of nobles, Charles proposed a campaign to conquer and convert the Avars, which was overwhelmingly approved by his vassals. He sent envoys to the chiefs demanding their warriors end the forays into his territory. When the tribal leaders refused to comply, Charles assembled three large armies of infantry and supporting cavalry, unleashing military strikes from the north, south and west. The attack from Lombardy was led by the king's second son, Pippin, whose troops stormed through the enemy's fortified walls, capturing and killing thousands. Charles commanded the offensive from the north, and when his troops reached the Avar frontier in the late summer he ordered them to spend the next three days observing Christian rituals asking for God's victory. The priests led the soldiers in prayers, Masses and recited penitential responses, while the men fasted. Following the religious services, in early September 791 a formidable force of Bavarian troops under Charles' personal command swept across the border, driving the Avars back into their interior with severe casualties, the Carolingian infantrymen charging into the pagan tribesmen with their deadly slashing swords and spears. By the end of the campaigning season, the Franks had occupied over half of the Avars' lands after winning numerous barbarous engagements and leaving a path of destruction.

In the spring of 792 Charles planned to rejoin his war against the Avars, but was compelled to send his dukes to renew the conquest while he personally intervened to defend the Church and end the uprising of the Saxons. The Saxons responded to the enactment of Charles' harsh laws following the surrender of Widukind by turning against the Church of Rome and the forced baptisms, returning to their pagan gods. While the resistance spread throughout the land, the Carolingian king took troops into Saxony to force their acceptance of his decrees and the Christian Church.

In the meantime, while the Carolingian king was engaged in the subjugation of the Avars, the unorthodox doctrine of Adoptionist Heresy was spreading from the Frankish-occupied territory in north-eastern Spain into neighbouring Aquitaine under the preaching of Bishop Felix of Urgel. The dogma stated that Jesus was not the natural son of God but a mortal being adopted by Him. The theory was in opposition to the Church of Rome's teachings and was considered heresy, being condemned by Pope Hadrian I, but the belief continued to grow. The town of Urgel was located in the kingdom of the Carolingian king, and he ordered the bishop to appear at an ecclesiastical court at his Regensburg palace. When Bishop Felix met with the court, he was declared guilty of heresy but was pardoned after promising to return to the Frankish lands in Spain and end his message of the doctrine. To ensure his compliance, Charles sent the bishop to the pope, where he again pledged to preach against the adoptionist dogma. Despite his vows against the doctrine, when the bishop arrived in Urgel he spoke out in favour of adoptionism with renewed enthusiasm.

As the Carolingian throne expanded its lands to the east against the pagan tribes under the direction of King Charles, in southern Aquitaine the monarch's son Louis came into increasing contact with the Muslims in northern Spain. In 785 the Franks again marched through the Pyrenees against the Moorish-held town of Gerona in north-east Spain. Louis' forces, under the command of Count William of Toulouse, assailed Gerona, overrunning the defensive fortifications and occupying the town. William was a trusted kinsman of Charles and had earlier defeated a large Moorish army as it moved into south-eastern France. Under the skilled command of William, the Franks expanded their presence in northern Spain, seizing additional towns. By 795 the Carolingians had conquered Cardona and Ausona. As Charles expanded his foothold in the Moorish-occupied region, he unified his newly won territory into the Spanish March under its own government. The Frankish conquests were aided by the frequent rebellions of the local Moorish governors against their king, Abdurrahman I. Later in the year, Louis' army moved against Barcelona, the principal city in Catalonia. As the Carolingians approached the city, the Moorish governor, Zaid, revolted against his king and surrendered to Charles' men. Barcelona was occupied by the Franks and incorporated into the Spanish March.

The Carolingian army in northern Spain continued to enlarge its occupied lands whilst the king's navy began intervening against the Saracens in the Mediterranean. He sent a naval force to conquer the Muslim-held islands of Corsica and Sardinia, and after defeating the

Saracens he occupied their towns with a Christian population. In 799 Charles renewed his offensive in the Mediterranean, driving the Saracens out of the Balearic Islands and reclaiming the region for Christendom.

Following the Carolingian regime's conquest of Barcelona, the Moorish king Hisham I recovered the city from the Franks in 797. When Louis learned of the city's capture, he assembled a large army of Aquitainians, Goths, Burgundians and Provencals, marching across the Pyrenees to lay siege against Barcelona. The Muslim garrison resisted the sorties of the Franks, with the siege dragging on for two years. After the Carolingians extended their siege lines around the defensive fortifications and repeatedly denied the Moorish inhabitants relief supplies, the city was compelled to surrender. The city's residents were forced to abandon their homes, the Franks repopulating it with people from southern France.

During the reign of King Pippin III, the Franks had subdued the Bretons in western France and had ruled the region with court-appointed royal counts. During the following years, the Bretons repeatedly broke their pledges of fealty, overthrowing the king's counts and assailing the Carolingian outposts along the border. The Franks were compelled to send military forces into Brittany to reimpose their sovereignty. In 786 the tribal chieftains of Brittany defied the Carolingians again, declaring their independence and refusing to pay their annual tribute. Charles ordered an army led by Count Audulf to reinstate his rule. The count unleashed a ruthless offensive against the Bretons, attacking their fortified villages while laying waste to the farmlands, compelling them to submit. Despite the Breton chieftains' pledges of loyalty, they continued to pursue their independence, raiding the settlements along the frontier. As the Bretons escalated their plundering raids, Charles ordered Count Guy of Nantes to intervene and subdue the tribes. Guy marched the Frankish army into Brittany, and in a ruthless campaign forced the Breton tribes to submit and pledge their loyalty. In 799 the count travelled to the Frankish court at Aachen, presenting Charles with the surrendered weapons of the Breton chieftains, signalling their submission to the Carolingian crown.

In the meantime, while Charles was occupied with the wars expanding his kingdom to the east and in northern Spain, in Constantinople Empress Irene, acting in the name of her minor son Constantine VI, had convened the Second Council of Nicaea on 27 September 787, which appeared to approve the worship of images for the eastern and western Christian Churches. However, when the report of the council's doctrine was translated from Greek to Latin for the Carolingian king to read, the original words' veneration of images was erroneously interpreted as adoration of images. Charles strongly disapproved of the practice of image worship, believing it was a return to paganism. In defence of Rome's religious beliefs, he organized the Council of Frankfurt to provide a forum to attack image worship and again try Bishop Felix of Urgel, who had broken his earlier promises not to preach the Adoptionist doctrine. On 1 June 794 he opened the council, attended by approximately 350 archbishops, bishops, prelates and representatives from the pontiff. Charles spoke to the gathered churchmen, strongly condemning the worship of images as approved by Empress Irene. Following his spirited speech, the delegates voted to denounce the practice.

In the aftermath of the vote against image worship, Bishop Felix was again tried on charges of heresy for preaching anti–Church beliefs. He was quickly declared guilty, but after again pledging to return to the approved dogma was absolved. Once back in northern Spain, however, he returned to the Adoptionist doctrine, forcing the Frankish king to remove him from Urgel and send him to Lyons, with instructions for the local bishop to keep Felix under close supervision in his church.

As the Carolingian king remained occupied defending the doctrine of the Roman Church, dissension spread throughout his lands. Under Charles' rule the Frankish kingdom had been involved in a near continuous series of wars, and the economy had deteriorated from the constant demands for men, food, equipment, horses and war supplies. While the king had expanded his personal powerbase, his vassals felt increasingly removed from the government, creating a feeling of isolation. The monarchy had also suffered the effects of plague and famine creating widespread misery. The conspiracy was organized by a small faction of high nobles, who had suffered the weight of the economic slowdown. In the climate of discord, the monarch's disinherited son by his first wife, Pippin the Hunchback, was drawn into the insurrection against his father. They planned to assassinate Charles and take control of the government by placing Pippin the Hunchback on the throne as a figurehead sovereign. Pippin was considered weak and easily controllable. Ever since his disinheritance, he held harsh feelings against his father and was quickly won over to the rebels' cause. As the conspirators prepared to strike in the name of Pippin, Charles was informed of the planned usurpation by a monk who overheard the nobles discussing their seizure of the monarchy. The Carolingian monarch ordered the arrest of his son and his co-rebels, who were quickly imprisoned. They were soon tried and convicted with the sentence of death. However, the king commuted Pippin the Hunchback's punishment to life in a monastery.

The monarch remained in his kingdom while the war against the pagan Avar tribes was fought by his oldest son Charles in the north and his son Pippin of Italy in the south. A large army of foot-soldiers and cavalry from all parts of the kingdom was led by Charles the Younger and Duke Eric of Friuli. The Frankish forces advanced against the pagans, attacking their fortified ring defences and engaging their horsemen with the elite Lombard cavalrymen. The Franks repeatedly outmanoeuvred the enemy troops, winning great victories. Duke Eric was killed during the fierce fighting and Prince Charles assumed command of the army. As the Avars were driven back by the prince's men, with the cavalry leading the vanguard, dissent erupted among the pagan chieftains. With their resolve to continue the war broken, Prince Charles penetrated the final ring of the Avar defences in 796, capturing the enemy's capital and the tribes' great treasury of gold, silver, precious stones and silk robes. He loaded the treasure on fifteen carts and hauled it to his father's palace at Aachen. The king richly rewarded his nobles, soldiers and Church, sending a large gift to Pope Hadrian I.

While Charles' son was overpowering the Avars in the north, Pippin led the Carolingian forces in the south, crushing the resistance of the barbarians. His troops ravaged the pagans' farmlands and settlements, devastating the population and leaving only a few scattered villages inhabited. The shattered Avar region was now annexed to the Frankish kingdom, extending Charles' realm to the Danube River in the east.

On Christmas Day 795 Pope Hadrian I died, and Leo III was elected his successor. The new pontiff was unpopular with the nobles and people of Rome and needed the support of the Carolingian king to secure his papacy. Soon after his election, he sent Charles a message to assure him of his allegiance and loyalty, enclosing the symbolic keys to the tomb of St

Peter and flag of Rome, signalling the king's authority as protector of the Church and Holy City. After receiving the correspondence, the Frankish monarch sent a messenger with a letter to Leo III, telling him: 'It is our duty to defend everywhere the Holy Church of Christ with help of divine love and with arms against the attacks of pagans and the devastations of infidels coming from abroad. To you most Holy Father belongs the task of assisting our army with your hands raised so that with the blessings of God the Christian world will be forever victorious over the enemies of the scared name of God.' In a second message, he encouraged the pontiff to live morally and follow the laws of the Roman Church.

While the Frankish king had given his support and protection to the new pope, a faction of Roman clergymen and nobles led by Pashalis and Campulus was organized to oppose Leo III. To encourage the fight against the pope, they circulated rumours in Rome accusing him of immoral conduct, crimes and acts of perjury. The insurrection gained momentum, and soon a plot to assassinate the pontiff was formed. The opportunity to murder Leo III arose on 25 April 799 during the religious procession in celebration of the feast of St Mark. Mounted on a horse at the front of the pageant, the pope was assailed by the plotters and dragged to the ground. In the resulting turmoil the spectators ran from the confrontation, while Leo III was carried unconscious by the conspirators to a nearby monastery. During the night some of the pope's faithful followers intervened, secretly entering the cloister and lowering him to the ground from his cell by a rope. Battered and beaten, the pontiff escaped to the safety of St Peter's Basilica with the aid of his supporters. When news of the pope's escape spread through Rome, an angry mob rioted in the streets, destroying the property of Leo III's friends. As the uprising continued, Duke Winiges of Spoleto intervened, his soldiers taking the pope to safety in his duchy. Winiges was a vassal of Charles, and in 789 had been appointed as the Carolingian crown's local lord to govern Spoleto in its name.

King Charles was at his palace in Paderborn, involved with the pacification of Saxony, when he learned of the attack against the pope. He issued instructions for Leo III to be brought to his court by a large escort of troops, led by his son Pippin. The Franks travelled to Spoleto, escorting the pontiff north without serious incident. When Leo III arrived at Paderborn, he was greeted by Charles, who knelt before the pope and then embraced him. They attended a Mass of thanksgiving in the local church before going to a great banquet in honour of the pontiff.

During the following summer months of 799, Pope Leo III remained with the king at the Paderborn palace, discussing every detail of recent events in Rome. While Charles talked with the pontiff, envoys were sent to Rome to gather information about the revolt and its causes. The conspirators claimed the pontiff's corrupt behaviour was beneath the dignity of the Roman Church and he should be deposed. After discussing the events in Rome with his advisors, Charles decided that Leo III had been placed on the papal throne by God, and only He could remove him. Despite the opposition of the Roman nobles, churchmen and citizens, the monarch chose to support Leo III to preserve the authority of the papacy and dignity of the office.

In the autumn of 799 the Carolingian sovereign sent Leo III back to the Holy See in the company of bishops and royal envoys, protected by a large detachment of soldiers. Emissaries had been dispatched by Charles to conduct a hearing on the criminal charges against Leo III, and had been ordered by the king to declare him innocent. As they entered the city, the citizens and nobles lined the streets to display their anger at his return. The outpouring was so strong against the pope that he was compelled to remain in the safety of St Peter's Basilica. A formal commission was convened and charges were brought against the pontiff, with witnesses testifying in his defence and against him. When the verdict was read, Leo III was cleared of the charges. Charles had hoped the open formal inquiry would end the dissent, but the people continued their opposition.

As Charles waited for the revolt against Leo III to subside, in 800 he visited the northern coast of his kingdom, which was now under increasing attacks by the Northmen from present-day Denmark, Norway and Sweden. The Vikings sailed into the North Sea in their longboats, raiding the Frankish coastal cities and inflicting havoc on the inhabitants. The king travelled to St Bertin, St Riquier and other towns that had been assailed, gathering information to combat the raiders. Utilizing the collected descriptions of the attacks, he ordered the construction of a fleet to patrol the harbours, while building a line of watchtowers along the coast and fortifications at the towns' entrances to guard against the marauding Northmen.

Charles remained involved with the papal conflict of Pope Leo III and the raids of the Northmen, while in Constantinople Empress Irene was at the centre of a revolt against her son Emperor Constantine VI. The empress ordered her son blinded and imprisoned, while she assumed the Byzantine crown. Throughout Western Europe, Irene's usurpation was unacknowledged and the throne of the Eastern Empire considered vacant. In Frankland the nobles and prelates now regarded Charles as head of the Christian world and ruler of a new Roman Empire.

As the animosity against Leo III escalated in Rome, Charles was compelled to personally intervene to secure the papacy for the embattled pope. In the autumn of 800 he travelled to Rome with a large party of nobles, churchmen and soldiers, receiving a triumphant welcome.

To resolve the ongoing revolt against Pope Leo III, he convened an assembly of clergymen and Roman nobles at St Peter's on 1 December. At the beginning of the synod, Charles addressed the nobles and prelates, telling them he had come to the Holy City to restore order to the Church and decide on the guilt or innocence of the pontiff. Following three weeks of testimony from the pope's supporters and enemies, the king announced his judgement, ordering Leo III to swear an oath of exoneration. On 23 December, before a large gathering of clergy and Roman citizens, Leo III placed his hand on the Holy Scriptures and declared his innocence of the charges. The oath of purification was declared by Charles to be sufficient to establish the virtue of the pontiff.

Following the absolution of Leo III, the nobles and high Church officials continued to meet, discussing the absence of a recognized emperor in the Eastern Empire after the seizure of power by Empress Irene. As the acknowledged ruler of Western Europe, and because God had granted him these lands, the Carolingian king was elected to the imperial title as emperor. On Christmas Day 800 Charles and his paladins, nobles and churchmen from all parts of his vast kingdom attended services at St Peter's Basilica. As Charles finished his prayers following the High Mass, Leo III came forward to place a golden crown on his head, calling out to the congregations: 'Long life and victory to Charles, the most pious Augustus, the great emperor and peacemaker, anointed by God.' The coronation signalled to the courts of Europe the creation of a new Western Empire, with Charles at its head. Emperor Charles remained in Rome for several months settling his affairs with the Roman Church before returning to his palace in Aachen.

In the aftermath of the rebirth of the Western Roman Empire, Empress Irene sought friendlier relations with the new emperor. While the two empires expanded their political contacts, Charles sent a proposal to the Byzantine court for his marriage to Irene to unite the western and eastern empires. A near constant flow of emissaries travelled between Aachen and Constantinople, carrying messages of friendship and bearing numerous gifts. As negotiations for the marriage continued, in 802 the empress was overthrown by a court faction led by Nicephorus I, who thereafter ruled the Eastern Empire. Under the reign of Nicephorus I, relations with Emperor Charles steadily deteriorated. To strengthen his position in the east against Constantinople, the western emperor opened contacts with Baghdad, sending envoys to negotiate a mutual assistance agreement against Byzantium.

While the negotiations with the caliph continued in Baghdad, Charles was compelled to intervene militarily against Emperor Nicephorus I. The Carolingian emperor appointed his son Pippin as commander for a large naval force, sending him to assail the Byzantines in Venice. The Carolingians were historically a land-based power, but as Charles expanded his empire across Europe he had begun a massive shipbuilding programme to defend his extensive coastal borders and river settlements. When the Byzantines ordered a fleet into the Adriatic Sea to protect their interests, Pippin advanced his ships against the Venetians. In the ensuing naval battle, the Frankish seamen were beaten back and compelled to withdraw. While the western regime had failed to enforce its rule militarily over Venice, Nicephorus I became increasingly threatened on his flanks by the new Caliph of Baghdad, Haroun al Raschid, and agreed to terms with the Franks, recognizing Charles as emperor of the west.

Under the direction of Charles, the Franks had expanded their presence across western Europe, while in the far north the Danes felt increasingly threatened by the Carolingians' aggressive usurpation of new territories. During his push into the north, Charles formed an alliance with Thrasco, King of the Obodrite tribe, for his military aid in suppressing the Saxons. In 798 the Obodrite Confederation overran the Saxon forces, seizing their lands for the Frankish throne. As a reward for the victory, Charles ceded part of the Saxon lands in Holstein north of the Elbe to Thrasco. The Franks continued their advance against the pagan tribes and in 804 penetrated as far north as the Eider River, Denmark's acknowledged southern borderline. To protect against further encroachments by the Carolingians, the Danes began launching marauding raids along the coastline of Aquitaine, assailing Charles' settlements and farmlands. The raiders were unwilling to challenge the military might of the hardened veteran Frankish soldiers, withdrawing quickly at the approach of their enemy. As hostilities grew more widespread, the Danish king, Godfrey, ordered the construction of an earthen fortification along his southern frontier. A high wall was erected, with deep trenches and topped by intermittent stockades. The vital trading centre at Hedeby, located on the Schlei Inlet of the Baltic Sea, was expanded and garrisoned with Danish troops. Over the next several years, King Godfrey expanded his forays across the frontier, striking as far south as the Seine River plundering Carolingian territory.

As the pillaging incursions of Godfrey intensified against his villages and coastal outposts, Charles was forced to build a fleet of warships to defend his shorelines, while reinforcing his defences in the Elbe region, which served as a primary artery for the Danish raiding parties. In 810 Godfrey led an attack with 200 longboats against the Frankish coast in north-western Germany, claiming the region for his Danish kingdom. To guard against future sorties into his north-western lands, Charles contracted with the Vikings to patrol the area with their longboats and drive off the Danes. Despite the growing protests of his vassals, the Danish king continued to assail the Carolingian settlements, but when he refused to end his pillaging raids deep into Frankish lands his chieftains rebelled against him, fearing a strong retaliatory attack by Charles. The Danish rebels seized their king and assassinated him. The successor to the Danish crown, Hemming, soon opened peace negotiations with the Franks, agreeing to a truce and ending the Danes' cross-border attacks.

In 806 Charles was sixty-four years old and began planning for the future restructuring of the Western Empire after his death. He issued a series of imperial decrees dividing his vast realm between his three sons. The title of emperor and all the Frankish land, Saxony, Thuringia and Burgundy were granted to his eldest son Charles the Younger, while

Louis was to rule in Aquitaine, Provence and the Spanish March and Pippin received Italy and Bavaria. The partition document also included rules for his three sons to follow in governing their separate kingdoms, stressing the importance of maintaining close cooperation. Remembering the near civil war that resulted after his father's death, the emperor emphasized the need for brotherly unity to keep the Holy Roman Empire intact. However, Charles' reorganization became outdated by the deaths of Pippin in 810 and Charles the following year. Under the revised division of the Western Empire, Louis was given the imperial title and the entire realm, with the exception of Italy, which was to become a vassal sub-kingdom of Bernard, the son of Pippin.

To better prepare Louis for the task of administrating a vast conglomerate of kingdoms, the heir-designate now spent more time with his father at Aachen learning the skills required for governing the multinational empire. Louis remained for nearly six months at the imperial court with the emperor and his advisors. He was told to always protect the Holy See from its enemies and establish friendly relations with the pope. The future emperor was warned to continually respond with a strong reply against rebelling vassals and foreign kingdoms. The emperor also instructed his son to appoint loyal and honest men to administer his counties.

In September 813 the paladins, aristocrats, nobles and high churchmen assembled for the coronation of Louis in the chapel at the Aachen palace. The emperor, dressed in robes of gold cloth studded with jewels, approached his kneeling son, placing the golden crown on his head an anointing him co-emperor of the Western Empire. After consecrating Louis, the aged emperor said: 'Blessed be Thou O' God, Who has granted me the grace to see with my own eyes my son seated on my throne.' By eliminating the clergy from the crowning of the new emperor, Charles was reinforcing the tenet signifying the head of the empire as a self-sustaining ruler. From the chapel, the attendees, led by Charles, were taken into the palace to celebrate the succession of the new emperor. Following the death of his father and his succession to the Carolingian throne in early 814, Louis I relocated his capital to Aachen to rule the Western Empire. During his twenty-six-year reign, he was beset with challenges against his emperorship, intervening against rebels in Brittany, the Spanish March, along his eastern frontier and against Viking raiders from the north. While defending his regime against external enemies, Emperor Louis I confronted numerous rebellions from his four sons, who relentlessly plotted to expand their designated inheritances. Following numerous revisions to his will, upon the death of Emperor Louis in 840 the Carolingian Empire was divided between his three surviving sons, with Louis the German ceded Bavaria and Lothair I the eastern fiefdoms, including Italy and the title of emperor, while Charles inherited West Francia, most of modern-day France.

Throughout his years as ruler of the Carolingian realm, Charles always exhibited an unrelenting interest in the arts and letters. He continually encouraged learned men to join his court at Aachen. Under the emperor's sponsorship, there was a revival in literature, architecture, education, government and visual arts. At the time of his succession to the crown, a foundation for a palace school existed but the emperor enlarged it and brought scholars in all fields of education to teach his sons and the pupils of the nobles and high churchmen. He was displeased with the correspondences sent to him by the clergy, writing: 'They are very correct in sentiment but very incorrect in grammar.' Charles questioned whether his priests had an adequate enough knowledge of Latin to understand the scriptures. Under his direction, new schools were established in every monastery for the instruction of local school-aged boys. He continued to monitor the progress of his schools, many of which developed into centres of higher learning. Emperor Charles took a special interest in preserving old books, and under his supervision many old heroic tales of the Franks, works of poetry and histories were copied, along with reproductions of the Old and New Testaments. His scholars also worked on new books of Latin and Greek grammar, biographies and classical texts. During his reign, the emperor was an enthusiastic collector of books on a wide variety of subjects, building a large library.

During the winter months, Charles returned to his palace at Aachen and frequently met with his circle of court scholars to discuss a wide range of topics. He was always eager to explore new fields of study, from astrology to religion and mathematics. From a young age, Charles was interested in music, both secular and ecclesiastical. During a visit to the papacy in Rome he became greatly attracted to Gregorian chants, bringing back choirmasters to his court to teach his churchmen the music. After designating Aachen as the capital of his empire, Charles was involved with the designs for the construction of his new palace and church, employing the best craftsmen. Under his direction, a grand imperial palace and magnificent cathedral were erected. While the palace has been destroyed by invading armies, enough of the original church has survived to show the beautiful Romanesque architecture. To more effectively govern his extensive empire, the Carolingian emperor ordered his engineers to improve the existing Roman infrastructural systems, resulting in the building of new roadways, canals and bridges, while existing ones were restored and enlarged.

To successfully rule his many diverse nations, reaching from the Atlantic Ocean to beyond the Elbe, required a highly centralized government. Charles divided his empire into numerous counties, each governed by a throne-appointed duke or count, and when new regions were annexed into the empire, they were divided into smaller counties ruled by an imperial vassal. Responsible only to the emperor, the duke or count administered Charles' justice, collected his taxes and provided men to fight his wars. The yearly assembly of nobles and high churchmen was continued, growing into an effective governing resource for the emperor.

In 812 Emperor Charles was seventy years old and knew that his death was nearing. To prepare for his acceptance into the Kingdom of God, he spent long hours praying and studying the Holy Scriptures, while continuing to attend church services three times each day. The emperor was a deeply pious ruler and considered abdicating his imperial crown to retire to a monastery and spend the remainder of his life in prayer. However, he strongly believed that God had appointed him to the emperorship and decided to fulfil his obligations. He began wearing a rough hair shirt to perform penance for his sins.

Following his coronation ceremony, Louis returned to Aquitaine to rule his kingdom, while Charles remained at his palace in Aachen. He soon left his court and set out into the forest around Aachen to hunt. The emperor spent several months hunting wild game, but in November returned to the palace to renew his studies of the Scriptures and discussions with the court scholars. In January 814 the emperor contracted a high fever and was compelled to retire to his bed. He had little faith in doctors, and prescribed for himself the avoidance of all foods. During the following week his condition deteriorated, with his body weakened by the fever and lack of food. On 27 January Charles received Holy Communion, expecting his imminent death. Lingering on through the night, in the early morning, after making the sign of the cross, the seventy-one-year-old Founder of the Holy Roman Empire died after ruling the Carolingians for over forty seven years. On the day of his death, Charlemagne was buried in the chapel of the palace at Aachen. A golden monument was erected over the tomb with an image of Charlemagne and the words: 'In this tomb lies the body of Charles the Great and Orthodox Emperor who gloriously extended the kingdom of the Franks and reigned prosperously for 47 years.'

Under the direction of Charlemagne, the Carolinian Empire had established the dominance of the Franks across Europe, creating an overpowering state that rivalled the former Roman Empire and challenged the Eastern Roman Empire in Constantinople. The Frankish monarch's greatest achievements, as they affected the future of Europe, were the regeneration of the Holy Roman Empire, which ruled a large section of the continent until 1806, the spreading of the Christian religion into the lands of pagan tribes and the creation of a trans-national integration that was not seen again until the age of Napoleon Bonaparte 1,000 years later.

Selected Sources:

Becher, Matthias, *Charlemagne*.
Chamberlin, Russell, *The Emperor Charlemagne*.
Gioia, Francesco, *The Popes – Twenty Centuries of History*.
James, Edward, *The Franks*.
James, Edward, *The Origins of France – From Clovis to the Capetians 500–1000*.
Komroff, Manuel, *Charlemagne*.
Matthews, John and Stewart, Bob, *Warriors of Christendom*.
McKitterick, Rosamond, *The Frankish Kingdoms Under the Carolingians*.
Norwich, John Julius, *Absolute Monarchs*.
Oman, Charles, *The Dark Ages*.
Rendina, Claudio, *The Popes*.
Riche, Pierre, *The Carolingians – A Family Who Forged Europe*.
Scherman, Kathrine, *The Birth of France – Warriors, Bishops and Long-Haired Kings*.
Williams, Hywel, *Emperor of the West*.
Wilson, Derek, *Charlemagne*.

Chapter Two

Alfred of Wessex

Founder of a United England

In the late eighth century Scandinavian warriors sailed their fleets of longboats south, unleashing savage plundering raids on Anglo-Saxon England with little opposition. In the 860s the Vikings' Great Heathen Army expanded its attacks, seizing English towns in the north and establishing the rule of the Danes. Most of England was under the occupation of the Northmen by 870, with only the southern Kingdom of Wessex remaining independent. In 877 the pagans invaded Wessex with a large army and the shire levies of King Alfred were hard pressed to repel the invaders' onslaught. In early May of the following year the king ordered his men to assemble at Egbert's Stone under the golden dragon standard to march against the Viking enemy. In the early morning light at Edington the Anglo-Saxons deployed into a unified line of interlocking shields, slamming into the pagan warriors who were under the command of King Guthrum. The battle raged throughout the day in violent and bloody fighting, the English finally breaking through the Vikings' defensive front and forcing them to withdraw, leaving hundreds of wounded and dead on the battlefield. The victory of Alfred at Edington ensured the survival of the Wessex kingdom, led to the eventual defeat of the Danes and the recovery of England from foreign occupation and hegemony.

At the time of Alfred's birth in mid-April 848, his father's Wessex kingdom was under attack by marauding warbands from Scandinavia. Alfred, the fifth son of King Aethelwulf and Queen Oshurh, was born at Wantage in Berkshire in south-eastern England. As the youngest of her children, Oshurh took a special interest in Alfred, lavishing him with attention and keeping him in her household. She established a palace school for her children and the sons of the Wessex aristocrats, and encouraged Alfred to excel in his studies. Growing up in the Wessex court, Alfred increasingly participated in hunting and falconry parties with his brothers and noblemen and attended horse and dog races, while learning to ice skate in the winter and swim in the warmer months. At night, by the light of fireplaces and candles, the Wessex prince joined his family in various board and dice games, and was entertained by the narrations of oral poets reciting new poems and familiar works of old pagan legends and epics of English literature, while listening to music played on harps and tubular wind instruments.

Despite the dangers of marauding pirates along the coastal waters and bandits across the land route, around the age of five Alfred was sent to Rome by King Aethelwulf on a religious pilgrimage to the Holy See. As a devout Christian, the Wessex king considered the pope as the living representative of God on Earth; the presence of his son at the papacy would confirm the dynasty's legitimacy, while enhancing its prestige throughout the European courts. In 853 Alfred set out on the long, dangerous journey to Rome with a large entourage of court advisors, noblemen and bodyguards. After crossing the English Channel to current-day France, the Wessex prince made a prearranged stopover at the Carolingian court of Charles II, king of the west Frankish realm. After spending several weeks recovering from the arduous trek across Francia, Alfred resumed his pilgrimage and was provided an armed escort by the king for safe passage to the Italian border. When the royal entourage reached Pavia in Lombardy, the prince rested at the hostel of St Mary, operated by the monastery of Brescia as a respite for pilgrims on their way to the Holy City. From Pavia the Wessex party travelled south to Rome.

As a young prince from rural England, where stone buildings were rare, Alfred must have been astonished as they approached the magnificent walled city with its many soaring brick and stone buildings, monuments and churches. Following his welcome by Pope Leo IV, the prince and his entourage were taken to St Mary's Church at the Saxon School, where rooms were ready for them. The school was located in the papal district and had been established as a centre for visitors from England. After resting from their strenuous journey, the Wessex pilgrims toured the city, visiting the Coliseum, numerous monuments to Christian martyrs and churches, praying before the saintly relics. Several days later, Prince

Alfred was taken to St Peter's Basilica for his blessing by Leo IV. In the majestic basilica at the altar of St Peter, the five-year-old Alfred knelt and was consecrated by the pontiff, receiving the sword and vestments of a Roman Consulate as a decorative honour. During the ceremony Leo IV served as the prince's godfather, establishing bonds of kinship between the Holy Church and the Wessex dynasty, signifying to the royal courts of Europe a personal relationship with the Vicar of Christ.

The Anglo-Saxon pilgrims remained in Rome for only a brief period following the ceremony at St Peter's Basilica, and by the spring of 854 Alfred had returned to his father's court. He was in Wessex for a short time before the Easter season, and was present with his parents and three surviving brothers for the court's religious celebrations at the village of Wilton in south-west England. During Easter at Wilton, the young Wessex prince and his fellow pilgrims to Rome were the centre of attention as they recounted their experiences in the Holy City and discussed the latest news from the continent.

King Aethelwulf was dedicated to the Christian religion and its representation of God's power through the pope. As a devout Christian, he was captivated by the stories of the religious travellers' visit to the centre of the Church in Rome, and his personal desire to make the journey as a pilgrim was re-energized. When reports reached him that Leo IV had died and Pope Benedict III had been elected to the papal throne, the king decided to make his personal pilgrimage to the Holy City, despite the many risks. The journey to Rome would provide the opportunity for Aethelwulf to reaffirm his relationship with the papacy and ensure the continued support of the new pope, while bringing him closer to God.

Aethelwulf began making preparations to leave his realm for a prolonged period, dividing his kingdom between his two eldest surviving sons. Aethelbald was named to rule Wessex, while Ethelred was assigned the eastern fiefdoms of Kent, Surrey, Essex and Sussex. To ensure the continued loyalty of the Wessex churchmen and warlords, the king granted many of them large tracts of royal land. With his arrangements for the governing of his kingdom finalized, the king set out for Rome, taking with him his youngest son, Alfred, along with numerous churchmen, Wessex aristocrats and a contingent of bodyguards.

In 855 the royal Anglo-Saxon entourage departed from Wessex, crossing the English Channel to the West Carolingian Kingdom of King Charles II. From the Frankish court, Aethelwulf and his party were personally conducted by Charles II through his lands to the Italian kingdom of his brother Emperor Lothar I. At the border the Francian king appointed a member of his court, Markward, to guide the Wessex pilgrims across the dangerous northern Italian region. Markward led Aethelwulf and his party safely over the mountainous territory to the hostel of St Mary of the Britons in Pavia. During his brief stay at St Mary's, the king presented a generous gift to the monks who managed the hostel. The royal entourage was soon travelling south down the pilgrimage route through several towns to the Holy City. When the Anglo-Saxons passed through the main gate into Rome, they were met by a papal escort, who took them to the Saxon School where Alfred had stayed two years before. The English quarter had changed dramatically since his earlier visit, Leo IV having rebuilt most of the district with funds provided by King Aethelwulf in appreciation of the pope's care and treatment of Alfred in 853.

Soon after the pilgrims arrived in the Holy City, the Wessex king and his seven-year-old son were taken to St Peter's Basilica and presented to the new pontiff, Benedict III. Alfred and his father approached the papal throne to receive the blessings of the Holy Father. During their visit with the pontiff, they discussed their long journey from England and the events unfolding in western Germany and northern Italy, where Emperor Lothar I was aggressively expanding his power. As part of his pilgrimage to Rome, Aethelwulf arranged for his anointment by the papacy as King of Wessex to gain acknowledgment from European rulers for his sovereignty through divine will. During his stay in the city Aethelwulf, accompanied by Alfred and the Anglo-Saxon magnates and churchmen, assembled at the throne of St Peter, where Benedict III, dressed in his papal robes, held the golden crown aloft and placed it on the monarch's head, thereby recognizing him as King of Wessex in the name of God.

The Wessex delegation remained in Rome for nearly a year, the king and Alfred visiting the hundreds of religious shrines and monuments located throughout the city. While the Anglo-Saxons were in the Holy City, Aethelwulf and the young Wessex prince were witness to the ongoing power struggle between the newly elected Benedict III and the supporters of Emperor Lothar I's choice for the papal crown, Cardinal Anastasius. Since the reign of Charlemagne, the acknowledged emperor of the Western Empire had played a major role in the election of a new pope. However, following Leo IV's death Benedict III was chosen pontiff by the high churchmen and the Roman people without conferring with Lothar I. In September 855 the anti-pope Anastasius entered the Holy City accompanied by his followers and an armed escort. Lothar I's usurpers went to the Lateran, where Benedict III was seated on the papal throne, arresting him and holding him captive. As the news of the usurpation of the papal crown swept through the city, the citizens rose up simultaneously in support of Benedict III, claiming his election had been conducted by canon law. Confronted by the fury of the Roman citizens, the imperial legates of Lothar I were forced to release Benedict and accept him as pope.

The victory of the Roman population and its ecclesiastical supporters established the independence of the Christian Church and reduced the influence of the imperial emperor. For the Wessex king and Alfred, the results of the power struggle strengthened the supremacy of the papacy, rendering its recognition and support more beneficial to a ruling sovereign. To further solidify their friendship with Benedict, Aethelwulf and the Wessex pilgrims presented him with gifts of a golden crown, goblets, candlesticks and many other items of worth.

In the spring of 856 the Saxon pilgrims ended their prolonged visit to the Holy City and, following a final meeting with the pope, began their long return journey to England. The Wessex king and Alfred, accompanied by the aristocrats and churchmen, followed their earlier route, travelling north through Pavia across the Alps into the Francian kingdom of Charles II. The Wessex party made its way to the king's palace at Verberie-sur-Oise north-east of Paris, where Aethelwulf and his son were reunited with Charles II. Several years before the Saxon ruler departed from Wessex on his pilgrimage to the Holy City, his wife Oshurh had died from unknown causes. Anxious to establish a diplomatic and military alliance with the Francian monarch, when the Wessex king first reached the Frankish court in 855 negotiations were begun for his marriage to Judith, the twelve-year-old daughter of Charles II. The marital union with the powerful Carolingian royal family promised to bring the Anglo–Saxon kingdom closer to the prestige and military might of the grandson of Charlemagne, securing a potential ally against the threat of the Vikings' subjugation of England and Wessex.

After arriving at the Carolingian court, the negotiations with the Frankish king were resumed for the marriage of Aethelwulf and Judith. The discussions dragged on for several months, while Alfred remained with his father learning the political skills of diplomacy and enjoying the grandeur of the Carolingian palace with its magnificent rooms and vast gardens. After the agreement was finalized, on 1 October 856, amid all the majesty and splendour of Charles II's Frankish court, Aethelwulf and Judith were married by the Archbishop of Rheims. Near the end of the ceremony, the archbishop placed a golden crown on the head of Judith, ordaining her by God as Queen of Wessex. However, in the Anglo–Saxon kingdom the sovereign's wife was not recognized as queen and Aethelwulf's new marriage caused a rebellion by a powerful coalition of noblemen and ecclesiastical magnates, led by the king's eldest son Aethelbald.

Several weeks after the marriage ceremony binding the Wessex House to the Carolingian dynasty, Aethelwulf's party departed for the Francian coast, crossing the Channel in calm weather. When the Anglo–Saxon king reached his realm, he discovered Aethelbald had asserted his rule throughout Wessex and was now recognized as the reigning sovereign. Aethelwulf was over fifty years old and lacked the support of the nobles, churchmen and people of Wessex, who considered him too weak to govern. The appearance of the new queen on her throne, which was against the traditions of the kingdom, gave reason for further dissent among the people. Negotiations between the two factions were arranged, and to avoid the threat of civil war, Aethelwulf agreed to abandon his claim to the Wessex throne and rule only the smaller eastern provinces as the under-king. When the treaty was presented to the Witan of powerful aristocrats and ecclesiastical magnates, the members voted to sanction the settlement. During the ongoing negotiations, Alfred observed the realignment of power in the Wessex kingdom unfold before him, gaining experience in the art of kingship which would be of great value in the future when he ruled his kingdom.

In the aftermath of the division of Wessex, Aethelwulf established his rule over the eastern fiefdoms, with Judith on her throne at his side as queen. The young Alfred remained with his father at court, continuing his academic education with scholars from the Church while learning the political skills of kingship. Around the age of ten, Alfred began his military training in the weapons of an Anglo-Saxon warlord, learning to fight with the sword, spear and throwing javelin, practicing his martial skills by hunting deer, wolves and boars in the surrounding woodlands.

After two years on the throne of the eastern region, in 858 King Aethelwulf died. As the oldest surviving son and next in line to the monarchy, Aethelbald continued to rule the Wessex realm, while in keeping with the Anglo-Saxon tradition the second-oldest son, Ethelbert, succeeded to the eastern provinces as sub-king to his elder brother. Aethelbald was readily accepted by the aristocrats, churchmen and citizens, ruling Wessex without opposition. However, his reign was brief and after only two years as sovereign he died in 860. Under the terms of Aethelwulf's will, the kingdom of Wessex and the eastern lordships were to be governed separately. The next in the line of succession to the crown of Wessex was Ethelbert, who seized control of both realms, defying the inheritance directives of his father. To solidify his usurpation, he summoned the Witan of aristocrats and high prelates, securing its approval for his actions. Alfred and his elder brother, Ethelred, were now forced to cede their rights of succession to the division of the kingdom and acknowledge their older brother as king of the united Wessex.

Following Ethelbert's usurpation of the Wessex throne, the twelve-year-old Alfred remained in the royal household, continuing his education with Church tutors appointed by the king, studying the Anglo-Saxon and Latin languages and basic arithmetic. During the reign of Ethelbert, the Northmen expanded their encroachments south into Wessex, assailing the capital, Winchester. As the raiders travelled back to their longboats ladened with plunder, they were ambushed by a combined army of militiamen from Hampshire and Berkshire. Taken by surprise, the Vikings were overrun and compelled to retreat. At the court of his brother, the young Alfred listened attentively to the stories of the fighting against the Danes near Winchester, learning the art of war from the king's soldiers. He stayed in the royal household with Ethelred, travelling to the palaces at Wantage, Wilton and Winchester, attending court and observing his brother's discussions with his royal advisors, nobles, churchmen and visiting foreign ambassadors. Following the zealous piety of his father, Alfred attended Mass every day in the palace chapel, celebrating the high Christian holidays with his family and courtiers. In the mornings Alfred and Ethelred usually joined the royal hunting party tracking down wild game in the forests, while practicing their martial skills as Saxon warriors. At night the princes sat at the monarch's table in the Great Hall for dinner before the roaring fireplace, eating deer and boar from the morning's hunt and vegetables grown on the realm's farmlands. After the dinner there was often singing from wandering minstrels performing tales of ancient heroes.

During Ethelbert's reign, the Northmen remained occupied largely to the north of the Thames, launching raids against villages and monasteries but leaving Wessex at peace. While Alfred continued his education and training as a warrior, in 865 the king died after ruling for five years. He died without any heirs, and as the eldest son of Aethelwulf, Ethelred succeeded to the throne of the unified Wessex, Prince Alfred becoming next in the line of succession to the crown.

While the new King of Wessex consolidated his rule over the monarchy, in the autumn of 866 the Great Heathen Army from Scandinavia, led by Ivar the Boneless and Halfdan, landed in East Anglia. In previous years the Northmen had sailed south in their longboats to England, plundering towns and churches before returning north, but Ivar and Halfdan came to overthrow the regional kingdoms and establish their rule. Quickly overwhelmed by the Viking onslaught, King Edmund of East Anglia was forced to seek terms with the Danes. For the invaders' pledge of peace, the East Anglan sovereign was compelled to provide the Great Heathen Army with provisions, arms, equipment and horses. The Danes remained in the kingdom for nearly a year before resuming their invasion in the autumn of 867, proceeding north across Lincolnshire to attack Northumbria.

In Northumbria the local Englishmen were embroiled in an ongoing barbarous civil war for control of the realm. The King of Northumbria, Osbert, had recently been driven out of the city of York by the army of the usurper Aella, and their continuing war weakened the defences of the kingdom against the Danes. Meeting little opposition from the Northumbrian army, on 1 November 866 Ivar the Boneless and Halfdan seized York after only scattered resistance. As the Danes expanded their occupation of Northumbrian lands, Osbert and Aella finally united against their common foe. They spent the winter months recruiting reinforcements and acquiring arms and supplies for a counter-attack against the pagan forces. On 21 March 867 the Northumbrians unleashed a surprise attack to retake York, catching the Northmen unprepared. As the Danes retreated into the defensive walls of the city in panic, they were pursued by the Englishmen. Inside the fortification, the Vikings rallied around Ivar and Halfdan, who led a counter-attack. During the savage ensuing fight, the barbarians steadily regained the initiative, beating the Northumbrians back with heavy losses. The battle raged for two days, with renewed assaults and counter-attacks, finally ending when Osbert and Aella were killed. Without the kings to command the Northumbrian army, the survivors abandoned the fight and fled into the woodlands. The victory at York left the Danes in control of the Northumbrian kingdom. To govern the newly conquered land in their names, Ivar and Halfdan appointed the local nobleman Egbert as their figurehead sovereign.

The Danes spent the spring and summer months in Northumbria continuing to plunder settlements and churches from their base in York, while preparing to renew their campaign of conquest southwards into the kingdom of Mercia. In the autumn Ivar the Boneless and Halfdan led their reinforced pagan army out of Northumbria to Mercia. When the Great Heathen Army first landed in England in 866, it had advanced peacefully through Mercia on its route north to Northumbria, local king Burgred freely permitting them to pass through his territory. As Ivar and Halfdan returned south, the Mercian king was taken by surprise, and while he attempted to muster his army, they captured his principal city of Nottingham with little resistance. With his lands now occupied by a foreign army, Burgred continued to assemble his troops to besiege Nottingham, while sending messengers to his brother-in-law, Ethelred of Wessex, appealing for military aid.

Alfred was now twenty years old and serving on his brother's royal advisory council. When the messengers brought the appeal from Burgred, Ethelred, on the advice of his counsellors, agreed to form an alliance with the Mercians against the Danes. As part of the agreement, Alfred was betrothed to Ealhswith, the daughter of a prominent Mercian nobleman.

After the terms of the alliance were finalized, the Wessex army set out north with Ethelred in command, and Alfred serving as his chief advisor.

Shortly after the royal Wessex forces joined Burgred at the siege of Danish-occupied Nottingham, Alfred was married to Ealhswith before a great assembly of guests. The celebrations continued long into the night, with abundant supplies of food and drink. As the festivities lingered on, Prince Alfred suddenly became ill with acute abdominal pain. Doctors were summoned but could not determine the cause of the illness. The condition persisted for several hours before slowly easing. While the immediate crisis was over, Alfred would suffer pain with recurring health problems in the coming years.

At Nottingham Ethelred joined the siege against the Northmen, placing his men in the siege lines. The Wessex forces at Nottingham included the noblemen with their professional retainers, while the majority of the army was levies from the countryside. The militiamen were poor farmers, whose time away from home was limited by the necessity of planting or harvesting their crops. As the investment against Ivar and Halfdan continued without any sign of surrender, and unable to penetrate the defensive walls, Ethelred and Burgred were compelled to negotiate a settlement with the Danish kings. For the payment of a large sum in gold, Ivar and Halfdan agreed to abandon the Mercian kingdom and relocate to York. Following the pagans' departure, Ethelred and Alfred led their army south back to Wessex, leaving the Great Heathen Army virtually intact and unbloodied.

While Prince Alfred remained with his brother in Wessex, sending their spies to monitor the activities of the Northmen, King Ivar stayed in York for nearly a year, reinforcing his army and collecting arms and supplies to resume his conquest of the Anglo-Saxons. In the autumn of 869 the Great Heathen Army broke camp, travelling across Mercia once more to East Anglia. The Danes moved against the small town of Thetford in Norfolk to establish their winter encampment. From the occupied town, the Viking king and his men plundered and burned the villages and farmlands of East Anglia. After destroying large areas, Ivar and his brother Ubba sent an envoy to the East Anglian king, Edmund, demanding a large annual tribute and acceptance of their overlordship. Edmund replied with a message of defiance, refusing to submit to the barbarians. The East Anglian king assembled his nobles and militiamen, advancing against the Vikings in defence of his kingdom. The Anglo-Saxon soldiers stormed into the ranks of the enemy behind their wall of shields, but were thrown back in barbarous and savage fighting. During the battle on 20 November 869, King Edmund was captured and tortured to death for refusing to renounce his Christian God. Edmund was later recognized by the Church as a martyr for his refusal to reject Christ and accept the pagan gods. Throughout the Middle Ages, Edmund's shrine in Suffolk was a holy site of worship for English Christians.

In the aftermath of the victory over Edmund, the Northmen stayed in the conquered kingdom, consolidating their rule and forcing the East Anglians to provide them with provisions and shelter. After remaining in East Anglia for a year, the Danish army, now under the command of Halfdan and Bagsecg, hastened south to invade Wessex. Shortly after reaching the southern realm, the pagans made camp east of Reading in Berkshire and began fortifying it with trenches and earthen ramparts. While the work on the encampment continued, a Viking forging party was attacked by the local Wessex earl and put to flight. When King Ethelred and his second-in-command, Alfred, learned of the skirmish, they assembled the Wessex army to advance against Halfdan and Bagsecg at Reading. Arriving at the enemy's fortified camp, the Anglo-Saxons surged forward but were driven off following a savage fight.

Ethelred and Alfred then withdrew their army, spending the next four days recruiting additional soldiers and preparing to renew the attack against the pagan invaders. In early January 870 the Anglo-Saxons marched against the Northmen again to force them out of their kingdom. When the English located the enemy, the Danes deployed into two sections along the high ground at Ashdown in Berkshire. Halfdan and Bagsecg commanded one of the divisions, while the other contingent was led by several of their lieutenants. With the enemy warband now divided, Ethelred took charge of half of the Wessex army, positioning it against the two Viking kings, while Alfred was given command of the remaining troops facing the warlords. As the Anglo-Saxon forces formed into formation, the early morning sun's bright rays were reported to have broken through the clouds and reflected off their shields and helmets. Before the peasant militiamen advanced forward, the two armies exchanged war cries, insults and shouts of, 'Out, out.'

While the Wessex army waited for the order to attack, Ethelred remained in his tent praying at morning Mass. Alfred sent a message to his brother urging him to quickly take command and lead the army forward. Despite his pleas, the king refused to leave Mass until the service was concluded. With the Anglo-Saxon forces in danger of losing momentum, Alfred took the initiative and ordered his men to advance up the slopes of the hill. When Ethelred heard the sounds of battle, he ran out of his tent to his troops, leading them forward in support of his brother's assault. The Wessex fighters stormed up the hill, their dragon banners flying in the morning breeze, meeting the Vikings near a lone thorn tree. The fighting raged around the tree throughout the day, with charges and counter charges, until darkness started to cover the battlefield and the Danes finally began to yield. As the Wessex forces of Ethelred and Alfred pressed forward, the barbarians' front first wavered and then broke, the Vikings fleeing under darkening skies and leaving thousands of dead and wounded on the battlefield of Ashdown. The English army pursued the withdrawing foe back to Reading, continuing the slaughter.

Although Ethelred and Alfred won their first encounter against the pagans at the Battle of Ashdown, the enemy forces had not been decisively defeated. From behind the protective fortifications of Reading, Halfdan and his brother reassembled their battered army and made preparations to renew their campaign of conquest. When Ethelred learned from his scouts that the Viking army had departed from Reading and was encamped near Basingstoke in Hampshire, he re-formed his nobles and militiamen, advancing against Halfdan. On 21 January 871 the Danes and Anglo-Saxons clashed again 2 miles from Basingstoke. The Great Heathen Army held a strong fortified line, but after his victory at Ashdown the Wessex king brashly ordered his men to attack the entrenched enemy behind their ditches and log fortifications. When the Anglo-Saxon militiamen collided with the Northmen, they were unable to penetrate Halfdan's defences, and despite the appeals of Ethelred and Alfred to rally for another assault, the Englishmen retreated after suffering major losses.

In the aftermath of their defeat, the battered Englishmen withdrew before regrouping to resume their campaign against Halfdan. In late March 871 the two armies clashed again at Meretun near the village of Wilton. At the approach of the Anglo-Saxons, Halfdan aligned his troops in two divisions along a strongly reinforced front. When the Wessex troops reached the waiting Danes, Ethelred and Alfred led their men forward, smashing into Halfdan's line of defences. The Viking warriors began to fall back under the might of the Anglo-Saxon assault. The Wessex sovereign and his brother pressed their attack, but in the late afternoon the pagans rallied around Halfdan and began to drive the English militiamen back in fierce fighting. As the Northmen intensified their assault across the open field into the English formation, Ethelred and Alfred were compelled to withdraw, abandoning their dead and wounded. During the fighting at Meretun, numerous Anglo-Saxon noblemen were killed and Ethelred mortally wounded. In mid-April 871 the Wessex king died of his wounds, and under the prior agreement signed at the assembly of Swinborg, the twenty-two-year-old Alfred succeeded to the throne, bypassing the two young sons of Ethelred.

Following the death of Ethelred, preparations for his burial were made and Wimborne Monastery in Dorset was chosen as the interment site. The funeral was attended by Alfred, his family and the high nobles and churchmen of Wessex. While at Wimborne, the Witan assembly of great landowners and high churchmen met to confirm Alfred's election to the Wessex kingship. The vote of the assembly was followed by the coronation of the newly sanctioned sovereign. The religious ceremony followed ancient Saxon tradition, with the service performed by the ranking bishop. At the church's altar, the bishop anointed Alfred with holy oil before crowning him king. The placement of holy oil on Alfred's head set him apart from his nobles, prelates and peasants, binding them to his overlordship with their fealty.

While the Wessex nobles and peers attended the funeral of Ethelred and the coronation of Alfred at Wimborne, a large contingent of troops was sent to monitor the movement of the Northmen at Reading. When Halfdan's scouts reported the presence of the English force, he assembled his army and unleashed a surprise attack against Alfred's men. The Anglo-Saxon warriors held their position against the Danish onslaught, but were outnumbered and after a spirited fight were compelled to retreat.

In the summer of 871 Halfdan's Great Heathen Army was reinforced by the Great Summer Army from Scandinavia, led by King Guthrum, and their combined forces advanced from Reading to renew their conquest of Wessex. When Alfred learned the Danes were in the field, he assembled his magnates and militiamen, marching to meet the enemy near Wilton. The English troops clashed with the pagans, with the new king, Guthrum, leading his men into battle from the front. The Anglo–Saxons formed their shield wall, charging across the field into the Northmen, while archers fired waves of arrows in support. Fierce fighting continued for hours, the barbarians driven to the rear only to rally and beat back Alfred's levies. Late in the day the Vikings feigned a retreat, and as the Wessex warriors charged forward in disorder, Halfdan and Guthrum unleashed a savage riposte, forcing the disorganized Wessex lords and militiamen to flee, their ranks shattered.

Alfred's succession to the throne of Wessex had been with the approval of the assembly of magnates and prelates, but his loss at Wilton weakened their support for the new king. To consolidate his assumption of power, the Wessex monarch needed a period of peace. To buy the needed time, he sent emissaries to Halfdan and Guthrum at Reading offering a sizeable sum of gold if they abandoned his kingdom. After negotiating with the English envoys, the Viking kings agreed to the terms. To raise the required funds, Alfred ordered his aristocrats, nobles and bishops to remit a substantial amount of money to the Wessex throne, while paying a large sum from the royal treasury. When the arrangements were approved, Halfdan and Guthrum took their armies from Wessex, moving against King Burgred in Mercia, where the government was in disarray under competing factions of nobles.

The Northmen established their encampment at London, while Alfred remained in his realm recovering from the war with the Danes, reinforcing and reorganizing his army and beginning the construction of a small navy. After the Vikings plundered the towns, farms and church properties in Mercia, they advanced again in the early summer of 872 into Northumbria, where the people had recently risen in revolt and overthrown the figurehead King of the Danes, Egbert. While the pagan army restored order, Halfdan and Guthrum encamped at the town of Torksey in Lincolnshire. From there the Danish troops pillaged Northumbria until the late spring of 873, and after extorting a large tribute from the nobles, towns and churches they moved back into Mercia. When the Northmen arrived in his realm again, King Burgred appealed to Alfred for military aid, but after his requests went unanswered he abandoned his subjects, retiring to Rome to live the remainder of his short life in peace.

All of Mercia was now under the hegemony of the Northmen, and they named Ceolwulf II as their puppet king. Ceolwulf, a weak nobleman from Burgred's court, was easily manipulated by the conquerors. Following the occupation of Mercia, the Danes split the Great Heathen Army into two sections in 874, Halfdan leading one force to the north to impose his rule while Guthrum remained in the south with the larger second division. From his court in Wessex, Alfred received a steady stream of reports detailing the victories of the Vikings across the Thames. While Guthrum moved his host south of the Thames, the remaining Danish forces marched into northern England, razing many towns and church properties and establishing their occupation forces. In Wales, the local king Rhodri Mawr steadily defended his borders against incursions by the pagans. While Alfred defended Wessex against the Northmen, Danish armies also advanced into Ireland, setting up a permanent base at Dublin and extending their supremacy into the countryside through military might.

The conquests of the Vikings continued into the Loire valley in France, with the invaders turning the abandoned city of Angers into an occupied stronghold fortified with strong wooden ramparts and blockhouses. Following the warbands' seizure of his town, the King of France, Charles II, assembled his army and moved against the Northmen at Angers. After failing to gain the surrender of the enemy forces by besieging the garrison, battering their defences with catapults and unleashing assaults supported by siege towers, Charles II ordered his engineers to divert the flow of the Maine River away from the fortification, depriving the Northmen of reinforcements and fresh supplies along the waterway. The barbarians were soon compelled to surrender, pledging to pay a large tribute and abandon Angers and the Loire area. After making the payment to the king, the Vikings withdrew from Angers but continued to stay in western France, pillaging and harassing the towns, farmlands and churches in defiance of the regime.

Meanwhile, in England, while the Vikings increasingly asserted their overlordship north of the Thames, to the south of the river, Wessex was the only remaining kingdom free of Danish rule by 875. Following the division of the Great Heathen Army, King Guthrum led his forces south to Cambridge, staying until the following year. While the pagans remained in the north, in the summer of 875 Alfred sailed his new fleet to engage a force of seven pagan ships. The Anglo-Saxons clashed with the enemy vessels off the Wessex shore, sinking one and compelling the others to flee. Soon after the victory over the Viking flotilla, a large Scandinavian army landed on the Wessex coast near Wareham, quickly seizing the fortified town. To contain the barbarian invasion, Alfred mustered his army of nobles and freemen and hastened against Wareham. When the Wessex peasant militiamen reached the town on the Frome River, King Alfred laid siege to the occupying forces. As the investment dragged on for several months, Alfred offered to pay a large remuneration to encourage the enemy to withdraw. The pagans accepted the offer, abandoning Wareham without a fight.

Following the withdrawal of the Northmen from Wareham, the Viking chieftain advanced his army to the Wessex town of Exeter, attacking and occupying it, despite his oath to abandon the kingdom sworn on the image of a golden pagan god. Alfred was again compelled to defend his realm, taking his men to Exeter and besieging the enemy behind its fortified walls.

As the Anglo-Saxons continued to press the siege, a large Viking fleet of over 100 ships was sent to the relief of the garrison. When the pagan vessels approached the coastline of Devon in Swanage Bay, they were attacked by the Wessex fleet. The king's seamen outmanoeuvred the barbarians with their knowledge of the coastal waters, destroying numerous ships, while a storm sank several more. In the wake of Alfred's naval victory, the Danish garrison commander made peace and swore to abandon the Exeter stronghold. In August 877 the Northmen marched out of the town, moving north to Mercia, where they drove the English out of their farmlands in the eastern part of the kingdom to establish their own homesteads.

In December 877 King Alfred spent the Christmas season at his palace in Chippenham with his family, high noblemen and church officials. With the senior earls and ecclesiastical prelates present, he met with the royal council, planning for the coming year and making appointments to his government. The battles against Guthrum had not gone well during the year, and the king was forced to make ever-increasing demands on his lords and bishops for more money to finance the war effort. A faction of powerful earls and churchmen led by the Archbishop of Canterbury, Ethelred, and Earl Wulfhere of Wiltshire favoured a settlement with Guthrum, similar to the Mercian and Northumbrian political agreements, which left the kingdoms under the rule of an appointed vassal monarch of the Northmen. During the Christmas festival at Chippenham, the royal Witan met in secret and, under the influence of a pro-Danish faction, voted to depose Alfred. Shortly after the king was notified of the council's decision, reports reached the court that the Viking warriors were fast approaching Chippenham. The king gathered his family and loyal followers, escaping into the cold night of January 878.

While the barbarians strengthened their hegemony over Wessex and began pillaging the surrounding villages and churches, Vikings from South Wales, under the command of Chief Ubba Ragnarsson, brother of Halfdan, sailed down the coast in twenty-three ships, landing in Devon in support of Guthrum. When the heathen warriors advanced against the local shire's troops, Earl Odda, who had remained loyal to King Alfred, ordered his men to withdraw to the abandoned fortification at Countisbury Hill. Ubba followed the retreating Anglo-Saxon freemen, besieging their fortified village. Inside the stronghold, the Wessex soldiers, cut off from reinforcements, relief supplies and water, chose to assail the enemy rather than face a slow death from dehydration and starvation. In the early morning, the Englishmen stormed out of the fort to attack the unsuspecting Northmen. During the ensuing battle, Ubba and over 800 of his men were killed, while the survivors fled into the woodlands in panic. The victory at Countisbury Hill strengthened Alfred's resolve to remain in Wessex and regain his throne.

As Guthrum expanded his rule over Wessex and the lords and churchmen in western Wessex increasingly pledged their fealty to him, Alfred refused to abandon his kingship, deciding to continue his fight against the Northmen from the marshes of Athelney in modern-day Somerset. In late March 878 Alfred, with the Earl of Somerset, retired with a small contingent of faithful men to the marshes, building a reinforced stronghold on the island of Athelney, surrounded by swamps and flood waters. The outlaw monarch's troops were supplied by local farmers, who brought fresh food and supplies, while there was abundant deer and boar in the forest to hunt for meat. During their exile in the swamplands, Alfred's soldiers left the security of their fort to ambush Guthrum's raiding and foraging parties, attack isolated outposts and harass the enemy's supply trains. The news of Alfred's defiance of the Danes spread across the kingdom and the Wessex people refused to lose faith in their king. Many legends grew out of Alfred's stay in the Athelney marshlands, spreading throughout his realm and becoming a part of his mystique. In one of the tales, the king, dressed as a minstrel, entered a fortified Danish encampment, entertaining the Viking warriors with his songs while collecting intelligence on their strength and defences.

In the spring of 878 Alfred's supporters spread the word through the surrounding shires that the Wessex army was mustering at Egbert's Stone to drive the pagans out of the kingdom. After remaining in the Athelney marshlands for nearly two months, Alfred assembled his men and advanced from the swamps to Egbert's Stone near Penselwood, the announced rallying point. Nobles and peasant levies from the shires of Somerset, Wiltshire and many freemen from Hampshire assembled at the king's call. Over 4,000 Wessex men abandoned their spring planting to answer the king's summons for the defence of their kingdom against the heathens. The next morning the English troops proceeded north-east to current-day Iley Oak near the village of Bishopstrow in Wiltshire, as additional men flocked to join his army.

As the Wessex farmers began leaving their fields in large numbers in early May, Guthrum was informed by his spies that Alfred's soldiers were mustering to regain their kingdom. After spending a day at Iley Oak, Alfred renewed his advance at dawn, leading his army to Edington, where his scouts reported the Danish were aligned along the high ground. Shortly after sunrise Alfred deployed his newly mustered army of Anglo-Saxon warriors in a line opposing Guthrum's troops. As the Wessex men dressed in their long tunics and pants waited for the order to attack, they hurled choruses of abuse at the enemy, who responded with yells of ridicule. The command to advance was then given and the Englishmen fashioned their wooden round shields into a solid line, marching forward under their golden dragon banners against the barbarians. The Anglo-

Saxon soldiers stormed up the hill. When they approached the Danes, they unleashed volleys of javelins and arrows into their ranks before ploughing into their foe's front with savage hand-to-hand fighting. The battle lasted throughout the day, the Anglo-Saxon peasant militiamen fighting the Northmen with their thrusting 7ft-long spears and slashing swords smeared with blood. As the sun began to drop late in the afternoon, and with his ranks thinned by dead and injured, Guthrum's line began to break under the constant pressure of the Wessex assault. As the Englishmen pressed their attack, the Vikings started to retreat in larger numbers with Alfred's warriors in close pursuit.

Following his defeat at Edington, Guthrum moved his battered army to the fortress at Chippenham some 14 miles away. As the despondent Northmen struggled back to the safety of the fortification, they were harassed by the pursuing English. Alfred ordered his men to besiege the stronghold, and siege lines were built around the defensive works, while attacks were launched against the defenders. After two weeks under siege, the Danes' food supplies became increasingly exhausted, compelling Guthrum to seek surrender terms from the Wessex king. During the talks with the Danes, Alfred pressed Guthrum and his chief warlords to disavow their pagan gods and convert to the Church of Christ to add validity to their promises of withdrawal. Following the negotiations, Guthrum agreed to a peace treaty pledging to abandon Wessex, give hostages to ensure his surety and accept Christianity. In early June Guthrum and thirty senior Northmen, dressed in white penance clothes, went to Aller and were baptized with holy oil. Alfred attended the ceremony, serving as Guthrum's godfather. During the religious ritual, a white band was placed around the part of the head that had been touched by holy oil. Eight days later Alfred and his royal council met with Guthrum and his chosen thirty warlords at the palace of Wedmore for the ceremony to remove the white strips. The removal of the bands marked the entry of the Vikings into the Christian faith.

The Danish forces remained in western Wessex until October before departing from the realm and relocating to East Anglia. The war against the Northmen had devastated Wessex, leaving it vulnerable to additional invasions from foreign enemies. The farmlands had been unattended, while nearly all trade had ceased. The villages and monasteries had been repeatedly pillaged and the royal treasury depleted by the expenses of the war. Virtually all education had come to an end after the destruction of the monasteries and lawlessness was widespread throughout the kingdom.

Assuming the powers of kingship again, Alfred initiated a series of reforms to ensure the safety of his kingdom against the threat of enemy invasion. Additional measures were decreed to rebuild villages, churches and monasteries and end the economic stagnation. In the recent period of crisis during the Viking war, the royal council of senior noblemen and ecclesiastical officials had turned against Alfred, and the first restructuring of his government enacted by the king was to replace these disloyal men. Seven Witan members were dismissed, with eight new earls and bishops who were devoted to Alfred appointed to the council. The composition of the existing Wessex army was inadequate to repel a force the size of the Great Heathen Army, and Alfred reorganized his military, creating a rotating system requiring half of the earls with their shire vassals to serve on active duty when summoned by the king, while the remaining peasant levies stayed on their farms to till their crops. In the event a campaign lasted a prolonged time, the soldiers in the field could be relieved by the men at home. This revised organization gave Wessex the beginnings of a permanent national army, instead of an improvised band of troops which were later disbanded after a crisis had passed. To increase the mobility of his new military forces, units of cavalry became a permanent arm, giving Alfred the necessary forces to perform reconnaissance and picket duties, conduct plundering raids deep in enemy territory and act as a courier service. The troops that remained on their farms were expected to guard their shires against enemy raiding parties and serve garrison duty at the local fort, while acting as a police force.

While the reforms to the Wessex military continued, Alfred began the construction of a national home defensive system. The Danes had repeatedly utilized great regional fortifications to protect their lands, and the king adopted their strategy. He planned to build numerous strongholds throughout his kingdom, fortified with earthen mounds, wooden blockhouses and deep trenches that could be utilized as shelters by the towns' residents and farmers when threatened by enemy armies or raiding parties. Most of the forts were built around existing villages and grew into larger settlements under the protection of the fortification. By the time of Alfred's death in 899, the planned defensive barrier had not been completed but had dramatically lessened the prospects of success for a potential invader.

To further strengthen the defences of his realm, Alfred ordered his engineers and craftsmen to build a fleet of coastal defence warships, in place of his commandeered trading vessels, to attack the Northmen at sea before they could land and launch their plundering raids. In the summer of 875 Alfred personally led a Wessex naval force against seven Viking longboats, capturing one and driving the others out to sea. He utilized his naval experiences to personally design the specifications for his new vessels, calling for craft that were nearly twice as long as the Danish longboats and faster, with sixty oarsmen. The Wessex flotilla was constructed as a manoeuvrable sea force, conceived as a troop carrier rather than an offensive weapon to strike enemy boats. The warships were built to engage the enemy's vessels by manoeuvring next to them and binding the two craft together with ropes. The Wessex seamen, armed with swords and bows and arrows, boarded the ship, clashing with the Northmen in man-to-man fighting. The king's construction of the fleet marked the beginnings of the British Navy.

In the aftermath of his victory over the Danes at Edington, Alfred spent the next eight years strengthening his overlordship and reinforcing his borders against a renewal of Viking attacks. Following his earlier settlement with the Vikings at Wedmore, the king negotiated a second agreement with Guthrum setting out the boundaries of Wessex to further secure his regime. The treaty also contained several provisions to resolve disputes between the two realms without resorting to war. As the result of his negotiations with Guthrum, Alfred's kingdom remained at peace with the Northmen, and restorations were made to the villages, churches and monasteries destroyed during the Vikings rampages, while trade with the rest of England and the continent was re-energized.

Alfred's wife, Ealhswith, was closely related to the royal family of Mercia, while his father-in-law, Ethelred, was a relative of a former king of the realm. Upon the death of the Viking figurehead monarch Ceolwulf II, the Northmen replaced him with Ethelred. The new Mercian overlord assumed the throne, ruling under the authority of the Scandinavians with the title of earl, instead of king. The Danes continued to reign in the eastern half of the kingdom, while their appointed token ruler governed the western region. To end the dominion of the Vikings, Ethelred utilized his connections with the Wessex crown to secure Alfred's overlordship and his protection against Guthrum. By recognizing Ethelred as his vassal, Alfred expanded his hegemony into western Mercia, while the Danes retained control over the east.

Alfred's intervention in western Mercia expanded his power into south-west England, with the Welsh border to the west. Soon after his recognition of Ethelred as his vassal, the Wessex king manoeuvred to expand his influence into southern Wales. The southern monarchies of Wales were in danger of being overwhelmed by the sons of Rhodri Mawr, who had assumed the governments of the northern Welsh regimes following their father's death. As the two brothers – Anarawd, King of Gwynedd and Powys, and King Cadell of Seisyllwg – prepared to invade the realms in the south, the sovereigns of Dyfed and Brycheiniog arrived at Alfred's court seeking his protection against the invasion of their lands. Alfred agreed to intervene in support of the two rulers and secure their kingdoms for them. After Wessex extended its influence into the two southern dominions, the kings of Gwent and Glywysing also appeared before Alfred petitioning his intercession against incursions into their Welsh lands by Ethelred of Mercia. By holding the Mawr brothers in place with his army and ordering Ethelred to withdraw his troops from Wales, the Wessex king expanded his supremacy as overlord across a large area. As Alfred's power in southern England continued to grow, he later agreed to support the two Welsh brothers against an invasion of their northern territories by a sizeable Danish force for their pledges of fealty. Through his forays into Wales, Alfred had gained control over most of the local monarchies. His presence in Wales had far-reaching consequences for the south-western lands, permitting later English kings to claim overlordship of virtually the entire region.

While Alfred was securing his kingdom against future Viking attacks, the Northmen invaded current-day France in large numbers, ravaging towns, church properties and farms for over five years. The barbarians pillaged as far north as Ghent in present-day Belgium and along the Somme to Amiens seventy miles north of Paris. The Danish forces remained in Amiens for a year, plundering the area of its wealth and food before separating into two warbands with one crossing the English Channel to assail the Anglo–Saxon trading centre at Rochester on the Kent coastline and the other heading farther inland into the kingdom of France. Rochester was a wealthy commercial and ecclesiastical centre with weak defensive fortifications built by the Romans. Located on the Medway River and close to the Channel, the Viking raiding parties could quickly strike in their longboats and escape on the nearby waterways before Alfred's troops could assemble and reach Rochester.

As the Scandinavian raiders waited on the coast of France for the weather in the Channel to clear, their expectations of a quick and easy victory over Rochester were high. After sailing across the Channel and landing on the shores of Kent, the pagans left their ships, advancing overland against the town. When the marauders reached Rochester, they were surprised to find a formidable defensive system surrounding the town, instead of the outdated and unstable Roman walls. The commander of the Vikings led an attack against the defenders, but was driven back. After discovering a well-fortified city with a determined garrison, the raiders were compelled to begin siege operations, believing Alfred's relief force would take many days to assemble and march to Rochester. Unknown to the invaders, Alfred had reorganized his army into two divisions, with one always on active duty while members of the other stayed at their farms and villages. When the king received reports of the Danes' siege, he hastened north to assault the besieging enemy forces. Upon reaching the outskirts of the town, he immediately unleashed a fierce attack against the Vikings, sending his warriors storming into the Danish formation with their wall of shields. The Northmen were surprised by the size of the Wessex army and its rapid arrival, abandoning their siege and withdrawing to their ships.

While the main body of the Northmen abandoned the invasion of Kent, a band of raiders remained in the area and began pillaging the coastal towns. The plundering party was soon joined by Danes from East Anglia who were part of Guthrum's occupation force. Together the two Scandinavian armies planned to plunder the coastal region of Alfred's lands. However, dissension quickly erupted between the two contingents of warriors, the 'French' Vikings recrossing the Channel to France while the East Anglians returned home.

Alfred responded to the renewal of plundering forays in his kingdom by sending a naval raiding force to assault the coastal towns of East Anglia as a message to Guthrum to end the attacks against Wessex ralm. As the Wessex king's ships pillaged along the coast, sixteen Danish warships sailed out from the mouth of the Stour River to defend their towns. The two fleets were soon locked in a savage sea battle. As the vessels moved closer together, the Wessex archers fired waves of arrows at the Vikings. When the Wessex flotilla manoeuvred to the pagan warships, Alfred's men stormed onto the enemy's decks, attacking the Northmen with their slashing swords and knives. During the violent encounter, all of the Scandinavian longboats were captured with numerous crewmen killed. As the king's naval forces prepared to leave the Stour area, the East Anglians assembled a fleet of warships to attack the Wessex vessels near the river. During the second battle, the Anglo–Saxon sailors were outmanoeuvred and overwhelmed by the Northmen. All of the captured ships were recovered by the Vikings, while many of Alfred's men were killed. The surviving Englishmen managed to escape from the enemy, returning to Wessex.

The town of London was built during the Roman occupation of Britain to serve as a port for trade with the coastal villages and the European continent. With its strategic location on the 215-mile-long Thames and close vicinity to the English Channel, the town grew into a thriving commercial centre. Following the fall of the Roman Empire in the fifth century, the city was abandoned and largely collapsed into ruins. As a highly successful mercantile site, the Anglo–Saxons later rebuilt London to the west of its original location, and over the following years it grew into a wealthy and densely populated commercial and manufacturing centre. The city's many artisans and craftsmen produced a wide range of products, from jewellery to iron goods. With its new-found wealth, the inhabitants erected new defensive works, including an earthen wall and deep trench, to discourage plundering raids by other English kingdoms and later the Vikings.

Following the invasion of Britain by the Danes, London was overrun by the Northmen and occupied by a garrison. As Alfred expanded his overlordship to the north, approaching the lands of Guthrum, he now believed the Vikings' continued presence in London posed an intolerable threat to his growing kingdom. In 886 he assembled his vassals and peasant militiamen to move against the Northmen in London. When the Wessex army entered Viking-occupied land, Alfred unleashed a vicious campaign of fire and fury, burning towns and destroying farmlands on his march to London. Upon reaching the city, he laid siege, surrounding the defensive works with a deep trench and parapets, while battering the walls with catapults. Under the pressure of the English attack, the Danish garrison was compelled to surrender after resisting for several months. The Northmen opened the gates of the city and Alfred accepted their submission.

While Alfred was securing his hold on the Thames, he ordered the city of London relocated to its prior site, a formidable defensive position, and the old Roman fortifications torn down and rebuilt. The original London had been constructed on a formidable defensive position and Alfred ordered its relocation to ensure his continued possession of the valuable city. The new London was laid out inside the defensive walls in a grid pattern.

The Thames originates far inland and flows eastward through much of Wessex and its overlordships. With its strategic location on the Thames and close to the river's confluence with the Channel, the possession of London was vital to Alfred's defence of his kingdom. With dominion over the city, the Wessex king controlled access to the passageway from the coast into the inlands of England, allowing him to repel any invading armies sailing up the waterway. To further monitor travel on the Thames, Alfred ordered his engineers to construct a bridge over the river with fortifications on the bank opposite London, enhancing his defensive coverage of the waterway.

Prior to the Viking invasions, the city of London had been under the rule of the kings of Mercia. The residents still considered themselves Mercians, and to secure his further overlordship of London Alfred gave control of the city to his vassal, Ethelred. To fortify his alliance with the Mercian ruler, the Wessex king arranged the marriage of his daughter Ethelflaed to Ethelred. Following the union between the Wessex and Mercian families, Ethelred took possession of London, ruling it for his father-in-law and keeping the city firmly under Alfred's authority.

After solidifying his power over London, Alfred renegotiated his prior treaty at Wedmore with Guthrum. Swearing oaths, the two kings pledged to respect the boundaries of each other's lands. Under the terms of their agreement, England was divided into two sections, with Alfred ruling in the south and the Vikings holding control of the Danelaw in the north. The borderline ran from London across England to Chester in the west, with Alfred's delegated overlordship acknowledged in Wales and western Mercia. Guthrum's kingdom included Essex, East Anglia, Northumbria and the eastern Mercian region. Following the signing of the treaty, Alfred held a great ceremony where all of his Wessex earls, vassals and the rulers of his subject kingdoms paid homage to him as their overlord. From this time forward, Alfred was considered King of the Anglo-Saxons, despite over half of the realm remaining under Danish rule.

In the wake of his treaty of friendship with the Danes, Alfred began compiling a set of laws for his subjects to live by. The king's code was based on the Ten Commandments from the *Bible*, the laws of his predecessors and advice from his secular and ecclesiastical advisors, and was to be observed throughout his realm. Alfred wrote in the preamble: 'I King Alfred collected the laws together and ordered to be written many of them which our forefathers observed, those which I liked and many of those which I did not like, I rejected with the advice of my counselors and ordered them to be differently observed.' The canon set out each crime in great detail, establishing its punishments. Acts of treason were considered the most serious and were punished by death, while a convicted murderer was required to pay a heavy fine to the victim's family as compensation. The code contained a long list of crimes for various injuries occurring during acts of violence, with their prescribed punishments. The payment to the victim for the loss of the third finger was greater than for the remaining fingers, while the cost of a severed thumb was still more severe. The same type of scale applied to the loss of other body parts. A different measurement applied for non-violent injuries, and the amount paid was determined by the pre-set value of the body part. For acts of theft, all convicted criminals were required to pay the same fine, except in cases of abductions of men, women or children. Charges brought against an individual were settled at a public meeting, with the local earl and bishop acting as judges. Over time, Alfred's code became the foundation for the British legal system.

To govern his vast southern English kingdom, Alfred needed educated and loyal agents who could be trusted to protect his interest. As his lands expanded, he required more men to administer his justice, act as envoys and collect his taxes. The creation of a new system of schools now became vital to train the representatives the king required to fill the positions in his administration.

The long-running military conflict with the Danes, with its demands for men and money, had resulted in the deterioration of learning in Alfred's kingdom. The Wessex king wrote about the condition of education in his lands, stating: 'Learning has declined so thoroughly in England that there were very few men who could understand their divine services in English or even translate a simple letter from Latin into English. There were so few of them that I cannot recollect even a single one south of the Thames when I succeeded to the kingdom.' With the realm's literacy at a low level, the king initiated a new effort to reform the educational system. He first began a recruiting programme to encourage scholars in England and on the continent to reside in his court and turn it into a centre of learning. The Bishop of Worcester quickly answered the king's call and was followed by additional educated men, who brought a wide range of learning skills. Soon after the Worcester bishop arrived at court he began the translation of the Latin classics into English. The abbey schools in Mercia had largely escaped the destruction of the Vikings, and the Wessex sovereign sent his agents there to recruit men of learning for his regime. The scholars at the Wessex court instructed the monarch by reading to him in Latin on a wide range of subjects. The king greatly enjoyed gathering with his favourite tutors to learn Latin grammar. Learned men from foreign courts were also employed by Alfred, who sent envoys to France to recruit the best scholars from the churches and monasteries.

After recruiting a wide range of learned men, King Alfred set up a palace school for his children and the sons and daughters of his nobles. Under the king's direction, his schools were to teach reading and writing in the English language to their pupils, plus Latin to those students who planned to take holy orders. He decreed that all government business was to be transacted in English, making a staff well-trained in the language essential. Additional schools were established in some of the larger monasteries. The palace school was for both the boys and girls of the king and his magnates. When boys reached the age of seven or eight, they began training in the weapons of a warrior, learning to fight with the spear, sword, javelin and bow and arrow, while mastering the skills of horsemanship. To practice their martial techniques, they frequently hunted in the dense forests of southern England.

During his reign Alfred was an active sponsor of the arts. He hired skilled artisans and craftsmen to fashion a wide variety of objects, from jewellery to decorative weapons. As the ruler of an extensive kingdom, he was expected to distribute gifts to his loyal vassals, churchmen and visiting dignitaries and envoys. To produce the high-quality art items the court required, the king encouraged the creation of new and elaborate items to impress the receivers of his rewards.

Through their over thirty years of marriage, Alfred developed a loving and devoted relationship with his wife Ealhswith, despite their arranged union. Ealhswith was from a noble family in the kingdom of Mercia and the daughter of a powerful and influential earl, but at the Wessex court she was content with her domestic duties and raising her children, taking no part in the affairs of state. Following the death of her husband in October 899, she founded the Convent of St Mary's Abbey in Winchester and spent the remainder of her life in the religious house.

Following the signing of the treaty of peace at Aller between Alfred and the Viking king Guthrum, Wessex was generally free of pillaging raids from the north. During the late 880s, Guthrum died and the Wessex monarch lost a reliable stabilizing force in East Anglia and along his northern borders. The potential for a renewal of war with the Northmen was further enhanced when the Danes in France suffered crushing defeats by the armies of the French. In the autumn of 892 the pagans began preparations to leave the French coast and sail to England. They loaded their families, animals and equipment onto over 250 vessels and crossed the Channel, landing along the Rother River area in south-east England. The Danes, forced out of France, were now in search of lands to conquer and inhabit as their new homes.

Soon after leaving their longships, the Northmen moved inland and quickly encountered King Alfred's fortified town at Eorpeburnan. Over 2,000 Viking warriors attacked the small outpost, rapidly overrunning the defensive works and slaughtering the garrison. The warband renewed its advance to Appledore near the Romney Marsh in Kent, where the barbarians built a town surrounded by strong defensive works. While Alfred was receiving reports of the destruction of Eorpeburnan, a second Viking fleet of eighty vessels, led by the chieftain Haesten, was sailing up the Thames with 800 men after crossing the Channel from Boulogne. Haesten, a veteran and brutal chieftain, was one of the Vikings' most successful leaders. He led Danish raiding parties and larger armies for over forty years, leaving a path of death and destruction along the rivers of the Seine and Loire, across the Low Countries and the towns and monasteries of the western Mediterranean before finally sailing to England. He landed his men and their families at the royal village of Milton Regis near the Isle of Sheppey on the Kent coastline. Alfred now faced two formidable mobile armies, plus the possibility that the East Anglian and Mercian Vikings would join the invaders from France. To meet the new challenge to his kingdom, he quickly mustered his vassals and militiamen, moving north into a position between both enemy warbands, where he could easily observe their movements. Alfred knew if he marched against one of the Scandinavian armies, the remaining wariors would be free to cause havoc in his realm. To give him time to attack the warband at Appledore, the king sent emissaries to Haesten to negotiate a peace agreement. A pact was reached between the two rulers, with Haesten pledging to have his two young sons baptized as Christians and abandon the Wessex crown's lands for a sizeable payment. The baptism ceremony was held in London, with Alfred and Ethelred serving as godfathers for the chieftain's sons.

In the wake of the religious ceremony at London and the payment of the bribe, Haesten withdrew his army from the Thames, relocating to Benfleet in Essex. While Alfred was monitoring the withdrawal of the Vikings from his lands, in the spring of 893 the leader of the Appledore Northmen sent a large marauding party west to ravage parts of Hampshire and Berkshire. When the raiders turned back toward their base, they were met by a veteran Anglo-Saxon army led by Alfred's eldest son, Edward.

The two forces clashed at Farnham, thirty miles south-west of London, where Prince Edward's soldiers overwhelmed the Vikings in a savage fight, compelling them to flee and abandon their plunder from the raid.

The survivors of the battle at Farnham escaped from the pursuing English troops, making their way to Thorney Island, where they quickly built a fortified encampment. The Vikings were compelled to remain on the island while their chieftain recovered from wounds suffered at Farnham. The Wessex king's son followed the enemy soldiers to Thorney Island and laid siege to the Danish camp, while his father advanced from the south with reinforcements. Meanwhile, the East Anglian and Northumbrian Northmen again broke their pledges of peace and, under the command of a pirate named Sigeferth, unleashed an attack against the town of Exeter in southern Wessex with 140 vessels, while a second naval force plundered the Devon coastline. With his kingdom under attack, Alfred was compelled to abandon his march north and turn to contend the Danes in Devon.

At the ongoing siege at Thorney Island, Prince Edward's position now became critical, with his food supplies running low and the term of active military service for his men ending. Despite the arrival of reinforcements from Mercia sent by Ethelred and a small force from his father, Edward was compelled to negotiate a settlement with the French Vikings. The Northmen made the usual promises of peace and gave hostages to the Englishmen before they were allowed to march out of their camp and leave Wessex. The Danes moved north to unite with Haesten at his newly built fortification near a small river at Benfleet, where they were joined by the surviving troops from Appledore. As the men from Thorney Island advanced to Benfleet, they were followed by the Wessex troops of Edward and Ethelred's Mercian forces. When the Wessex militiamen and their Mercian allies reached Benfleet, Haesten was away on a plundering raid with a large part of his army, leaving only a small garrison to protect the fort, his wife and two sons, and the women and children of his soldiers. Edward quickly ordered an attack against the fortress and his troops broke through the walls to enter the village. The Benfleet garrison was easily subdued and the women and children captured, along with their fleet. Haesten's wife and two sons were sent to Alfred, while most of the Danish ships were taken to London and Rochester and the remaining vessels destroyed. When Alfred received the Viking chieftain's family, he ordered them sent to Haesten, instead of holding them for ransom, in a gesture of Christian friendship.

In the wake of the loss of Benfleet, Haesten withdrew his warriors to a new base at Shoebury, where he was joined by a large force of East Anglian and Northumbrian Vikings. After uniting the two armies, he left the women and children at his fortified encampment and moved westward to find a new site to inhabit permanently. Soon after, concluding the Wessex men were determined to defend their lands and Alfred's defences were too strong to overrun, the Danish chieftain decided to relocate his men and their families to western Mercia near Buttington.

Buttington was situated close to the Welsh border, and the Viking chieftain sought the intervention of the local princes against the Wessex king, but Alfred had previously formed an alliance with the Welsh and they remained loyal to him, refusing to rise up against their recognized overlord. The west Mercian warlords were ordered by Alfred to assemble their vassals and militiamen and move against the threatening Danes. The five regional lords mustered their men and were soon joined by Ethelred, who led their advance against Haesten. The formidable Mercian force was joined by troops from the Welsh princes, and the reinforced army marched toward Buttington to eliminate the threat of the Northmen. As the allied forces approached the enemy camp, the Vikings retreated into the protection of the fortified village. When Ethelred reached the fortress, he ordered his soldiers to surround the defensive works and keep the barbarians bottled up. The English farmer-warriors threw up wooden siege ramparts around the fortifications, patrolling the walls to prevent the Northmen from slipping out to search for provisions. Denied freedom to forage and pillage for food supplies, the pagans were compelled to slaughter their horses and eat them to survive. As the English siege wore on, Haesten and his Danish troops made an attempt to force a breakout. The Vikings opened the gate and stormed toward the Anglo-Saxons, crashing into the English shield wall, but were thrown back after fierce fighting. Ethelred's men pushed forward, slaughtering hundreds of Haesten's troops and crushing their resistance. With the battle lost, the surviving Danes fled to the east back to Shoebury.

After reaching the fortified encampment at Shoebury, Haesten and his soldiers were joined by warriors from Northumbria and East Anglia, who had again broken their pledges of fealty to Alfred to plunder the English towns for booty. Alfred was determined to finally eliminate the threat against his kingdom, ordering his army to pursue the enemy forces. With Ethelred and his English troops now advancing toward Shoebury, the Danish chieftain abandoned the fortified camp and Wessex territory, marching north-west along the old Roman road of Watling Street to the deserted ruins at Chester. The Anglo-Saxon army continued its pursuit, following them to Chester. The Wessex militiamen besieged the warband's camp, while men were sent into the surrounding area to collect farm animals and crops to deny them to the Northmen. Following a short siege, the English left Chester and returned to Wessex, leaving the Vikings to struggle through the advancing winter with acute shortages of provisions.

In the spring of 894 the surviving Vikings at Chester were compelled by hunger and disease to leave Mercian territory, withdrawing into northern Wales to find food. Haesten led his men into the fiefdom of Prince Anarawd, where they launched pillaging raids to gather provisions. The pagan army stayed in Wales, devastating the princedoms of Gwent, Brycheiniog and Glywysing, burning towns and farmlands. After remaining in Welsh lands for over nine months, living on what they could plunder, the warband turned south-east through Danish-held Northumbria and East Anglia, where they found support from Scandinavian sympathizers. Following their long trek across the Midlands, the Danes reached Mersea Island in Essex, north-east of London.

While his allies fought the Vikings in the north-west, Alfred was engaged against a Danish fleet from East Anglia and Northumbria that was raiding the coastline of Devon. The Northmen attempted to break into the king's fortified villages along the coast, but were repeatedly pushed back by the strong garrisons and formidable defensive works. In the spring of 894 the Viking leaders abandoned their pillaging attacks after failing to provide booty for their warriors. On their voyage north to their homeland, the squadron from East Anglia halted at Alfred's fortified town of Chichester to launch one more attempt to find plunder. The raiders moored their longboats on the coast and hastened inland against the town. The Viking warriors formed into battle formation, storming across the open ground and attempting to penetrate the defensive walls with their battering rams. Despite repeated attacks, the Northmen failed to break through the defences and were forced to withdraw to their ships, leaving hundreds of men dead and wounded on the bloody battlefield. The raids along the southern coast of Wessex had been unsuccessful because Alfred's fortified settlements were too strong for the marauders to breach.

Meanwhile, the Viking warriors on Mersea Island had remained at their encampment a short time before rowing their ships down the coastline in the autumn of 894 toward London, under the command of Haesten. When the raiders reached the Thames, they rowed up the waterway before turning onto the Lea River tributary searching for a new site to build a village. After moving up the Lea a short distance, the Danes moored their fleet and set to work constructing a fortified camp about twenty miles north of London. From their encampment, the Vikings began ravaging the countryside for food and plunder. With their close vicinity to London, the Northmen posed a direct threat to the security of the important commercial centre. When Alfred learned of the presence of the Danes so close to London, he ordered soldiers from the London garrison to drive them away. Arriving at the well-fortified campsite, Alfred's commander rashly ordered his Wessex men to take the enemy position by storm, but following a fierce fight were beaten back with many casualties.

During the London troops' attack against the warband on the Lea River, Alfred had been occupied relieving the siege of Exeter, but after driving the Danes away, in the summer of 895 he moved his army against the camp on the Lea. He ordered his engineers to drain the lower reaches of the Lea to eliminate the Vikings' use of the waterway as an escape route to the Channel, while sending men to protect the region's farmers against plundering raids. Once the Northmen realized the consequences of Alfred's draining of the Lea, they abandoned their fortified settlement and withdrew.

In the aftermath of their defeat on the Lea, the surviving Danes abandoned their ships and rode west across Mercia, with the English mounted troops in close pursuit. In the winter of 895, when the Northmen reached Bridgnorth on the Severn River, they secured a strong defensive position. When Alfred with his vassals and peasant militiamen reached the fortified site, they besieged the Vikings, encircling their camp with ramparts and lines of sentries. As the investment at Bridgnorth continued through the winter, Alfred sent the Earl of Somerset, Ethelnoth, on a diplomatic mission to the Danes occupying Northumbria and East Anglia to eliminate their continued support for the invaders. Meeting the Danish envoys at York, Ethelnoth convinced them to abandon their backing of the Bridgnorth warband. When the warriors on the Severn learned of the treaty negotiated at York and realized that Alfred and his earls were too strong to permit them permanent settlement in their lands, they divided their army into two divisions, with one going to East Anglia and the other to Northumbria, while a small contingent crossed the Channel to join the Vikings in France along the Seine. Alfred's siege at Bridgnorth ended the four-year war against the Scandinavians, with the enemy driven out of southern England. The king's reorganization of his army and the building of a system of strategically placed fortified towns with strong garrisons had proven too powerful for the Danes to conquer. While the conflict against the invading Northmen was over, during the remaining years of Alfred's life there were repeated flare-ups with the Vikings north of the Thames. Wessex and its supporting allies largely remained at peace with their northern neighbours until the reign of Alfred's successor, Edward the Elder.

Alfred had earlier begun an initiative to improve the education of his subjects by making books available to them in their language of English, and he returned to the project after the last Danish warrior crossed the border into the Danelaw or had sailed to France. Throughout lulls in the wars against the Vikings, the king, with the assistance of the Bishop of Worcester, had continued working on the rewriting of the Latin text of Pope Gregory I's *Dialogues* into English. After securing peace with the Northmen, he returned to his translations of the pope's writings. The four books of the work were a collection of various miracles, wonders and healings performed by holy men in Italy during the sixth century. When the undertaking was completed, he sent copies to the bishops in his realm.

During the remainder of his reign, six more Latin books were translated into English by the king or under his direct supervision. Following the completion of the *Dialogues*, Alfred and his fellow scholars began work on Gregory I's *Pastoral Care*, which served as a set of instructions for the bishops to bring the word of God to their worshippers, while including a description of the qualities of a good prelate. The next Latin book rewritten into English was the *Ecclesiastical History of the English People*, written in 731 by the Venerable Bede at his monastery of St Peter in Jarrod, Northumbria. Bede was a renowned Anglo–Saxon historian and scholar, well-known for the writing of the Church history of early England. The monk's masterpiece begins with Julius Caesar's invasion of Britain in 55 BC and ends with an account of the state of Christianity during the eighth century. King Alfred's translation of the manuscript brought the people of Wessex the heroic story of England's history and the part played by the Christian Church. The next book translated was *Seven Books of History Against the Pagans*; the original manuscript was written by a Portuguese priest named Paulus Orosius in 418, a narrative of the wars, epidemics, famine, storms and crimes which had befallen mankind in the pagan age. Rewriting his translation of Orosius's manuscript, the king added a section near the beginning discussing the geography of Germany and Scandinavia. Following his work on the barbarian history, Alfred rewrote *The Consololation of Philosophy*, compiled around 520 during the reign of King Theodoric of Rome by Boethius, a renowned Roman senator, consul and philosopher of the early sixth century. The book was a philosophical thesis on fortune, death and unfairness, the story of a man's struggle against injustice and his final triumph through perseverance in truth through the Christian God. The fifth translation made by the king was from a work by Augustine of Hippo entitled *Soliloquies*, a description of man's search for knowledge of God and the human soul. Augustine, a Christian theologian and philosopher in the early fifth century, was known as one of the founders of the Christian Church, and through his many writings adopted classical thought into Christian teachings to create a spiritual system of great influence. Alfred deleted parts of Augustine's original work, substituting numerous illustrations to describe the quest to discover God. In one of his examples he wrote: 'He who would see wisdom with the eyes of the soul must climb upward little by little, as a man climbing some cliff on the seashore, step by step. When at the top he can now look out upon the view over shore and sea lying below his gaze.' The final book translated into English by

Alfred was *Psalms* from the *Bible*. Alfred had heard the verses of *Psalms* since his early childhood and could recite many of them. In ninth-century Britain, the people widely believed King David of Israel had written the *Psalms*, and with his monarchy beset by foreign invasions and internal rebellion, Alfred closely identified with the Biblical hero. When the Wessex sovereign translated, 'Why do the kings of the earth rise up, and noblemen come together against God, and against him whom He chose as lord and anointed?', it must have reminded him of the many adversities he had overcome during his reign as king. While Alfred continued his translations of classical books into English for his noblemen and subjects, he commissioned the compilation of a new history of England from 60 BC to AD 892 in a year-by-year account of life in the kingdom, entitled the *Anglo-Saxon Chronicle*. The work was authorized to highlight the rule and power of the Wessex kings, especially Alfred. The monarch was personally involved in the project, ensuring Wessex was presented as a victorious and just kingdom.

In the final years of his life, Alfred continued to strengthen his fortified towns and enacted decrees to make them successful commercial centres by stimulating local trade. In 898 he met with his council of nobles and bishops to authorize the restoration and rebuilding of London into a regional commercial site. From about the age of twenty, Alfred had suffered from frequent recurring bouts of abdominal pain, and in October 899 became seriously ill with another attack. The court doctors were unable to save the king, and on 26 October he died at the age of fifty-one. As Alfred approached death, he called his eldest son Edward to his side, telling him to 'Love God and St Cuthbert and to place in them his hope, as he himself had done and still most zealously was doing'. Alfred and his wife had five surviving children. The oldest child was their daughter Ethelfleda, who had been married to Ethelred of Mercia in a politically arranged union to enhance the monarch's relationship with the northern kingdom. The heir to the Wessex monarchy was Edward, who like his father was both a warrior and scholar. After his father died, Edward's succession to the Wessex throne was challenged by his cousin, Aethelwald. To assert his rights by birth to the crown, Edward assembled his loyal troops and marched against the usurper, forcing him to flee to the Vikings at York. With the support of the East Anglian Northmen,

Aethelwald returned south to challenge Edward's kingship but was killed at the Battle at Holme. Edward spent most of his reign driving the Danes out of southern England, and by his death in 924 was ruler of Wessex, East Anglia, the Midlands and Mercia. Alfred had two additional daughters, one of whom, Ethelgeda, entered a nunnery and later became Abbess of Shaflesbury. The final daughter, Elfthryth, was married for political reasons to the Count of Flanders, Baldwin II, to strengthen relations with the important continental countship and support the Flemish expansion into southern France. Alfred's youngest child was a boy named Ethelweard, who inherited his father's love of learning and literature and served his brother loyally during Edward's reign.

Alfred was buried in Winchester in the Old Minster. His body remained there until 903, when it was transferred to the New Minster, where he lay next to his wife, Ealhswith, until the arrival of the Normans. Following the seizure of the English throne, King William I of Normandy ordered the bones of all prior kings collected and removed to Winchester Cathedral, with the exception of Alfred, who was reinterred at Hyde Abbey. His remains stayed at the abbey until it was converted into a house and the location of the burial site was forgotten. When the house became a prison in 1788, the prisoners uncovered Alfred's tomb while clearing the land. The convicts emptied the stone crypt, scattering the fragments of the king's bones over the ground.

Selected Sources:

Ault, Warren O., *Europe in the Middle Ages.*
Brooke, Christopher, *The Saxon and Norman Kings.*
Cannon, John and Hargreaves, Anne, *The Kings and Queens of Britain.*
Duckett, Eleanor Shipley, *Alfred the Great – The King and His England.*
Ferguson, Wallace K. and Bruun, Geoffrey, *A Survey of European Civilization.*
Horspool, David, *Alfred the Great.*
Humble, Richard, *The Saxon Kings.*
Peddie, John, *Alfred the Great – Warrior King.*
Pollard, Justin, *Alfred the Great – The Man Who Made England.*
Rendina, Claudio, *The Popes.*
Smyth, Alfred P., *King Alfred the Great.*
Roberts, Andrew, *Great Commanders of the Medieval World.*
Whitlock, Ralph, *The Warrior Kings of Saxon England.*

Chapter Three

Cnut

Ruler of the North Sea Empire

In September 1015 Cnut sailed across the North Sea from Denmark, landing his 200 longships on the English coast at Sandwich and launching his invasion of the Anglo-Saxon kingdom with an army of 10,000 Danes and Norwegians. He advanced his Vikings against the enemy forces, and by early 1016 had gained control over large regions of Wessex, Mercia and Northumbria. As the Danes continued their campaign of conquest in the south, they clashed with the English, led by King Edmund II, at Ashingdon in Essex. Cnut deployed his men on Canewdon Hill, while the Anglo-Saxons were aligned on nearby Ashingdon Hill. In the afternoon of 18 October, Cnut stood in the centre of his line of soldiers, alongside his battle standard flying a black raven on a white background, as the English troops in a formation of locked shields began advancing down the hillside. Cnut now led his warriors forward, and approaching the enemy unleashed a storm of spears into the English ranks. The charging Anglo-Saxons collided with the Vikings, swords and axes clashing and men falling in a savage fight. In the late afternoon, the line of English and Welsh soldiers, led by Ealdorman Eadric, began to flee, soon joined by hundreds more as the Anglo-Saxon front wavered and broke under the relentless assaults of the Northmen. Cnut's victory at Ashingdon won the English crown for him, and by 1028 he had created the North Sea Empire, ruling the kingdoms of England, Denmark and Norway, along with parts of Sweden.

Cnut was the second son of Swein Forkbeard and Gunhild, daughter of the Duke of Poland, and was born around 995 in Denmark. When King Swein was defeated by Eric the Victorious of Sweden and his lands occupied, he was compelled to temporarily abandon his homeland, sending Gunhild to Poland with Cnut. While the Danish king sought allies in Norway and England to reclaim his throne, his son was taken from Poland to the Danish enclave in Pomerania and raised in the Viking tradition in the household of the northern warlord Thorkell. At the court of the Viking warrior, the young Danish prince was taught the basics of reading and writing, later receiving instruction in Latin. Under the guidance of Thorkell, Cnut was trained in the battle skills of a Viking warrior, learning to fight on foot with axe, spear and sword and to defend himself with a wooden shield. He practiced throwing the spear and shooting arrows, preparing for combat by stalking wild boar and deer in the dense northern forest. As the son of a Danish king, he was also taught the skills of sailing and navigation, while learning to swim, hunt with hawks and play various childhood games with the other boys.

While Cnut grew into a tall and formidable Viking warlord, Swein Forkbeard recovered his Danish throne and with his monarchy unchallenged began sailing across the North Sea to unleash plundering raids against the coastal towns of England. In 1003 he landed on the English east coast with a large army, moving inland to the west and seizing control of the town of Exeter before swinging into the southern shires, raiding villages and laying waste to the countryside, while terrorizing the townspeople. After wintering along the English coast, Swein moved his army into East Anglia, sacking the city of Norwich. The Earl of East Anglia, Ulfcetel, then negotiated a truce with the Northmen for the payment of a large tribute. After receiving the agreed money, the Vikings soon broke the agreement, attacking and sacking Thetford. Ulfcetel responded to the breach in the truce by assembling his army of militiamen, attacking the Danes as they returned to their longships, but following a hard-fought fight they were beaten back. After the defeat of the English, the Danish king led his fleet back to Denmark, ending his prolonged campaign of pillage in England.

While Cnut remained with Thorkell, the Danes returned to England in 1006 to resume their raids. The longships landed at Sandwich on the coast of Kent, burning and killing as they advanced inland. The English king, Ethelred II, mustered his militia in Wessex and Mercia, setting out to intercept the Northmen, but Swein escaped to his camp on the Isle of Wight. In midwinter the Vikings returned to the mainland, proceeding north-east to Reading, pillaging as they advanced. When Swein's troops began to make their way back to the southern coast, the English mustered an army and clashed with the Vikings near the Kennet River, but were driven back following a brief skirmish. The Danes returned to the encampment with their plunder. Shortly after his victory, Swein again agreed to end his pillaging and return to Denmark after Ethelred offered to pay a sizeable payment in gold and silver.

During the next several years Swein Forkbeard remained in the north ruling his Danish kingdom, while in England Ethelred II initiated measures to re-energize his realm to repel the anticipated renewal of Viking raids. The inability of the Anglo-Saxon king to prevent the repeated attacks of the Northmen had caused a widespread loss of confidence in his rule. To strengthen his regime's resistance, he reorganized his administration, appointing new ealdormen and issuing orders to reinforce the defences. In mid-May 1008 the king summoned his high magnates and churchmen to Eanham in Hampshire to discuss better ways to confront the northern raiders and regain the trust of his subjects. The law-making council drafted a set of statutes designed to unite the English people against the raids of the Vikings.

Ethelred II's new defensive measures for his kingdom were soon tested, when the Northmen from modern-day north-western Poland began landing at Sandwich in July 1009. An army of over 4,000 men under the command of Thorkell the Tall advanced into the southern counties, pillaging and burning before spending the winter plundering as far north as Oxford. The marauders returned to their longships and set sail up the coast to East Anglia. As Thorkell's men disembarked and moved inland, they launched a surprise attack against the East Anglian and Cambridgeshire forces of Ulfcetel at Ringmere south of Norfolk. While the English were forming their battle line, the Northmen attacked and beat them back in fierce fighting. As the Danes pressed forward, the East Anglians began fleeing the battlefield, leaving the men from Cambridgeshire to struggle alone against the Vikings. Thorkell's veteran warriors charged into the depleted English line, quickly overpowering them. The defeat of the Anglo-Saxons at Ringmere broke the renewed spirit of the English, allowing the Northmen to freely ravage through much of southern England. Ethelred II was now forced to begin negotiations with Thorkell to end his campaign of plunder. Under the resulting pact, the English king agreed to pay a tribute, while the Northmen pledged to leave England. When the payment was raised, the king convinced Thorkell and his soldiers to serve as mercenaries in the Anglo-Saxon army. The Vikings were sent to establish their encampment in East Anglia, where it was expected that, over time, they would follow earlier Northmen and settle on the land as loyal subjects of the king.

While Thorkell the Tall was agreeing to serve the Anglo-Saxon regime, in Denmark, in the town of Roeskild, Swein Forkbeard was making final preparations for the return of his Danes to England. Cnut was now seventeen years old and ready to begin his calling as a Viking warlord, joining his father's expeditionary force. To rule his kingdom during his absence, Swein named his eldest son, Harald, as interim ruler. In the midsummer of 1013 the Danish troops boarded their ships and set sail for England. The Northmen pulled on their oars and the square shaped sail caught the morning breeze propelling the longships toward England. The Viking fleet landed at Sandwich, and following a brief raid into East Anglia, the Danes proceeded up the coast to the mouth of the Humber near present-day Hull. The Viking king led his men up the river to its confluence with the Trent, and journeyed south-west to the town of Gainsborough in the Danelaw. The Northmen disembarked and were welcomed by the local inhabitants. The region had been populated by Vikings from previous expeditions, and they rallied to Swein, pledging their fealty. Soon after the Danes' arrival at Gainsborough, the Earl of Northumbria, Uhtred, submitted to Swein without a fight. As Swein and his army advanced into the Danelaw, the principal towns accepted him as overlord and in a short period the area north of Watling Street, the recognized border between southern England and the Danish-dominated region, had acknowledged him as sovereign.

With the north of England now under Danish hegemony, Swein proceeded south with his army to impose his overlordship, leaving Cnut in the north to guard the ships and monitor the activities of the English. Swein renewed his campaign of subjugation, encountering only sporadic resistance and quickly taking Oxford and Winchester. He then led his warriors against London. The city was defended by a formidable garrison of English and Viking troops led by Ethelred II and his ally Thorkell. The Danes laid siege to London but were unable to penetrate the strong walls and break the determined resistance of the Anglo-Saxons and their northern mercenaries.

Unable to break into London, Swein ended his siege and moved his army unopposed west to Bath, where the magnates from the south-western shires led by the Ealdorman of Devon, Ethelmer, submitted and gave their oaths of homage to the Danish king. After procuring hostages from the shires to ensure their loyalty, Swein took his soldiers back to Gainsborough to prepare for the coming winter. He demanded provisions and money from the shires and spent the following months along the Trent.

While the Viking king was securing the overlordship of south-western England, the wife of Ethelred II, Emma, crossed the Channel to the Norman duchy of her brother, Richard II, seeking his armed intervention in England. When military support from Normandy failed to arrive, Ethelred, with Thorkell at his side, fled his kingdom from the Isle of Wight, joining Emma and their two sons at the court of Richard II. After the flight of their king, the municipal officials of London submitted to Swein, who was now acknowledged ruler of Denmark and England.

Shortly after gaining the homage of the Anglo-Saxon realm, Swein I arranged the marriage of Cnut to Lady Elfgifu of Northumbria to secure the succession of his second son to the English throne. Elfgifu was the daughter of the Earl of Northumbria, and the union with the foremost noble family closely united the royal Danish court to the Anglo-Saxon nobility and strengthened the new monarch's hold on the crown. The marriage was the result of a negotiated contract between the two families and was not sanctioned by the Church. Cnut had two sons with Elfgifu, Swein and Harald, born in 1016 and 1017. Harald later succeeded his father to the English monarchy, while Swein was acknowledged as King of Norway.

As Swein I consolidated his reign over England, on 2 February 1014 he suddenly died less than two months after his conquest of the kingdom. After learning of the death of their king, the soldiers of the large Danish army at Gainsborough recognized Cnut as his successor. While Swein had been accepted as monarch by the high English lords and churchmen, he had not been elected by the Witan or crowned by the Church, which weakened Cnut's claim to the kingship. Many Anglo-

Saxon warlords considered Cnut inexperienced and untested, sending envoys to Normandy to petition the exiled Ethelred II to reclaim the English throne. The banished Ethelred responded by sending an embassy to England in March under the nominal leadership of his young son Edward to negotiate his assumption of the monarchy. At the conference the prince brought friendly greetings from his father and the promise of fair treatment for all Englishmen, while pledging to be a dedicated and supportive sovereign. After agreeing to the return of the Anglo-Saxon king, the nobles swore their allegiance to him. In mid-April 1014 Ethelred crossed the Channel to reclaim the crown with a new Viking ally, Olaf the Stout, and his men. The English people rallied to the monarch and a large army was soon assembled to move against Cnut. The Northmen had remained at Gainsborough and were largely unaware of the resurgent support mobilized by Ethelred II's regime. As Cnut gathered supplies and prepared for a spring offensive in the south against the Anglo-Saxons, the English king, with Thorkell and Olaf leading the mercenary troops, advanced north against the Danes, catching them by surprise. They fell on Cnut, overrunning his unprepared forces and compelling them to flee to their ships and sail back to Denmark.

Cnut was welcomed at the Danish court by his brother King Harald and began preparations to regain the kingship of England, collecting a fleet and troops with the assistance of his older brother. Cnut, who had earlier been assigned the southern region of Norway by his father, made contact with the local Norse earl, Eric. As his overlord, the Danish prince called upon Eric to provide soldiers and ships for his invasion of England. While he continued his arrangements for the recovery of the English crown, in early January 1015 Anglo-Saxon troops launched a surprise attack, led by Ulketel of East Anglia, against the unsuspecting indigenous Vikings in London and East Anglia, killing several hundred of them. Among the dead was Thorkell's brother Heming. Shortly after the slaughter of the Danes, Thorkell abandoned the English regime and returned to Denmark with his soldiers, pressing Cnut to invade England to avenge his brother's death.

While Cnut remained in Denmark securing support for his conquest of England, Ethelred II grew increasingly frail and inactive. The king remained isolated in London as his allies and vassals abandoned his regime, and his eldest surviving son, Edmund, began to challenge for the kingdom. In the absence of any royal intervention against his usurpation of the Anglo-Saxon throne, Edmund advanced into Mercia with his troops, securing the support of the people. He started issuing charters under his name as king of England.

As England stood on the verge of civil war between the proponents of Ethelred II and Edmund, Cnut and his army of over 10,000 veteran warriors sailed for England. The Viking ships were approximately sixty feet long and fifteen feet wide, with a shallow draft allowing their use in rivers, and carried a crew of thirty to forty men. For propulsion the longships were fitted with oars along almost the entire length of the craft and carried a single mast with a square sail. The prows of the ships were brightly decorated with figureheads of dragons, snakes and bulls, while ornamented shields were placed along the top edge of the boat. Following a three-day voyage in fair weather, the Danish flotilla made landfall at Sandwich and sailed up the Frome River. After travelling several miles upriver, the Vikings disembarked and advanced against the fortified town of Wareham. The English had constructed strong walls on three sides of the town, but had left the riverfront unprotected. Cnut ordered his sailors to beach the vessels and sent his warriors charging across the open field into Wareham. The garrison, unprepared for the assault, was soon overpowered by the attack of the Danes and their Scandinavian allies. After sacking Wareham, the Northmen proceeded farther inland, plundering more towns. As Cnut and his army continued to harry the south-west of England, the local municipal officials submitted. With winter approaching, Cnut set up his encampment in Wessex, signalling a warning to Ethelred II and Edmund that he had come to regain the English throne by force of arms.

Early in 1016 Cnut proceeded north, crossing the Thames into Mercia and resuming his campaign of conquest. The Viking king was joined by the soldiers of Ealdorman Eadric of Mercia, who had submitted to the invaders in late 1015. While the Danes and their Mercian allies subjugated new areas, Edmund attempted to raise an army to defend England, but without the presence of the king the men refused to fight, leaving Cnut unopposed. After his failure to unify the English lords, the Anglo-Saxon prince advanced his household forces into Northumbria to form a union with Earl Uhtred. They united their troops and marched into Mercia, harrying the lands of Eadric. As Edmund and his ally continued their offensive, Cnut moved his warriors into Northumbria. When Uhtred learned of the attack against his territory, he returned to Northumbria and, lacking the troop strength to fight the Danes, surrendered to Cnut, giving hostages to guarantee his loyalty. To further secure his possession of the northern lordship, Cnut had Uhtred killed, appointing Eric of Norway as the new earl.

Following the conquest of Northumbria, Cnut hastened south, moving through the western counties and gaining the local warlords' oaths of loyalty. Meanwhile, Edmund had marched his army to London and joined forces with his father. As the Englishmen made preparations to attack the Northmen, on 23 April 1016 King Ethelred II died. In the wake of the king's death, an assembly of high lords and churchmen met and elected Cnut as the successor to the English throne, while in London the Witan, with support from the city's citizens, chose Edmund II as the new monarch.

To assert his kingship over England, in early May 1016 Cnut advanced his army against King Edmund II in London. The Danish soldiers and their Scandinavian allies boarded their vessels at Greenwich, sailing up the Thames. The fleet bypassed the city's defensive works and dug a channel on its southern side, dragging their ships to the west to gain control of the entire waterway. The invaders dug ditches and built battlements around London to blockade the city. The Danes unleashed several attacks against the garrison but were repeatedly thrown back by the defenders. The siege dragged on through May and into June, the Northmen pressing their assaults but unable to break through the formidable walls.

While Cnut and Eric of Norway continued the siege, Thorkell was sent with a large contingent of warriors to harass Edmund, who had earlier escaped from London and was raising an army in the southern lordships. The Danes advanced south-west and came upon Edmund and his newly recruited troops at Penselwood in Dorset. In a brief skirmish, Thorkell's men were driven back and compelled to retreat, giving Edmund a much-needed victory. Thorkell's men and Anglo-Saxon forces collided again several weeks later at Sherston near Malmesbury in Wiltshire. In the early morning of 24 June, King Edmund led his soldiers forward into the solid wall of Viking shields. The battle raged throughout the day, with neither side giving ground. The onslaught was renewed the following day, but after more brutal fighting both the Northmen and Edmund withdrew, ending the inconclusive encounter. Following the fighting at Sherston, Thorkell rejoined Cnut at the siege of London. However, during Thorkell's campaign in the south-west, Eadric of Mercia deserted the Vikings and rejoined the army of Edmund II with his men.

With his army reinforced by the defection of Eadric and his martial victories in the south, Edmund moved north-east to relieve the siege against London. As the English approached the city, Cnut lifted his siege and made his way to the fleet. During the withdrawal, the Viking rearguard fended off an attack by Edmund at Brentford as Cnut and his troops escaped to their ships.

Shortly after his withdrawal from London, Cnut returned to the city when Edmund left to raise troops in Wessex. The Vikings renewed their siege, attacking the defenders by land and from the river, but were unable to penetrate the strong defensive walls. With his provisions and supplies now nearly depleted, Cnut abandoned the siege and sent Eric of Norway with a detachment of troops into Mercia to plunder the lands of the traitor Eadric, while the remainder of the Northmen proceeded to their encampment on the Isle of Sheppey fifty miles east of London at the mouth of the Thames. After Eric's raid into Mercia, in the late autumn the Vikings boarded their longships at the Isle of Sheppey, sailing up the coast to the Orwell River and westward to Mercia, where they launched an offensive against Eadric. The Vikings freely pillaged through the region. The local crops had been recently harvested and the Danes and their allies quickly gathered a large cache of supplies for the winter. Cnut sent the infantrymen back by ship to the Isle of Sheppey, while the cavalry rode to the campground. After Edmund learned of the division of the enemy's army, he assembled forces from all regions of his kingdom and set out after the Vikings. The English intercepted the Danish horsemen at Otford in western Kent. The Northmen, encumbered with the plunder from Mercia, were forced to manoeuvre around the Anglo-Saxons to avoid battle, hurrying to Sheppey. The English king's pursuit of Cnut's men was delayed by his dispute with Eadric, allowing the invaders to escape following a brief skirmish.

In the wake of his return to the Isle of Sheppey, Cnut rested his army and in mid-October ordered his soldiers to again board their longships and sail up the coastline to East Anglia. The Vikings moved inland, plundering settlements and laying waste to the countryside. While the Danes devastated East Anglia, Edmund set out in pursuit, catching the raiders at Ashingdon in Essex. The Anglo-Saxon army occupied Ashingdon Hill and in the early afternoon of 18 October 1016 the English king aligned his forces into three divisions, placing the elite soldiers in the front line behind a wall of shields, while Cnut was positioned on nearby Canewdon Hill. As the Anglo-Saxons advanced forward under a barrage of arrows, Cnut led his men down the hill, clashing with the English in a bloody melee until nightfall, when the troops of Eadric of Mercia began to flee. The retreating Mercians were joined by hundreds of English as their defensive line collapsed. With his army in flight, and the flower of English nobility killed defending their king, Edmund was compelled to abandon the field, securing the victory for Cnut. Following the retreat of the Anglo-Saxons, the Danes and their allies combed the battlefield for plunder and in the morning buried their dead, while leaving the slain Englishmen for the wild animals.

The Anglo-Saxon sovereign collected his demoralized men after the battle at Ashingdon, moving to Gloucestershire with the hope of recruiting Welsh troops to his banner, while Cnut began his pursuit of the English. When Edmund's attempts to raise a new army in the south-west were largely unsuccessful, at the urging of his advisors, emissaries were sent to Cnut's encampment to discuss terms for peace. The Vikings had been fighting a strenuous campaign for over a year, and with recruiting in a hostile region difficult, Cnut was compelled to agree to a settlement with the Anglo-Saxons. The two kings met on Ola's Island on the Severn River near Deerhurst. Under their negotiated treaty, the kingdom was partitioned with Cnut ruling the northern counties, while Edmund was recognized as sovereign in Wessex, the Thames serving as the boundary. The city of London was granted to Cnut and the two kings pledged to maintain the peace. It was further agreed that the survivor would inherit the kingdom after the death of the other. King Edmund II's reign was short; he died on 30 November 1016, leaving the southern region of the realm to Cnut.

The new king of the united England established his court at Winchester and celebrated the Christmas season with his family, friends and the magnates and prelates of England. Following the holidays an assembly of high nobles met in London, acknowledging Cnut as sovereign. Cnut's reign was now unchallenged, with no English nobleman for the people to rally around. The children of Edmund II were too young to challenge for the throne, and the two sons of Ethelred II were in exile in France. England had been involved in internal strife for the past thirty years and the populace were ready for peace, accepting the government of a Dane. At the start of his reign, the king relied on the counsel of three prominent men to guide him through the perils of kingship, naming Thorkell, Eric of Norway and Ealdorman Eadric as his counsellors. During his time in England at the court of Ethelred II, Thorkell the Tall became well acquainted with the Anglo-Saxon nobles and churchmen and gained widespread knowledge in governmental affairs. Closer to the monarch was Eric of Norway, who had shown unquestionable loyalty to Cnut and noble character. The final advisor was Eadric of Mercia, who, despite uncertain faithfulness, was well experienced in many areas of government. With these advisors, the monarch set about solidifying his rule over the English.

As Cnut established his sovereignty over his recently conquered lands, he divided the English kingdom into four districts with different warlords at the head of each. Thorkell was given authority over East Anglia, Northumbria was granted to Eric of Norway, while Mercia went to the dangerous and unreliable Eadric, who still maintained a powerbase in the earldom. The king retained control in the wealthy and dominant area of Wessex. Cnut rewarded the warlords who supported his conquest of England, making generous gifts of land, titles and money. The Viking chieftain Eglaf was given properties in the Severn valley for his loyalty and service in Thorkell's army. The son of Eric of Norway, Hakon, was placed in control of Worcester to rule in the name of the king. Cnut created a policy to reconcile the Danes and English and issued laws based on the enactments of his Anglo-Saxon predecessors, while appointing Northmen to earldoms throughout the kingdom to ensure his continued reign. To unify his kingship further, in late 1017 he ordered the elimination of many powerful and influential Anglo-Saxons who posed a threat to his crown. Among those killed was Eadric of Mercia, who was accused of plotting against the throne. During the purge, Cnut moved against the surviving members of the royal Anglo-Saxon family. In 1018 the leading Englishmen and Danes were summoned to Oxford by the king, where they pledged to live together in peace.

Meanwhile, in the north, the Scots crossed the Tweed led by King Malcolm II and Owen the Bald of Strathclyde to invade the Earldom of Northumbria. The local earl, Eadulf Cudel, began assembling an army from the region around Durham, but before mustering the entire force his men were attacked by the Scots. The Northumbrians, caught by surprise, were hard-pressed to defend their lands. The forces of Malcolm II overwhelmed the earl's host, his victory expanding the Scottish border to the Tweed. During fighting at Carham, Eadulf was killed by the Scots. Cnut was too occupied in the south with the establishment of his new regime to send a relief army to his subjects in Northumbria, who were left under the rule of Malcolm.

Soon after his assumption of the English throne, the Viking king opened negotiations with Duke Richard II of Normandy for marriage to his sister, the dowager Queen Emma. The union with the former wife of Ethelred II and mother of his two sons, Edward and Alfred, would neutralize their inheritance rights to the Anglo-Saxon kingdom and closely associate his new monarchy with the previous dynasty. She was described by comtemporaries as a lady of the greatest nobility with a delightful charm and beauty. Cnut was at least ten years younger than his new wife but they developed a close relationship and she frequently aided him in the administration of the regime. Following the negotiations, a marital contract was signed, with the duke stipulating the issue of Cnut and Emma would succeed to the English crown. Unlike the first marriage to Elgifu, the second was performed and sanctioned by the Church and Emma was anointed Queen of England. The politically motivated union resulted in the birth of two children, with their only son, Harthacnut, rising to the kingships of Denmark and England.

To further enhance his hold on England, Cnut established a permanent army of 3,000–4,000 men named the Housecarls, who were responsible for the defence of the realm and maintenance of internal order. The Housecarls served as the sovereign's personal guard and were organized as an elite heavy infantry force. The guards were stationed at the royal court and spread throughout the kingdom, especially in Wessex, where the threat of rebellion was the greatest. Scandinavian warriors comprised the majority of the Housecarls, but Anglo-Saxons were permitted to enroll. The Housecarls performed both a military and administrative function in their service to the monarchy. The guards were armed with an iron-headed spear used for thrusting and throwing and carried a powerful two-handed battle-axe capable of decapitating a man with a single blow. The elite soldier also went into battle with a broad two-edged steel sword, used for slashing and stabbing, and typically carried a round wooden shield for protection. A standing naval force was also created to protect the coastline against raiders and serve as a first line of defence against foreign invasion. When a fleet of Viking longships landed a raiding force on the eastern coast of England in 1018, they were quickly overwhelmed by Cnut's professional army, while his navy destroyed their flotilla. The royal attack was a devastating defeat for the Northmen, ending their future plundering activities. To finance the military expenses, Cnut authorized the collection of a yearly tax on the people. The new taxes were a heavy burden on the English, but with the two military forces in place they brought back internal and external peace that had been absent from the kingdom for many years under the Anglo-Saxon sovereigns.

To protect the western boundary of his kingdom, Cnut was forced to counter the relentless raids by the Welsh, who were crossing the border into his realm to pillage. He created new earldoms along the frontier and appointed loyal Danish warlords to defend his lands against the repeated plundering attacks. The aggressive forays of the earls severely limited the marauding activities and secured the king's acknowledgement as overlord from the southern Welsh princes. When the princes broke their pledges of peace, the monarch's earls retaliated by crossing into Wales to harry their towns and farmlands in a devastating counter-attack.

To further reinforce his relations with his English subjects, Cnut assembled the great lords and prelates at Oxford, where they agreed to adopt the laws of the former Anglo-Saxon king, Edgar. The restoration of the previous statutes allowed the people to keep the laws they had previously lived by, instead of new Danish edicts, and once enacted was popular in the earldoms. The king remained in Wessex for several months, travelling around the southwest and by the force of his presence and personality asserting his authority over the heartland of England. He frequently journeyed to various parts of the kingdom with his court, dispensing justice and ensuring the local lords were acting in his best interest. This enabled the sovereign to be seen by his subjects, binding him closer to them. To further unite his reign with the Anglo-Saxons, he introduced reforms to promote economic growth in agriculture and commerce, while the coinage system was put on a uniform and standardized basis. Over time the new changes produced an increase in prosperity, along with a stable regime. Through his newly enacted measures, Cnut's monarchy won the support of the English people, allowing him to look across the North Sea to further his ambitions for land and power. His Danish homeland was under the rule of his brother Harold II, and the Norwegians had recently reasserted their control over their lands, but changes were stirring that would propel Cnut to the overlordship of the North Sea Empire.

In 1018 King Harold II of Denmark died, leaving no heirs to the throne, and after securing his sovereignty over England, Cnut began preparations to claim the vacant crown. The following year he mustered an army of less than 1,000 soldiers, setting sail for his homeland after naming Thorkell as regent in England and leaving some of the Housecarls to protect his monarchy. The kingdom of Denmark was strategically located between the European mainland and Scandinavia, and possession of it would give the English king control over the entrance and exit to the Baltic Sea. Denmark was also an important commercial centre, its merchants travelling across Europe and into the Mediterranean to trade their goods of walrus tusks, furs, slaves, flax and amber. Following the death of Harold II, several political factions developed to fill the void of a recognized ruler, and these Danes now opposed Cnut's attempt to take the throne. During his quest for the Danish crown, Cnut carried out an attack on the Danes living in Pomerania located on the southern coastline of the Baltic Sea. The Pomeranians had disputed Cnut's right to the kingship, but after crossing the Baltic the king's troops overwhelmed them, enforcing his claim to the kingdom. During the operation, the English Earl of Wessex, Godwin, led a successful night raid against a rebel Danish settlement. The attack was made without the knowledge of the king, but Godwin's defeat of the Pomeranian insurgents with English troops won the favour of Cnut, who rewarded the earl with titles, land and appointment to his inner council. Godwin's son, Harold, would later succeed to the English monarchy as the last Anglo–Saxon monarch.

After imposing his kingship over Pomerania, Cnut returned to Denmark, joining his army with his local followers and spending the winter asserting his supremacy over the rebellious warlords. By the spring of 1020, through the payments of bribes and the use of military might, Cnut was recognized as his brother's successor to the Danish crown. Following the elimination of all local resistance, he began preparations to return to England, but before sailing from Denmark he appointed his brother-in-law, Ulf, as regent to administer the kingdom and protect his sovereignty. During Cnut's absence in Denmark, a conspiracy of several earls developed in south-west England, led by Ethelwerd, Earl of Devon, creating a challenge to the regime's rule. Shortly after his return to England, the king summoned the lords to meet at Cirencester to reassert his authority. At the assembly, he received pledges of fealty from his magnates and banished the Earl of Devon for his insurrection. While at the Cirencester assembly, Cnut issued a proclamation to the English people promising them a future of good government and their recognition by the crown as citizens rather than conquered subjects. In the document he wrote: 'I make known to you that I will be a kind lord and loyal to the rights of the Church and secular laws.' He issued an order to his earls, telling them, 'To govern my people justly and give right judgements by the witness of the shire bishops.'

The recognition and endorsement of the English Church was vital to Cnut's continued support from his subjects. When the spiritual leader of the English Church died in 1019, the king appointed his friend and ally Ethelnoth as the new Archbishop of Canterbury. As Cnut re-established his rule, he outlawed heathen practices in his kingdom, encouraged pilgrimages to holy sites and promoted the adoration of the saints to bind him further to his Christian subjects. Churches and monasteries that had been destroyed by Viking raids were rebuilt under the monarch's sponsorship. In 1020 the newly built church at the battlefield of Ashingdon was consecrated by Archbishop Wulfstan, with Cnut attending the ecclesiastic ceremony along with many bishops and abbots. The Ashingdon church was the first of many new holy houses constructed during the king's reign, while large endowments were granted to numerous religious foundations, enhancing his relationship with the clergy.

Thorkell the Tall, who had earlier been appointed Earl of East Anglia and served the monarch as his English regent during his campaign in Denmark, was the foremost earl in England, a skilled and experienced Viking chieftain. During Cnut's absence in Scandinavia, he continued to expand his territory, becoming more powerful and wealthy. Possessing a private army and navy, he was now a threat to the throne of Cnut. As Thorkell's powers in England grew and more Northmen and English warlords joined his forces, in November 1021 King Cnut banished him to Denmark.

In the aftermath of his expulsion from England, Thorkell and his retainers quickly established a new powerbase in Denmark, posing a potential threat to Cnut's sovereignty. In 1023 Cnut travelled to his northern kingdom to safeguard his realm against the exiled earl's usurpation. He met with Thorkell, forging a reconciliation with him and naming him regent after his pledge of fealty. In the late autumn the king departed for England with his Danish kingship again secure.

By the end of 1024, King Cnut was the uncontested ruler of England and Denmark and now looked to Norway and Sweden for new conquests. Olaf II Haraldsson had assumed the monarchy of Norway in 1015 by force of arms, while Anund Jacob had succeeded to the Swedish throne following the death of his father. The kingdom of Denmark was again under the control of Ulf after the death of Thorkell, and to more closely associate his family to the Danish crown Cnut sent his son Harthacnut to rule as king. Harthacnut was still young and served as figurehead monarch, Ulf continuing to govern as his advisor.

As the overlord of England and Denmark, Cnut possessed great wealth and military might, posing a threat to the continued autonomy of Norway and Sweden. In 1024 the Anglo–Danish king sent an embassy to Olaf II's court demanding possession of the Norwegian kingdom. Upon reaching the royal residence at Tunsberg, the envoys were presented to the king after being forced to wait for several days. In the presence of Olaf II, they claimed the Norse realm for their king, asserting that his ancestors had possessed the land before him and he was now the rightful ruler. Cnut offered peace and pledged not to advance into Norway with his army if another choice was possible. He offered to appoint Olaf II as his vassal to rule Norway in his name. The Norwegian monarch sent a reply to Cnut that he would defend his regime and never pay tribute for his kingdom.

In the autumn of 1025 Cnut assembled a large Danish and Anglo-Saxon host in England, sailing to Denmark. He spent the next few months preparing for the campaign against the Norwegian monarchy. To protect his throne against an attack by the Anglo-Danish regime, Olaf II formed an alliance with the Swedish king, agreeing to unite his army and naval forces with the Swedes for their mutual defence. During the winter Cnut sent envoys to King Anund's court assuring him of peace and independence if he renounced his coalition with the Norwegians. The offer was quickly rejected by the Swedish monarch, who pledged to remain faithful to Olaf II.

As the Scandinavian allies prepared for the war against the Anglo-Danes, in the spring of 1026 Cnut returned to England, leaving his northern kingdom under the rule of Ulf. Following the departure of the king, Olaf II and Anund met at Kingscrag in south-east Norway to discuss their alliance against Cnut. They agreed to strike first, and a sea and land attack was planned. While the Anglo-Danish sovereign remained in England, he began bribing the Norwegian chieftains with gold and silver to gain their support. As rebellion and dissatisfaction spread in Norway against Olaf II, Cnut recruited additional soldiers and prepared for the campaign to subjugate the Norse.

Meanwhile, Queen Emma was plotting to secure the Danish monarchy for her son, and acting under her influence, Ulf summoned the great lords to Viborg, where he announced it was Cnut's desire to have his son Harthacnut proclaimed King of Denmark. At the large gathering of nobles, he successfully argued that the kingdom had always been ruled by a king within its borders, and that the present regency administration was ineffective. The assembly approved the proposal and Harthacnut was declared monarch in defiance of Cnut.

Following the meeting at Kingscrag, Olaf II raised a large host in his kingdom and set out for the agreed assembly point with the Swedish fleet at the mouth of the Throndhjem Firth in east central Norway, while Anund gathered his ships on the Scanium coast. The Norwegian flotilla sailed southward as additional longships joined the expeditionary force against the Anglo-Danish enemy. Olaf II personally led his men from his flagship, *Bison*, which was decorated with the golden figure of a bison. When the Norse king learned from his spies that Cnut was still in England preparing for the voyage north, he reduced the size of his navy, sending the older and slower vessels home, and sailed for the muster with Anund on the coast of Zealand in eastern Denmark with over sixty well-armed ships.

In the meantime, in England, King Cnut was finalizing his preparations for the offensive against the allied forces. In the summer of 1026 a great fleet of ships set sail from southern England, journeying up the coastline and across the North Sea, with the Anglo-Danish king in command of the expeditionary force. Cnut's vessel was approximately 250 feet ling, propelled by 120 oarsmen and a large sail painted with blue, red and green stripes. The flotilla sailed up the eastern coast of Denmark, joining Ulf and his forces at Lim Fjord in northern Jutland. Earlier in the year, as the allies prepared to attack the Danes, Ulf had been in contact with Olaf II and Anund, encouraging them to invade Cnut's kingdom. When the Anglo-Danish monarch disembarked at Lim Fjord, he was met by Ulf and his son Harthacnut. Cnut had learned of the Danish regime's rebellion and quickly forgave his son, who knelt at his feet in submission. He refused to reconcile with Ulf, but ordered him to take his troops and join the campaign against the Scandinavian enemy.

As Olaf II waited for the arrival of Anund in September 1027, he attempted to gain the support of the local Danes to his cause. As he addressed an assembly of Danes, spies informed him that a large fleet was coming from the south. At the approach of the hostile forces, Olaf set sail to the east to unite with the Swedes on the Scanian coast. Cnut ordered his fleet to pursue the Norse vessels and managed to engage part of the flotilla near Stangeberg in southern Sweden. Soon after the inconclusive naval clash, Cnut came upon the combined navies of the enemy at the Holy River, a small outlet for a group of inland lakes in Scania. When the allied monarchs heard from their scouts that the Anglo-Danes were approaching, they decided to form their warships for battle east of the river, while Olaf II went inland to prepare an ambush against Cnut. The Norwegians found the area where the river formed, and under the command of Olaf his men began building a dam of timber and earth. The work on the dam continued for several days until couriers from Anund alerted him of the approaching Anglo-Danes. When Cnut neared the outlet of the Holy River, he saw the allied ships aligned for battle, but it was too late in the afternoon to attack. He sailed most of his flotilla into the harbour at the river's mouth for the night.

The next morning, Cnut began landing his troops on the shore for an attack against the Norwegians. At the same time Olaf ordered his men to open the dam, causing a torrent of water to surge down the river into the enemy's fleet. The water and debris slammed into the vessels, while overflowing onto the shoreline and drowning many of the king's soldiers. The sailors on Cnut's flagship struggled to cut their tether ropes to escape the turbulent water. They managed to free the dragonship and floated out to sea toward the hostile naval force. The Norwegians and Swedes recognized the vessel of Cnut, rowing toward it and hurling a storm of spears, arrows and stones, killing many seamen and soldiers. While Cnut's men engaged the hostile vessels, the ships of Ulf joined the fight. At the approach of Ulf's squadron, the allied monarchs broke off the encounter, withdrawing to the east. While the naval battle at Holy River ended in a stalemate, the Swedes were discouraged and showed little interest in continuing the fight in the spring. Meanwhile, in Norway many Norse lords became disillusioned with Olaf II following his failure to defeat the Danes and their English allies, compelling him to be on guard against internal revolt.

In the aftermath of the battle at Holy River, Cnut returned to his Danish kingdom, establishing his royal residence at Roeskild. Shortly after his arrival, he attended a lavish feast prepared for him and his court by Ulf. During the night an argument erupted between the king and his earl over a chess game, and they parted with harsh words. After spending a restless night concerned about the king's rage, Ulf went to the Holy Trinity Church seeking refuge from the priests against his assassination. When Cnut awoke in the morning, he became angrier, ordering a nearby bodyguard to kill the earl. The guard entered the church and murdered Ulf, violating the asylum of the sanctuary. Cnut and his Danish ruler had been at odds over his perceived rebellion, the chess game serving only as the pretext to his murder. The monarch's slaying of Ulf in the church had violated papal dogma and incurred the displeasure of the Holy See.

In 1027 many great magnates and churchmen in Western Europe were preparing to attend the coronation of Conrad II in Rome as emperor of the Holy Roman Empire. After discussions with his advisors and archbishops, Cnut decided to travel to the Holy See and join the other rulers at the anointment ceremony. As he made arrangements for his journey to Rome, the death of his earl was a consideration in his decision to leave his Danish and English kingdoms to make the long and dangerous pilgrimage. His attendance in Rome would provide the opportunity to repair his relationship with the Holy See following the murder of Ulf and develop a friendship with the emperor. He set out with the staff and scrip of a pilgrim, accompanied by a large entourage and horses laden with bags of gold and silver. Along the route south through Flanders, Francia and Italy, the travellers stopped at numerous monasteries for the night, where Cnut gave generous offerings to the monks as penance for his sins. Upon reaching the Eternal City in early spring, he met with Pope John XIX and secured significant tax exemptions for the English Church. The pope agreed to abandon papal demands on English monasteries and bishoprics for donations in exchange for Peter's Pence, which was a tax of one penny levied on every household each year on 1 August. During his stay in Rome, the Anglo-Danish king made a vow at the Tomb of the Apostles to amend his life, possibly related to his quest for forgiveness and reconciliation with the Church after ordering the assassination of Ulf. On 26 March 1027 Cnut, along with prominent nobles and churchmen, attended the crowning ceremony of Conrad II and his wife Gisela in the Church of the Holy Apostles. In the final act of the service, Pope John XIX held the magnificent crowns of gold and jewels up high, placing them on the heads of Conrad and his wife proclaiming them emperor and empress, to the acclaim of the congregation. At the close of the elaborate service, Conrad left the church with Cnut and King Rudolf III of Burgundy walking at his side. At the Holy See, Cnut secured the blessing of the pope and papal recognition as the rightful King of England. During his stay, he met with Conrad II, reinforcing their friendship and securing his eastern borders against attack. The Viking sovereign negotiated a commercial agreement with the emperor, gaining substantial reductions in the tariffs charged to his merchants as they travelled through German territories.

In early April Cnut began his return journey to Denmark, eager to reach his northern kingdom before the expected resumption of the war against Norway and Sweden. After reaching his homeland, he took personal charge of the government while preparing to contend with the allies. When the expected hostilities failed to occur, the king set sail for England upon receiving reports that King Malcolm II and the Scots were moving into his realm in Northumbria. The Norwegian monarch was overlord of the Orkney Islands and Scottish coastal lands located to the north of Malcolm II's domain, and he actively encouraged the Scots' attacks into northern England to distract Cnut away from his ambitions in Norway. Cnut made contact with the Scottish sovereign, securing an agreement for him to retain possession of the occupied lands as the vassal of the English crown.

During Cnut's absence in Rome and his intervention with the Scots, his envoys in Norway were actively working to undermine the loyalty of the Norse warlords to Olaf II. They travelled throughout the kingdom bribing the Norwegians to gain support for the Anglo-Danish regime. By 1028 Cnut was ready to attack Olaf, sailing from England with fifty ships and a large army made up of his Housecarls and militiamen from the English earldoms. The king's fleet made its way across the North Sea into Lim Fjord, joining the waiting Danish vessels and soldiers. As the Anglo-Danish forces approached, Olaf ordered the mustering of his navy and army, but his edict was answered by only a small number of men. The Anglo-Danish king sailed along the Norwegian coastline, stopping at key towns to receive the fealty of the chieftains and inhabitants. Before leaving the towns, he appointed trusted local lords to administer his newly claimed territories. When the combined Anglo-Danish flotilla reached Nidaros, present-day Trondheim, on the western coast of central Norway, Cnut summoned a great assembly of Norwegian lords to accept their proclamation as king.

Following the meeting of the Norwegian chiefs, the Overlord of the North called the great magnates from Denmark, England and the newly acquired Norwegians to assemble and set royal policy. At the gathering, he announced the creation of a system of ruling vassal kings and earls. He named his nephew Hakon as regent for Norway, and the Danish kingdom was given to his young son Harthacnut, with Harold, son of Thorkell, acting as guardian and advisor. After the required hostages were given to ensure the fealty of the rulers, the monarch sailed south, stopping at towns bypassed on the earlier northern voyage to secure their submission. He resumed his journey southward along the coastline to the Oslo Firth and up the waterway to the town of Sarpsborg, fifty-five miles below modern-day Oslo, where he received the fealty of the local chieftains. After remaining at Sarpsborg a short time imposing his sovereignty, he returned to Denmark for the winter.

When Olaf learned of Cnut's departure from Norway, he went to Tunsberg and tried to rally the Norse chieftains to his royal banner, but few warriors answered his call. While the deposed king attempted to raise troops to reclaim the Norse crown, Cnut's ally and ardent supporter Chief Erling Skjalgsson assembled a large host and sailed to attack Olaf. As Erling neared the rogue forces, his dragonship was intercepted by the deposed king's flotilla. Olaf's longships pulled alongside the chieftain's vessel and his soldiers clashed with the loyalists in furious hand-to hand fighting. Erling's troops were overpowered, compelling him to surrender and agree to a reconciliation with the dissident monarch. While the two men negotiated a settlement, a bodyguard of Olaf walked behind the chief and killed him with an axe blow.

Reports of Erling's death spread rapidly through Norway with the magnates rallying to the support of Cnut's kingship with calls for revenge. As the sons of the murdered chieftain moved against the followers of the dethroned king in the south and Earl Hakon mustered a large host in the north, Olaf abandoned his quest for the Norwegian monarchy and fled to safety across the mountains to Sweden.

When King Olaf II summoned his vassals and retainers to regain the throne, Kalv Arnesson and his men had earlier joined his army. The Arnessons were a wealthy and powerful family that had always remained loyal to the Norwegian king, but after Olaf fled to Sweden, Kalv made peace with Hakon and swore allegiance to Cnut. The Anglo-Danish monarch realized his continued hold on Norway was tenuous and considered his current regent weak, non-energetic and unreliable. He summoned Kalv to his court in Winchester and ordered him to lead a campaign against the anticipated return of Olaf from Sweden, promising him the Norwegian regency with the title of earl. Kalv sailed back to Norway with his ship laden with gifts. A few months later, Hakon was ordered to England and sent to the recently acquired Orkney Islands as regent. During the voyage to the islands, he was killed when his ship was sunk by a violent storm with all lives lost.

In the meantime, Cnut altered his plans for Norway and decided to appoint Swein, his son by his first wife Elgifu, as earl to strengthen his ties to the kingdom's nobles, churchmen and people. Kalv had earlier been promised the earldom, but remained loyal to the king and when news reached him that Olaf II was returning to reclaim the monarchy, he assembled the navy and army to defend Cnut's crown. The royal forces were divided, with the southern warlords ordered to safeguard their region, while the host led by Kalv and Thor the Dog held the northern region of Norway. In the summer of 1030 Olaf travelled with 3,600 men from Sweden over the mountains and into the valley of Verdal in western central Norway. In late July Kalv's forces made contact with the army of Olaf on the farmlands at Stiklestead, and on the morning of 29 July prepared for battle with the enemy. In the early afternoon, the exiled Norwegian king led his men into the fray, carrying his battle axe named *Hel* after the Viking goddess of death. The troops of Olaf advanced toward the king's men shouting their battle cry, 'Forward, forward, men of Christ', as they slammed into Kalv's wall of shields. When Olaf spotted Kalv at the centre of the line under his flying standard, he rushed toward him. As he reached the banner, he was cut down by a spear in his lower chest and the slash of Kalv's sword across his neck. The victory at Stiklestead and the death of the pretender to the crown solidified Cnut's authority over Norway and firmly established his North Sea Empire.

While his regents ruled in the northern kingdoms, Cnut remained in England, maintaining peace and governing with the approval of his subjects. He established his royal court in the heartland of England at Winchester in the Earldom of Wessex. From his capital, the king began to increasingly rely on the military and political skills of Earl Godwin. In the wake of the death of Edmund II in 1016, Godwin quickly pledged his allegiance to the new Anglo-Danish monarchy and was rewarded for his loyalty and substantial abilities through the following years with grants of titles, estates and wealth. During Cnut's campaigns against rebellious lords, the Wessex earl joined his militiamen with the crown's army. Through his military service to the king, he became the pre-eminent warlord in Wessex. He was appointed to the realm's inner council and was recognized as the monarch's chief advisor. During Cnut's numerous absences from the capital, Godwin served as regent of England.

Cnut's marriage in 1016 to Queen Emma, the sister of the Norman Duke Richard II, had been the foundation for his policy of preserving peace with the duchy. When the duke died ten years later, relations between the regimes became increasingly strained under the new Norman duke, Robert I. The duke aggressively promoted the inheritance claims to the English throne of the two sons of Ethelred II and Emma, Edward and Albert, who had been exiled to the Rouen court. In 1030 Robert sent emissaries to Winchester demanding the English monarchy for his two wards. Cnut received their report with great contempt, refusing to consider the claims. When the envoys returned to Rouen with the king's reply, Duke Robert assembled his army and navy and made preparations for an invasion of England. While the Normans made ready for their campaign against England, war broke out between Robert and the Duke of Brittany, Alan III, preventing the expeditionary force from being utilized in the cross-Channel attack. Relations between the two realms remained hostile until 1035, when Robert I died on his return to Normandy from a pilgrimage to Jerusalem.

During Cnut's pilgrimage to Rome in 1027, friendly contacts were established with the Emperor of the Holy Roman Empire, Conrad II. The two regimes maintained close relations, their continued association serving to protect the southern borderlands of Cnut's empire. The Anglo-Danish king made the preservation of cordial relations with Conrad's government the uppermost priority for the safeguarding of his empire. To further strengthen their bond, negotiations were initiated for the marriage of Cnut's young daughter Gunhild to the emperor's son Henry, which was finalized in 1036 with their wedding. In return for his friendship, Cnut was ceded the March of Schleswig to secure the southern border between the Schley and Eider rivers, while extending the frontier lands of Cnut's empire into Germany.

The endorsement of the English Church was vital to the success of Cnut's rule, and policies were adopted to ensure his continued alliance with the clergy. Cnut's 1027 pilgrimage to the Holy City strengthened his bond with the papacy and the local prelates. The friendship of the Church could best be achieved by the king's careful selection of abbots, bishops and archbishops who were likely to retain their support of his monarchy. When vacancies occurred in the Church administration, priests who were known to the king and in his favour were appointed to the office. Winchester was the site of Cnut's court and an important English commercial city, with direct access to the Channel by the Itchen River. When the Bishopric of Winchester became available, he named Bishop Elfwine, who was a member of his inner circle, to the post. In 1033 Bishop Dudoc, whom Cnut had earlier met in Germany during his return from Rome and had returned to England with him, filled the vacancy in the Wells Bishopric following the death of the bishop. The English monarch appointed several of his court priests and advisors to ecclesiastic positions. During his reign, Cnut made frequent generous gifts of gold and land to the English monasteries and churches. In Denmark, meanwhile, the See of Bremen was responsible for the administration of the Danish churches. When Cnut attempted to send English clerics to Denmark, the Archbishop of Bremen strongly opposed his initiative. The festering dispute was mediated by the Archbishop of Hamburg, who persuaded Cnut to recognize the Bremen archbishop's primacy for religious affairs in Denmark and later Norway.

In the later years of his reign, King Cnut enacted numerous new laws regulating the practices of the Christian faith in his empire. He replaced the old ecclesiastic rules and gave protection to the priests by declaring outlawry as the punishment for the slaying of a churchman. Religious holidays and Sundays were to now be properly observed, with no commerce or public business to take place on these days. Under the monarch's enactments, all Christians were required to understand the teachings of the Church and pay their required dues without delay.

In a visual display of his humility, Cnut allegedly ordered his courtiers to place his throne on the seashore, and sitting on it he ordered the incoming tide to stop and not wet his feet. When the tide rushed in around his chair, he said to his courtiers: 'Let all men know how empty and worthless is the power of kings, for there is none worthy of the name but He whom heaven and earth and sea obey by eternal laws.' He reportedly took off his crown and placed it on a crucifix, never wearing it again. By his illustration to his courtiers, Cnut was showing them all that secular power was in vain compared to that of God.

While the Anglo–Danish king was securing the allegiance of the Church, Malcolm II had expanded his powers in Scotland and began moving south into England, challenging the kingship of the English regime. In 1031 Cnut assembled a large army and proceeded north to defend his sovereignty. As the English Housecarls and militiamen neared the Scottish border, Malcolm agreed to negotiate a treaty of friendship. Cnut met with the Scottish monarch, demanding the return of his seized lands. Confronted by the formidable Anglo–Danish martial power, Malcom was forced to abandon the territory, re-establishing the English realm's control in the north.

Meanwhile, Magnus Olafsson, the young son of the deposed Olaf II, became the symbolic head of a revolt led by dissident Norwegian chiefs. An embassy was sent to Russia to escort Magnus back to Norway to lead the uprising against the rule of the foreign Danes. In the spring of 1035, Magnus arrived in Norway under the protection of the Norse chieftain Kalf. As Magnus travelled through Norway, the Viking warlords and their retainers rallied to his standard, pledging their fealty. Norway was under the rule of Cnut's son Swein, who summoned his troops to defend his father's realm. As the return of the Olafsson family was popular with the Norwegians, Swein's call to arms was largely ignored and the troops that answered the summons were unreliable. Confronted by the loyal and determined soldiers of Magnus, Cnut's son abandoned his resistance and fled to the protection of his half-brother Harthacnut in Denmark. Cnut made no attempt to dislodge the new king and his return to Norway marked the termination of the Anglo–Danish reign in the kingdom, with Magnus ruling for the next twelve years.

In 1035 Cnut began to show signs of being seriously ill, and during a progress through Wessex he died on 12 November at the town of Shaftesbury of unknown causes. Before his death he was likely given the last rites by his priests commending his soul to God, while making the sign of the cross. The king's clothing was removed by nuns, and following the removal of the internal organs, his remains were wrapped in a woollen burial garment. From Shaftesbury the body was taken to Winchester in a solemn procession. Later in the month, he was buried at the Old Minster in a service attended by his English heir, Harold, and the great lords and prelates of England, led by Earl Godwin of Wessex, Leafric from Mercia and the Northumbrian Earl Sigurd.

During his reign Cnut had sent his son Harthacnut to rule Denmark, while Swein was named as regent for Norway and Harold remained at the English court preparing to assume the crown. Before his death the king did not designate a clear successor to his three kingdoms, creating a succession crisis. To enforce his perceived rights to the English monarchy, Harold pursued his coronation by the Archbishop of Canterbury to fulfil the legal requirement to become king. Despite Harold's offers of money and intimidation, his request was denied. As the head of the English Church, the archbishop forbade any of his bishops from conducting the ceremony and Harold remained an uncrowned monarch. With England still without an acknowledged king, the Witan was assembled at Oxford in January 1036 to choose a successor. When the magnates and prelates met, Harold was chosen to rule as regent until Harthacnut could settle his affairs in Denmark and come to England to present his appeal for the kingship. While the nobles and churchmen waited for Harthacnut's arrival, the mother of Harold and Cnut's first wife, Elgifu, began intriguing to secure the English realm for her son. During the delay Harold and Elgifu forged an alliance with the Mercian and Northumbrian earls, while Emma became allied with Godwin of Wessex to support the rights of her son Harthacnut. Through bribes and pleas, Elgifu gained the support of many powerful warlords in the north, binding them to her son by oaths of allegiance, while Emma laboured in the south. Harold was now recognized as king in large areas of Mercia and Northumbria, and Emma, with the backing of Godwin and his army, governed in Wessex as regent for Harthacnut. In the *Anglo-Saxon Chronicle* it was written that, 'Godwin and the lords of Wessex opposed the rule of Harold for as long as they could but could not do anything against it.' By 1037 many of the southern lords had abandoned the Danish king's quest for England, and Emma was forced to flee to Bruges in Flanders. Harthacnut was compelled to remain isolated in Denmark to protect his realm against the expected invasion of Magnus of Sweden, while his mother continued to conspire with her allies for her son's rights to the English kingship.

Finally, in 1039 Harthacnut negotiated a settlement with Magnus permitting him to pursue his quest for the English regime. With peace now restored in the north, the Danish monarch assembled an army and fleet of sixty-two ships, joining his mother in Flanders. Before his flotilla set sail for the invasion of England, on 17 March 1040 King Harold died at Oxford aged only twenty-four after a reign of four years. In the wake of Harold's death, the Witan appointed a commission of magnates and bishops to travel to Bruges and offer the crown of England to Harthacnut. In mid-June the king designate, along with his army, crossed the Channel in his fleet, landing in Sandwich. From the coast the royal party proceeded to London, receiving a triumphant reception from the inhabitants as he rode through the streets. Several days later he was anointed King of England. Shortly after his coronation, he had the body of his half-brother Harold disinterred from Westminster Abbey, beheaded and thrown into a swamp in revenge for his cruel rule. Harthacnut ruled in England for the next two years and his death in 1042 marked the end of the Anglo-Danish hereditary line in England begun by Swein I Forkbeard in 1013 and the return of the Anglo-Saxon kings, while in Denmark the monarchy was seized by Magnus.

Selected Sources:

Ashley, Mike, *British Kings and Queens*.
Bartlett, W.B., *King Cnut and the Viking Conquest of England 1016*.
Henry of Huntingdon, *The History of the English People 1000–1154*.
Larson, Laurence, *Canute the Great*.
Lawson, M.K., *Cnut – The Danes in England in the Early Eleventh Century*.
Matthews, Rupert, *The Popes*.
Roberts, Clayton and Roberts, David, *A History of England – Prehistory to 1714*.
Trow, M.J., *Cnut – Emperor of the North*.

Chapter Four

William I

Conqueror of England

In 1066 King Edward III, the Confessor, died without a direct heir, creating a succession crisis for the crown of England. Shortly after the monarch's death, the Witan elected Harold Godwinson to the throne. However, Harold II's claim to the monarchy was challenged by William, Duke of Normandy and cousin of the deceased king. William considered himself the rightful heir by birthright, and assembled his barons, knights and peasant troops to seize the kingdom by force of arms. After crossing the English Channel, he landed his soldiers in south-east England and proceeded north to Hastings, where his army of 7,000 men clashed with Harold II on 14 October. The English occupied Senlac Hill and repelled the repeated assaults of William in fierce and bloody fighting. The battle dragged on, with the Normans and their French allies unable to break the Anglo-Saxon front until Harold was mortally wounded. Following the death of their king, the English militia fled the battlefield, securing the victory for William. In the aftermath of Harold's defeat, the Witan elected William I as sovereign, and on 25 December 1066 he was crowned at Westminster Abbey. The triumph of William I at Hastings changed the course of English history, deciding the fate of the nation.

William was born in western France at the ducal castle of Falaise during the summer of 1027, the illegitimate son of Count Robert of Hiemois and Herleve, the daughter of a master tanner. He was a direct descendent of the Norwegian pirate Rolf the Viking, who had been granted lands in western France by Emperor Charles III in 911 that over the next 100 years were expanded into the Duchy of Normandy by his successors. Little is known about William's early childhood, but he likely spent his first years in the Falaise household of his mother. In early August 1027 the ruling Norman duke, Richard III, died unexpectedly and was succeeded by his brother, Robert of Hiemois. The questionable circumstances of the duke's death cast a shadow over his brother's possible involvement, resulting in civil war between Robert's loyal vassals and the advocates of the young son of Richard III. While the duke was solidifying his power, the young William was brought to the castle in Rouen to reside with him. During this period of turmoil Robert formed numerous political alliances with powerful feudal warlords and neighbouring fiefdoms to further secure his reign.

By 1031, with the support of the Archbishop of Rouen and other magnates and churchmen, the duke had imposed his overlordship on the Norman nobles and Church. After usurping the ducal crown and establishing his rule, in late 1034 Duke Robert suddenly announced to the court his decision to depart on a pilgrimage to Jerusalem to seek penance and absolution for his sins. The duke's declaration was met with surprise and disapproval by the Norman barons and bishops, who tried in vain to alter his decision, noting the lack of an heir if he failed to return from the dangerous journey and the resulting political turmoil. During the meeting with his lords and churchmen, Robert presented his seven-year-old son and persuaded his Norman vassals to acknowledge him as the lawful heir. Before departing for Jerusalem, Robert appointed the Rouen archbishop, Robert, the Count of Brionne, Gilbert, and Alan III, Count of Brittany, as his son's guardians and advisors to govern the duchy during his absence. In 1034 Duke Robert I assembled his vassals to pledge their fealty to William, and they came forward swearing their allegiance. Soon after the ceremony, Robert left his duchy never to return, dying the next year in the city of Nicaea in present-day Turkey.

Shortly before the departure of Robert on his pilgrimage, the King of France, Henry I, gave his consent for William's succession to the Norman demesne, and the heir travelled to the royal court to offer homage to his overlord. While the young duke had secured the acknowledgement of the king and pledges of fealty from his magnates and ecclesiastical lords, his position of power was precarious following the death of his father. As the threat of rebellion escalated, the Archbishop of Rouen became the stabilizing force in the realm, asserting the rule of William. Under the influence of Archbishop Robert, the duchy remained peaceful, with the great feudal lords respecting the duke's authority. It was only after the death of the archbishop in March 1037 that Normandy was beset with internal dissent, as a wave of assassinations and kidnappings swept through the ducal land and the feudal families fighting for control of the crown.

Throughout the following twelve years, numerous political factions discarded their oaths of allegiance to William to conspire for control of the realm. The duke, under constant threat of kidnap and murder, was taken from Rouen to the castle at Vaudreuil in north-west France for his protection. The ruling Norman administration quickly became fragmented and weak, as the demesne was plunged into anarchy. Numerous warlords disregarded the ducal crown's authority, engaging in private wars and plunder. As the turmoil escalated across Normandy, the young duke was frequently moved from castle to castle for his safety. There were several attempts to kidnap William, resulting in the murders of several of his guardians and relatives. In October 1040 Count Alan III of Brittany was killed by assassins and the newly named chief tutor, Count Gilbert of Brionne, was murdered, while the duke's steward, Osbern, was slain by rivals. Longstanding feuds between the great landed families were renewed as the violence continued unabated. William remained under the protection of his guardians, who provided his security, education and military training. He heard numerous stories of his father's exploits from his court-appointed tutors, learning the art of diplomacy and politics and the use of military force to secure his objective. The duke's academic education was severely limited by the ongoing violence, and his knowledge of reading and writing was at a rudimentary level. While his formal education was largely ignored by his tutors, William was trained by masters of arms to fight with the weapons of a feudal warrior, becoming skilled in the use of the broadsword, lance and battle-axe, while training to attack enemy soldiers on horseback. Throughout his turbulent youth, he grew into a charismatic warlord of piety and dignity. During his minority years, William's personal power remained weak, forcing him to depend on the continued support of loyal Norman factions and his French overlord, King Henry I. As he grew older, William began to slowly assert his authority, choosing his own advisors and taking actions on his own initiative.

The unrelenting lawlessness in the ducal fiefdom had been instigated by numerous magnates seeking to settle past grievances or expand the feudal lands under their control. In 1046 the political instability, which had ravaged the duchy for over twelve years, began to change under the leadership of the rebellious Count Guy of Burgundy. The count was a direct descendant of the ruling Norman dynasty, with a rightful claim to the succession of the duchy. Guy had acquired great wealth and power, attracting a large following of Norman nobles, knights and towns. A formidable faction of warlords and mounted warriors from the district of Singlis, located between Caen and Falaise, added their support to Guy's growing army. In the summer of 1047 the rebel magnates moved against William while he was visiting the town of Valognes. Friends of the duke warned him of the impending danger and he managed to escape, making his way to safety at the castle of Falaise. With a large part of western Normandy allied against him, the duke was compelled to appeal to his overlord for reinforcements. Travelling from his demesne, he located the French king at Poissy, prostrating himself before him and asking for his intervention against the conspirators. The Duchy of Normandy was an important fiefdom of Henry I's kingdom and he ordered his army to hasten west to rescue William from Guy of Burgundy's attempted usurpation.

As the French troops approached Caen, they were met by Duke William with a small force of his loyal vassals. The combined army marched north, encountering the rebels on the plain of Val-es-Dunes in central Normandy, six miles from Caen and close to the Orne River. Before the battle began, Seneschal Ralph Tesson defected from the Burgundian count, taking his knights and soldiers to attack the rebels from the rear. While Tesson's forces fought Guy's army, the cavalry of King Henry and the duke against the enemy with the French shouting, 'St Denis,' and the Normans, 'God be our aid'. They made a series of fierce charges against the insurgent horsemen. During the fighting the king was unhorsed by an infantryman and saved by Rogier, Count of Pol, and a contingent of French knights, while William collided with Lord Hardeg of Bayeux, slashing his sword through the rebel's chain-mail and killing him. After the rescue of King Henry, the Count of Pol led the French horsemen in a counter-attack, crashing into Count Guy's men. As the royal allies pressed their attack, Guy's troops began to retreat, leaving hundreds slaughtered on the battlefield.

With the tide of battle turned against them, Guy's men attempted to escape the carnage by fording the Orne River, with the French and Normans in close pursuit. As the king and William intensified their attack, the rebels at the river crossing began to panic and many were drowned trying to reach the opposite bank. During the retreat, the wounded Guy made his way to his fortress-town at Brionne. The castle was constructed on an unapproachable hilltop, surrounded by high stone walls and towers armed with archers. William followed the rebel leader to his fortification and besieged the garrison. The investment dragged on for three years before the count agreed to surrender. Guy was pardoned by his overlord and forced to return to his native Burgundy.

Following the decisive victory over the rebels at Val-es-Dunes, William summoned his prelates to Caen, proclaiming the Truce of God to preserve the peace gained on the battlefield. The Holy Church of Rome had instituted the doctrine to end the acts of violence directed against churchmen, the poor and ecclesiastical properties during designated holy days. The assemblage at Caen approved the law, swearing on holy relics to obey the Truce. Under the terms of the Caen Truce, private wars were prohibited from Wednesday evening to Monday morning and during several religious holidays. The penalty for violating the terms of the agreement was excommunication, but the French king and Duke William were excluded from the canon.

While the siege against Count Guy of Burgundy continued at Brionne, Duke William had been forced to remain in Lower Normandy to enforce his rule over potentially rebellious lords. As the duke kept a close watch on his vassals, to the south-east the Count of Anjou, Geoffrey II Martel, had begun expanding his demesne toward Normandy. In August 1044 he defeated Count Theobald of Blois, seizing control of the towns of Tours, Chinon and Langeais. After securing his rule over the Loire Valley, in 1047 the Count of Anjou marched north into the countship of Maine, gaining possession of Le Mans. Geoffrey II now moved north-east, occupying the castles at Domfront and Alencon, close to the Normandy border. As the count continued to enlarge his holdings in northern Maine, in the autumn of 1051, with the approval of his French overlord, William entered the countship with his army to protect his border. When the duke advanced against the castle at Domfront, Count Geoffrey mustered his forces to defend his newly won territories. The two armies clashed near the fortified town, and after fierce clashes Geoffrey was compelled to withdraw.

In the aftermath of the Count of Anjou's retreat, William proceeded with his army to the fortress at Domfront. The town and its castle were built on a rock overlooking the Varenne River and surrounded by strong defensive works. Unable to take the fortification by storm, William was forced to besiege it. He gave instructions for his men to construct siege towers to attack the stronghold and dig a deep entrenchment to isolate the garrison from reinforcements. While the siege dragged on, William left a contingent of troops to watch the fortress and took the remainder of his army to capture Alencon. As William approached the stronghold's outer defences, Geoffrey II's soldiers placed several oxen hides over the walls, ridiculing William's illegitimate birth with repeated shouts of, 'Hides, hides for the tanner's son'. At the sight of the hides, the duke became enraged, ordering his troops to assault the outpost without mercy. The Normans stormed the fortification killing many of the defenders and taking the remainder prisoner. When the captives were brought to William, he ordered their hands and feet cut off. The severed bloody limbs were thrown over the walls of the Alencon fortress, signalling to the inhabitants that a similar fate awaited them if they did not surrender. The residents and garrison quickly submitted and William honoured his word, sparing them the horrible savageries suffered by the outpost defenders. Following the capture of Alencon, William left a Norman garrison in the town and returned to the siege at Domfront. When reports of the atrocities at Alencon reached Domfront, the garrison quickly agreed to surrender. With his occupation of the two fortifications, Duke William had created a formidable defensive barrier against future attacks by Geoffrey II.

Duke William had waged his war against Geoffrey with the permission of King Henry I and had successfully driven the count back into his own territory. The Count of Anjou and the French king had for many years been rivals, but in the autumn of 1052 they forged a reconciliation, which had future implications for William's survival. While William closely monitored the relationship between the two former enemies, his continued suzerainty of Normandy became more precarious when his vassal, Count

William of Talou, revolted against him, threatening the duke's authority in Upper Normandy. The Count of Talou and his brother, Archbishop Mauger of Rouen, were the dominant rulers in northern Normandy, and their rebellion threated the duke's overlordship of the area. The count and Mauger were uncles of the young duke, and had plotted to overthrow their nephew. With the intervention of Archbishop Mauger, the Count of Talon formed an alliance with the French king against Normandy. Duke William was in the region of Cotentin in north-western France when the news of the count's uprising reached him. He quickly collected a small force of knights and soldiers, riding to confront the rebels at the castle of Arques. He sent forward a contingent of lightly armed troops who, approaching the stronghold, unleashed an attack against the count's followers, driving them back into the walls of Arques. The fortification was too strong to take by storm, and after receiving reinforcements, the duke besieged it. With William of Talou's castle surrounded by loyal Norman troops, William assembled a large army to meet any relieving French forces from the king. As he monitored the northern border area, in August 1053 Henry I entered Normandy at the head of an army in support of his Talou ally. When the king advanced deeper into Upper Normandy, the duke's troops ambushed the French advance party, inflicting heavy casualties. In the aftermath of his stinging defeat, Henry I withdrew his men back across the border. The siege at Arques continued until late 1053, when, with no relief force coming, Count William surrendered after the duke pledged to spare the rebels' lives. The capture of Arques gave the duke a formidable military presence in rebellious Upper Normandy, helping to secure his rule as the victorious defence of his ducal lands gave him added status among his vassals.

While William was enforcing his overlordship in northern Normandy and defending his frontier against encroachment by Geoffrey II, in 1052 he married Matilda, daughter of Count Baldwin V of Flanders. The marriage between the duke and Matilda had been announced in 1049 but was delayed when the Church of Rome refused to sanction the union because it was within the prohibited degree of relationship. It was held by the Church that William and Matilda were cousins and both directly related to Rolf the Viking. During the following three years William, increasingly challenged by powerful enemies within Normandy and along his borders, needed the added security of a loyal ally. Consequently, despite the rulings of the Church, the wedding ceremony was performed at Eu in north-west Normandy. The union was finally authorized by Pope Nicholas II in 1059. Matilda was described by contemporaries as a princess of grace and intelligence, renowned for her many acts of generosity and piety. The future of the ruling Norman dynasty was secured in 1053 with the birth of a son, Robert. William and his wife had a total of nine children, with four sons and five daughters. Two of the sons became kings of England: William Rufus in 1087 and Henry I in 1100.

After years of animosity between Henry I of France and Geoffrey II of Anjou, in 1054 the French king negotiated an alliance with him for a united campaign against Normandy. The monarch issued a decree nullifying the original charter granting Normandy to Rolf the Viking and his descendants, claiming the duchy for his royal throne. Henry mustered a formidable expeditionary force of his vassals with their retainers, along with discontented Norman barons and troops from Geoffrey II. The French king led his great military force along the Seine toward Normandy. As he approached the duchy, his army was divided into two: Henry retained command of one division deployed along the left bank of the river, while his brother Odo was entrusted with the soldiers on the right bank. Following the course of the Seine, the monarch set out for William's capital city at Rouen, ravaging the towns and farmlands in his path. When the duke received reports of the French encroachment from his scouts, he assembled his vassals and levies to defend his lands. Confronted with two advancing forces, he split his troops into two armies, taking charge of the men facing Henry I, while his half-brother Robert of Mortain was given command of the Normans on the right flank. As the Norman armies hastened toward their foe, Robert made first contact with the French and their allies, attacking them at dawn at the village of Mortemer. Odo's barons and militia were taken by surprise, struggling to form a defensive line. Fierce fighting lasted for over nine hours, as Robert's levies slaughtered thousands while taking many knights prisoner.

News of the great triumph was rushed to William, who had remained on the left bank of the Seine preparing to assail the king and his host. The duke, still the vassal of Henry I, was reluctant to attack his overlord. To avoid battle with the French and their allies, William sent a messenger to the king announcing his victory over Odo at Mortemer and encouraging him to withdraw. The next morning, the duke's scouts returned to the Norman encampment with news that the enemy was retreating back to France. Shortly after returning to his kingdom, Henry sent emissaries to the duke proposing peace talks. Under the negotiated agreement, William pledged to return the captured knights from the battle at Mortemer, while the monarch agreed to recognize the duke's rights to Normandy and possession of certain castles along his south-east border.

The formidable fortress at Ambrieres, one of the castles ceded to William by King Henry by the Treaty of Mortemer, was built on the Norman border with Maine. With his right to the stronghold confirmed by the French monarch, the duke garrisoned the outpost with his men to protect the frontier against encroachments by Geoffrey II of Anjou. As the Normans worked to enhance the defensive works of Ambrieres, the count suddenly appeared with his militiamen and allies from Aquitaine, besieging the fortification. Duke William, informed of the siege, quickly gathered his army and returned to Ambrieres. When Geoffrey was warned of the approaching Normans, he abandoned his investment and withdrew. After reaching his castle, William pursued the fleeing count, forcing him to turn and fight. In the ensuing battle, William's forces overwhelmed the enemy troops, taking Geoffrey and William of Aquitaine prisoner. The count was held captive until he agreed to acknowledge William as his overlord in Anjou, expanding Norman rule south into the countship.

Over the next three years William ruled his demesne without intrusions by King Henry or Count Geoffrey. However, humiliated by his defeat and capture by William, the count met the king at his capital in Angers to reconcile their differences and form a coalition against their common enemy. In the summer of 1057 they set out from Angers to attack William. Warned of their approach, William went to Falaise to assemble his army to meet the invaders. As the French and their Anjou allies marched through Normandy, they ravaged and burned. When the French king's army reached the small settlement of Varaville near the town of Caen, they began fording the bridge over the Dives River. The waterway flows to the north-west into the English Channel, and as they moved across the ford, the tide started flowing in from the coast, flooding the river. Henry and the count, on the right bank, watched helplessly as the rising water stranded over half of their army on the opposite side. With the forces of the French and their allies now split, William ordered his men to attack the isolated soldiers who had not passed over the Dives. His foot soldiers, armed with 7ft spears, and cavalrymen with lances and swords tore into the French and Anjou troops, driving them back as the Norman archers and crossbowmen fired volleys of arrows into the enemy's ranks on the crowded road. The allied troops that managed to escape from the rising river and onslaught of the Normans were pursued mercilessly and thousands were slaughtered. While the fighting continued on the left bank of the Dives, the king and Geoffrey abandoned the battle, retiring to their lands. The clash at Varaville was Henry I's final invasion into Normandy. Three years later both the king and his ally were dead. The French kingdom was now ruled by the eight-year-old Philip I under a regency government led by Count Baldwin V of Flanders, Duke William's father-in-law and ally. With the kingdom administered by the count, William remained at peace with the regime until 1072 when Baldwin died.

With his ducal lands finally at peace, William devoted his resources toward solidifying his control over his vassals. He travelled relentlessly throughout his demesne, holding court in numerous towns and castles to enforce his rule. After receiving the oaths of loyalty from his barons, the duke reorganized his government, placing all power and authority in his hands. He appointed loyal viscounts to collect taxes and impose his laws. A chancery administered the duchy in the name of the duke, while a central law court settled all judicial issues. William defied papal protocol, appointing his own Church officials and resolving all ecclesiastical matters. He was a generous benefactor and devoted protector of the Church, building a strong relationship with his bishops. Under his reign, an effective centralized government was created which was responsive and loyal to him.

The duke had earlier begun expanding his territorial holdings into Maine, taking control of several strategic areas. Geoffrey II of Anjou had previously overthrown the ruling count of Maine, Walter II, occupying his lands. Following the death of the Anjou ruler, William negotiated a treaty with the deposed Count of Maine agreeing to intervene to protect his rule in return for his fealty. The agreement was guaranteed with the pledge of marriage between William's son Robert and the count's young daughter. The union between the two families never took place, but under existing law the betrothal was accepted as the equivalent of marriage. Possessing a legal claim to Maine, William prepared to invade and impose his sovereignty, but before his campaign was launched, the bishop and people of the capital city of Le Mans chose Walter of Vexin as their new ruler. Numerous other warlords also pledged loyalty to Walter. Mustering his forces, William advanced into Maine to challenge Walter of Vexin, who withdrew his army to the capital while the duke ravaged the countryside and captured numerous castles. After consolidating his hegemony, William hastened to Le Mans to lay siege to the city. With no possibility of relief from friendly forces, Walter surrendered to the Norman besiegers, giving William a position of dominance in Maine.

While William had received oaths of loyalty from many Maine barons, the Lord of Mayenne, Geoffrey, refused to accept Norman overlordship, withdrawing with his vassals to his formidable castle. The fortress was constructed on a steep hill overlooking the town of Mayenne, fortified with strong defensive works and a determined garrison. The duke moved his army from Le Mans to attack the rebellious warlord and eliminate the last resistance to his rule in Maine. Reaching Mayenne, he sent his foot soldiers and cavalry charging against the castle's walls but was repeatedly thrown back. Catapults were built and battered the stone walls, but could not force a breach. Unable to take the stronghold by storm, William sent several men secretly over the walls into the town to set fire to the wooden buildings. When the inhabitants attempted to extinguish the flames, the Normans attacked, scaling the walls with ladders, overwhelming the defenders and compelling Geoffrey to surrender. After receiving the lord's oath of loyalty, William returned to Le Mans, garrisoning the castle with loyal troops and ordering his engineers to reinforce the defences. By the beginning of 1064 he had secured his hold over Maine.

Duke William's Norman predecessors had a long history of maintaining friendships with the English court and had negotiated numerous marriage alliances between the two regimes. In 1014 Duke Richard II gave sanctuary to the deposed Anglo-Saxon king Ethelred II after his overthrow by the Viking warlord Swein and his son Cnut. Ethelred was married to William's great-aunt, Emma, giving the Norman duke a claim to the English throne if the reigning Saxon king died without an heir. Ethelred and his wife were forced to remain at the Norman court, and their sons Alfred and Edward grew up under the protection and care of the dukes. When Swein unexpectedly died, his son arranged his marriage with the widowed Emma to give legitimacy to the Danish seizure of the English crown. In 1042 Cnut's successor, Harthacnut, died without a direct heir and the English Witan elected Emma's son, Edward III, as successor to the monarchy. William continued to maintain close contact with his blood relative, later visiting him at his English court.

While William was enforcing his feudal rights in and around Normandy, in England King Edward III, known as the Confessor, became reconciled with the Godwinson family after its banishment from court for acts of rebellion. In 1052 Godwin and his eldest son Harold reclaimed their vast estates and wealth. Seven months after his restoration, Godwin died and Harold succeeded him as Earl of Wessex. Harold increasingly gained the favour and confidence of Edward, and after the Welsh rebelled against the English was given command of the royal troops. He unleashed a relentless campaign against the recalcitrant Welsh, establishing himself as the most popular and powerful warlord in the kingdom.

In 1064 Harold was sent to Normandy by the Anglo-Saxon regime on a diplomatic mission. During the crossing of the English Channel his small fleet of three ships encountered stormy weather and was wrecked on the French coast. The earl was captured and held for ransom by Count Guy of Ponthieu. William intervened, securing Harold's release and gaining an ally in his quest for the English monarchy. He took the earl to his palace at Rouen, entertaining him lavishly with banquets and martial tournaments to win his friendship. William and his guest travelled extensively throughout Normandy, while the duke flaunted his formidable castles and magnificent churches and monasteries.

During the earl's extended stay at the Norman court, he was invited by William to take part in the Norman campaign against Count Conan II of Brittany, who had attacked the duke's friend and ally Baron Ruallon of Dol. Harold advanced with the Normans into Brittany, fighting alongside William against Conan II's garrison at Dol. The Anglo-Saxon earl remained with the Norman army, sharing its hardships and dangers. The Normans now advanced to besiege the Bretons at their capital of Rennes.

The besiegers quickly overpowered the defenders and then moved to capture the count's stronghold at Dinan, which surrendered after token resistance. Unable to resist the onslaught of the Norman host, Conan met with William at Dinan, submitting and pledging his fealty. With his victories in Brittany, William's borders were now secure and his supremacy over western France made him the dominate ruler in the region.

Following the surrender of the Bretons, Harold was knighted by the duke on the battlefield and during the ceremony the earl pledged his fealty to William. From Dinan the duke and Harold rode to Bayeux with a large escort of knights and lords, spending the night at the ducal castle. During their stay at Bayeux, William held a meeting of his grand council, inviting Harold to attend. At the assembly of great lords and prelates, Harold repeated his earlier oath to support William's quest for the English throne, swearing with his hand on holy relics. The earl then departed for England, understanding the significance of his pledge on the bones of saints to defend Duke William's hereditary rights to the crown as his English supporter.

By 1065 William had secured his rule as Duke of Normandy and safeguarded his borders through military might and negotiated political alliances with the surrounding lordships. As he maintained his vigil against rebellious barons and governed his ducal lands, events in England were unfolding that would change the course of European history. Edward the Confessor was now sixty years old and in poor health. As the king approached death, he acknowledged Harold Godwinson of Wessex as his heir, despite Harold's pledge to support William of Normandy. Aware King Edward was dying, in December 1065 the Witan assembled in London, electing Harold monarch without opposition. On 5 January 1066 Edward the Confessor died surrounded by his wife, Lady Edith, Harold of Wessex, his chamberlain and the Archbishop of Canterbury, Stigand. He was buried at the newly constructed Westminster Abbey on 6 January, and later that day Harold was anointed by the Archbishop of Canterbury in the abbey as King of England. As Harold II accepted the English crown, his continued rule was challenged on three fronts. In the north the King of Norway, Harold Hardrada, claimed hereditary rights to the throne, while across the Channel, William of Normandy prepared for a campaign to enforce his inheritance through the bloodlines of his great-aunt, Emma. Harold's brother, Tostig, was also conspiring against him for the crown.

Following the death of Edward the Confessor and the coronation of Harold II, Norman spies in London sent a messenger to William at Rouen with the recent news. The duke was surprised at Harold's desertion of his pledge to support his claim of kingship. He dispatched envoys to King Harold demanding his renunciation of the monarchy. When his first message was ignored, a second was sent suggesting the union between the two realms be sealed with the marriages of Harold to the daughter of the duke and the English king's sister to a Norman baron. When the second proposal was met with mockery, the enraged duke began planning for the overthrow of Harold Godwinson by force of arms.

William summoned his chief advisors and preparations for the conquest of England were begun. As the duke prepared his army and naval forces for the invasion of England, he sent envoys to Rome to gain the approval of Pope Alexander II. William had been a benevolent sponsor of the Church in Normandy and was deemed a pious lord. In Rome the Norman delegation accused Harold of profaning the relics of holy saints, usurping the English crown and being involved in the murder of Edward III's brother Alfred. William's cause against Harold was further supported by the Papacy's policy of favouring the succession of kings by hereditary right, and Godwinson's election by the Witan violated the Holy See's principle. After hearing the emissary's pleas, Pope Alexander II authorized Duke William to carry out his seizure of the Anglo–Saxon crown, provided the English Church was subjected to the new stricter reforms of the Holy See. Before the Normans departed from Rome, they were presented with a consecrated flag of St Peter to be carried during the campaign along with the hair and tooth of the saint. The duke was further empowered to deliver a bull of excommunication against Harold II and his supporters. After receiving the pope's blessing for the war against England, the embassy returned to Rouen.

Meanwhile, in Normandy, William summoned his great warlords, prelates and landowners to gain their approval for the English expedition. At first the men refused to take part in the campaign, but after the duke pledged they would all share in the spoils of the conquest, the Normans agreed to his request for men, ships, arms and money. News of the venture then spread through the duchy and was met with widespread enthusiasm. Reports of the duke's invasion reached the French kingdom, Brittany, Flanders and other fiefdoms, as knights, foot soldiers and archers from all parts of western France soon began joining Duke William's army.

As William finalized his preparations, the rebellious younger brother of the English king, Tostig, ravaged the eastern coastline of England with his supporters before sailing to Scotland and the court of his friend and ally King Malcolm III. After spending the summer with Malcolm, the deposed English earl travelled by ship to the Norwegian realm of King Harold Hardrada, a great and powerful warlord in the north. Tostig met with the king, offering him the rich southern half of England in return for their combined invasion of the kingdom. Under Tostig's proposal, Hardrada would rule as monarch, while the earl would govern the north as his sub-king. The Norwegian king readily accepted the offer and began assembling men and ships.

While Tostig and his Norwegian ally prepared their English invasion, in Normandy Duke William gave orders for the construction of a large fleet, sending agents to purchase ships from French and Flemish harbours. Each of the expedition's vessels was a Viking-style longship measuring approximately eighty feet long and fifteen feet wide, with a single mast fitted with a triangular sail and carved dragon's head on the bow. They were propelled by the wind and oarsmen. From the early spring of 1066 until late summer, the duke's artisans and craftsmen were busy building ships from timber cut in the local forests. The Norman flotilla assembled along the coastline near the mouth of the Dives River and other surrounding ports. The exact size of the naval force is unknown, but is estimated at 800 troop and cargo ships. Over 7,000 soldiers, 2,000 horses and several tons of armour, weapons, shields, equipment and supplies were procured. Each of the great barons had a quota from the ducal administration for the number of vessels to be provided for the duke's navy. The duke's half-brother, Odo, Bishop of Bayeux, provided 100 ships and a contingent of armed men. William's flagship, called the *Mora*, was the largest and fastest vessel in the fleet and was a gift from his wife Matilda.

In early August 1066 William began mobilizing his ships and soldiers at the mouth of the Dives. Before departing from Rouen to his invasion fleet, he appointed his wife regent to administer the duchy, entrusting a council of barons and prelates to advise Matilda. While the duke waited for favourable weather for the Channel crossing, an English scout sent by King Harold was captured at the assembly point. When the spy was brought before the duke, he was told: 'Take back to Harold this message. He will receive no damage from us and he will live tranquilly the rest of his days if he sees me not within the space of one year.' The reply to Harold by the duke was also a message to his reluctant barons that he was confident of victory against the English.

After the troops and fleet were assembled, the invasion was delayed by contrary winds and over the weeks of waiting the men grew increasingly concerned that the duke had lost the backing of God, who prevented favourable weather. As the discontent grew in the army, William travelled to the nearby monastery of St Valery, asking the abbot to bring the holy relic of the church to his gathered soldiers. The monks paraded the shrine through the encampment as the troops knelt in prayer, asking the saint to change the wind's direction. During the night their appeals were answered, when the breezes began shifting from the west to a southerly direction.

In the early morning of 27 September the duke gave the order to load the ships. During the day the soldiers, horses and supplies were brought aboard the vessels, and at nightfall the crews set sail for England. In the *Mora*, William led his ships to the south-west through the darkness, guided by the light of his rear lantern. However, when the duke looked for his fleet the following dawn, the *Mora* was alone. A sailor was sent up the mast to search for the flotilla, but replied: 'I see only the sky and sea.' The duke ordered the seamen to throw out the anchor to slow the vessel. After a brief period, another crewman climbed the mast, yelling: 'I see a forest of masts and sails.' The fleet reassembled and the voyage resumed over a calm sea with favourable winds. The Norman fleet made landfall on the Sussex coast at Pevensey Bay at 9.00 am on the morning of 28 September. The ships were beached and the army disembarked on English soil unchallenged.

While the Normans had been delayed at Dives by the weather, in southern England King Harold's militiamen were mustered and stood ready to drive off the invaders, while English ships patrolled the Channel eager to assail the approaching Norman fleet. After four months of waiting, and anxious to return to their farms and trades, the men grew restless, threatening to desert and forcing Harold to disband his army.

As Harold was demobilizing his troops in the south, Harold Hardrada sailed toward England with his massed Viking army. The Norwegians stopped over at their colonies in the Orkney and Shetland Isles, where they were joined by ships and warriors from the Scottish king. When the northern fleet reached the Tyne River in northern England, it was united with Tostig and his soldiers. The 8,000 invaders now ravaged and pillaged the region's towns unopposed by King Harold. The Northmen sailed up the Ouse, anchoring near the city of York. Edwin, Earl of Northumbria, and Morcar, Earl of Mercia, attempted to defend York but were driven off, compelling the city to surrender to the Vikings. While the Norwegian king and Tostig were plundering northern England, Harold was informed of their invasion and headed north with his mustered knights and militiamen. On 25 September the Englishmen clashed with the Northmen at Stamford Bridge near York. As Harold's host approached the invading troops, the Vikings were taken by surprise, throwing up a wall of shields in a half circle for protection. The English king sent his Anglo-Saxon warriors charging across the open ground into the enemy's formation. A savage struggle lasted through the day. During the early fighting Hardrada was killed by an arrow through his neck, leaving Tostig in command of the invaders. In the late afternoon the English foot soldiers crashed into the shield wall time and again before finally breaking through. After Tostig was killed, the surviving Northmen and their confederates abandoned the battlefield, fleeing to their ships.

Following the victory over the Northmen, Harold reformed his men returning to York and stayed several days to rest his exhausted soldiers. While at York, he received reports of William's landing on the southern coast. After rapidly moving north to face the Vikings, the English royal army was now compelled to hastily return 240 miles to southern England. On 6 October they reached London, where Harold remained for six days to recruit reinforcements and rest his men, while tending to the affairs of his kingdom.

While Harold was defeating the Vikings and their allies in the north, William was pillaging the Pevensey Bay region to draw the English king into fighting for his kingdom. Following a short stay in Pevensey, the

Normans moved to a more defensible site at Hastings. A wooden stockade was erected with a deep trench, while the duke's scouts reconnoitred for the English army. Harold II remained in London until 12 October, when he marched his army south to Hastings and took up a defensive position on a steep hilltop named Senlac Hill, seven miles from the invaders' camp.

Harold had an army of approximately 7,000 soldiers made up of his Housecarls, militiamen and lightly armed local peasants. The 3,000 Housecarls were the king's elite troops, specially trained and heavily armed with Danish axes to form the core of the royal army. To protect the English front line, the king's men dug a trench and threw up a barrier of stakes to hold back the advance of the Normans. On the crest of Senlec Hill the lightly equipped peasants held the right flank, while the Housecarls were deployed on the left. The monarch's battle banner, depicting a fighting warrior on a field of gold, was unfurled in the middle of the Housecarls' formation. The Norman host was slightly smaller than the English army and comprised heavily armed infantrymen, archers, slingers and cavalry. The heart of the Norman force was the mounted troops, dressed in long coats of mail and equipped with swords and lances. William aligned his army with the Breton troops of his half-brother Odo on his left and the Normans holding the centre, while the French and other allied soldiers were positioned on the right flank.

The night before the battle the English spent the evening singing their traditional songs and drinking ale under the light of the waning half-moon, while the Normans attended Mass and received sacraments from the numerous priests and monks who had joined the expeditionary force. At dawn on 14 October, Pope Alexander II's flag of St Peter was unfurled and the knights, mounted troops, archers, slingers and crossbowmen, followed by the priests, set out on the road to Hastings. As the invaders came over the crest of Talham Hill, they saw the deployed Anglo–Saxon army along the top of Senlac Hill. William aligned his army for battle, placing the archers, slingers and crossbowmen in front of the first line of infantrymen, who were armed with spears and swords, while the cavalry was positioned in the rear. Around 9.00 am the invading army advanced at the blast of trumpets and loud war cries. The fighting began when the Norman bowmen fired volleys of arrows into the ranks of the Englishmen, as the foot soldiers moved up the slope of the hill to attack the shield wall.

Harold's forces fought back with spears and swords, and the Housecarls swung their heavy axes at the approaching foe. As the infantry struggled to break the Saxon shield wall, William's cavalry unleashed an assault up the hill. Holding the high ground and fighting behind their barrier of kite-shaped shields, the English continued to repel the Normans and their allies. While the Normans in the centre and the French and Flemish on the right wing pressed their attacks, the Bretons on the left flank began to abandon the battle after failing to penetrate the Anglo-Saxon line. As the men of Bishop Odo fell back, the whole advancing front fled down the slopes of Senlac Hill. Following the enemy's withdrawal, the English warriors discarded the protection of their shield wall to pursue William's forces.

The Norman were further disheartened when news spread that Duke William had been killed. Seeing his army in danger of being destroyed, the duke rode up to the fleeing men, taking off his helmet and shouting to them: 'Look at me, I still live, and with God's help I will conquer.' After seeing their duke alive, the knights and militia turned around to crash into the pursuing Englishmen. The Anglo-Saxon foot soldiers had cast off their shields and were now easy prey for William's horsemen. After slaughtering hundreds, the cavalry rushed up Senlec Hill into the ranks of the Housecarls, who continued to hold their line. William's knights made repeated assaults but failed to penetrate Harold's front as casualties mounted on both sides.

Unable to breach the Anglo-Saxon defences, William ordered his horsemen to feint a withdrawal. Believing the enemy forces were in retreat, the English went storming down the hill. The Normans and their French allies then turned to attack the unsuspecting pursuers, killing many of them. The duke's men resumed their attack, overrunning Harold's flanks. The English king managed to hold his position, protected by the resolve of his Housecarls. To finally break Harold's line, William ordered his archers to fire volleys of arrows into their formation. The hail of arrows fell into the ranks of the Saxons, one striking Harold in the eye. Wounded, he continued to fight protected by the Housecarls. The Norman mounted troops intensified their attack, overrunning the English position and killing the king. Seeing their monarch dead on the battlefield, the militiamen and peasant soldiers fled, while the Housecarls fought on with their bloody axes cutting down many of the advancing Normans. By nightfall the invaders had gained control of Senlac Hill to claim victory, despite continued isolated resistance. The battle at Hastings had decided the fate of the English kingdom.

Following his victory over King Harold, Duke William remained at Hastings to rest his men and wait for additional soldiers from Normandy before advancing against London. On 20 October he moved slowly north-eastward, capturing Dover and occupying Canterbury after the inhabitants surrendered without resistance. At Canterbury the duke was struck down by a mystery illness and was compelled to wait in the city for a month before fully recovering. In mid-December he was well enough to renew his march, taking his army in a wide sweep around London to ravage the towns and lay waste to the countryside in Surrey, Sussex and Hertfordshire, leaving a wide path of devastation. The Normans crossed the Thames at Oxford, while in London numerous factions of nobles and prelates struggled to find enough support to attack the invaders. William turned his forces south, occupying Wallingford, where he was met by the Archbishop of Canterbury, Stigand. The prelate offered his fealty to the duke and pledged to return to London to secure his election by the Witan as successor to Harold. The great English churchmen and earls, including Edwin of Mercia and Morcar of Northumbria, met Duke William at Berkhamsted. They swore loyalty to him and offered hostages to secure their conduct. While the high nobles and churchmen now supported the duke, the city of London continued its defiance. The army was ordered to move toward the capital, continuing to plunder and burn. When the invaders approached London, a delegation of citizens came to the duke to surrender the city. After occupying London, the chief prelates presented the English crown to William, pledging their allegiance. At first the duke refused to accept the offer, but agreed after his army voiced its approval.

Before William's coronation as king, he ordered the construction of a stronghold inside the city's walls as protection against an uprising by the London citizens. On Christmas Day 1066, at Westminster Abbey, William was crowned King of England by Archbishop Aldred of York. William I claimed the English kingship not as a conqueror but the legitimate hereditary successor to Edward III. While the Normans and their French allies had gained control over most of south-east England, the rest of the kingdom remained defiant and unconquered.

As construction of the first Tower of London continued, William I located his court at nearby Barking, where he was visited by Edwin of Mercia and Morcar of Northumbria, who pledged their northern earldoms to the new king. To solidify his rule over southern England, William toured the shires, visiting towns and establishing his government. He ordered the erection of numerous castles at strategic points to protect his conquest. During the eleventh century most of the early Norman castles were made of timber. Wooden strongholds could be built quickly, and, under constant threat of attack, speed of construction was vital to their protection. The fortresses were surrounded by earthworks, and deep trenches added an extra layer of protection. Most of the fortifications were manned with small garrisons and built on sites with a commanding view of the surrounding countryside. Many of the king's loyal barons were placed in charge of the conquered shires. To his half-brother Odo of Bayeux, the sovereign gave command of Dover and the Earldom of Kent. Less than six months after sailing from Normandy, King William had enforced his sovereignty over much of southern England.

William remained in England until February 1067, returning to Normandy to reassert his ducal authority. Before departing he appointed Odo of Bayeux as lieutenant general for the region south of the Thames, with William Fitz-Osbern made responsible for the north. William sailed with a small fleet carrying a large entourage of English barons and prelates held as hostages against a potential uprising by rebellious warlords. After reaching Normandy, the king travelled to Rouen to receive a hero's welcome from the people. He set out with Matilda to visit strategic towns and ensure their loyalty. From the rich plunder taken in England, the regime gave gifts of land, gold and silver to the nobles, churches and monasteries. The captured battle flag of King Harold was sent to Pope Alexander II in recognition of his support. William celebrated Lent at Fecamp, where he was met by a delegation of magnates from King Philip I of France, sent to congratulate him on his conquest of England. With his rule over the duchy secure, in December the king returned to England, where rebellion was beginning to fester. While in Normandy, he again named Matilda regent, assisted by their son Robert and an advisory council of barons and churchmen.

Following William's return to England, the lands and possessions of the Anglo-Saxon knights who had fought against him were declared forfeited to the monarchy. Prior to the departure of the expeditionary force from Normandy in September 1066, the king had promised all of his men a share of the English plunder, and now it was distributed to them. The great shires were given to the powerful Norman warlords, who became the largest landowners in the realm to create the new Anglo-Norman nobility.

Before returning to Normandy, William I had instructed his two lieutenant generals, Odo of Bayeux and William Fitz-Osbern, to rule with tolerance and moderation, but during his absence they governed with cruelty and arrogance, creating a spirit of rebellion among the Englishmen. The first revolt against the Norman occupiers occurred in Dover. The city council elected Count Eustace of Boulogne as its overlord, in defiance of William. The count crossed the Channel with his small army, joining forces with the rebellious Dover townspeople. The French and their English allies attacked the Norman garrison but were quickly repelled. After several days of failed assaults, Eustace became convinced of the invincibility of the stronghold, withdrawing his men. As the attackers pulled back, the Normans rushed to the gates, attacking Eustace's rebels and killing many of them, while the survivors fled in panic. This first attempt to throw-off the rule of the Normans was quickly quelled, but other regions of England were ready to challenge the power and resolve of King William.

Following the subjugation of Dover, the inhabitants of Exeter in western England began reinforcing their defences in preparation for rebellion against the crown. The townsfolk had earlier formed a league with other cities to oppose Norman occupation by military might. When William learned of the growing opposition, he sent a message to the town council asking members to come to his court and give their oaths of allegiance. The citizens replied that they would never swear loyalty to a foreign invader or allow him inside their walls. The king answered: 'It is not my custom to receive my subjects on such conditions.' He ordered his army to march to Exeter to enforce his rule, and as they approached the town the magistrates submitted. The offer was accepted, but when the delegation returned to Exeter with news of the surrender, the citizens refused to accept the terms. With the gates to the town closed, William was compelled to lay siege to it. After eighteen days of resistance, the inhabitants capitulated. Despite their defiance to his rule, the monarch granted the people a pardon, but built a stronghold inside the walls garrisoned by Norman soldiers to impose his kingship.

William resumed his suppression campaign in the west against members of the rebel league, marching to Cornwall and putting down the revolt with little opposition. The formidable Norman presence in the western shires and their occupation of Exeter and Cornwall convinced the remaining rebel towns to surrender to the king. While William was enforcing his rule in the south, York became the focus of revolt in the north. Edwin of Northumbria and Morcar of Mercia disregarded their earlier pledges of loyalty and fled from London with their English followers to York, challenging the king's power. As the threat against the Norman throne gained momentum, William advanced toward York with his army, erecting a series of castles in the area to deter the insurrection. Intimidated by the size of the fortresses and their garrisons, the two earls submitted to the king and without their leadership the uprising soon fell apart. By the end of 1068 William was in York and his reign over the north again seemed secure.

Early the following year the Norman crown's appointed earl at York was overthrown and slain by rebelling English forces under the banner of Edgar Etheling, a distant cousin of Edward the Confessor and last living member of the old Anglo–Saxon royalty. A large northern army was soon raised by the local warlord, Cospatrick, in support of Etheling Edgar, who had earlier fled to the protection of the Scottish king, Malcolm III. When William learned of the uprising, he sent Robert, Earl of Cemines, to impose his rule. The earl moved quickly to the north with 500 knights and their retainers. On 28 January he spent the night inside the walls of Durham, but as his men slept the English surrounded the town and set fire to the houses, killing most of the Norman troops. After clearing the region north of the Ouse of Norman forces, the Englishmen proceeded south to York, assailing the king's garrison in the castle. The York citizens declared their fealty to Edgar Etheling, who left King Malcolm III's court to join the rebellion. As the English soldiers pressed their siege against York, the garrison commander sent a messenger to King William requesting reinforcements. William quickly mustered his forces and hastened to the north. By a series of forced marches, he surprised the rebels with his unexpected arrival, overrunning their defences and killing many of the English troops. With York again under his control, he named William Fitz-Osbern as the new garrison commander and ordered the construction of a new fortress to reinforce his defensive works around the city.

After the northern magnates and prelates had been defeated twice in their attempts to overthrow the Norman throne, and with Edgar Etheling considered a weak and ineffective leader, the rebels began negotiations with the Danish king Sweyn II for his usurpation of the monarchy. Sweyn II was the nephew of the former English king Cnut, and represented an institution still popular in northern England, especially among the Vikings' descendants. With the promise of gold and military support, the Danish king agreed to invade England. In the autumn of 1068 he sent a fleet of nearly 250 ships and a large army reinforced with English exiles, under the command of his brother Osbern, down the east coast of England. Osbern sent his army ashore at Dover, but following an unsuccessful attack against the Norman stronghold withdrew his soldiers, sailing north to plunder several coastal towns. When the Danes and their English allies landed on the banks of the Humber River south-east of York, they were welcomed by descendants of Scandinavian immigrants who joined their expeditionary force. As the invaders moved toward York, they were merged with a powerful English army under the command of Cospatrick, Earl of Bernicia. The Anglo-Danish army now hastened against the Norman garrison at York. At the approach of Osbern's soldiers, the troops from the two Norman fortresses marched out to attack them, but were overwhelmed by the superior forces of the Anglo-Danes and routed.

Rebellions broke out in other areas of England after reports of the Danish victories in the north spread through the realm. English rebels in Cornwall and Devon attacked Norman castles, threatening to overpower the defenders. Behind their wooden castle walls, the garrisons repelled the attacks of the rebels. In Somerset, the insurgents assaulted the royal castles, but with reinforcements from London and several other loyal towns, the king's commander, Bishop Geoffrey of Coutances, compelled the English to withdraw.

In the early winter of 1069, to put an end to the rebellions, King William took his army to York to attack the Anglo-Danish forces. When he neared the city, his scouts reported the Danes and their English allies had returned to the Humber and the security of their ships. The king divided his army into three divisions, sending one to reoccupy the city of York and a second contingent to monitor the Danes on the river, while he led the third force of knights and infantry against the rebel English. He advanced against the rebels, overrunning the English camps, burning their farms and crops and laying waste to the countryside, murdering thousands of men, women and children, in what became known as the 'Harrying of the North'. He continued his campaign of fire and fury over the winter, relentlessly pursuing the insurgents throughout Northumbria and forcing their submission. The devastation was so great that it led to a widespread famine which killed more than one-in-ten of the population. A chain of strongly garrisoned castles was erected to enforce the rule of the king over the subdued North.

As William was suppressing the northern uprising , the Danes remained on the Humber in their ships, allowing the Normans to reoccupy York without opposition. The two destroyed castles were rebuilt and garrisoned with loyal troops. William spent Christmas at York with his court celebrating the season with religious ceremonies and banquets. He renewed his pillaging campaign in January 1070, advancing north to the Tees River to hunt down the rebels. During the king's campaign, many of the insurrectionists' leaders, including Cospatrick, submitted their allegiance to him.

Meanwhile, to the south-west, rebels led by Edwin the Wild were besieging Shrewsbury Castle and bands of English and Welsh rogues were raiding throughout Mercia. William reassembled his battered and exhausted army of royalists and French mercenaries marching to Chester, where he built a wooden castle with deep trenches to secure the surrounding region for his regime. He left a reinforced garrison and set out to pursue the rebels. Under his relentless campaign, the Mercia was brought back under Norman control. Lord Hugh of Auranches was given the Earldom of Chester and ordered to continue the aggressive offensive against the insurgents, unleashing attacks along the Welsh border and conquering the area for the Norman throne.

In the aftermath of his 'Harrying of the North', King William travelled to Winchester, celebrating Easter with his family and court. During his stay in the city, he was visited by three cardinals sent by Pope Alexander II to honour him as a son of the Holy Church and to depose Archbishop Stigand from his sees of Canterbury and Winchester. With the three papal envoys, William presided over an ecclesiastical council that voted to dethrone the archbishop. With the Canterbury archbishopric now vacant, the king arranged for the appointment of his advisor and friend Lanfranc to the office.

During the winter the king continued to monitor the activities of the Danes on the Humber, but took no action to drive them off. However, in the spring of 1070 the hostile forces were joined by King Sweyn II, who brought additional ships and soldiers. The Northmen had spent the winter building a fortified encampment on the Isle of Ely in East Anglia, while continuing to plunder the region around the river. The stronghold became a refuge for English outlaws and rebel lords. From their sanctuary the Danes and their English allies intensified their pillaging raids, attacking several towns. With the rebels firmly entrenched on the island, William negotiated an agreement with Sweyn II for his return to Denmark after a large payment of gold and silver was made. The remaining insurgents on the island, led by Hereward the Wake, resumed the attacks against the Norman occupiers, burning settlements and laying waste to the countryside. In the spring of 1071 numerous English patriots, including the son of the Earl of Morcar, joined Hereward's campaign. In the summer William finally moved against the rogues' camp. Using a secret pathway revealed to him by local priests, the king attacked the Englishmen, catching them by surprise. The Normans penetrated the defences, killing many men and capturing numerous prominent Anglo-Saxon warlords.

The king spent most of the following year at peace in his English realm, enforcing his rule and laws. In 1072 he launched a punitive campaign against Malcolm III of Scotland in retaliation for his support of the rebels and his numerous pillaging raids across the border. When the Normans and their English allies advanced into the Scottish kingdom, Malcolm offered to negotiate a reconciliation. In the ensuing Treaty of Abernathy, the Normans recognized Scotland's rights over the northern territories, while Malcolm offered his fealty to King William.

With his kingdom finally pacified, William I began the process of building a governing institution based on Norman feudalism. The lands of the Anglo-Saxon rebel lords were confiscated by the throne, with a share granted to the king's vassals and the remainder retained by the monarchy. By the end of William's reign in 1087, only a few Anglo-Saxon lords or bishops maintained possession of their properties. Under the king's direction, the tax system was modified and an annual levy based on the value of the land was instituted. The existing English courts continued to be utilized, but were augmented by the introduction of regional Norman legal institutions. The office of sheriff was enhanced and was now led by prominent noblemen, who enforced the crown's justice. The king's regime brought Norman laws, institutions and culture to the English people, creating the foundations for a highly effective centralized government, while producing an era of stability, national unity and prosperity.

The Norman regime's reforms were extended to the English Church. The existing ecclesiastical structure was reformed, new monasteries and churches were built and leading Anglo-Saxon churchmen replaced by loyal Normans. William's advisor, Lanfranc, was appointed Archbishop of Canterbury and under his direction the Church was transformed. After the new pope, Gregory VII, objected to William's appointment of his own prelates in England, Archbishop Lanfranc travelled to Rome to defend the king's right to name them. When the pope later issued a decree claiming papal suzerainty over the European thrones, William responded that he would pay no homage that his predecessors had not offered. During the king's absences in Normandy, Archbishop Lanfranc ruled the kingdom as regent, continuing William's policies. Like all aspects of Anglo-Norman society, the control of the Church remained the prerogative of King William.

While the Norman monarch remained occupied in England suppressing the revolts of his English nobles, his friend and ally the Count of Flanders, Arnult III, was killed at the Battle of Cassel in February 1071 and succeeded by his uncle, Count Robert the Frisian. The victorious Robert seized control of the Flemish throne, but was not acknowledged as ruler by William, enflaming relations between them. As William was increasingly threatened by hostilities from Flanders, Anjou to the south of Normandy was ruled by the bellicose Count Fulk IV, who began to scheme to intervene in Maine in opposition to William's authority. In early

1073, after Count Fulk was invited by the citizens of Le Mans to intervene in Maine, William was compelled to return to Normandy and reimpose his overlordship. Fulk advanced into Maine, and with the support of local troops seized control. When William landed in Normandy, he marched immediately into Maine with his hastily assembled army, augmented by soldiers from England. Encountering little resistance, he overran several towns before turning to attack Le Mans. His forces laid siege to the city, forcing the inhabitants to surrender after offering little resistance. With his hegemony in Maine re-established, William returned to Normandy to face the growing danger of the French monarchy under Philip I and the hostility of Flanders.

In 1067 Philip I had assumed the crown of France and began a diplomatic and martial campaign to regain his feudal rights over his Norman vassal. To reclaim his overlordship of Normandy, Philip formed an alliance with Robert the Frisian of Flanders, the regent of Brittany, Hoel V, and Fulk IV of Anjou. For the remainder of his reign, William was continually under the threat of attack by members of the French league. While he kept watch on events in western France, Ralph, Lord of Gael and Earl of Norfolk, who held lands in both Brittany and England, rebelled against William. English forces under the command of Lanfranc moved against the rebel, compelling him to retreat to his stronghold at Norwich. Ralph soon departed for Denmark to incite the Northmen to invade England, leaving his wife Emma, the daughter of William Fitz Osbern, in charge at Norwich. The castle was besieged and following token opposition surrendered to Lanfranc. Shortly after the capitulation at Norwich the Danes reached England, but with the revolt crushed they returned after pillaging several coastal towns. At Christmas 1075 William sailed back to England, celebrating the season in a peaceful kingdom.

Early in 1076 King William was once again back in Normandy, preparing to invade Brittany. Having returned to Brittany, Ralph Gael found refuge with Hoel V and joined his son, Alain Fergant, at Dol to defend the fortress against attack by William. Dol was near the frontier and a constant danger to the Norman regime. In September the Normans advanced against Ralph, besieging him in the castle at Dol. Despite repeated Norman assaults and the continuation of the siege, the

Bretons, led by Ralph, defiantly held out. As the investment continued, Philip I led a large army to the relief of Ralph in October, driving off the Normans after fierce fighting with infantry and cavalry charges and counter charges. William's failure to defeat the Bretons allowed Ralph and Hoel V to consolidate their power in Brittany and Philip I to take control over the Vexin region, tightening the ring around the continued independence of Normandy.

In early 1077 Fulk IV resumed his campaign of conquest into Maine advancing his army against the countship of Le Fleche ruled by Count John. Hard pressed to hold his stronghold, the count sent messengers to his ally, William I, asking for his intervention. While the Le Fleche count continued to repulse the attacks of Angevin forces, the Normans came to his assistance ploughing into the invaders with their veteran infantrymen and horse soldiers compelling them to withdraw. During the fighting Fulk IV was wounded and was now agreeable to a truce with the Normans, which was followed by a treaty between Philip I and the Anglo–Norman regime later in the year.

Before his departure to England in 1066, Duke William had recognized his eldest son, Robert Curthose, as his heir to Normandy. When his father was in England, Robert ruled Normandy, with his mother as co-regent. As Robert approached the age of majority, he was described by contemporaries as impatient and ambitious for his assumption of the ducal throne. In early 1078 he demanded independent authority over Normandy, in defiance of his father's continued suzerainty. When the king ignored his overtures, Robert withdrew from court with his followers, attempting to seize control of Rouen. After the garrison withstood his attacks, King William ordered the arrest of his son and his followers. Robert fled to the court of Philip I with many of his young lords from the great houses of Normandy. Through the intervention of the French monarchy, contingents of knights and soldiers from France, Anjou, Maine and Brittany rallied to Robert's growing revolt, seriously threating William's rule.

As his son's insurgency expanded, William summoned his loyal vassals and retainers to march against the rebels. He first attacked the renegades defending the castle at Remalard, overpowering the defenders. The Norman army followed the survivors to the stronghold at Gerberoi on the eastern border. William ordered his men to besiege the fortification, and as the garrison continued to hold out their provisions became depleted. Cut off from supplies and reinforcements, the rebels were compelled to open the gates and charge against William's army. During a violent and bloody battle, the king was unhorsed and his forces put to flight. Following his unexpected defeat, William returned to Rouen and, through the mediation of a faction of influential barons, opened talks with Robert for a reconciliation. In early 1080 father and son were reunited, with Robert again named successor to the Norman duchy. While William was in Normandy protecting his ducal lands, in England the Scots under Malcolm III resumed their pillaging raids along the border, forcing the loyal northern lords to enforce the crown's control.

Meanwhile in England, Bishop Odo of Bayeux plotted to take advantage of the ongoing turmoil in Rome between Pope Gregory VII and the anti-pope Clement III, who had the backing of the Holy Roman Emperor, Henry IV. In 1082 the bishop conspired with the Roman Curia to gain its support for his usurpation of the Holy See from the embattled Gregory. The continued friendship of the papacy was vital to King William's rule in Normandy and England, and after learning of his half-brother's intrigues, he crossed the Channel and ordered the arrest of the bishop to protect his relationship with Rome.

In 1085 the King of Denmark, Cnut IV, revived the Scandinavian claim to England and began preparing for an invasion of the kingdom. He formed an alliance with Robert, Count of Flanders, for a combined attack against William's realm. When the king learned of the Danish preparations, he ordered the coastal regions of England laid to waste to deny enemy forces access to food and supplies. He left Normandy with a large army of ducal knights and French mercenaries to protect his kingdom. To fund the cost of the military force, the crown imposed a heavy tax on all Englishmen. The king ordered a national survey to collect the revenue necessary to pay for the expected Danish war. The amassing of a kingdom-wide census was needed to provide an accurate account of land ownership following many years of property transfers under the Anglo-Norman regime. During 1086 royal agents were sent to every shire with instructions to assign values to each household and farm by recording its size, number of labourers, livestock and crops to determine the appropriate tax. This became known as the *Domesday Book*. However, as the English prepared for the Danish onslaught, in July

1086 Cnut IV was murdered at the church of Odensee and the campaign against England was abandoned.

While William was occupied in England with the expected Scandinavian attack, Philip I took advantage of the distraction to resume his hostilities against Normandy. The French monarchy financially supported Robert of Normandy, who had again broken his pledge of fealty to rebel against his father. As the rebels in western France continued to oppose William, the barons in the Vexin were encouraged by the French regime to plunder Norman borderlands and harass towns loyal to William.

As the incursions into his ducal lands escalated, William sailed back to Normandy and established his court at Rouen. In the summer of 1087 the French garrison at Mantes crossed the frontier to plunder Normandy at the prompting of King Philip. William assembled his army to retaliate against the raid, advancing into Vexin in August. He moved first against Mantes, besieging the castle. When the garrison opened the gates and charged out of the fortress at the king's forces, they were beaten back in a bloody melee. The Normans pursued the rebels into the castle, overpowering them and seizing control of the town. Mantes was brutally sacked and burnt by William's men. As William rode through the streets of the burning city, he was suddenly struck by a sharp abdominal pain. As the illness grew worse, he was taken back to Rouen and attended by the court doctors, but to little avail. To escape the harsh summer heat, the monarch was taken to the hilltop priory of Saint Gervais. William's health continued to deteriorate, and nearing death, he acknowledged Robert Curthose as his successor to the duchy of Normandy, while his second son William Rufus was given the English kingdom and the youngest son, Henry, was awarded 5,000 pounds of silver and several estates and castles in England. Laying on his deathbed, the king received the sacraments from the Archbishop of Rouen, and in the early morning of 9 September 1087 he died at the age of fifty-nine. His last recorded words were: 'I commend myself to Mary the Holy Mother of God, my heavenly Lady, that by her intercession I may be reconciled to her Son our Lord Jesus Christ.' He was carried from the priory to Caen and buried in the Abbey of Saint Stephen.

Following the death of his father, Robert was acknowledged duke by the Norman lords and Church. The new duke was, however, considered a weak and ineffective ruler, and was unable to establish his authority over his rebellious vassals. As Robert struggled to control his warlords, in 1091 his younger brother, King William II of England, invaded Normandy to reunite his father's two crowns. In the ensuing campaign, Robert was defeated and forced to cede two Norman countships to the king. After making peace with William, the two older brothers agreed to jointly attack the lands of their youngest brother Henry, seizing parts of Maine. As the warriors of Europe assembled for the First Crusade in 1096, Duke Robert summoned his knights and soldiers to join the expeditionary force. To fund the cost of his campaign, the duke mortgaged Normandy to William II, who now ruled the duchy as regent. Bishop Odo of Bayeux accompanied his nephew to the Holy Land, dying en route in February 1097 at Palermo in Sicaly. Duke Robert fought with distinction against the Muslims at the Battle of Dorylaeum on 1 July 1097 and the siege of Antioch, and was present at the fall of Jerusalem to the crusaders in 1099. In 1100 King William II was killed in a hunting accident, and with Robert still on crusade, their younger brother Henry took the English throne unchallenged. Learning of William's death, Robert hurried back to England to claim the kingdom from Henry I. He invaded the realm in 1101, but was defeated and compelled to abandon his rights to the English crown for an annual payment of 3,000 marks. As relations between the brothers remained strained, in 1105 Henry renewed hostilities against Duke Robert, crossing the Channel with his army to take Normandy. At the Battle of Tinchebray in 1106, Robert was defeated and taken prisoner. He spent the next twenty-eight years imprisoned in England at the castles of Devizes and Cardiff, dying aged eighty in 1134.

Selected Sources:

Bates, David, *William the Conqueror*.
Brooke, Christopher, *The Saxon and Norman Kings*.
Chambers, James, *The Norman Kings*.
Douglas, David C., *William the Conqueror – The Norman Impact upon England*.
Fraser, Antonia, *The Lives of the Kings and Queens of England*.
King, Edmund, *Medieval England*.
Rendina, Claudio, *The Popes*.
Rex, Peter, *William the Conqueror – The Bastard of Normandy*.
Roberts, Andrew, *Great Commanders of the Medieval World*.
Slocombe, George, *William the Conqueror*.
Smith, Goldwin, *A History of England*.

Chapter Five

Frederick I Barbarossa

Unifier of the Holy Roman Empire

In 1152 Frederick I Barbarossa was elected King of Germany and opened negotiations with the Holy See of Rome to secure his recognition as Holy Roman Emperor. The Treaty of Constance was signed on 25 March 1153 by representatives of the German regime and Pope Eugenius III, confirming Frederick I's rights to the imperial throne. Under the provisions of the agreement, the papacy pledged to anoint Frederick I as emperor of the Holy Roman Empire and overlord of northern Italy, while the German monarchy agreed to intervene in support of the pope against the rebellious citizens of Rome and southern Italy. Acting under the terms of the treaty, Barbarossa marched his army into Lombardy and Tuscany, enforcing his imperial rule over the princes and city-states. After securing the fealty of his vassals, he travelled to Rome to meet the newly elected Pope Alexander IV. Frederick rode into the Holy City on 18 June and dismounted at St Peter's. He removed his armour and, dressed in his coronation robes, entered the basilica. He walked toward the confessional and knelt before the pope. Adrian IV anointed Barbarossa with holy oil and celebrated Mass in honour of the Virgin Mary. In the final act of the coronation ceremony, he conferred the sceptre and sword to the emperor and placed the golden crown on his head. The congregation then loudly acclaimed him as Emperor of the Holy Roman Empire.

Frederick was the son of Duke Frederick II of Swabia and Judith, the daughter of the Bavarian duke, Henry IX, and was born in late 1122 at Haguenau in present-day south-eastern France. Frederick's father was a member of the Hohenstaufen dynasty, while his mother was from the Welf family; with his birth uniting the two rival families. He was raised in the ducal household under the care of the duchess and her servants.

Monks from the monasteries provided his limited education and the young lord was taught the basics of reading and writing, while studying Latin grammar. As was common practice in feudal Europe, around the age of seven Frederick began his military training for knighthood under the guidance of a master of arms. He was taught the fighting skills of a foot soldier and mounted warrior. The young lord practiced long hours with the sword and spear of an infantryman, while learning to ride a horse in battle formation and charge into the enemy's ranks as a cavalryman. Frederick routinely hunted with the bow and arrow in the forests of southern Germany to practice his martial skills, while participating in various field sports and games with the children of other noble families. As the Swabian lord grew older, he was described by contemporaries as medium in height with broad shoulders, muscular body, blond hair and reddish beard, while presenting an overall manly bearing. When Frederick first travelled to Italy, he was called Barbarossa by his vassals and militiamen for the reddish tone of his beard.

While Frederick had received little formal education, he was exposed to the routine governing of the Swabian realm by the duke, acquiring political and administrative skills. As heir-designate, he attended council meetings, met with visitors and envoys from neighbouring fiefdoms and witnessed his father's interaction with his Swabian vassals. When his uncle Conrad III was elected King of Germany in March 1138, Frederick visited his court, gaining further governmental exposure and experience, while making contacts with powerful warlords.

As Frederick reached his mid-teens, he began participating in his father's punitive campaigns against rebellious Swabian warlords and enemies of King Conrad III. In 1146 he was given an independent command and led his army into Bavaria to subdue Count Henry of Wolfratshausen and his allies, who had continued to defy the Swabians. Frederick unleashed a surprise attack against his enemies, catching them outside their defensive works. The Bavarians quickly formed a front to repel Frederick's first charge, but as his knights and soldiers pressed their assaults, they drove Henry's forces into the castle. During the battle the young lord's troops captured Conrad II of Dachau, who had fought courageously and valiantly. Despite many of his men encouraging him to seek a large ransom for the return of Conrad II, Frederick ordered his release to spread the message of his knightly virtues to the German people.

Shortly after enforcing his rule over Henry of Wolfratshausen, the young Frederick mustered his host and moved against Duke Conrad II of Zahringen in south-west Germany. After overpowering the duke's forces at Zurich, the Swabians were reinforced with troops from Bavaria and ravaged the region to the castle at Zahringen, near current-day Freiburg in Baden Wurttemberg, Germany. Frederick continued his campaign of subjugation, seizing the castle. As the Swabian soldiers and their allies remained in his lands, Conrad II was compelled to sue for peace at the court of Duke Frederick II, agreeing to pledge his loyalty to secure the withdrawal of the Swabians.

While Frederick continued to attend council meetings at court and enforced his father's feudal rights, in December 1145 Pope Eugenius III issued a papal bull for the monarchs of Europe to reclaim the Christian enclaves in the Levant recently lost to the Muslims. The papal legate, Bernard of Clairvaux, arrived in the imperial territories in October 1146 to persuade King Conrad III to participate in the Second Crusade. The legate met the king in late December at Speyer, convincing him to take the cross of a crusader and unite his German army with the French forces of King Louis VII in a great expedition against the Muslims. When Frederick learned of his uncle's decision to travel to the Holy Land, he joined the pope's campaign, while many nobles and peasants flocked to the call of the papacy.

As the Germans and the monarchs of Europe prepared for the crusade, in early April 1147 Frederick II died and was succeeded to the Swabian throne by his son, who became Duke Frederick III. After assuming control of the ducal regime, Frederick III appointed regents to govern in his absence and continued his preparations for the Levant expedition. At the end of May 1147, the German crusaders set out overland for the crusader states, known as Outremer, planning to travel through the Balkans, Byzantine Empire and Asia Minor. The papacy's summons for Christian soldiers to defend the Holy Land had attracted a large following, Conrad III's army numbering nearly 20,000 men and pilgrims. The German contingent of the multinational force was led by Duke Frederick III. Conrad III was now over fifty years old and in declining health. He was too incapacitated to control the frequent outbreaks of friction between the Germans, Slavs and Bohemians, delegating most of his authority to his young nephew.

The German army passed through Regensburg, Vienna and in June into Hungary. The journey thus far had been made with little difficulty and was supported by the local populations with donations of food and supplies, but when the crusaders entered the lands of the Byzantine Empire there were frequent outbreaks of violence between the inhabitants and soldiers. Despite the delays, the Christian troops pushed on, proceeding through Sofia in modern-day Bulgaria to Constantinople, as the plundering by the crusaders continued unabated. When a German warlord was murdered by bandits, Frederick III responded by destroying a monastery, killing the monks and worshippers. To end the escalating violence, the Byzantine emperor, Manual I Comnenus, persuaded Conrad III to transport his troops across the Bosporus by ships to Asia Minor.

After reaching the coast of western Asia Minor, the crusaders hastened to Nicaea, where they collected fresh provisions and supplies for the journey south. As the German forces neared the site of the First Crusade's victory over the Muslims at Dorylaeum half a century earlier, they were ambushed in late October by the Seldjuk Turks. The Saracens fell on the Christians, their lightly armoured horsemen charging into the crusaders and wheeling back into the bloody fray, firing volleys of arrows from horseback and decimating the German ranks. Conrad and Frederick attempted to rally their infantry and knights, but by nightfall the German survivors were in full flight on the road to Nicaea. At the second Battle at Dorylaeum in north-west Turkey, the German host was decimated with over half of the troops slain. While the crusaders fled north-west, they were harried by the Turks with thousands more killed. After reaching the safety of Nicaea, the majority of the surviving Christian soldiers deserted the army, returning home and leaving Conrad and his nephew a greatly depleted force to continue the crusade against the Muslims.

While the Germans were withdrawing to Nicaea following their disastrous defeat, Louis VII and the French had reached Constantinople and passed over the Bosporus into Asia Minor. Learning of the Capetian king's presence, Frederick III was sent to the French camp to orchestrate a meeting between the two kings. Louis VII hastened to the German encampment, and after discussing the options with Conrad III they decided to advance toward the crusader kingdom by the coastal route through the mountainous region of Anatolia, with the French in the van and the greatly depleted German forces a day's march behind. When the combined armies reached Ephesus, Conrad became seriously ill and was transported by ship to Constantinople with Frederick III and a large entourage, while his half-brother Otto of Freising assumed command of the host. In the Byzantine capital the German monarch was treated personally by Emperor Manuel I, who had studied medicine under renowned local physicians. The crusaders remained at the emperor's court until the king recovered, and on 7 March 1148 embarked on imperial ships sailing to the Christian enclave at Acre. After reaching the fortified town in mid-April, the Germans were welcomed by the local leaders and began planning their campaign against the Muslims in defence of the crusader kingdom. While remaining in Acre, Conrad and his nephew visited Jerusalem and were greeted at the city's gate by King Baldwin III. The German entourage was escorted through the streets to the sounds of hymns and chants, and later toured the sacred sites of the city.

On 24 June the rulers of Germany, France and Jerusalem, along with warlords from powerful fiefdoms in Europe and the Levant, met in Acre and decided to seize the Muslim-held city of Damascus in present-day south-western Syria. With the German crusader army having suffered large losses in manpower and equipment during the arduous march from Nicaea, the unified Christian forces were not strong enough to capture a well-fortified and defended Muslim city. In prior years the defenses of Damascus had been weakened by two Christian sieges and its capture would strengthen the Europeans' presence in Outremer, while depleting the powers of the Muslim leaders. When a faction of barons from the Latin East objected to the choice, the three kings insisted the attack be made against Damascus, emphasizing it was an important Christian city.

In mid-July the great crusader army set out from Galilee, with the soldiers from Jerusalem in the vanguard, followed by Louis VII's French knights and infantrymen and Frederick III with the Germans in the rearguard. They arrived before Damascus later in the month and encamped on the south side of the walled city near the edge of large gardens and orchards. When the Emir of Damascus, Unur, learned of the crusaders' advance, he collected troops from his provincial towns and sent messengers to Aleppo for help from Nur ed-Din, Muslim ruler of the Syrian province. In the early morning of 24 July, as the crusaders resumed their march, the Muslims attacked them near the village of al-Mizza but were beaten back behind the walls of their city by the fierce assaults of the Christian spearmen and cavalry. Under orders from King Baldwin III, the army of Jerusalem stormed into the orchard in the afternoon, clearing the area of enemy soldiers, while the Germans captured Rabwa close to the city walls. The Europeans moved closer to the defensive works, cutting down trees from the orchard to build stockades. On the following day, as the Christians renewed their sorties into the Saracen fortifications and attempted to break into the city, Muslim reinforcements arrived from Aleppo and their combined forces drove the crusaders back. Unur continued his attacks, regaining control of the orchards in a fury of bloody and savage fighting decimating the ranks of the Europeans and compelling them to move eastward onto an open plain. As Unur pressed his assaults, the three kings were forced to abandon the siege and on 28 July they began withdrawing to Galilee, with Duke Frederick leading the depleted German contingent. On the long march back to Acre, they were harassed by Muslim horsemen pouring volleys of arrows into their ranks. In early August the defeated and humiliated expeditionary force reached Acre, and in early September Conrad III with his nephew and entourage sailed to Constantinople, ending the Second Crusade.

After remaining in the court of Manuel I Comnenus for several months, Duke Frederick III returned to Germany, travelling overland by way of Bulgaria and Hungary and arriving in April 1149. Back in Germany, the duke resumed control of his duchy and ruled his lands following the policies of King Conrad III. The humiliating failure of the Second Crusade convinced the young duke that only a ruler with great personal power could enforce his suzerainty over his frequently rebellious vassals, and following his return to Swabia he took measures to render his retainers subservient to him. He enforced the existing feudal system, requiring military service and loyalty from the warlords in return for protection and just treatment. Frederick gained the support of the Swabian towns by granting them special privileges and exemptions. By the use of negotiations, intimidation and armed attacks, the duke's authority over the Swabians was now unchallenged.

While the Swabian duke was imposing his overlordship, his maternal uncle Welf VI of Bavaria sent his troops into the lands of Conrad III's two sons to challenge the authority of the Hohenstaufen family. As Welf expanded his attacks, his forces were defeated and forced to withdraw. To prevent an escalation of the conflict, Frederick arranged a reconciliation between his two uncles. Under the agreement, Welf swore to forgo any future hostilities, while the German king promised to transfer the income from several royal towns to him. Frederick's choice as arbitrator to restore peace between the two rulers elevated his standing among the feudal warlords and knights, enhancing his power and supremacy.

On 15 February 1152 King Conrad III died at Bamberg, and in early March at Frankfurt the German princes elected Frederick his successor, with little opposition. On 9 March the kingdom's bishops escorted him from Charlemagne's palace in Aachen to the imperial chapel, and Archbishop Arnold II of Cologne crowned him Frederick I, King of Germany, in the presence of the great magnates and prelates. Before the death of Conrad III, Frederick met with his uncle's closest advisers to gain their support for his election to the crown. Utilizing the endorsement of the highly influential bishops, he met in private with the potential challengers to the throne to secure their backing, promising the duchies of Saxony and Bavaria to Henry the Lion, while Welf was assured possession of the Margraviate of Tuscany, Duchy of Spoleto and several other Italian properties, and the Zahringen family was guaranteed influence in Burgundy.

Shortly following his coronation, King Frederick summoned the great princes to his private rooms in the palace to discuss the state of the German kingdom. He informed the nobles and churchmen that his first goal was to unify the kingdom and restore the Holy Roman Empire in Germany, Italy and Burgundy to its former glory. To secure the continued support of the Holy See, he sent two bishops with a letter to Pope Eugenius III in Rome advising him of his election and the continued allegiance of the German realm, writing: 'We assure our Holy Mother, the Roman Church, and all her noble sons of our prompt and sure attention to justice and of our protection.' The king further notified the pontiff of his desire for a closer association with the papacy. The pope had earlier petitioned Conrad III for military aid against the ongoing rebellion of the citizens of Rome, known as the Roman Communes, and in his reply to the new king, he renewed the request. Not willing to become bogged down in Italy, Frederick refused to commit to an immediate campaign until Germany was again under the control of the throne. Frederick continued negotiations with the Holy See, pressing the pope to finalize the arrangements for his coronation in Rome as Emperor of the Holy Roman Empire.

At the time of Frederick I's succession to the German crown, the kingdom was beset with internal turmoil and lawlessness, and in May 1152 the king issued his Peace of the Land Charter to restore order. He assembled his vassals, making each one swear to observe the peace and maintain loyalty to the regime. The charter prohibited all peasants from bearing arms, while only nobles were now allowed to settle personal disputes by fighting a duel. Penalties were established for the crimes of murder, assault and theft, while fines were set for lesser offences. When the new law came into effect, farmers and merchants were forbidden to settle disputes by acts of violence. The king met with his magnates, instructing them on the proper enforcement of his charter to ensure justice for all his subjects.

During the reign of King Conrad III, the German realm was rife with private wars between the princes, so after taking the crown Frederick adopted measures to restore peace. He transferred the Swabian duchy to his cousin Frederick of Rothenburg to settle the ongoing dispute over its rightful titleholder. In June at the Diet of Regensburg, he granted Welf VI the Italian lands earlier promised at Frankfurt. To end the hostilities over the Duchy of Bavaria, Frederick gave the support of his regime to Henry the Lion. As part of his reassertion of the throne's powers, he intervened in disagreements for the elections of clerics and asserted his right to name bishops without approval from Rome. Soon after announcing his new powers over ecclesiastic disputes, the king ordered the election of Rother of Malberg to the office of abbot for Prum Abbey, despite his rejection by a majority of prelates. The king later moved against disloyal bishops, removing them and appointing his chosen churchmen to their posts.

By the autumn of 1152 Frederick had made his powers felt by the magnates, prelates and peasants, and now pressed his ongoing talks with

Pope Eugenius III to reassert his authority over northern Italy. The king's earlier marriage to Adelaide of Vohburg had remained unhappy and childless, and to secure the succession of his family in Germany he was impatient for the papacy to approve its annulment. He sent a petition to the Holy See requesting the abrogation of the union, which was quickly granted on grounds of too close a kinship. The pope, hard-pressed in the south of Italy from the attacks of King Roger II of Sicily and in Rome by the ongoing rebellion of the citizens, offered to negotiate a treaty of mutual assistance with the German king. The negotiating parties met in Constance in late 1152, and on 25 March 1153 a final settlement was signed. Under the terms of the Treaty of Constance, the pontiff pledged to honour Frederick I as emperor and assist him in the fulfilment of his office, while the emperor agreed to use his army to enforce the papacy's rights over the citizens of Rome and to not declare a truce or negotiate peace without the consent of the Holy See. Both parties promised not to cede any territory to the Byzantine Empire, and to unite to repel its forces from Italy if the eastern emperor invaded the peninsula. By signing the treaty, Frederick gained the pope's support and approval to enforce his rule in northern Italy, while Pope Eugenius III secured the German military forces necessary to quell the uprising of the Roman citizens.

In the months following the Constance accord, Frederick prepared for his campaign into Italy. In early July 1153 Pope Eugenius III died and was succeeded by Anastasius IV. The new pontiff had little interest in attacking the Roman Commune, adopting a conciliatory approach to the rebellious citizens. The pope was devoted to religious matters, putting the fulfilment of the Constance Treaty's terms in jeopardy. Despite the papacy's apathy, the king continued his preparations for the Italian expedition, and in October assembled his army near Augsburg.

The German forces marched south, crossing the Alps through the Brenner Pass into northern Italy. King Frederick I Barbarossa led his knights and soldiers into Piedmont and set up his winter quarters at Roncaglia on the Po River. While at the town, the German king held his first Italian diet with members of the nobility, Church and towns. Having advanced into Lombardy with only a small army, he summoned his local vassals to assemble with their troops. If a prince failed to answer the call of his overlord, his lands were seized by the crown. At the meeting

Frederick renewed the constitution forbidding the sale of a fief without the permission of the vassal's lord. The charter increased the supremacy of the high magnates, which reinforced the king's policy of collaboration with the great warlords. At Roncaglia the king met with nobles and town envoys, resolving disputes between them as their overlord. He ordered the Milanese and citizens of Pavia to end their ongoing armed conflict.

At the conclusion of the diet with his Italian vassals, Barbarossa asked the envoys from Milan to guide his expeditionary force through Milanese territory and provide provisions and shelter for his soldiers. When the Milanese failed to secure adequate food for the Germans, the king perceived it as a deliberate act of defiance against his rule. He struck out against the Milanese, ordering his men to destroy their outer defensive works at Resate while sending his knights to attack the city's gates. The Germans and their Italian allies continued their punitive campaign against Milan, burning two wooden bridges and demolishing several outlying fortresses. After imposing a sentence of outlawry on Milan, he headed west to Chieri to burn the rebellious town, which had been outlawed at the Roncaglia diet.

From Milan the expeditionary force advanced southwest to the mutinous city of Tortona, which had ignored the summons to appear at the royal court to answer charges of hostility against Pavia. The citadel was located on a mountain top, protected by massive surrounding walls and towers. The German army, reinforced with militiamen from Pavia and Montferrat, besieged Tortona, which was defended by Milanese knights and archers. On 17 February 1155 Duke Henry the Lion's men and the Pavian troops stormed into the city, forcing the inhabitants to flee to the citadel for safety. Barbarossa's troops built siege engines and battering rams to assault the defensive works. They hurled large boulders into the city and against the walls, while pounding the fortified gates with battering rams. When the Germans and their allies attempted to tunnel under the walls, they were thwarted by the defenders in a fierce and bloody fight. As the siege continued, the garrison frequently unleashed surprise forays against the Germans, but Barbarossa refused to abandon the campaign. After over two months the garrison finally surrendered and terms were negotiated by the Abbot of Chiaravalle.

In the aftermath of his victory, Barbarossa advanced to Pavia in south-western Lombardy at the invitation of the townspeople to celebrate the destruction of their enemy. As the king rode through the main gate, he was greeted by wildly cheering crowds and escorted through the streets to the Church of St Michael. At the high altar he was anointed King of Italy and crowned with the Iron Crown. After remaining for three days of celebrations, he rode to Bologna to receiving homage before moving south through Romagna and Tuscany, where many fortified towns submitted to him.

Frederick Barbarossa and his army reached the outskirts of Rome on 8 June and were met by the new pope Adrian IV and his cardinals at Sutri. When Barbarossa advanced toward the pope to offer homage, he refused to hold the stirrup and bridle of his horse, as was customary when first meeting him. Greatly offended by the break with protocol, Adrian IV dismounted from his horse and walked to his temporary throne. The German king moved forward, prostrating himself before the pontiff and kissing his feet. Barbarossa expected to receive the kiss of peace from Adrian IV, but he refused to perform the ritual until the king agreed to fulfil the customary honour of leading his horse. Their first meeting ended at an impasse, but a second audience was quickly arranged by the cardinals, where the king observed the expected ceremony. Adrian IV replied by bestowing the kiss of peace on Barbarossa.

The pope was satisfied by Frederick's act of reverence, agreeing to proceed with the imperial coronation. On 18 June 1155, Barbarossa rode into Rome and dismounted at St Peter's Basilica, removing his armour and dressing in his coronation robes before entering the church. He walked to the confessional, kneeling at the feet of the pope and swearing: 'Before God and the blessed Peter, to be with divine help, at all times, to the best of my ability and intelligence, and in all good faith, the protector and defender of the Holy Roman Church and of the person of the pope and his successors.' Adrian IV anointed Frederick with holy oil and celebrated Mass in honour of Mary. In the final act of the coronation, he conferred the sceptre and sword to the emperor and placed the golden crown on his head. Barbarossa was then loudly acclaimed Emperor of the Holy Roman Empire.

While Frederick I was receiving the ceremonial crown of the Holy Roman Empire, the citizens of Rome rioted against the papacy. When learning of the uprising, Barbarossa immediately came to the defence of the pope, ordering his soldiers to assemble and advance against the rioters. The imperial troops rushed to the Castel Sant'Angelo, attacking the Romans and beating them away from the Vatican. The fighting lasted until nightfall, with over 1,000 killed and many more wounded or captured. The exhausted Germans spent the night close to St Peter's in the fortified Leonine City, where they encamped. In the morning the emperor renewed his assault against the insurgents, marching his forces against the rebellious towns in the vicinity of Rome and seizing control of them. When the imperial army reached the town of Tivoli north-east of Rome, the citizens quickly surrendered and gave homage. The town had earlier been under the protection of the pope, and Barbarossa, in a gesture of friendship, returned it to him. He continued his assaults around Rome imposing imperial authority. At Albano, fifteen miles south of Rome, the emperor halted his campaign and moved into the mountains to rest his men in the cooler weather away from the threat of plague.

After imposing his rule over his Italian vassals and securing the support of Pope Adrian IV, Barbarossa set out for Germany. On the journey north, the imperial army halted at Spoleto to sack the city, which had defied the emperor by paying its required tribute in counterfeit coins. From Spoleto the imperialists proceeded to Ancona on the Adriatic coast, where he met envoys sent by the Byzantine emperor, Manuel I. The eastern emperor offered Barbarossa a large sum of gold for a joint expedition against the Sicilian king, William I. The German army, exhausted and ill-equipped from the summer campaign, having suffered large losses in men and supplies from fighting and disease, was too small and weak to invade southern Italy. At Ancona the host was disbanded and in September 1155 the emperor headed north through the Brenner Pass into Germany.

During Barbarossa's absence in Italy, his realm was beset with rampant disorder and instability without his strong rule. In Germany the forces of Henry the Lion and Henry Jasamirgott fought each other for control of Bavaria. To restore order to the duchy, the emperor invested Henry the Lion with the fiefdom in October, transferring the March of Austria to his cousin's rival. He strengthened his influence in the Rhineland by ceding the Rhine Palatinate to his half-brother Conrad, and sent imperial troops to enforce his sovereignty. Following his return to Germany, the emperor worked tirelessly to impose his rule and peace, enacting new laws to enhance his powers while personally interceding to quell disputes between his warlords. He travelled extensively throughout his lands, seizing the castles of rogue princes and ensuring his vassals were committed to fulfilling their feudal obligations to him.

Barbarossa, having earlier secured the annulment of his first marriage, was now anxious to find a suitable spouse. While in Italy, he had sought Emperor Manuel I's daughter in marriage, but the Byzantines wanted to make the union conditional on imperial cooperation in the conquest of southern Italy. Unable to negotiate a contract with the Byzantines, Barbarossa turned to the young Countess of Burgundy, Beatrice. The union with Beatrice would give the emperor control over the strategic countship and provide additional soldiers for his imperial army. The ceremony took place at Wurzburg Castle on 9 June 1156, attended by the great princes and prelates of the empire. At the time of the wedding, Beatrice was just thirteen years old and the acknowledged ruler of Burgundy. She was described by contemporaries as a beautiful woman with long golden hair, medium in height and well-educated. During her reign as empress, she was a patron of literary works and sponsor of courtly principles. Beatrice frequently accompanied Frederick on his military campaigns, travelling throughout the empire with him. She was anointed empress on 1 August 1167 in Rome by the anti-pope, Paschal III. Despite being a politically arranged marriage, Frederick and Beatrice were well-suited to each other, developing a close and loving relationship. Empress Beatrice gave birth to eleven children, with her second son succeeding to the imperial crown as Henry VI.

Meanwhile in Rome, Pope Adrian IV had negotiated a treaty with William I of Sicily giving him acknowledged rights to certain lands in southern Italy and formally investing him with the Sicilian kingdom, while the pontiff received a yearly tribute and homage from his former enemy. The terms of the agreement effectively terminated the Treaty of Constance, further straining relations between Barbarossa and the papacy and leaving the emperor feeling betrayed. While holding court at Besancon in Burgundy in the early summer of 1157, Barbarossa received a letter from the pontiff insinuating that his empire was a grant given by the papacy. The emperor replied that the Holy Roman Emperor was not a vassal of the pope but an independent lord chosen by God. Adrian IV's attempt to expand his power and influence added to the growing dissent between the two rulers. The conflict was later minimized when the German bishops, in support of their emperor, dispatched a letter to the pope advising him to write another message to Frederick to further clarify his intent. In June 1158 Adrian IV sent several cardinals to the imperial court, where they explained he had not intended to imply the papacy's temporal suzerainty over the empire.

While Adrian IV was securing his authority in the Papal States, in February 1157 Barbarossa and his new wife travelled to her court in Burgundy. After arriving at Besancon in eastern France, he met with Burgundian nobles and prelates, accepting their homage and asserting his suzerainty over the region. He placed the larger French churches under his personal protection and confirmed their ancient privileges.

After asserting his power over the Burgundians, Frederick I was drawn into the family dispute for the overlordship of the Duchy of Poland. In early August 1157 he assembled his army at Halle in south-east Saxony and proceeded toward Poland to reinstate the displaced Grand Duke Wladyslaw, who was married to his aunt. The usurping grand duke, Boleslaw IV, had failed to offer fealty or pay tribute to the emperor, giving Barbarossa personal reasons for the campaign. As the imperial forces marched deeper into the duchy, they were joined by contingents of Russians, Prussians and soldiers from Pomerania. Facing the powerful imperial army, the Poles withdrew east, scorching the land and demolishing fortifications to deny them to the enemy, while the allies ravaged Breslau and Posen. Unable to stem the imperial advance, Boleslaw agreed to meet with Barbarossa and forge a peace treaty. In September the two rulers met and Boleslaw offered homage, vowed to pay tribute and pledged to accept the Diet of Magdeburg's decision for the rightful Grand Duke of Poland. After agreeing to the grand duke's terms, Barbarossa returned to Germany to await the December meeting of the Magdeburg assembly. When the diet assembled, Boleslaw failed to attend and ignored his pledges to the emperor. Barbarossa, involved with preparations for his second campaign in Italy, was forced to delay a response to the grand duke's defiance.

In January 1158 Barbarossa attended the German diet at Regensburg to settle unresolved disputes with his warlords and prelates and continue his preparations for the Italian expedition to reaffirm his authority. Before departing south he sent two emissaries to Italy with instructions to encourage his vassals' resistance to Milan and secure the allegiance of various uncommitted city-states. In June the emperor assembled his multinational army of Germans, Poles, Bohemians and Hungarians, setting out from Augsburg. Crossing the Alps through the Brenner Pass and entering Italy, the imperial forces were reinforced with contingents of knights, cavalrymen, spearmen and archers from Pavia, Como, Lodi and Cremona. Barbarossa led his forces against Milan, laying siege to the well-defended city. The Milanese had built an enormous three-mile long earthen rampart around the city, surrounded with a water-filled moat. The imperial troops pounded the massive walls with siege engines and battering rams, while the Milanese launched sorties to disrupt their attacks. The residents of Milan resisted for a month, but opposing a large well-equipped army and weakened by famine, they were compelled to seek terms on 1 September. Under the provisions of the agreement, the Milanese were forced to pay a large fine, provide hostages for their continued fealty and give oaths of homage.

After remaining in Milan for several months, Barbarossa travelled to Roncaglia to attend the diet of his leading Italian vassals and cities. At the assembly he named four jurists to compile a registry of the imperial entitlements assigned to the emperor. The long listing of rights that were under the authority of the emperor included control of the roads, rivers and ports, levying of taxes, appointment of magistrates and many other items infringing on the prerogatives of the nobles, churchmen and towns. Many of the lords and bishops had documents excluding them from the new law, but the towns were unable to provide proof of their rights. To further expand his powers, Barbarossa issued a separate law requiring all males between the ages of eighteen and seventy to swear an oath to maintain the peace.

The Edict of Roncaglia placed a large burden on the towns and many refused to abide by its provisions. In early 1159 Milan violated the terms of the earlier treaty with Barbarossa, renewing its attacks against Lodi and Como, while Brescia and Crema supported the uprising against imperial rule. To break the resistance of the rebelling citizens, the emperor marched his army to Crema and opened siege operations. The town was protected by a large trench, two encircling walls and a garrison reinforced with 400 infantrymen and a contingent of knights sent from Milan. Barbarossa ordered his engineers to construct a 100-foot tall siege tower with a drawbridge at the top and mounted on large wheels to breach the defenses. In September the tower was slowly rolled forward to the walls as archers and crossbowmen fired hails of arrows at the defenders and a battering ram smashed a hole in the outer wall, but they were unable to break into the town. As the siege dragged on with no end in sight, in January 1160 the town's chief engineer defected to the enemy, recommending they construct a second tower with a bridging platform. On 21 January the emperor's men advanced again with the two towers under a wave of arrows, spears and stones hurled from the wall. The Germans and their allies drove the defenders from the outer walls, pressing their attack and storming into Crema. Unable to check the allies, the garrison commander was compelled to surrender. Barbarossa ordered his troops to raze the town but spared the lives of the inhabitants.

The listing of imperial entitlements announced at the Roncaglia Diet spread fear and apprehension through the papacy, forcing Adrian IV to adopt an anti-German policy. The pope responded by establishing closer relations with King William I, who provided him with enough money to reinforce the defensive works of the Holy City. In return Adrian made contact with Emperor Manuel I, convincing him to end his campaign of conquest against the Sicilian lands of William I. The Papal State also began secret negotiations with Milan and the northern cities, encouraging them to resist German intervention. The pontiff sent two cardinals to the imperial court proposing they return to the provisions of the Treaty of Constance. When Barbarossa countered with the proposal to create a committee of six cardinals and six German bishops to resolve the conflict, the pontiff dismissed the offer as unworkable. Another attempt to reconcile the impasse was proposed by the papacy, but the emperor's counter-overture was rejected. With no resolution seemingly possible, in August 1159 Barbarossa received a document from Adrian threatening to excommunicate him in forty days unless he ended his expansionist campaign. With the papal and imperial relations at a stalemate, on 1 September 1159 Pope Adrian IV died, propelling the standoff into further turmoil.

When the cardinals assembled at the Sacred College to elect the new pope, Barbarossa sent envoys to meet with the prelates and pressue them to vote for a pro-German candidate. After three heated votes, the two

Charlemagne

**Charlemagne Anointed
Holy Roman Emperor
by Pope Leo III**

Throne of Charlemagne

Source: Photo by Author – Aachen Cathedral.

Tomb of Charlemagne

Source: Photo by Author – Aachen Cathedral.

Frederick I Submitting to Pope Alexander III

Source: Spinello Aretino fresco at The Palazzo Publico in Siena, Italy (public domain).

Frederick I Barbarossa

Source: Photo by Author – Frankfurt, Germany.

Frederick I

Source: Photo by Author – Emperor's Hall – Frankfurt, Germany.

Richard I

Source: Photo by Author – Westminster, London.

Tomb of Richard I

Source: Photo by Author – Fontevraud Abbey, France.

Frederick II

Source: Photo by Author – Emperor's Hall – Frankfurt, Germany.

Robert the Bruce

Source: Photo by Author – Bannockburn Battlefield, Scotland.

Main Gate Stirling Castle, Scotland

Source: Janfrie, 1988 (public domain).

Empire of Charlemagne – 814

Source: Map by Author.

England During The Reign of Alfred – 878

Source: Map by Author.

North Sea Empire of King Cnut

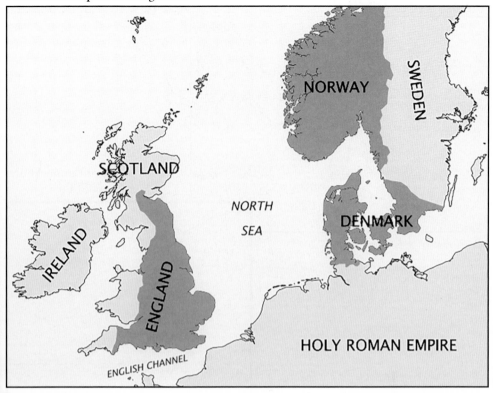

Source: Map by Author.

Battle of Hastings – 14 October 1066

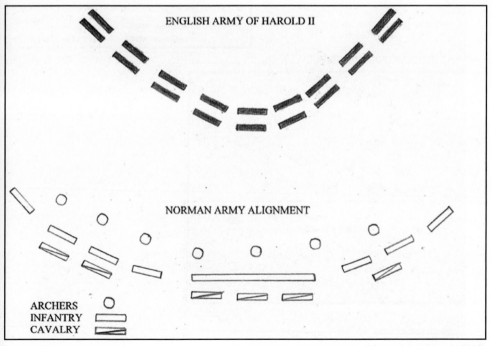

Source: Map by Author.

Empire of Emperor Frederick II

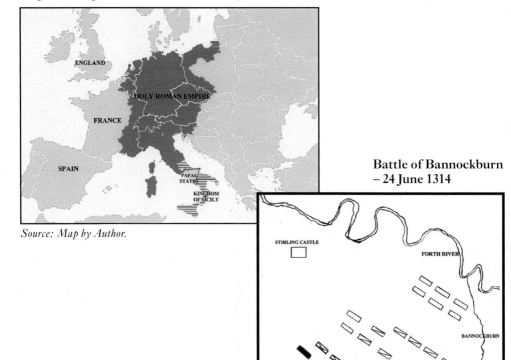

Source: Map by Author.

Battle of Bannockburn – 24 June 1314

Source: Map by Author.

Crusades to the Levant of King Louis IX

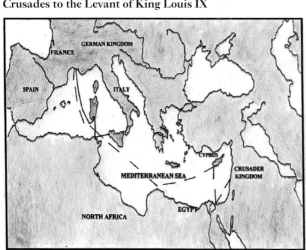

1248-1254 FIRST CRUSADE — —
1270 SECOND CRUSADE ——

Source: Map by Author.

surviving nominees each claimed victory, with Pope Victor IV in the pro-imperialists' party and Alexander III in the anti-German faction. The emperor threw his support behind Victor IV, using all his powers to enforce his election among the lords and prelates. To give legality to Victor IV's papacy, Barbarossa convened a synod at Pavia to decide the new pontiff. With Barbarossa acting as arbitrator, Victor IV was declared the successor to Adrian IV. When Alexander III learned of the assembly's decision, he immediately excommunicated Barbarossa.

In the aftermath of the pro-German pope's election, Barbarossa decided to assert his imperial power over all of Lombardy and then advance south against the Kingdom of Sicily. In the spring of 1161, after receiving reinforcements from his German and Italian allies, the Holy Roman Emperor set out to destroy Milan, the leader of the anti-imperialists in northern Italy. In May Barbarossa mustered a large army and proceeded to Milan. The city was surrounded and besieged. He sent his cavalrymen to ravage the farms and crops and to patrol the roads, preventing anyone from carrying relief supplies to the blockaded city. The confederation of Italian and German troops relentlessly pursued the siege, and by 1 March the inhabitants, beset with disease and starvation, agreed to submit. In retribution for their prolonged defiance, Frederick ordered the population dispersed, Milan's churches, houses and defensive works destroyed and the trench filled in. When reports of the destruction of Milan spread through northern Italy, the rebellious cities quickly offered their fealty. The emperor enacted lesser punishments against Milan's allies, but all were forced to pay a large indemnity and their governing consuls were subject to approval by the regime's representatives. With his power reasserted, Frederick I issued an edict proclaiming imperial sovereignty over the entire region of northern Italy.

After concluding his campaign of subjugation, Barbarossa began preparations to invade the Kingdom of Sicily. The expeditionary force against the Sicilians required ships and the emperor sent agents to negotiate with the maritime cities of Pisa and Genoa. They agreed to provide fleets of ships and naval stores, while the imperial regime granted them liberal trade concessions. As the arrangements for the invasion accelerated, Barbarossa was forced to postpone the attack when Pope Alexander III fled to France, seeking the support of the French and

English in his quest to secure the papal throne. With the pope in France, the emperor decided to wait until his ally Victor IV was firmly established in the Holy See before embarking on the Sicilian expedition.

Barbarossa now moved decisively to secure the papacy for Victor IV, summoning a diet to Lodi to reaffirm the election of his cardinal. To bolster support for Victor, the emperor sent envoys to the nobles in regions bordering France to gain their recognition of his pope. He also made contact with friendly French bishops, establishing a pro-German faction, while Alexander III dispatched legates to the court of the English king, Henry II, seeking his sponsorship. Barbarossa hastened north from Lombardy to Burgundy to personally intercede in Pope Victor IV's favour. In early September 1162 Frederick I held a synod at Dole, where the assembled princes and prelates acknowledged the pro-imperialist as pontiff. The French king closely monitored events at the diet, and when asked to meet with the emperor to determine the rightful pope agreed to attend the conference. However, instead of personally meeting with Louis VII, the emperor sent his chief adviser, who lost his temper during the discussions, calling him a petty king. Negotiations were quickly broken off and several days later the French monarch acknowledged Alexander III as rightful successor to the papacy. While events were unfolding in France, Henry II also announced his support for the anti-German pontiff.

In the aftermath of the French and English recognition of Alexander III as pontiff, Emperor Frederick I departed from Burgundy for Germany. The emperor remained committed to Victor IV's succession to the papal throne in the Holy City, and before returning to Rome to enforce his candidate's coronation, he settled ongoing disputes in his German realm. The city of Mainz had rebelled against the emperor's appointed archbishop, and in retaliation Barbarossa ordered the city's privileges revoked and its defences demolished. When the warlords in Bavaria revolted against his cousin, Henry the Lion, the emperor sent troops to support the campaign against the rebels, while compelling Boleslaw IV of Poland to cede the usurped countship of Silesia to the rightful heirs. In October 1163, after restoring peace to his lands, Barbarossa assembled the imperial army, marching south and crossing the Alps into Italy with the objective of placing Victor IV on the throne of the papacy in the Holy City.

Prior to leaving Germany, Frederick sent envoys into central Italy to rally support for the papacy of Victor IV. Many towns in Tuscany were won over to the imperialists' pope, pledging loyalty to Barbarossa and agreeing to supply troops for the attack against Rome. German forces were now garrisoned in strategic castles, and loyal Italian and German princes were appointed to high offices throughout Tuscany. When the emperor entered Tuscany, he was welcomed by the lords and prelates as the master of the region. While he had gained dominance over much of central Italy, the Republic of Venice sided with the papacy of Alexander III, negotiating an alliance with William I of Sicily out of fear of German supremacy and the loss of independence. The Venetian doge, Vitale Michiel II, began to openly endorse Alexander III in Tuscany in opposition to the Germans, sending money and troops while encouraging the northern cities to defy the emperor. As resistance to the imperialists multiplied, in April 1164 Venice joined the cities of Verona, Vicenza and Padua in a league opposing Barbarossa. When the supporters of the emperor attacked Grado in north-eastern Italy, the doge ordered a Venetian fleet to aid the town. The Venetians landed their troops and overpowered the imperial forces, taking over 700 prisoners. Barbarossa reacted to the threat against his rule in northern Italy by granting liberal privileges to Ferrara and Mantua, and in June advanced his army of German and Italian soldiers against Verona. He ravaged the countryside, destroying numerous fortifications and towns around Verona. Barbarossa had been able to muster only a small army and lacked the troop strength to continue the campaign. He withdrew his soldiers from around Verona and in October returned to Germany, determined to return with a strong and well-equipped military force.

While Frederick I Barbarossa was in northern Italy, Pope Victor IV died on 20 April 1164 at Lucca. The emperor's chief counsellor quickly arranged the election of Cardinal Guido of Crema as the new pontiff, taking the name of Paschal III. The choice of the Holy Father was made without consultations with Barbarossa, but he sent his approval to avoid further turmoil. The emperor's endorsement was made without notifying the German bishops and was highly unpopular in the kingdom, with many churchmen now voicing their support for Alexander III.

Barbarossa spent the summer of 1164 in Germany solidifying his sovereignty and sending envoys to Italy to ensure the military support of his vassals for the new campaign to enthrone Paschal III. Before returning to Italy, Frederick summoned the lords and bishops to a diet at Wurzburg to promote the papacy of his candidate. At the synod he announced that Henry II of England was now recognizing Paschal III as pope, making the acceptance of his nominee more likely. During the meeting, the emperor swore an oath to only acknowledge Paschal III as the Holy Father and never accept the papacy of Alexander III or his successors. He told the princes and prelates that the schism could only end with the expulsion of Alexander. To further strengthen his hold over the German churchmen and warlords, they were required to swear a similar pledge. Not all of the assembled imperialists agreed to the oath, however, switching their allegiance to Alexander.

In November 1165 Pope Alexander III returned to Rome following the election of a favourable Roman Senate, and immediately began to assert his rule over Italy. He appointed a new archbishop for Milan, ordering him to rally the local princes and towns to his papacy, while negotiating a treaty of alliance with the Byzantine Empire and reaffirming his friendship with the Sicilians. As the pope accelerated his offensive to secure the papacy, Barbarossa finalized his preparations for the expedition to Rome. The imperial army was assembled at Augsburg in late summer, marching across the Alps through the Brenner Pass. At the end of November, the Germans reached the friendly city of Lodi, where they were reunited with their Italian allies. After spending the winter at Lodi, Frederick passed through the Romagna region north of Florence and moved to besiege the town of Ancona on the Adriatic. The garrison, reinforced with Byzantine troops from Manuel I Comnenus, continued to repel the emperor's attempts to break into the town. While the Germans and their allies battered the defences of Ancona, a second contingent of imperial soldiers moved against the Holy City, defeating the Roman army on 29 May. Barbarossa lifted his siege and rushed to Rome to press his attack against the allies of Alexander III. On 25 July he sent his troops against the defences of the Castel Sant'Angelo, but were driven back after heavy fighting. Barbarossa reformed his forces, launching them against St Peter's. The basilica had been fortified with a ring of trenches and turned into a citadel by the Roman supporters of Alexander III. The papal soldiers held out for over a week before the Germans and their Italian allies smashed through the great bronze doors in the nave leaving the floor scattered with the bodies of the dead and dying.

With the imperialists now in control of the entire right bank of the Tiber, Alexander abandoned the city, escaping to the castle of Frangipani to rally his soldiers. Emperor Frederick I sent a message to the anti-German pope, proposing both nominees to the papal throne abdicate and a new council of cardinals assemble to elect a new pontiff. When Alexander refused, the Roman citizens turned against him, forcing the pope to flee to the Sicilian court and leaving Barbarossa in control of the city. On 30 July 1167 Paschal III was anointed at St Peter's and held his first Mass as pope. Two days later Barbarossa was invested as Patrician of Rome, signifying his assumption of power. Following the ceremony, the members of the Roman Senate pledged their fealty to the emperor. He had now gained hegemony over northern Italy, Burgundy and Germany, recreating the Holy Roman Empire of Emperor Charlemagne.

While the imperial soldiers remained in Rome, the emperor sent envoys across the Tiber to negotiate a settlement with the survivors of the Roman army. In early August the provisions of the treaty were signed, giving Barbarossa control over the entire city. As the Germans and their Italian allies celebrated their triumph, on 2 August Rome was struck by a violent rainstorm that swept through the imperialists' encampments, contaminating the water supply. Almost immediately soldiers became sick with high fever, intestinal pains and severe dysentery. The epidemic spread throughout the army, with thousands dying. On 6 August Barbarossa ordered his troops to leave Rome and move to the cities in the north, but during his retreat the disease continued to decimate the army.

The supporters of Alexander III seized upon the disaster as a sign of God's displeasure at the pro-German factions' enthronement of tainted cardinals, as many princes, prelates and towns abandoned Paschal III in favour of his rival. Barbarossa advanced his greatly depleted army to Pavia, resting his troops and reimposing his suzerainty over many cities now openly opposing him. The rebellious towns were divided into two factions: the Ghibellines, who were revolting against the Germans' harsh government, and the Guelphs, who were resisting the emperor in the name of Italian liberty. While Barbarossa remained in Pavia disengaged from events unfolding in Italy, the rebels came together on 1 December and put aside their differences, agreeing to unite in the League of Lombardy against the rule of the imperialists. The alliance was made up of sixteen cities, who took an oath to regain their independence and make no separate peace with the Germans. The envoys from the sixteen cities approved the creation of a communal assembly to rule northern Italy and elected two rectors to administer laws.

Confronted with the unified league and lacking the troops to enforce his sovereignty, the emperor was compelled to return to Germany. With much of Italy up in arms against him, in March 1168 he travelled west with his army into Burgundy. In his wife's countship, Barbarossa found most of the local magnates and prelates were now proponents of the anti-German faction. The imperialists stayed in the countship for a short time before travelling to their homeland. In an unbelievably short period, all of Frederick I's gains in northern Italy seemed to be lost as Alexander III's alliance steadily gained power.

In Germany, Frederick I Barbarossa quickly reasserted his power over his subjects, ensuring their continued loyalty and willingness to fulfil their feudal obligations. He rebuilt his military forces and strengthened his defences, constructing additional strongholds at strategic locations throughout his realm. The emperor reorganized his government, dividing the realm into districts with their own governors, who enforced crown policies and collected taxes. He further enacted laws following the rules promulgated at Roncaglia. New measures were also put in place to increase imperial control over the Church. The regime intervened frequently in episcopal elections, making sure the churchmen were friendly to the emperor's administration. Barbarossa took an interest in promoting economic growth by encouraging the creation of new villages and clearing of forests for farmlands, and reducing travel restrictions. The crown later authorized annual trade fairs at four towns to stimulate commercial expansion. To retain the fealty of its most powerful princes, the imperial throne granted them additional privileges and exceptions to the crown's laws. During the years before Barbarossa's return to Italy, he actively sanctioned measures to strengthen his hold on his German subjects, imposing a strong hand on his vassals. In late June 1168 he appointed his infant second son, Henry, as his successor-designate, passing over his invalid eldest son to ensure the Hohenstaufen family's assumption of the throne. On 15 August Henry was crowned King of the Romans at Aachen, where the high nobles and churchmen pledged their fealty to the four-year-old heir.

While Frederick I reinforced his suzerainty over his German subjects, in northern Italy the members of the Lombard League had grown stronger and more unified. Many new cities had joined the confederation, and in December 1168 the participants adopted a new charter rejecting the rule of the emperor. To enlarge the region under their administration, the league attacked Ghibelline towns and expelled pro-German bishops, replacing them with supporters of Alexander III. The Lombard League was further strengthened when Pope Alexander III decided to form an alliance with the member cities. As the league became more dominant in the north, in an act of grand defiance it began constructing a new city named Alessandria in honour of the pontiff. Alessandria was protected by formidable defensive works, and in 1168 was occupied with several thousand residents from nearby villages.

The League of Lombardy continued to expand its hold on northern Italy, while magnates and towns in the central area of the peninsula remained loyal to the emperor. Frederick I fortified his administration in Lombardy, sending aggressive new German consuls to enforce his rule. The league lacked the power to unseat Paschal III, and when he died in September 1168 a successor was named by a small group of schismatic cardinals in Rome, taking the name of Pope Calixtus III. To retain his present position and prevent any further deterioration until he could raise a new army, in 1169 Barbarossa began negotiations with Alexander III to end the schism. Two abbots were sent to meet with the anti-German pontiff in Sicily. After listening to the emissaries, the pope dispatched a message to the emperor agreeing to talks on the settlement of peace for all of Italy. A second meeting was held the following year, with representatives of the Lombard League present. Barbarossa proposed to end all personal attacks against Alexander III and acknowledge the bishops appointed by him. In return the pope was to abandon the league and make peace with the imperialists. Alexander quickly replied, refusing to accept the terms and ending the negotiations. To reaffirm his unity with the League of Lombardy, he sent a papal bull to the cities stressing his continued support for their cause. Despite the failure of his diplomatic mission with the Holy See, Barbarossa sent envoys to France and the Byzantine Empire seeking to recruit new allies in his conflict with Pope Alexander, while continuing to rebuild his army for the next Italian campaign. In the autumn of 1173 the emperor announced he was ready to lead a new expeditionary force into Italy.

In September 1174 Barbarossa set out from Burgundy with his army of 8,000 men, made up of soldiers from his German vassals and a large contingent of mercenaries. After passing through the Mont Cenis Pass into northern Italy, he marched to Susa, overpowering the defences and destroying the town. The imperial army continued its advance, and after accepting the submissions of Turin and Asti moved against Alessandria. In October the Germans and their allies laid siege to the town, which was protected by large earthworks topped with a parapet and surrounded by a wide water-filled trench. Shortly after reaching Alessandria, the weather became cold and rainy. The imperial camp turned into a quagmire, with the rains thwarting the Germans' sorties against the city. After suffering through the bitter winter months, in spring the weather improved and the emperor sent a large battering ram to break through one of the gates. The small Alessandria garrison of 150 soldiers withstood the assaults, driving the attackers back. After his forays were continually thwarted, Barbarossa instructed his craftsmen to build a large siege tower, but when the imperialists pushed the structure toward the defences, the defenders again forced them to withdraw with volleys of spears, stones and arrows. Unable to break through the fortified works, the emperor ordered his men to dig a tunnel under the fortifications. The Alessandrians detected the noise of the digging and slaughtered the Germans as they emerged out of the tunnel. In the resulting confusion, the league's troops charged out of a gate, burning the siege tower. On 13 April 1175 Barbarossa burned his camp and set off for Pavia.

Following his failure to destroy Alessandria, Barbarossa sent emissaries to the Lombard League offering to negotiate a settlement. A truce was quickly arranged and talks continued at Montebello. On 17 April envoys from the league presented their proposal for peace, offering to acknowledge Barbarossa's imperial rights as his predecessors had obtained but demanding a reconciliation between him and Alexander III and the acceptance of Alessandria as a member of the confederation. Barbarossa quickly rejected the proposal, and utilizing the provisions from a prior treaty with the cities he referred the terms of a peace settlement to envoys from Cremona for arbitration. When the commission put forward their compromise treaty, it was rebuffed by the league. With negotiations deadlocked, the emperor tried once again to forge a reconciliation directly with Pope Alexander III but their differences were too great to resolve and Frederick was forced to resume the war against the Lombard League.

After the truce with the Lombard League expired, Barbarossa sent messengers to his German allies summoning reinforcements. He made an urgent appeal to his cousin, Henry the Lion, asking for his intervention. Henry had just returned from the crusader kingdom with his army and refused to aid the emperor, claiming his troops and resources were exhausted. Denied the support of his powerful cousin's army and with many of his vassals only responding with minimal assistance, the emperor was compelled to rely on his Italian allies for a large part of his armed forces.

In the spring of 1176 Frederick I set out from Pavia with 3,500 knights and foot soldiers, making his way to Milan from the north, while a second army led by Christian of Mainz hastened from the south. When the league learned of the emperor's movements, they advanced to oppose him. In the early morning of 29 May, the Lombards sent a reconnaissance patrol of 700 knights to search for the fast-approaching enemy forces. Near Legnano, Barbarossa's vanguard intercepted the league's cavalry in a brief and bloody clash. As the German army neared Legnano, the Lombard patrol withdrew, reporting the presence of the imperial forces. The Holy Roman Emperor led his army forward slamming into the forces of the League of Lombardy with his cavalrymen driving them back in confusion. The league's spearmen rallied around the Milanese sacred battlewagon containing the city's standard and cross of its archbishop. The fighting lasted for over six hours, with the league's infantrymen holding their front, as a flood as carnage swept across the battlefield. The resistance at the battlewagon was spearheaded by the Company of Death, a Milanese social order of volunteers sworn to fight to the death in defence of the wagon. In the afternoon the reorganized Lombardy cavalry struck the Germans from the rear, breaking through their lines. Barbarossa rode forward to rally his men, but in the ensuing melee was knocked off his horse and fell to the ground unconscious. At this his soldiers panicked, fleeing the battlefield, and were cut down by the enemy cavalry. The survivors from Legnano returned to Pavia bringing reports of the emperor's death to Beatrice and the gathered imperial court. Beatrice was mourning the death of her husband when he suddenly appeared at the Pavia gate several days later, wounded and exhausted.

The battle at Legnano was a crushing reversal for Barbarossa, but despite the defeat his Italian allies remained loyal to him. Lacking the military strength to resume the war, he asked the consuls of Cremona to mediate a resolution to the conflict with the Lombard League. The negotiations continued into late July, the Lombard League refusing to accept any agreement without the recognition of Pope Alexander III. With discussions with the Lombards again at an impasse, the emperor resumed direct contact with the pontiff to work out a reconciliation. In late October emissaries from both parties assembled in Anagni, south of Rome, to resolve their ecclesiastic differences and settle the future of Italy. Following two weeks of talks, a settlement was hammered out, the emperor recognizing Alexander III as pontiff and without reservations pledging to restore the properties seized during the schism to the Church. In return, the pope consented to acknowledge Frederick as emperor and grant him responsibility for all churches in Germany. In a final provision, Barbarossa promised to forge a separate peace treaty with the Lombard League, and if negotiations failed he agreed to accept the decision of an arbitration committee.

While the church officials from each faction worked on the resolution, Barbarossa began negotiations with several members of the Lombard League, offering them his protection and special privileges in exchange for their defection from the confederation. He renewed his political campaign, securing the allegiance of additional league members and independent towns. As the pro-German faction continued to expand, Barbarossa sent his envoys to meet with the pope's representatives at Modena, where they decided the two rulers would meet at Bologna. When the emperor rejected the city the city as too anti-German, the emissaries settled on Venice. In May the envoys from the pope, Lombard League and Holy Roman Empire assembled in the Venetian Republic, and on 21 July 1177, after prolonged discussions, finally signed the Treaty of Venice. The three parties agreed to a six-year truce, and on the same day peace was arranged between Pope Alexander III and Emperor Frederick I Barbarossa. The pontiff acknowledged Barbarossa's overlordship of the imperial churches, while the emperor accepted Alexander III as pope and recognized his authority over the Papal State. Three days later Barbarossa entered the city, escorted by Doge Sebastiano Ziani to St Mark's Basilica. Upon reaching the entrance, the emperor prostrated himself as a sinner before the pope and kissed his feet. Alexander raised the emperor to his feet and gave him the kiss of peace. As the German churchmen sang a *Te Deum*, Frederick I conducted the pontiff to the choir of St Mark's and received his blessing. On the next day Barbarossa joined the pontiff at St Mark's for Mass, and following the service he held the stirrups of Alexander's horse in an act of penitence. Several days later he exclaimed to the gathered princes and prelates: 'Let it be known to the entire world that although we are clothed in the dignity and glory of the Roman Empire, this dignity does not keep us from human error, imperial majesty does not preserve us from ignorance.' While in Venice, Barbarossa renewed the imperial treaty with the doge, promising to preserve the peace with the republic and its vassal towns. In mid-October Alexander III departed for Rome, escorted by the emperor's chief advisor, Christian of Mainz. In the Holy City the pontiff received the homage of the senators on 29 August, and Calixtus III was forced to resign his office. Through protracted negotiations Barbarossa had finally brought peace to the Italian peninsula, albeit for only six years. In the aftermath of the setback at Legnano, he established a reconciliation with the Holy See, reduced the strength of the Lombard League and put it on the defensive, while retaining his supremacy over Germany.

Emperor Frederick I Barbarossa remained in northern Italy to solidify his sovereignty over his Italian princes and vassal towns. He began an extended tour of his loyal towns, visiting Ancona and the Duchy of Spoleto and enhancing his support among the citizens. The emperor proceeded to Tuscany and later Lombardy, where he was received with great approval by the people. In Piedmont he reorganized his government, appointing loyal officials to administer the region. From Turin, Barbarossa travelled north into Burgundy. At the city of Arles, he received the local magnates in great majesty and on 30 July 1178 was anointed King of Burgundy. After spending the summer months in Burgundy touring the region, he returned to Germany, arriving at Spires in late October.

While Frederick I was in Italy, his cousin, Duke Henry of Saxony and Bavaria, had been granted rich estates by the Bishop of Halberstadt, who was a supporter of Pope Calixtus III. Under the terms of the emperor's treaty with Alexander III, the duke's lands were now to be returned to the Church and a new bishop named. Henry refused to comply, and at the Diet of Spires on 11 November Barbarossa endorsed the rights of the newly appointed Bishop Ulrich to the properties. Barbarossa pressed the duke to relinquish the estates, ordering a second diet to meet at Worms to rule on the rightful owner. When Henry refused to attend the hearing, the representatives declared him an outlaw of the realm. A second trial was held after the duke failed to respond to the verdict, where the emperor presented the charges against him. Henry the Lion again ignored the assembly and all of his properties were declared forfeited to the regime. Henry's estates were seized and partitioned to loyal followers of the emperor. The title of Duke of Saxony was transferred to Bernard of Anhalt, while the Duchy of Bavaria was ceded to Otto of Wittlesbach. Through his skilful political manoeuvring, Barbarossa had retaliated against the duke's refusal to send troops to Italy and eliminated a powerful potential rival.

Following the confiscation of his estates, Henry the Lion mustered his troops to regain his properties by force of arms. Many of the duke's vassals refused to answer his call to arms and when Barbarossa advanced into his lands, the imperialists quickly overpowered their rivals. The city of Brunswick was quickly captured and Luback besieged. While the emperor maintained the siege, Henry the Lion fled to the castle at Stade in northern Saxony, sending envoys to his cousin asking for a pardon. Frederick agreed to meet with Henry at the Diet of Erfurt in November 1181. On 11 November the deposed duke prostrated himself before his cousin and was granted the cities of Brunswick and Luneburg, but was not restored to his former duchies and fiefdoms.

After increasing his feudal powers in Germany, Barbarossa further asserted his authority in Poland, Bohemia and Hungary, ensuring his rights and laws were enforced. In Germany he expanded the lands of his family, buying properties in Swabia, Saxony and Thuringia. As the emperor moved to enhance his control over the magnates and towns, he tightened his hold over the Church. He intervened in ecclesiastic elections, ensuring loyal churchmen were elected to episcopal sees. When bishoprics became vacant, he took measures to make sure his supporters were rewarded with the offices.

While Barbarossa enforced his feudal rights over Germany, his representatives in Lombardy were steadily solidifying his rule over the city-states. In March 1183 he authorized three imperial envoys to initiate peace negotiations with the Lombard League. The issue of the continued existence of Alessandria as a municipality remained a deterrent to a resolution, and to resolve the impasse the emissaries signed a separate agreement requiring the citizens to temporarily depart from their city before returning to the newly named Caesarea. On 30 April a preliminary covenant was signed at Piacenza, with Barbarossa granting the privileges previously approved by him and his predecessors and acknowledging the league, while the members were to assist the emperor against all enemies and respect the peace. The cities gained the right to choose their own consuls, who were to be invested with their offices by an imperial representative. On 23 June Barbarossa personally ratified the treaty at the Diet of Constance in the presence of the cities' envoys, papal legates and his German magnates. In the aftermath of the signing of the treaty, the Lombard cities remained loyal to the emperor and became his faithful allies in the new conflict with the papacy.

Following the Diet of Constance, Emperor Fredrick I Barbarossa resumed his preliminary negotiations with the Kingdom of Sicily. Relations between the two realms had improved following the signing of the Treaty of Venice, and as the Sicilians increasingly feared the ambitions of the Byzantine Empire along the eastern Italian coastline, closer links with the Germans were established. The emperor agreed to acknowledge the ruling Norman family as sovereign and offered his son Henry in marriage to the daughter of King Roger II of Sicily. The marriage was officially announced in Augsburg in late October 1183, giving the imperial throne greater influence in southern Italy and advancing its hold over the regime.

In late August 1181 Pope Alexander III died and was succeeded by Lucius III. The new pontiff was anxious to maintain cordial relations with the imperial crown and resolve several unsettled issues. While negotiations between the papacy and Barbarossa continued, the Roman Commune rose up against the pope, forcing him to flee the city. From the town of Velletri south of Rome, he appealed to the emperor for his intervention. After receiving the pope's request, in early September 1184 Barbarossa set out from Regensburg for Verona and his meeting with Pope Lucius III.

After passing through the Alps into northern Italy, Barbarossa reached Verona in October and soon began talks with Lucius to resolve their outstanding issues. From the beginning of the meeting, the pontiff was in a non-conciliatory temperament and responded negatively to the emperor's agenda. Frederick had earlier exercised his feudal rights under the Concordat of Worms, naming Rudolf of Wied to the vacant see of Treves. Despite his repeated requests, the pope would not recognize the new bishop, believing the emperor was attempting to usurp total authority over the German Church. After failing to resolve the dispute, they discussed the clergy ordained during the schism, whom Barbarossa wanted recognized by the new pontiff. Lucius refused to accept the proposal, referring the request to a special church council. When Barbarossa undertook to have the pope crown his heir, Henry, as co-emperor of the Romans to secure his succession, Lucius rejected the appeal. The meeting with the pontiff ended in deadlock, as relations between the two steadily deteriorated.

Barbarossa departed from Verona in early November and proceeded to finalize his ongoing negotiations with Milan for a defensive and offensive alliance. To regain the friendship of the Milanese, he moved against its rival city, Cremona, blaming its officials for the destruction of Crema and the usurpation of imperial lands. Confronted by the powerful alliances of the emperor, Cremona was forced to submit and sue for a pardon, which was granted for the payment of a large indemnity. With their rival city now pacified, the Milanese agreed to a confederation with the imperial throne, pledging to support the emperor against his enemies, while Milan regained its feudal privileges. Barbarossa remained in central Italy during 1185, supporting the magnates and prelates against the city-states and appointing new imperialists to the government. Within a short time he had gained control of the region, while in the north the Milanese intervened to compel other city-states to accept imperial authority.

In late November 1185 Pope Lucius III died and the cardinals elected the Archbishop of Milan to the papal throne, taking the name of Urban III. The new pontiff was a fierce opponent of Barbarossa and showed little desire to alter papal policy toward the Holy Roman Empire. Shortly after his election, he was petitioned by the emperor to crown his heir, Henry, as co-emperor. In a display of hostility, the pope refused. Nevertheless, to enforce his rule, Barbarossa had Henry anointed emperor on 27 January 1186 at Milan by the Patriarch of Aquileian. To further solidify Hohenstaufen power, Henry was crowned King of Italy and married to Constance, daughter of King Roger II of Sicily.

As relations between the papacy and the imperial crown deteriorated further, Urban III denounced the feudal Rights of Spoils, which gave Frederick the temporary administration of a bishopric's lands during the period between the death of its bishop and the appointment of a successor. In the wake of additional disputes, the emperor sent Henry with an army to besiege the pontiff at Verona. In retaliation Urban named Archbishop Philip of Cologne as his papal legate to Germany, knowing he was a strong opponent of the imperialists. The archbishop had earlier been ceded large estates by the imperial throne but now raised a rebellion against Barbarossa in support of the pope. He formed a grand confederation with discontented German magnates and bishops, along with the kingdoms of England and France, while Henry the Lion was also suspected of joining with Archbishop Philip. After learning of the growing uprising, Barbarossa rushed back to Germany, summoning the princes and clergy to meet at the Diet of Gelnhausen. At the assembly he defended his actions and reproached Lucius III for creating dissension among the Lombardy cities and opposing his feudal rights. The diet fully supported the emperor, and the bishops sent a letter to the pontiff petitioning him to make peace with the German regime.

While Frederick I was winning the support of his nobles and churchmen in Germany, Urban III declared him guilty of the charges earlier brought against him and was ready to declare him an outlaw when on 24 October 1187 he suddenly died. Meanwhile, in Germany, Philip of Cologne was preparing to mount an attack against the imperial regime, but without the endorsement of the pope and the ensuing defection of many of his allies was forced to make peace with the emperor.

In the aftermath of the death of Urban III, the College of Cardinals gathered in Rome to elect another new pope. A large party of cardinals, anxious to reach a reconciliation with the German regime, chose the aged Albert of Morra as pontiff, who took the name of Gregory VIII. The new pope quickly wrote to Barbarossa informing him the purpose of his papacy was to serve God and not make war. While the two men were preparing to meet in Rome to resolve their differences, Gregory VIII also died and was succeeded by Clement III. The new pontiff had been a supporter of his predecessor's policies for peace with the Holy Roman Empire, sending a message to the imperial court asking the emperor's heir, Henry, to accompany him into Rome for his investment as pope in a demonstration of peace and unity between the two former enemies. When Henry reached Rome, he met with the pontiff and quickly negotiated a settlement to their long outstanding differences. While his son made peace with the Holy See, Barbarossa restored his imperial order over Germany. Meanwhile, in Italy, the imperial partisans had defeated the emperor's enemies, enforcing his feudal rights in Italy and with the papacy. Frederick was now free to announce to his subjects that he had taken the cross of a crusader to recover the recently lost city of Jerusalem from Muslim control.

In early 1187 the army of the Kingdom of Jerusalem was virtually destroyed by the Muslim forces of Saladin at the Battle of Hattin. Saladin advanced against Jerusalem, compelling the garrison to surrender after a short siege. The Holy City had been under the control of the Christians for nearly 100 years, and Pope Gregory VIII was committed to the recovery of the Holy City, sending an appeal to the princes and prelates of Europe for the Third Crusade. Following the death of Gregory VIII on 27 December 1187, the newly elected Clement III renewed his predecessor's quest for the crusade and Barbarossa decided to lead a German army to the Holy Land. He began preparations for the Third Crusade in 1188, appointing his son Henry as ruler of the empire in his absence. He summoned his vassals to a diet at Mayence, where a letter from Clement III was read summoning the knights of Christendom to recapture Jerusalem from the Muslims. At the diet the emperor, his second surviving son, Frederick of Swabia, and thousands of knights ceremonially took the cross of a crusader. Barbarossa made extensive preparations for his expeditionary force, decreeing only men capable of equipping themselves were allowed to join the army and sending envoys to the rulers of the lands on his overland route announcing the coming of the crusader army. He made special efforts to assure the Emperor of Byzantine, Isaac II Angelus, that the objective of the campaign was the Holy Land and not his eastern empire.

On 11 May 1189 the German crusader army of over 12,000 men set out from Regensburg on the long overland march to the Levant, agreeing to join forces with King Richard I of England and Philip II, King of France, for the campaign against the Muslims. While the French and English sailed to the Outremer, the Germans travelled by land making their way through Vienna and Belgrade with support from the local rulers. After reaching Branicevo in modern-day Serbia, the crusaders followed the old Roman road into the Balkans. When they reached the Byzantine Empire, they were confronted by a hostile Emperor Isaac II Angelus, despite the earlier attempts by Barbarossa to assure him of his peaceful passage. Frederick I ordered his troops to press forward in battle formation, overpowering the Byzantine fortresses that blocked his route and repelling raiding patrols. As the eastern emperor continued his hostilities, Frederick threatened to sack his capital, Constantinople. When the crusaders attacked additional fortified towns, Isaac II Angelus sued for peace and on 21 January 1190 agreed to provide the Germans with provisions and end his attacks in return for their pledge to bypass Constantinople.

In March 1190 the crusader army crossed the Dardanelle Straits from Gallipoli on ships provided by Isaac II Angelus, landing in Asia Minor. The emperor set out for Iconium, present-day Konya in south central Turkey. Upon reaching the city, the Germans were compelled to take it by storm and force the sultan to provide them with food supplies. The crusaders set out for the Principality of Armenian Cilicia on their way to the Christian enclave at Antioch. After crossing the border into Armenia, the emperor was welcomed by envoys sent by the local ruler, Leo II. As Frederick I Barbarossa rode through Armenia in dreadful heat heading toward the town of Seleucia, on 10 June he decided to swim in the nearby

Saleph River to cool off and likely suffered a heart attack, dying aged sixty-seven after a reign of thirty-eight years. Shortly after the death of the emperor, his army broke up into several contingents, with many German princes returning home and some sailing to Antioch, led by Frederick of Swabia, while still others marched overland to current-day Syria. A large force of German troops later participated in the siege against Acre with Richard I and Philip II, compelling the Muslim defenders to surrender. In the aftermath of the death of Emperor Frederick I Barbarossa in Armenia, the Holy Roman throne was occupied by his eldest son, who became Henry VI. The new emperor ruled the empire for seven years and during his reign resumed the aggressive policies of his father, gaining control of the Kingdom of Sicily-Naples, reducing the lands subject to papal control in Italy to only the Duchy of Rome and securing his power in Germany and Burgundy.

Selected Sources:

Bryce, James, *The Holy Roman Empire*.
Ferguson, Wallace K. & Becker, Carl L., *A Survey of European Civilization – Ancient Times to 1660*.
Heer, Frederick, *The Holy Roman Empire*.
Henderson, Ernest F., *A History of Germany in the Middle Ages*.
Matthews, John & Stewart, Bob, *Warriors of Christendom*.
Matthews, Rupert, *The Popes*.
Munz, Peter, *Frederick Barbarossa – A Study in Medieval Politics*.
Norwich, John Julius, *A History of Venice*.
Otto of Freising, *The Deeds of Frederick Barbarossa*.
Pacaut, Marcel, *Frederick Barbarossa*.
Rendina, Claudio, *The Popes*.
Roberts, Andrew, *Great Commanders of the Medieval World*.
Rodes, John E., *Germany: A History*.
Runciman, Steven, *A History of the Crusades, Volume III*.
Smith-Riley, Jonathan, *The Crusades*.

Chapter Six

Richard I

The Lion Heart Ruler of England and Western France

On 8 June 1191 King Richard I of England landed his army at Acre on the shores of the Holy Land, joining the ongoing siege against the well-fortified city held by the Muslim troops of Saladin. The city had been besieged for two years by the King of Jerusalem, Guy of Lusigan, but his small forces lacked the military might to overpower the defenders and Richard I and his soldiers were part of a larger relief army that had answered Pope Clement III's call for the recovery of the Holy Land. The English troops joined the French crusaders of King Philip II, and together they pounded the defensive works with siege engines and dug tunnels under the walls, causing them to collapse. As the holy warriors relentlessly battered the walls, on 11 July the garrison was compelled to surrender. Following the occupation of the fortified city, Philip II returned to France, leaving the English monarch to resume the campaign. After garrisoning Acre, he set out for Jerusalem, moving south while seizing control of towns on the coastline to Jaffa. After fortifying the city, he made two attempts to capture Jerusalem but was thwarted each time and forced to withdraw. Unable to take the holy city, the English king held talks with Saladin, agreeing to a three-year truce and unrestricted Christian access to Jerusalem. After fighting for over sixteen months, Richard had failed to return the city to Christendom but had regained possession of the coastline from Jaffa north to Acre, and had re-energized the campaign to recapture Jerusalem from its Muslim usurpation, while securing safe passage to the city for pilgrims.

Richard Plantagenet, the third son of King Henry II and Eleanor of Aquitaine, was born on 8 September 1157 at Beaumont Palace in Oxford, England. The first son of the king, William, had died the previous year, and Richard was recognized as second in the line of succession behind

Henry the Younger to the vast lands of the Plantagenets in western France and England. The young prince spent his first five years in the household of the queen at Oxford, cared for by her servants. After relocating with his mother to Aquitaine in western France, eminent instructors from the Church were appointed for Richard's education. The prince's tutors concentrated his studies on grammar, rhetoric, Latin and theology, while familiarizing him with arithmetic, geometry, astronomy, music and social graces. He developed a great fondness for music and poetry, later writing popular poems and composing music. While the Plantagenet prince continued his academic education, he began training as a feudal knight under the instruction of experienced masters of arms. At a young age he learned to ride a horse and routinely practiced the tactics of a mounted soldier, while learning to fight with the weapons of an infantryman. As Richard grew older, he began to travel with his father and mother throughout the extensive territories of the throne, learning political skills. As the queen's favourite, Richard spent most of his adolescence at her court in Poitiers, the administrative centre of Aquitaine. While at the Poitiers court, he was frequently exposed to Eleanor's administration of her inherited lands, attending meetings with her advisors, while listening to discussions with her magnates, prelates and visiting foreign emissaries, gaining experience in the art of kingship. The prince was a natural leader with a charismatic personality, evolving into a skilled statesman and master of warfare. Through the strong influence of Queen Eleanor, Richard developed an energetic and life-long allegiance to Aquitaine, and in January 1169 was acknowledged duke designate for the duchy by Henry II. Three years later, at the age of fifteen, he was formally invested at the Church of St Hilary in Poitiers as Duke of Aquitaine by the Archbishop of Bordeaux.

King Henry II had earlier invested his eldest son, Henry the Younger, as successor to England, Normandy and Anjou, while Richard was ceded Aquitaine and the third son, Geoffrey, was granted the Duchy of Brittany. Despite their endowments, the king refused to relinquish any sovereignty to his heirs, and the lack of independence gave cause to their rebellion as they grew older. In March 1173 Henry the Younger broke away from his father, fleeing to the French court of King Louis VII, who welcomed him as an ally against the Plantagenet king. From Paris he summoned his two brothers to join him in revolt against their father. At the encouragement of Queen Eleanor, Richard agreed to participate in the insurrection. After he joined his brothers in Paris, they formed an alliance with the Capetian regime and recruited dissenting warlords from western France for their insurgency. While in Paris, the sixteen-year-old Richard was knighted by Louis VII, signifying his status as a feudal warlord.

In preparation for their attack against the Plantagenet throne, Richard and his two brothers pledged not to make a separate peace with the regime nor secure their father's oath to transfer sovereignty to them for their individual princedoms. With encouragement and the promise of military assistance from King Louis, the Plantagenet princes recruited rebellious magnates from Blois, Boulogne and Flanders for their campaign. The coalition forces, with support from the French king, first moved against Henry II's castle at Aumarle, where after a short siege the defenders submitted. The attack against the fortress was Richard's first experience in battle, facing the dangers of an armed enemy. In July they launched an assault into eastern Normandy to reduce Henry II's frontier fortifications, seizing Neuf-Marche and Vermeuil, while in the north numerous warlords joined the growing rebellion. After garrisoning the strongholds, the brothers proceeded to Driacourt surrounding the defensive works and besieging the fortress. The garrison held out for a month before surrendering on 21 July. As the uprising spread in his lands, Henry raised an army of knights and soldiers from Gascony and Anjou, also hiring a force of mercenary troops. The English king advanced against the mutineers in the north, and after overpowering them shifted his men to the east, compelling the three brothers to retreat back into France.

The invasion into Plantagenet lands had failed to make any appreciable gains, and in September Duke Richard and his brothers sent envoys to their father offering to resolve their revolt. The king agreed to meet at Gisors and offered Richard control of four castles in Aquitaine and half the annual revenue from the duchy, but no transfer of autonomy. Similar proposals were made to Henry the Younger and Geoffrey, but the offers were rejected by the three princes on the advice of Louis VII and hostilities were renewed. In November Henry II led his mercenaries south of Chinon, capturing three rebel castles and occupying Poitiers with his troops. During the sweep around Chinon, the Plantagenet king's men captured Eleanor, as she attempted to join her sons. Now that his mother was no longer in control of the county of Poitou, Richard advanced his army into her Aquitaine duchy, moving against the city of La Rochelle, but the defenders remained loyal to the Plantagenet crown and compelled him to swing his army forty miles south-east to attack the fortress at Saintes. In May 1174 he sent his soldiers slamming into the defenses taking the town by storm. Duke Richard established his headquarters in Saintes but was hard-pressed by his father's troops and forced to flee to Geoffrey's castle at Taillebourg. At the Battle of Saintes, Richard lost most of his army and could make little headway against the king's soldiers in Poitou. When the duke learned that his older brother had submitted to the Plantagenet throne, he met his father in Poitou, falling to the ground and asking for clemency. Henry raised his son to his feet and granted him his pardon. Under the terms of the peace treaty, Richard pledged loyalty to the king and was granted half of Aquitaine's revenues as previously offered, but was given control of only two castles instead of four.

In the aftermath of his submission to his father, Richard returned to govern the Duchy of Aquitaine, while his mother remained the prisoner of Henry. During the recent civil war, many barons in Aquitaine had risen up in rebellion, seeking to regain their independence from the duke in the vacuum created by the absence of an energetic ducal government. With the conflict against Henry resolved, Richard assembled his army and proceeded north to quell the revolt of the warlords and punish them for their disobedience. After sacking several castles and leaving them in ruins, he moved against Lord Arnold de Boville's fortress at Castillon-sur-Agen. When the Aquitaine army advanced into his lands, Arnold gathered a force of his allies and vassals, strengthening his castle's defences against the anticipated attack by Richard. The duke brought up his siege engines, battering the walls of the formidable stronghold with large projectiles. As the Aquitaine troops intensified their assaults, the garrison of thirty knights and a contingent of foot soldiers surrendered in August 1175. By the end of the year Richard had regained control of much of northern Poitou and looked to the south where a mighty coalition had united against his rule.

Confronted by the powerful league in the south of his duchy, led by the sons of the Count of Angouleme, Richard lacked the military power to defeat the rebels and was forced to return to England to ask his father for martial support. In April 1176 he reached the royal court, meeting with King Henry and discussing the growing threat to the crown's supremacy in Aquitaine. The king agreed to provide money for mercenary troops to defend his realm. While the duke was in England, Vulgrin of Angouleme assembled his private army, augmented with hired knights and foot soldiers, and moved into Poitou, ravaging the towns and farmlands. When Richard returned to his duchy, he struck against Vulgrin, marching his reinforced army into his lands and defeating him near Barbezieux in a fierce and bloody pitched battle. After the victory over Vulgrin, Richard continued his subjugation campaign, advancing his army to impose the crown's will over the town of Limoges. In June 1176 he laid siege to the town, held by Viscount Aimar of Limoges. The viscount resisted Duke Richard's assaults for several days before agreeing to submit.

In the wake of his victories over the now weakened rebel alliance, Richard travelled back to Poitiers, meeting his older brother, who had been sent by Henry II to help suppress the revolt. After remaining in the town for a few days, the duke and Henry the Younger moved into Angouleme with the Aquitaine army to renew the offensive against the rebellious barons. To secure their lines of communications with Poitiers, the brothers laid siege to the enemy's castle controlling the roadway north and south through Angouleme. After the fortification was captured following a two-week siege, Henry the Younger abandoned Richard's campaign, straining relations between the brothers. The Aquitaine troops continued their expedition, seizing the stronghold at Moulineuf after a short investment, and proceeded to the key castle of the insurgnets at Angouleme. Gathered behind the walls of the fortress were the leaders of the rebellion: Count William IV of Angouleme, his son Vulgrin and Lord Aimar of Limoges. Richard besieged the fortification, but after only six days Count William agreed to submit and surrender all his principal fortifications to the duke, accepting ducal suzerainty over his lands. Following his conquest of Angouleme, Richard swept south, leading his army in a lightning offensive to take control of enemy castles and secure the road to Spain. After reasserting Plantagenet rule, Richard returned to

Poitiers in early 1177, reporting the results of his campaign to his father in England.

In August 1177 King Henry II boarded a ship in England, crossing the Channel to join Richard at Poitiers. Henry the Younger and Geoffrey were summoned to a family meeting to discuss the ongoing revolt of the rebels in western France. Remaining in France, Henry II held separate discussions with Louis VII, agreeing to a non-aggression pact, to settle border disputes by arbitration and to participate in a new crusade to the Holy Land. With his borders now secure, Henry II took Richard and advanced the army into Limousin to punish insurgents for their rebellion against the throne. They assailed the hilltop fortifications of the rogue barons, razing many and devastating their lands. While in Limousin, King Henry II purchased the large Countship of La Marche, adding it to Richard's already substantial holdings in Aquitaine.

In the aftermath of his humiliating defeat by the Plantagenets, Count William IV decided to make a pilgrimage to Jerusalem to beg for God's forgiveness, leaving his eldest son Vulgrin as his regent. When Vulgrin was called to the Saintes court to pledge his homage to Richard, he refused the summons, forming an alliance against the duke with Geoffrey III of Rancon and several other dissident barons. In defence of his feudal rights, Duke Richard led his troops and mercenaries against the rebel fortification at Pons in south-western France. The castle was in the domain of the Rancon family, and Geoffrey prepared the defences for an attack by the Plantagenet forces. When the duke besieged Pons, his troops were unable to breach the formidable defensive works. As the siege dragged on, Richard left a large force of knights and infantrymen to maintain the investment, leading his remaining men north to capture and demolish five castles in a swift campaign to weaken the resolve of Geoffrey III's allies.

Duke Richard continued his offensive against the rogue barons, proceeding against the formidable castle at Taillebourg, which was considered unassailable. The fortification was built on a rocky outcrop overlooking the valley of the Charente River, and was approachable from only one side, protected by a series of three stone walls, while the remaining three sides were built along a steep cliff. On 1 May, Richard moved his siege engines forward and began battering the defensive works with large projectiles. While the artillerymen hammered the castle, Richard's soldiers were ordered to pillage the surrounding countryside, ravaging the farms and villages. After learning of the destruction of their properties, the citizen-soldiers of Taillebourg sortied from the stronghold, clashing with the besiegers in hand-to-hand fighting. The Aquitaine men steadily pushed the enemy back toward the gates, with Richard leading his soldiers in the melee. When the rebels' line wavered and then broke, they fled to the open gates, Richard and his troops following them into the fortification. The garrison took refuge in the citadel, but with no hope of relief soon submitted. After Geoffrey heard of the loss of his great fortress, he surrendered Pons and submitted to the duke. Following the capitulation of his ally, Vulgrin agreed to terms with the Plantagenet prince, surrendering his strongholds at Angouleme and Montignac, which were levelled to the ground. Duke Richard's victory at Taillebourg greatly enhanced his reputation among the Aquitaine barons as a ruthless martial commander, intimidating the remaining rebel warlords and forcing their submission.

In the wake of his conquest of the Aquitaine rebels, Richard remained in Poitou enforcing Plantagenet rule against sporadic uprisings by rogue barons and loyally administering the duchy for his father. Under the firm control of the duke, his lands remained peaceful until June 1182 when Vulgrin died, leaving an infant daughter as his only successor. As her overlord, Richard claimed the right of guardianship for the heiress, but her uncles, William and Ademar, disputed his entitlement. When the two brothers attempted to seize the county by force of arms, they were driven out by soldiers of the duke. William and Ademar fled to the court of their half-brother Aimar of Limoges. To enforce their perceived right of inheritance to the county, they made an alliance with Viscount Elie of Perigord and several recalcitrant barons. With his vassals again in rebellion, Richard mustered his forces, proceeding into Limousin pillaging and burning the villages and farms. As the duke was razing the countryside, King Henry II came to Aquitaine, summoning the rebels to meet at Grandmont to resolve their revolt. The leaders of the uprising met with the king to present their charges against the duke, who defended his ducal privileges. The rightful guardianship of the heiress remained unresolved, and Henry the Younger was ordered by the king to aid his brother in the suppression of the rebel warlords. The two brothers marched their army first into the lands of Aimar, occupying his castles and estates. They resumed their campaign against Viscount Elie, overpowering him and forcing his submission. As the dissident coalition began to break apart, Aimar sued for peace and pledged his fealty to Richard.

Henry II had earlier given Richard and his third son, Geoffrey, their lands to govern autonomously as his vassals, while Henry the Younger had been ceded England, Normandy and Anjou but was deprived of independent power. Denied sovereignty by his father, he looked for an opportunity to intercede against his brothers to secure his self-rule. Richard had repeatedly suppressed the rebellions of his barons, who began sending messages to the eldest son offering to recognize him as Duke of Aquitaine. When King Henry summoned his sons and vassals to Caen for the Christmas celebrations in 1182, Henry the Younger was still vying for his autonomous rule. The king asked Richard and Geoffrey to pledge their fealty to their older brother to ensure the continuance of the Plantagenet empire following his death. Geoffrey quickly agreed, but Richard refused to submit. When pressed by his father, the duke finally consented, but only after the regime acknowledged him and his heirs as the rightful rulers of an independent Aquitaine. Henry the Younger rejected Richard's terms, announcing he would now support the Aquitaine rebels against his brother. As the dispute threatened to spiral into civil war, Henry II interceded, summoning his sons and the rogue Aquitaine barons to meet at Micebeau. When Geoffrey was sent to Limousin to make the arrangements, he joined the rebellion against Richard. As new insurgent warlords pledged to participate in the revolt, Henry the Younger left the royal court to join his brother at Limoges in early February 1183. After reaching Limoges he was recognized as Duke of Aquitaine by the rebellious barons. They assembled an army of knights and foot soldiers, augmented with a large force of mercenaries. While the two brothers were mustering their troops, a second contingent of hired soldiers from Brittany was ordered by Duke Geoffrey to assail Poitou from the north. With his properties under attack from two fronts, Richard moved swiftly against the Breton mercenaries, defeating them and ravaging Geoffrey's lands in retaliation. Duke Richard now turned to attack his brothers and their forces. He caught Aimar's mercenaries at Gorre, routing them and executing many of his prisoners in revenge.

As Richard was protecting his duchy, Henry II rode to Aixe in the hope of ending the fighting between his sons. He met with his eldest son, who attempted to defend his rebellion but the king refused to listen. Henry the Younger returned to Limoges and prepared his defences for a siege. While Henry II and Richard attempted to negotiate a settlement with the rebels, messengers were sent to Poitou to bring the royal army to Limoges. When the troops arrived on 1 March, Richard marched against the insurgents at Limoges, besieging the citadel of St Martial, but Geoffrey of Brittany and Viscount Aimar resisted the assaults. The conflict dragged on with no end in sight. During the siege, Henry the Younger was in the county, raising money to pay his mercenaries and attacking loyalist castles. While he was travelling through the countryside, he was stricken with dysentery and died on 11 June. The death of Henry the Younger ended the coalition against Richard, who, as the oldest surviving son, became the successor-designate to the Plantagenet throne.

In the aftermath of the death of Henry the Younger, Richard expected to be crowned co-king and given authority over parts of the Plantagenet realm. In 1183 Henry II summoned Richard and his youngest son, John, to Normandy to discuss changes in the governing of the domain. The king ordered Richard to assign Aquitaine to John, while transferring Normandy and Anjou to him. The duke refused to transfer any part of the duchy to his younger brother after spending the last eight years fighting to gain sovereignty over the barons. He withdrew from the royal court, returning to Poitiers. During the early months of 1184, the king continued his efforts to convince his heir to give up Aquitaine but the duke refused his offers. Finally in frustration he gave John permission to attack Aquitaine. In the summer John allied with Geoffrey of Brittany unleashed harassing raids into Poitou, while Richard retaliated by sending soldiers to pillage Geoffrey's Breton lands. When Henry II learned of the outbreak of fighting, he ordered his three sons to England, where an uneasy peace was restored at Westminster Palace. Richard remained at the Plantagenet court until after the Christmas celebrations, returning to Poitiers to take control of the duchy.

Shortly after returning to Aquitaine, the war between the brothers erupted again along its borders, and Richard was occupied mounting raids against Geoffrey's lands. In April 1185 Henry II crossed the Channel to Normandy and sent for Queen Eleanor. When she arrived at court, a message was sent to Richard demanding the surrender of Aquitaine to his mother. He was compelled to obey his father's order and left his duchy for the royal court in Rouen. Duke Richard remained at Rouen, playing the obedient son. When the king returned to England, Richard was sent south to subdue Raymond V of Toulouse, who had attacked Aquitaine lands in Limousin in support of Viscount Aimar. He advanced his veteran army of ducal troops and mercenaries south, invading Quercy and quickly overwhelming the rebel forces.

Richard remained in Toulouse, attacking Raymond V's castles and desolating his lands, then in April 1186 the political alignment in western France was dramatically altered when Duke Geoffrey was killed during a martial tournament in Paris. King Philip II claimed guardianship of the duke's two daughters as overlord of Brittany, in opposition to Henry II. As the two kingdoms moved closer to war, the kings of France and England met in October, agreeing to a truce and compelling Richard to withdraw his forces from Toulouse. When the ceasefire expired, the Capetian and Plantagenet regimes again began preparing for war. In the summer of 1187 Philip II sent his armies into Berry, south of Orleans, but after papal legates intervened a two-year peace was arranged. Following the signing of the agreement, Richard journeyed to Paris with the French king and over several months developed a close friendship with him. While at the Capetian court, he was continually pressed by Henry II to return to the Plantagenet kingdom. The duke finally departed from Paris to join his father at Angers, where he publicly gave homage to alleviate his father's fears of revolt. As the duke remained with the monarch in Angers, rebellion again erupted in Aquitaine and Richard was ordered to advance with his army and mercenaries to Angouleme and Toulouse to impose Plantagenet sovereignty. He unleashed a campaign of fire and storm against the recalcitrant warlords demolishing their stronghold and towns forcing their surrender.

After Aquitaine's mercenary troops ravaged Toulouse, Philip II claimed the campaign was a breach of the ongoing truce and sent his army sweeping into Berry, threatening to overrun the countship. The French quickly broke through the defensive works at the formidable stronghold of Chateauroux and captured numerous other castles. Richard rushed his men to defend his lands, while King Henry assembled a large army in England, crossing the Channel to join his son. When the Englishmen reached Normandy, Philip withdrew his men to defend his borders, leaving Richard free to recover his recently lost properties. The duke's men regained possession of most of the fortresses, but the great castle at Chateauroux repulsed their repeated assaults. While Henry remained immobile in Normandy through illness, Philip took the initiative, advancing his forces into the Loire Valley. With the French threatening to overrun the Loire, Richard led his troops toward them. Not willing to risk a pitched battle, the Capetian sovereign retreated and returned to his Paris court.

In the wake of the French withdrawal, King Henry moved his army toward Mantes in late August 1188, Richard riding at his side. Travelling through the region, the Plantagenet forces laid waste to the countryside. As the war wore on, Philip sent a messenger to Henry asking for a peace conference at Bonsmoulin in north-west France. On 7 October the monarchs and Richard met to set the conditions for peace, but after fiery discussions they could not come to terms. Following the failure to find an agreement, Richard met privately with the French king to negotiate a compromise. Under the new proposal, Philip would abandon his recent territorial gains, while Henry would acknowledge Richard as king-designate in England and western France and approve his marriage to the Captain monarch's sister, Alice. When presented the treaty, the English monarch again refused to accept the terms. Before leaving Bonsmoulin, the kings negotiated another truce, lasting until 1 January 1189.

When it was time to renegotiate the ongoing truce, Henry II was unable to attend the conference due to illness so Philip ordered his troops to renew the war. The Bretons were the first to revolt, attacking several Plantagenet castles and towns. The English king sent repeated messages to his heir, asking him to return to court and lead the counter-attack into Brittany. As the fighting spread into other parts of western France, Pope Clement III sent his legate to negotiate a resolution. Through his intervention, the warring factions met in Maine in the spring, Richard and King Philip joining together against Henry and presenting their terms. These demands were quickly rejected by the English king and the conflict resumed. Duke Richard and the French king unleashed a surprise raid into Maine, capturing several castles before attacking the fortified town of Le Mans. As the allies continued their offensive, King Henry rode to his ancestral home at Chinon to rally his vassals. He was exhausted and ill from the constant campaigning, offering little resistance to the attacks of his son. While he remained in Chinon, his rivals overran Maine and Touraine, and in early July they captured the strategic city of Tours. With his empire crumbling, Henry met with Richard and the Capetian monarch and agreed to their terms. When the conference ended, King Henry was carried in a litter back to Chinon, where he died on 6 July 1189, leaving Richard I, King of England, Duke of Normandy and Aquitaine and Count of Poitou, Anjou and Maine.

At the start of his reign Richard I fought to assert his fealty over rebellious barons and struggled against his family's attempted usurpation of his lands, while in the Levant the Saracen sultan, Saladin, destroyed the Christian army at the Battle of Hattin and seized Jerusalem. When Pope Gregory VIII issued a proclamation calling for a new holy war to reimpose Christian sovereignty in the Holy Land, King Richard took the cross of a crusader, pledging to participate in the reconquest of Jerusalem. Following his assumption of the Plantagenet empire, he was eager to begin preparations for the crusade but first had to safeguard his rule in western France and England. Following his father's funeral, Richard first journeyed to Rouen and was formally acknowledged as duke by the local archbishop. After receiving vows of homage from his Norman vassals, he hurried to meet King Philip II and negotiate the security of his borders with France. They met on 20 July near Chaumont, quickly coming to an agreement. Under the terms of the treaty, Richard pledged to marry the Capetian king's sister Alice, with the dowry of Gisors, and to honour his father's earlier promise to pay the French regime a large remuneration in silver. The two kings agreed to jointly take part in the Third Crusade and depart in the early spring of the following year.

In the wake of the treaty of non-aggression with the French crown, Richard returned to Normandy and received the fealty of the people to solidify his assumption of power. In early August he sailed to England for his coronation as monarch. He was joined by his mother, who had served as his regent for England after the death of Henry II. As the king made his way to London for the coronation, he was welcomed by large and enthusiastic crowds at each town he passed through. On 1 September the royal party arrived in London, and two days later Richard entered Westminster Abbey dressed in his coronation robes. The magnificent procession of bishops, abbots, barons and knights preceded the king down the nave, which was filled with the foremost noblemen and court officials of England. Richard took his place at the front of the altar, and after making three oaths to protect England from its enemies took off his robes to dress in royal vestments. He was led to the altar, where the Archbishop of Canterbury, Baldwin of Exeter, poured oil on his head, chest and right shoulder, signifying knowledge, valour and glory, then crowned him King of England. The sovereign was escorted to the throne to hear Mass and receive communion. At the conclusion of the ceremony, he was taken out of the abbey by several bishops, to the acclaim of the large gathered crowd. The coronation was followed by a banquet celebrating Richard's assumption of the English crown.

After securing the fealty of his English and western French subjects, King Richard began to raise the funds necessary to finance a large well-equipped military force for the campaign in the Latin East. England was the Plantagenet regime's wealthiest domain and was expected to subsidize a major portion of the cost of the expeditionary force. The Saladin Tithe was a ten per cent tax on revenue implemented in England by Henry II in 1188 to finance his participation in the Third Crusade. The king died the following year without withdrawing the money, and now Richard seized it for his crusade. To supplement the revenue from the Saladin Tithe, a royal decree was proclaimed stripping all English officeholders of their positions and requiring the payment of a fee to the treasury to regain them. Monasteries were compelled to make large donations to retain their privileges, and cities found generous charters could be secured for a price. The king readily sold royal castles, manor houses, titles and privileges to anyone who had enough money. Richard remarked to a courtier: 'I would sell London, if I could find someone rich enough to buy it.' While the English kingdom provided the bulk of the money needed for the expedition, the Plantagenet princedoms in western France were also required to make sizeable contributions to the war effort. As the funds began pouring into the treasury, the regime made purchases of equipment, arms and supplies for the crusade, while making arrangements for a fleet to carry the troops to the Outremer. To supplement his army, Richard recruited mercenary soldiers, hiring professional cavalrymen and elite infantrymen.

As the preparations for the crusade continued, King Richard made arrangements for the administration of his English and French domains. To rule England during his prolonged absence, he divided his kingdom into two, appointing justiciars to govern in the north and south. To appease his brother John's ambitions for wealth and power, he supplemented the fiefdoms previously given to him by adding the English counties of Cornwall, Devon, Somerset and Dorset. However, Richard's generous donations only created a larger base of operations for John to plot against his brother's crown during his time in the Holy Land. Before departing from England, the king banished John to his lands in Normandy for three years to curb his aspirations.

While the money continued to flow into the royal coffers in England, on 12 December 1189 King Richard crossed the Channel to meet the French king at Nonancourt in Normandy to complete their plans for the crusade. They agreed on a joint campaign against the Saracens and to share all spoils equally. The monarchs arranged to assemble their armies at Messina at the invitation of King William II of Sicily, who was married to Richard's sister Joanna. They pledged to respect the demesne of the other and resist any attack against their sovereignty. In mid–March Richard summoned Queen Eleanor, along with his brother John and prominent English magnates, to meet with him at Nonancourt to finalize the arrangements for the governing of England. The choice of regents was confirmed, and to protect the king's interests in England, Prince John was required to vow not to travel to the kingdom. They discussed various measures to ensure the proper administration of England and the enforcement of Richard's rights as sovereign. Near the end of the meeting, the dowager queen convinced the king to allow John to visit the realm, which would later have profound consequences for the regime. The English chancellor, William Longchamp, was ordered to collect the ships for the voyage to the Holy Land using parts of the royal fleet and vessels from the port cities of the Plantagenet monarchy. Richard remained in western France, touring his lands and making appointments to governmental posts, granting privileges and favours to secure his reign. The final preparations for the expedition took longer than anticipated, with the departure time extended, but after the unexpected death of Philip II's wife, Queen Isabella, it became necessary to advance the date forward again.

As the date of departure to the Outremer neared, on 27 June 1190 King Richard was invested at Tours with the insignia of a pilgrim by the archbishop. Shortly after the ceremony, he began his journey to Vezelay in central France for his reunion with Philip II. The monarchs travelled together with their armies to Lyon, where the French advanced separately to the port-city of Genoa and the English moved overland to Marseilles for the sea voyage to the Levant. After reaching the Mediterranean port on 31 July, Richard expected to find his transport fleet of over 100 vessels waiting, but it failed to arrive. The troops could not stay in the city, and after waiting a week Richard divided army into two forces, sending one contingent led by Archbishop Baldwin of Canterbury directly to the Holy Land on hired ships, while he took the remaining soldiers down the coast of Italy by boat, putting in at Genoa, Rome and several other ports. When the king reached Salerno, he learned that his fleet was now sailing to Messina in Sicily after a prolonged delay in Lisbon. He set out overland for part of the journey along the Italian coastline, later re-embarking and arriving at Messina on 23 September for the reunion with the French king and his army. He was met by Philip and King Tancred of Sicily, and escorted into the city in a grand procession. The English king later conferred privately with Philip, discussing the next phase of the passage to the Latin kingdom and offensive operations against the Muslims. At the Sicilian court, Richard was graciously entertained by Tancred but his friendly reception soon deteriorated.

As the crusaders had made their preparations in England and France for the expedition to the Levant, King William II of Sicily died in November 1189 and the pope appointed his illegitimate cousin, Tancred, as his successor. Richard's sister Joanna had been married to William II, and when her brother demanded the return of her dowry, Tancred refused. As the two kings faced off against each other, the citizens of Messina rose up against the English soldiers, attacking them in support of their king. The Plantagenet sovereign ordered a force of 2,000 knights and 1,000 archers to seize the town. In the afternoon of 4 October, Richard, dressed in armour, led his men forward at the sound of the trumpets. As they approached the city's walls, Tancred's bowmen unleashed volleys of arrows into the ranks of the crusaders. Under a storm of arrows, the Plantagenet archers replied, firing at the defenders and driving them back. The king's knights charged the gates, breaking into the city with battering rams. The crusaders continued their assault, overrunning the Sicilians and capturing Messina. After his garrison troops and volunteer soldiers from the town were decimated, Tancred was forced to submit, agreeing to reimburse Joanna for her dowry, and upon receipt of payment a peace treaty was signed. Near the city's ramparts, Richard built a fortress to keep watch on the Sicilians.

It was now late in the year, and with frequent winter storms in the Mediterranean posing a threat to the crusader fleet, Richard was compelled to spend the next six months on Sicily. The army built its winter quarters outside the city walls, living in tents and suffering the effects of rain, cold and disease. During Richard's preparations for the crusade, he had visited the kingdom of Navarre on his southern French border to reinforce his friendship with King Sancho VI. To bind his demesne closer to Navarre, he negotiated his marriage to Sancho VI's daughter Berengaria. While the crusaders remained on Sicily, in March Queen Eleanor arrived with Berengaria. On 30 March Richard escorted his mother and future wife into Messina, while King Philip departed for the crusade to Acre. Eleanor remained at Messina, visiting her eldest surviving son for only three days before journeying back to England by ship, leaving Berengaria with Richard.

The next week was spent with final preparations and the loading of men, supplies, equipment and arms on the 219 ships of the fleet. On 10 April, with fair winds filling the white sails, the flotilla set out from Messina for the East. After a week, a lookout sighted the island of Crete, the halfway point of the journey to Outremer, and the vessels put in to the harbour. Following a brief stopover, the ships resumed their voyage and reached the island of Rhodes, where the crusaders remained for ten days to allow stragglers to rejoin the fleet and Richard to recover from a fever.

While on the island, Richard made inquiries about the political state of Cyprus, the next point on their journey. He was told by local officials that its self-imposed emperor, Isaac Comnenus, had seized control of the island by force, and the people were unhappy with his tyrannical rule. The occupation of Cyprus would give Richard a secure nearby base of operations for his expedition to the Holy Land, while its wealth could be utilized to supplement his expenses. On 1 May he set out to conquer Cyprus.

During the passage from Rhodes, over twenty of the English ships were blown off course by a storm and landed on the coast of Cyprus, where the crews were imprisoned by Isaac. The vessel carrying Berengaria and the king's sister was part of the flotilla, and after anchoring in the port of Limassol they were in danger of being seized by the island's ruler. After Richard learned of their plight, he immediately sailed to Cyprus, landing on 6 May, reuniting with Joanna and Berengaria and sending a message to Isaac demanding the release of his men. When the emperor refused, the monarch disembarked his troops and forced Isaac's mercenaries to abandon the town. After capturing the port, Richard opened negotiations with the emperor. While the talks continued, on 11 May the deposed King of Jerusalem, Guy of Lusignan, accompanied by several Latin princes, arrived at Limassol to encourage the king to hurry to the ongoing siege at Acre. While the Latin princes remained on Cyprus, on 12 May Richard and Berengaria were married in the Cypriot Chapel of St George and following the ceremony she was anointed Queen of England. She was described by contemporaries as a queen of beauty, nobility and wisdom. Soon after their marriage Berengaria traveled with her husband to Acre, remaining in the Levant during the crusade. During their time in the Holy Land, they became estranged and were never fully reconciled, with each living separate lives. Their marriage produced no children, giving cause to claims of Richard's homosexuality, although no supporting evidence has been found. The wedding had been followed by a great celebration and feast. Soon after the festivities, the king met again with Isaac Comnenus, presenting his demands for peace. The emperor, refusing to accept the terms, withdrew to Famagusta with his Cypriot militia to defend his rule. Richard split his army, sending Guy of Lusignan overland with a large contingent of troops to the fortress, while he sailed up the coast with a second force to meet him. When the reunited crusaders reached the fortified town, it was abandoned; Isaac had escaped to the fortification of Nicosia. The English marched on Nicosia, and as they approached the stronghold they were ambushed by Isaac. The disciplined Plantagenet army quickly formed into battle formation, overwhelming the enemy troops and compelling Isaac to flee to the castle of Kantara. During the fighting, Richard recognized Isaac in the melee and charged toward him on his horse, but the emperor managed to slip away. As the Plantagenet forces were defeating the Cypriots, King Guy led a second contingent of Richard's men, capturing the fortresses at Kyrenia and Didimus.

At Kyrenia, the young daughter of Isaac was taken prisoner and held for ransom. When the emperor learned of her capture, he surrendered to Richard, begging for the safety of his daughter. The young girl was brought to see her father and later placed in the household of Queen Joanna, while Isaac was sent in chains to the great castle of Marqab in Syria. In less than a month Richard had conquered Cyprus and enthroned himself as king. With the island now under his rule, he boarded his ship on 5 June and set sail with his fleet for the Levant to reunite with Philip in the crusade against the Muslims.

The crusader fleet ploughed through the blue waters of the Mediterranean before making landfall in Syria and sailing down the coast to reach the ongoing siege at Acre on 8 June. The English were welcomed by the besieging forces of King Guy and Philip II. The fortified town was first besieged by Guy in 1189, but he lacked the troop strength to overrun the defenses. When Philip arrived at Acre, he assumed command of the expeditionary force and put his men to work building siege engines and battering the defensive works, launching sorties against the defenders. Acre, built on an inlet overlooking the Mediterranean, was protected by steep cliffs and two formidable walls with towers on the landside. Relations between the English king and Philip II had been strained at Sicily, but now they deteriorated further when Richard offered to pay four gold coins a month to any knight who would serve under his battle flag, while the French king was paying only three.

When Richard departed from Sicily for the Levant, he dismantled his fortress guarding Messina and carried it by ship to Acre. He rebuilt the fortification, locating it near the Saracen defences. His archers positioned in the tall tower fired volleys of arrows at the defenders, as a line of siege engines launched large rocks at the defensive works. Richard remained with his troops, encouraging them and directing their operations. During the investment he was stricken with a high fever and confined to bed. Despite the illness, he continued to direct the fighting from his sickbed. As the siege continued with no end in sight, Richard sent a message to Saladin without conferring with Philip, offering to meet, but the offer was rejected. The independent communication without the approval of the French further strained the relationship between the two kings.

After a week Richard recovered from his illness and returned to the fighting, ordering his siege engines forward to fire at the walls, while sending his engineers to dig tunnels under the walls to weaken them. The Muslims in Acre were hard-pressed to hold the city, as the sappers and siege engines forced large sections of the walls to crumble. Saladin stayed in the hills around the city, but his repeated sorties against the crusaders were repelled. He was unable to break through the Christians' lines to relieve the defenders, and after a two-year resistance the garrison was compelled to submit. Under the terms accepted by Philip and Richard, the Saracens agreed to surrender Acre, pay a large indemnity, release 1,500 prisoners and return the True Cross, which had been seized at the Battle of Hattin in 1187, while the garrison remained as hostages until the provisions of the treaty were fulfilled.

Shortly after the agreement with the Muslim defenders was finalized, Philip announced he was returning to France. Despite the deterioration in their once cordial relationship, Richard begged him to stay and lead the French army in the recapture of Jerusalem. On 3 August the Capetian sovereign set sail for home after pledging not to attack any of Richard's lands. While the crusaders waited for the Saracens to fulfil the terms of the treaty, Saladin was having difficulty raising the indemnity and Richard agreed to accept the money by instalments. Impatient to resume the expedition to the south, Richard feared that the sultan was deliberately delaying the payment for time to reinforce his army. When Saladin failed to make the first instalment, on 20 August the Plantagenet monarch ordered the Saracen prisoners to be taken out in groups and massacred. Two days later the Christians moved out of Acre, leaving a reinforced garrison to hold the fortification.

Richard led his multinational crusader army down the coastal road toward Jaffa, modern-day Tel Aviv, the slow-moving baggage train on the seaward flank and the infantry and cavalry positioned on the landward side to repel the expected sorties of Saladin. Shortly after leaving the protection of Acre, the Christians were harassed by the sultan's cavalry, but Richard refused to allow his men to counterattack. The journey to Jaffa was also made difficult by the lack of water and food, choking dust storms and intense heat, which caused the death of many soldiers. The crusaders wore heavy jackets fitted with metal plates for protection against Muslim arrows, adding to the discomfort of the journey. After traveling for several miles, the Christians had their first encounter with the enemy, as Saladin's cavalry swept in from the desert to attack the baggage train. After learning of the attack, King Richard and his personal escort galloped into the Muslims' ranks in a fury of thundering charges, driving the attackers away. After clearing the roadway, the army continued south, camping near the Kishon Stream later in the day, and on the following morning resumed the advance, reaching the town of Haifa, where the soldiers rested for a few days.

On 27 August the Christian army resumed its advance after Richard realigned the order of march, placing the cavalry in the centre and the infantrymen, pikemen and archers on the landward side to prevent the Saracen horsemen from penetrating the column. When the flank was attacked, the king ordered his men to keep marching and not engage the foe. Unable to isolate and destroy small bands of Christian soldiers, the sultan withdrew his troops, moving ahead of the column to block the road at Arsuf. The Muslims occupied the high ground, and as the Christian army approached with the Knights Templars in the vanguard and Hospitallers in the rear, Saladin sent wave after wave of cavalrymen thundering down the hills, followed by his pikemen and archers. With his column under assault, Richard again refused to allow his forces to respond, but as the Saracen onslaught intensified, numerous knights broke ranks to charge at the Muslims. Richard responded quickly, ordering his men to counterattack. With a contingent of knights, he galloped to the support of the Hospitallers in the rear, slamming into the Saracen cavalry and infantrymen, cutting them to pieces. Saladin threw his reserves into the melee, assailing the centre of the Christian column.

Richard ended his pursuit of Saladin's cavalry and led his horsemen back into the battle in the middle of his line, overwhelming the Muslim troops and forcing them to withdraw, leaving hundreds of dead and wounded on the battlefield.

The following morning the crusaders resumed their march, arriving at Jaffa three days later, while the Saracens continued to harry their flank and rear. After reaching the town, the Christians encamped and rested from the arduous journey from Acre. The defensive works at Jaffa had been demolished by the Muslims and the king put his men to work repairing and rebuilding the fortifications. Meeting with his council of advisors to decide the next move, he was persuaded to make Jaffa his main base of operations and launch his campaign to seize Jerusalem from the town.

Richard, realizing the advance and capture of Jerusalem was a formidable task, decided to achieve his objective through negotiations with Saladin. Messages between the two rulers were exchanged, but Saladin rejected the crusaders' terms. Despite the refusal, Richard sent additional letters to the Muslim leader and finally an arrangement was made to meet with al-Adil, brother of the sultan. During their talks the two rivals developed a cordial relationship, becoming friends. Richard continued to demand the return of Jerusalem, but after no settlement was reached he proposed the marriage of his sister Joanna to the sultan's brother, with the two of them ruling Jerusalem and the recently conquered coastline as co-monarchs. When Joanna was informed of the offer, she refused to marry an infidel and no resolution was found.

With his negotiations with the Muslims at an impasse, in late October the Plantagenet king decided to take Jerusalem by force. He moved his host to the east, but his progress was slowed by rain and the Saracens' harassing attacks against his foraging parties and lines of communications. Marching through the winter rains for nearly a month, the army was still 15 miles from the city. The storms now intensified, forcing the king to encamp at Ramleh, the men enduring living in saturated tents and mud, while forced to eat rotting food. During the march down the coast, the crusader army had suffered large losses, and with many of the soldiers also pilgrims, who planned to return home after seizing Jerusalem, Richard believed the crusaders could not hold the city if it was captured.

Given the reality of the military situation, he halted his army, ordering his men to withdraw to Jaffa.

The dispirited soldiers trekked back to the west in the continuing cold rains over almost impassable muddy roads. The crusaders had nearly reached the city that they had left their families and risked their lives for, only to have their dreams shattered with their quest almost in sight. During the march, Richard decided to swing his army south-westward to the town of Ascalon and rebuild its defences, which had been destroyed by the Muslims. He remained in the town for the next four months, transforming Ascalon into a formidable fortress, which gave him a base of operations to launch raids against Saladin's lines of communication with Egypt.

While the crusaders were rebuilding Ascalon, in Acre hostilities erupted in the multinational garrison for control of the city, with the French and Genoese battling the troops from Pisa over the rightful King of Jerusalem. The French and their allies rallied around Marquis Conrad of Montferrat, while the Pisans supported Guy of Lusignan. To reunify the Christians, Richard summoned the leading crusaders to Ascalon to resolve the impasse. On 16 April the men unanimously elected Conrad king, putting an end to the festering dispute. To compensate Guy for his loss, Richard arranged for him to assume the monarchy of Cyprus. Conrad's reign was, however, short, and after only a week on the throne he was assassinated. The king's wife, Isabella, was acknowledged as successor and soon married Count Henry of Champagne, who became King of Jerusalem. Henry's rule was widely accepted by the Christians and there was no resumption of hostilities.

After reunifying the war effort in Acre against the Saracens, in the spring Richard set out south from Ascalon down the coastal road, seizing the Muslim fortress at Darum. The capture of the town allowed the king to expand his attacks against the Saracen supply lines to Egypt. While in Darum, Richard received a message notifying him that his brother John was stirring up trouble in England, while Philip II was active in Normandy with his army. With his presence needed in Europe to protect his lands, the king decided to make one more push for Jerusalem. On 6 June he set off, and in five days reached the location where the army had earlier been forced to withdraw. As the Christians proceeded forward, scouts located a contingent of Saracens on the roadway ahead and Richard took a strong force of knights to charge into them. He quickly overpowered Saladin's men, compelling them to flee. The crusader horsemen pursued the Muslims, and as they reached the summit of a large hilltop, the city of Jerusalem was visible in the distance. The view from the hill was King Richard's first and only sight of the holy city. After returning to his encampment, he held a meeting with his lieutenants to discuss whether or not the campaign against Jerusalem should continue. The defences of Jerusalem were formidable and well-garrisoned by Muslim soldiers, with Saladin in personal command. Lacking the troop strength to take and hold the city, Richard ordered his men to fall back once more to Jaffa.

Following his return to Jaffa in July 1192, Richard left a strong garrison to defend the fortified town and returned up the coastal road to Acre. Upon reaching the city, he reopened peace negotiations with the Muslims. After exchanges of messages, Saladin agreed to leave the captured coastal towns under Christian control and grant pilgrims safe access to Jerusalem if Richard destroyed the fortifications at Ascalon. The king refused to demolish the town and the talks reached an impasse. While negotiations to find a resolution continued, on 27 July the sultan launched a surprise attack against Jaffa. He besieged the town, breaking through a large section of the defensive walls on the second day. The crusaders rallied around the breach, driving back the enemy troops in a savage hand-to-hand struggle. The Christians held the walls through the night, but during the next day were compelled to withdraw into the citadel. When the king learned of the battle, he assembled a small force of knights, spearmen and archers, sailing down the coast and arriving at the siege on 31 July. He beached his galleys and waded ashore. The crusaders charged into the occupied town, quickly overwhelming Saladin's men and forcing them to flee. The Christians redeployed to the outskirts of Jaffa, establishing a defensive line, while the Saracens fell back several miles. During the morning of 4 August, the sultan's cavalrymen and infantry unleashed another attack against the encampment. As the enemy charged, the king formed his troops into a half-circle, with the foot soldiers kneeling in the front rank with their spears forming a deadly defensive barrier, while the archers and crossbowmen fired volleys of arrows at the fast-approaching Muslims, beating them back. The Saracens charged again and again, but were unable to penetrate the crusaders' line. As the sultan's soldiers withdrew, Richard led a counterattack with his spearmen and horse soldiers, compelling the Saracens to abandon the battlefield and retreat to Jerusalem, leaving their dead and wounded behind.

While Richard stayed at Jaffa repairing its defences, peace negotiations were renewed with Saladin through his brother al-Adil. The talks dragged on through August until Richard finally agreed to abandon Ascalon. Under the treaty's terms, a three-year truce was approved, the Christians were granted unfettered access to the holy sites in Jerusalem, while the captured coastal towns and surrounding countryside were to remain under crusader control. After the agreement was signed, the Plantagenet monarch turned over the government of the Kingdom of Jerusalem to Henry of Champagne, and on 9 October 1192, after spending sixteen months in the Holy Land, departed from Acre, never to return. While the Third Crusade had failed to recapture Jerusalem, Richard had re-established a large part of the Crusader Kingdom, which remained in Christian hands for most of the next 100 years.

Richard departed from Acre, planning to sail to Marseille and proceed through the French Duchy of Toulouse, then overland across his domains to Normandy. During the voyage west, he altered his course, making for the island of Corfu after learning that the Count of Toulouse, Raymond V, was preparing to capture him. The count was a vassal of the king, but relations between them had been strained for over six years. When the crusader fleet reached the harbour at Corfu, Richard made contact with the captains of three pirate ships, hiring them to transport him and a small party up the coastline to the town of Ragusa in south-eastern Italy. After coming ashore near Ragusa, the crusaders entered the town disguised as returning pilgrims from the Holy Land. Remaining in the area for several days, Richard became increasingly concerned the authorities would recognize him and hired ships to take his group farther up the coastline. During the voyage the small fleet was struck by a violent winter storm and the vessels were thrown against the shore. Abandoning their ships, the king and his companions continued their journey and moved inland. When they were questioned by local officials, Richard told them they were merchants travelling home from the Levant. As they advanced farther north toward Vienna, they were recognized and arrested by representatives of the Duke of Austria, Leopold V.

King Richard was taken from Vienna to the fortress at Durenstein and held for ransom. Leopold V, who had earlier been the leader of the German contingent at the siege of Acre, had been humiliated by the English king for placing his personal banner on the captured walls of the fortress alongside those of Richard and Philip II. By his actions he was claiming his equal status with the two kings, and was forced to remove the flag. With the king now in his custody, the duke was determined to collect a large ransom for his earlier embarrassment. Under orders from Leopold, Richard was placed under constant guard within the formidable walls of the hilltop fortress overlooking the Danube. When the duke's overlord, Emperor Henry VI, was informed of the English king's capture, he demanded possession of him. In mid-February 1193 Richard was moved to Regensburg at the court of the emperor. While he was held in captivity, Philip II sent envoys informing him that he was no longer considered a vassal of the Capetian regime and their treaties were now void, which gave the French freedom to attack Plantagenet lands in western France. Richard began personal negotiations with the emperor for his release, refusing to accept his initial demands. Following further discussions, he agreed to pay a large indemnity of 50,000 pounds in silver, while Henry VI pledged to act as intermediary between the French and English kings to restore peace. After the terms were settled, in March Richard began raising the large sum of money from Speyer in Germany for his release, making contact with his government officials, nobles and churchmen. In England the justiciars imposed a new tax requiring all subjects to pay a quarter of their yearly revenues to the crown, which was collected by the sheriffs in the counties and the bishops from the churches. Queen Eleanor was made responsible for the supervision and accounting of the ransom moneys and the selection of hostages demanded by the emperor. As the English continued to collect the ransom during the summer and autumn of 1193, Richard was compelled to make a separate agreement with the French regime to prevent King Philip from exerting pressure on the emperor to keep him in captivity. Under the terms of their treaty, Philip secured the right to retain the lands he had recently occupied in the Plantagenet fiefdoms, while Richard was required to offer homage to the Capetian crown for his French fiefs, pay an indemnity and provide four castles as security for the satisfaction of the agreement. By December the transfer of the ransom funds had begun, and on 4 February 1194 at Mainz, King Richard was released from imperial custody in a grand ceremony attended by numerous high-ranking English and German churchmen and magnates. Following the festivities, Richard and Henry VI sent letters to Prince John and Philip II demanding they return to the Plantagenet realm the lands, castles and towns seized by them.

In the aftermath of his release, Richard and his English entourage proceeded down the Rhine to Antwerp, from where they sailed across the Channel, landing at Sandwich on 13 March 1194. Three days later he made his formal entrance into London amid widespread rejoicing. He rode through the city, gaily decorated with bright banners and thronged with hundreds of cheering spectators. At the cathedral of St Paul's, the clergy symbolically celebrated the reunion of the sovereign with his realm.

During Richard's absence in the Holy Land, Prince John, with a force of mercenary troops, broke his pledge of fealty, seizing several castles in northern England and was recognized as king by several barons. Following the celebrations in London, Richard set out to the north to reimpose his sovereignty over the rebellious magnates who had acknowledged John as their overlord. He first advanced against Nottingham, forcing the rebels to take refuge in the citadel. Realizing that Richard had returned from the crusade and was at the head of his army, they surrendered without opposition. As the king resumed his campaign of subjugation in the northern counties, the leader of Prince John's supporters, Robert de la Mare, agreed to unconditionally submit after learning of Nottingham's capitulation, surrendering his stronghold at Tickhill in Yorkshire. The quick capture of the two fortifications ended the revolt, with the followers of Prince John offering fealty to their overlord. Shortly after enforcing his rule over the English lords, the king travelled to Southwell to meet with the King of Scotland, William I. The Scottish monarch wanted territorial concessions in northern England for lands that had earlier been part of his realm. Richard refused to return the property but offered the Scots monetary concessions, which were accepted. Following his negotiations with the Scots, Richard rode to Winchester, where in the cathedral on 17 April he was anointed King of England by the Archbishop of Canterbury, signifying his reunion with the English kingdom. The coronation ceremony was attended by the dowager queen and her court, William I of

Scotland, high earls and barons and a multitude of commoners. Queen Berengaria was not in attendance and had not been with Richard for nearly two years, increasing the rumours of his homosexuality.

After securing his authority in England, Richard prepared to leave for the continent to regain his territories lost to the French during his absence in the Outreme. After a final flurry of appointments and meetings with his English churchmen and court officials, on 10 May he boarded a ship and set sail for Normandy with his army. Two days later the fleet of 100 ships landed at Barfleur in Normandy. From the port the English troops proceeded inland to Lisieux, east of Caen, where the king met his brother John, forgiving him for his rebellion in England. With familial peace restored, Richard moved his army into Aquitaine before swinging east to Vendome in search of the French king. At the small town he received reports from reconnaissance patrols that Capetian forces were only 10 miles away. He quickly mustered a contingent of fast-moving light infantry and cavalry, setting off to attack the enemy. He caught the rearguard, forcing them to retreat and leave their baggage train, including part of Philip II's treasury.

With the Capetian army withdrawing into the safety of the French kingdom, Richard marched his troops into Aquitaine to force the barons, who had transferred allegiance to King Philip, to submit. Geoffrey of Rancogne was an enthusiastic supporter of the French regime and the English king first advanced against him, overrunning his lands and seizing his castles in a lightning operation. He continued his campaign in Aquitaine, capturing additional fortified towns. As the Plantagenet offensive gained momentum, Philip agreed to resume peace talks. Under the guidance of a papal legate, an agreement was reached at Tillieres giving the French kingdom the territories currently held by its forces, while Richard was permitted to reinforce the towns he occupied and a general truce was to last until 1 November 1195.

Following the signing of the Treaty of Tillieres, the Plantagenet overlord returned to Normandy and after Philip disbanded his army Richard repudiated the agreement. Richard remained on the continent, travelling from castle to castle with his court, administering his empire and raising money to resume the war against the French, while also spending time hunting, playing games at night and listening to the music of travelling minstrels with his courtiers. During the interlude from the war, Richard became closely associated with many known homosexuals; warnings from the clergy to change his ways were repeatedly ignored. As the sovereign continued his association with his friends, in late March 1195 he became critically ill. Facing death, he called his priests to his bedside, confessing his sins and receiving absolution. As the king slowly recovered from his illness, he summoned Berengaria from Poitou and she once again became part of the royal household. To further gain forgiveness, the king made sizeable donations to churches and monasteries and regularly attended Mass.

In mid-July 1195 the English and French kings met near the castle of Le Vaudreuil to negotiate a permanent peace. As the discussions continued, Philip ordered the defensive works of the fortress destroyed to prevent their use by the English. When the walls suddenly collapsed, Richard ended the peace talks and attacked the French, pushing them back. As the English continued their attack, Philip quickly withdrew his forces over the Seine, destroying the bridge behind him and escaping.

While Richard waited for an opportunity to attack the French army, he sent the captain of his mercenaries, Mercadier, into Berry to reimpose Plantagenet rule over the southern region. During the following months there were only several brief skirmishes between the rival armies ,and in early August peace negotiations were reopened. After several months of failed talks, the war was renewed, when Philip II ordered his troops into Normandy destroying the town of Dieppe, while he led his forces into Berry and besieged the castle of Issoudun. Richard responded by taking a large contingent of knights and infantry into Berry, driving the French away from Issoudun. After Philip was compelled to abandon the siege, he sent messages to his rival proposing the renewal of talks. On 5 December the kings met alone and agreed to a temporary truce lasting until 13 January 1196. The treaty also included a clause for them to meet again on the expiration date of the truce to negotiate a permanent peace treaty.

After spending the Christmas season at Poitiers, in the new year Richard and his counsellors journeyed to Louviers in Normandy to resume peace talks with Philip. The Plantagenet negotiators met with their French counterparts for a week, hammering out an agreement that was accepted by both kings. Richard ceded his rights to the territories of Gisors and the Norman Vexin to the French, while Philip yielded his claims to Gascony, Berry and Eu. The boundary between both realms was established and a mutual exchange of prisoners was arranged. The Treaty of Louviers gave King Richard authority over most of Henry II's former demesne.

With peace restored to the borderlands, in April 1196 King Richard began to conspire to recover control over Brittany, which had regained a large measure of its former autonomy during his absence in the Third Crusade. To enforce his sovereign privileges, he claimed the right of guardianship over the ten-year-old Count of Brittany, Arthur, as his overlord and uncle. To retain their independence, the Breton warlords refused to turn over the young count to the English, sending him to the court of Philip II, where he was given sanctuary. Thwarted in his attempts to peacefully impose his rule, Richard marched his army into Brittany and by 19 April had enforced his authority. The king now claimed that by giving refuge to Arthur, the French had violated the terms of the Louviers Treaty and began building a series of fortifications to protect the strategic Vexin. The largest and strongest of his new castles was Gaillard, which guarded the approaches to Rouen. The hilltop castle was constructed on the summit of a large outcropping and was considered impregnable.

As construction on Richard's many castles continued, in July Plantagenet troops seized the fortress at Nonancourt, while King Philip besieged the stronghold at Aumale. After his forces seized control of Nonancourt, Richard journeyed to Aumale to break the siege, but his attacks were repelled. He next redeployed his men to the fortress at Gaillon and laid siege to it. During the fighting, the king was struck in the leg by the bolt from a crossbow and was immobile for a month while the wound slowly healed.

While Richard was at war with the Capetian kingdom in north-west France, to the south in Toulouse its new count, Raymond VI, rebelled against the overlordship of the Plantagenets. He attacked the forces of Richard and his allies in Toulouse to regain his lost independence. Richard, preparing for a large offensive against the French, needed loyal allies in the south. When he was approached by the Toulouse count's envoy suggesting peace talks, he quickly agreed. Under the terms of their resulting treaty, Richard abandoned his rights to Toulouse, while the count consented to his marriage to the king's sister, Joanna, strongly binding his countship to the Plantagenet regime. While negotiating with Raymond VI, the monarch also forged alliances with the Count of Boulogne and Baldwin IX of Flanders, securing additional allies in his fight against the French realm.

In the aftermath of Richard's treaty with Count Raymond VI, he intensified his preparations for the offensive against Philip. He ordered reinforcements from England and Wales, while strengthening his defensive works in his French territories and hiring additional mercenaries. New taxes and levies were imposed, and England was again hard-pressed for money. Richard spent the first half of 1197 building new fortifications and remaining for long periods at Gaillard, supervising the construction of the castle. While the building of the defences continued, he unleased harassing attacks against the French, burning the town of Saint-Valary and sending troops to seize fortifications in Berry, while in May his brother John and Mercadier captured the long-time ally of the Capetian throne, Bishop Philip of Beauvais.

In August 1197 the Plantagenet ally Baldwin IX unleashed an incursion against the town of Arras in north-western France. With his city under siege, King Philip brought his army to the relief of the defenders. As the French neared Arras, Baldwin IX withdrew his forces from the siege, ambushing the enemy's troops as they followed him. In the battle Philip's contingent of troops was outmanoeuvred by the count and compelled to surrender. At the ensuing meeting with the count, Philip agreed to confer with Richard near Gaillard in mid-September to discuss peace terms. When the two rivals and Baldwin met, they agreed to a truce running until 13 January 1199 and to retain their current territorial holdings.

During the next year peace in France was preserved and Richard was occupied preparing for the resumption of hostilities. He ordered additional reinforcements from England, demanding more taxes from his subjects. As the Plantagenets in western France strengthened their fortifications and built a stronger army, the Holy Roman Emperor Henry VI died, leaving his infant son as heir. Richard was resolved to prevent the French king from securing an ally on his eastern border and conspired to procure the kingship of Germany for his nephew Otto of Brunswick. When a rival faction in Germany began promoting Henry VI's brother Philip of Swabia for the German crown, Richard sent envoys to Rome to influence Pope Innocent III to sponsor his candidate. King Philip actively supported the inheritance rights of the Swabian duke, sending representatives to the Holy See to promote his interest. While the pope was listening to the arguments of the rival factions, Richard was occupied using his influence in Germany with his allies and friends to advocate for his nephew. In the early spring of 1198, Pope Innocent III announced his choice of Otto as the next King of Germany. With the endorsement of the papacy behind his candidacy, Otto of Brunswick was elected King of Germany by the diet. With Richard's nephew now on the German throne, relations between the regimes became extremely close. Through his political manoeuvring, the king had succeeded in further isolating the realm of Philip II.

Following the signing of the truce at Gaillard in September 1198, the Plantagenet and French regimes honoured the agreement until the peace was broken a year later, when Richard's ally Baldwin IX laid siege and captured the castle at Saint-Omer. Learning of the loss of his stronghold, Philip retaliated by unleashing a punitive raid into Normandy, burning towns, terrorizing the inhabitants and destroying crops. The hostilities escalated further, when Richard led his army into the territories of the French kingdom besieging two castles. Philip brought up a force of 300 knights and infantry to break the sieges. After receiving reports from his patrols that Capetian forces were moving against him, Richard assembled a contingent of soldiers from his army and advanced to assail the foe. He deployed his troops to ambush the approaching French host. As the main force of the army waited for the French, Richard took a detachment of knights, riding ahead to search for the enemy. When he located the French, he led his mounted troops forward crashing into the Capetians and forcing them to flee toward the protection of their castle at Gisors. The Gisors fortress was protected by a moat, and as King Philip and his horsemen galloped over the bridge, it suddenly collapsed, throwing the king into the water. He was rescued by his men after nearly drowning. Following the encounter at Gisors, the Plantagenet and French soldiers continued to clash in several skirmishes until the Archbishop of Rouen intervened to mediate another peace agreement. The archbishop failed to secure a settlement but arranged a truce extending until mid-January

1199, when the two monarchs pledged to meet again and attempt to negotiate a permanent peace.

Richard spent the Christmas season of 1198 at his Domfront stronghold, where he was joined by Pope Innocent III's legate, Cardinal Peter of Capua. Before the scheduled January peace conference, the papal legate met with both monarchs to begin the talks. When the two rulers gathered on 13 January 1199, Peter of Capua joined the meeting to act as mediator. At the urgings of the cardinal, both kings agreed to a five-year truce but failed to reach terms for a permanent peace.

With the truce agreement now in place, King Richard decided to proceed to Aquitaine. While at Chinon, he heard that valuable figurines of gold and silver had been found by a local farmer and claimed by Viscount Aimar of Limoges. As the viscount's overlord, Richard demanded possession of the treasures. When Aimar only turned over part of the valuable discovery, Richard mustered a small force of knights and foot-soldiers, moving against the viscount's castle at Chalus and placing it under siege. He began mining the fortress's walls and prepared his men to attack, as his archers fired a steady stream of arrows at the defenders. During the fighting, Richard was struck in the left shoulder by the bolt from a crossbow. After the tip of the missile was removed, the wound became inflamed. The infection spread and gangrene set in. Richard's condition became steadily worse, and after receiving the last sacraments, he died on 6 April 1199. The Plantagenet ruler of England, Normandy, Aquitaine and Anjou was buried at Fontevrault, near the tombs of his father and mother. King Richard I died without a direct heir, and before his death named his brother Prince John as successor. John ruled the Plantagenet lands for seventeen years that were defined by wars with the French monarchy and his barons in England and western France. By 1206 he had lost Normandy, Anjou and parts of Aquitaine to Philip II, and over the following years, as discontent escalated in England against his regime's policies, civil war broke out. When the rebels seized control of London, King John was forced to negotiate a peace agreement, meeting the barons at Runnymede on 19 June 1215. In the resulting *Magna Carta*, he agreed to limits on his royal powers and assured the magnates of their feudal rights. Soon after signing the agreement, John repudiated the *Magna Carta* and the civil war resumed, continuing until his death in October 1216.

Selected Sources:

Barber, Richard, *The Devil's Crown – A History of Henry II and his Sons.*
Bingham, Caroline, *The Crowned Lions – The Early Plantagenet Kings.*
Bridge, Anthony, *Richard the Lionheart.*
Brundage, James A., *Richard Lion Heart.*
Frazer, Antonia, *The Lives of the Kings and Queens of England.*
Gillingham, John, *Richard I.*
Harvey, John, *The Plantagenets.*
Matthews, John and Stewart, Bob, *Warriors of Christendom.*
Miller, David, *Richard The Lionheart – The Mighty Crusader.*
Saul, Nigel, *The Three Richards.*

Chapter Seven

Frederick II

Lord of the World

In 1236 the reigning Holy Roman Emperor, Frederick II, summoned a diet to Piacenza to reimpose his authority over the increasingly rebellious northern Italian city-states. When the assembly was thwarted by the intervention of Pope Gregory IX, the emperor began preparations to invade the mutinous cities. In August 1237 he crossed the Alps from Germany with 2,000 knights to enforce his sovereignty over the recalcitrant Lombard League. After reaching Verona, the emperor united his forces with his loyal Italian allies and moved against the rebels. As the imperial forces marched against the rebel city of Mantua, they were reinforced with over 6,000 horsemen and infantrymen from Frederick II's Kingdom of Sicily, which included a large contingent of Apulian Saracen archers and slingers, augmenting his army to over 15,000 soldiers. After securing the peaceful submissions of Mantua and Bergamo, Frederick invaded the territory of Brescia. While the imperial forces were capturing several towns, the leader of the troops from the Lombard League, Pietro Tiepolo of Milan, mustered an army of nearly 10,000 men and hastened to meet Frederick. In late November 1237 the imperial vanguard clashed with the Lombards near the town of Cortenuova. Taken by surprise, Tiepolo withdrew his soldiers into Cortenuova, establishing a defensive line centred on the Carroccio, a four-wheeled war wagon used as an alter adorned with the Milanese standard and religious relics. The imperial cavalry charged into the Milanese defenders and inflicted heavy casualties. The rebels rallied around the Carroccio, fighting valiantly and holding their position, despite repeated attacks. During the night, Tiepolo ordered his surviving men to abandon the fray and fall back. As the Lombards retreated at dawn with the Carroccio, Frederick ordered his infantry and cavalry to attack them. The withdrawing enemy was quickly overwhelmed, with many thousands killed or captured and the sacred war wagon seized. Following his victory Frederick made a triumphant entry into the city of Cremona, with the Carroccio pulled by an elephant. He was now at the summit of his reign, ruling a vast empire that included Germany, Burgundy, most of Italy and the Kingdom of Jerusalem.

Emperor Frederick II was an extraordinary ruler of ambition, energy, ability and culture, contemporary chroniclers calling him 'The wonder of the world and first European'. Frederick was heir to his father's vast empire and recognized as king-apparent to Germany and southern Italy and emperor of the Holy Roman Empire. He was the only child of the German King Henry VI, of the Hohenstaufen family, and Queen Constance of Sicily, and was born on 26 December 1194 at Jesi in central Italy. The birth of the child took place in a tent in the town square, witnessed by numerous cardinals and bishops to assure the legitimacy of the royal heir. Constance was over forty years old and had borne no previous children, making the unusual precautions necessary. Frederick spent his first three years at Foligns in the household of a noble Italian lady, while Henry VI and his queen attended to the affairs of state.

Frederick's future inheritance of Italy and Germany was thrown into turmoil in September 1197 when Henry VI died at Messina after being stricken with malaria. Frederick had earlier been acknowledged as successor to the Holy Roman throne, but Pope Innocent III voided the decree. In the wake of the decision civil war erupted in Germany between the forces of the Hohenstaufens and German princes, while in Sicily a wave of anti-foreign sentiments swept through the kingdom. As the daughter of the former Norman King of Sicily, Roger II, Constance was recognized as regent for her minor son, ruling the realm in his name. She had spent many years of her life in a convent and lacked the training and experience of a skilled ruler. The defence of the monarchy in Sicily became her primary objective and she saw no advantage in pressing her son's rights to Germany. The queen surrounded herself with local counsellors and laboured to exclude her husband's German advisers from her government. Constance abandoned Henry VI's policy of confrontation with the Holy See, readily accepting Pope Innocent III's advice and assistance. As the queen struggled to safeguard Frederick's Italian inheritance, in early 1198 she suffered a serious illness. Facing death, she arranged the joint coronation of herself and her son at Palermo. She intensified her contacts with the papacy and opened negotiations to secure Innocent III's acceptance of the guardianship of Frederick. A settlement was reached after Constance agreed to appoint Bishop Walter of Pelear as head of the regency council. After a reign of fourteen months, Queen Constance died in late November 1198 and the bishop took custody of the four-year-old Frederick in the name of the pope.

Following Queen Constance's assumption of the regency council in 1197, she had been compelled to contend with escalating hostilities of the German knights who had accompanied Henry VI south into the Kingdom of Sicily. Proceeding under her powers as regent, Constance tried in vain to force the Germans from the realm. Led by Markward of Anweiler, the knights ignored the banishment decree and established a powerbase in southern Italy in Ancona, aggressively challenging the regency council. In the aftermath of Constance's death, the civil war was resumed with a new fury, and for his protection Frederick was forced to move from one safe haven to another. During the continuing hostilities, Markward produced the alleged last will of Henry VI, which named him regent of Sicily and guardian for Frederick. Acting as the rightful ruler of Frederick's kingdom, Markward invaded Sicily in November 1199, and with ships provided by the Count of Malta landed his troops at Trapani in the west of the island. As the Germans advanced eastward with the objective of seizing the capital at Palermo to enforce their perceived rights, Markward aggressively sought the assistance of the local Muslim population for his military campaign. When informed of the invasion, Innocent III sent a letter to the Sicilians notifying them that Markward was a supporter of Muslims and a threat to Christians, and should be strongly opposed. The retention of Sicily by forces friendly to the Holy See was vital to the pope's plans for a new crusade to recover Jerusalem from the Saracens. To encourage resistance to the knights' attack, Innocent III granted the same privileges as a crusader to all Sicilians who fought against Markward.

The papacy lacked the military might to carry the fight to the invading knights and formed an alliance with the French Count Walter III of Brienne, whose wife was the daughter of a previous Sicilian king. With the promise of the Principality of Taranto and County of Lecce, Walter

III entered the fray in the service of the Holy See. Under Walter's command, the papal army was assembled, supplemented with the count's French forces of sixty knights and forty mounted sergeants. The papal troops marched against the Germans, who were led by Markward's ally, Dipold of Acerra, defeating them at Capua and Canne on the Italian mainland, giving the pope control over much of southern Italy. After imposing his authority in the north, Walter sailed to Sicily, landing on the west of the island near the city of Monreale, his knights and mounted sergeants leading the way. The Holy See's soldiers advanced against Monreale, compelling the garrison to surrender after a brief siege. While the pope's forces had gained a foothold on Sicily, Markward was steadily consolidating and widening his powerbase in the island. Struggling to dislodge the strongly embedded Germans with only a small papal army, the pope's local representative, Bishop Walter of Pelear, offered to divide the Kingdom of Sicily, giving the island to Markward while the monarchy's mainland territories would remain under the rule of Innocent III as regent for Frederick. When the offer was accepted, the bishop departed for the mainland, leaving Frederick in the care of his brother, the Count of Manopello, at Palermo.

Markward soon abandoned the papal agreement and in the spring of 1201 moved his army against Palermo, which had remained under royal rule. The city offered only token resistance before opening its gates to the Germans. When the invaders broke into the royal palace, the seven-year-old Frederick was seized by Markward after valiantly attempting to defend himself. With possession of the king, Markward could now rule the kingdom in the name of Frederick with a degree of legality.

In late 1202 Markward died near Messina in Sicily and the German warlord, William of Capperon, assumed command of the army. Frederick, under the guardianship of Capperon, spent the next several years passing intermittently from the control of one regent to another. During William's rule, an agreement was negotiated with the Holy See giving Innocent III authority over Sicily, while the Germans' hold on the island was acknowledged by the Church as its overlord. Capperon managed to retain power in Sicily until 1208, when his hold on the government was briefly challenged by Dipold of Acerra before Bishop Walter of Pelear forced him out of the regime and seized control in the name of the Holy See. The pope had been forced to deal with the hostile German rulers of Sicily, but now with Walter as his papal representative in Palermo he regained control of Frederick and the monarchy. Innocent III continued to act as Frederick's regent until late 1208, when the king reached the age of majority at fourteen. During the period of the regency, several different tutors were provided by the guardians for Frederick's education. As Frederick neared the age of three, Cardinal Cencio Savelli, who later became Pope Honorius III, was appointed as his first instructor. Frederick was a highly precocious student, excelling in all of his studies. With the royal court in frequent turmoil, he never experienced a systematic education, receiving only irregular tutoring. Growing up in the multinational port of Palermo, the king was exposed to the culture of Muslims, Byzantines and native Italians, which laid the foundation for his self-taught education. In the port-city's marketplaces, he encountered Normans, Saracens, Jews, Greeks and Italians, learning their customs and speech. Frederick learned to speak six languages: Sicilian, German, Latin, Greek Arabic and French. Exposure to Muslim culture in Palermo guided the future king's mind to an appreciation of the arts, literature and science, providing a broad view of philosophy, while greatly influencing his character. He was taught to read and write by his infrequent tutors and studied history, mathematics, religion, science and philosophy. Under the instruction of German knights, he became skilled in the handling of the sword and spear and spent long hours practicing archery. He was particularly skilful in fencing and equestrianism. Throughout his life he had an interest in learning and was always anxious to discuss a wide array of subjects with noted scholars.

While Frederick was in Sicily under the protection of his regents, in far-away Germany a power struggle for the German monarchy developed after the death of Henry VI. As the only child of the king, Frederick had the strongest right to the German throne, but his uncle, Philip of Swabia, and the Duke of Saxony and Bavaria, Otto, challenged for the title. When Otto agreed to respect papal rights in Sicily and Philip continued to claim his inheritance over the kingdom, Pope Innocent III sided with the Duke of Saxony and Bavaria. With the support of Rome, Otto defended his entitlement to Germany but lacked the military power to win acceptance as sovereign. As more German princes united in support of Philip, he sent an army into Italy under the Bishop of Worms, Liupold, to regain control of the central region of the kingdom, which had recently been recovered from Germany by the Holy See. Innocent III soon realized his continued promotion of Otto was dangerous and negotiated a reconciliation with the Swabian duke As Philip's claim to Germany grew steadily stronger, in 1208 he was murdered by an embittered former supporter. With the elimination of Philip's threat, Otto IV was acknowledged as King of Germany by the majority of princes and on 4 October 1209 was crowned Holy Roman Emperor in Rome by Innocent III, greatly reducing Frederick of Sicily's chances of ever ruling the northern kingdom. However, many supporters of Philip refused to acknowledge the new sovereign and turned to the Sicilian king as their claimant to the German throne.

In early 1209 Frederick was crowned King of Sicily and began his independent rule of the realm, with Innocent III retaining suzerainty over the kingdom. While still regent for Frederick, the pope negotiated the young king's marriage to a woman ten years his senior, Constance of Aragon, the widow of the Hungarian ruler. The Sicilian monarch signed the marriage contract in 1209. While negotiations with Aragon were being held, Frederick was leading his army in a campaign to impose his authority over rebellious barons along the eastern coast of Sicily. Constance arrived at Palermo in the summer with 500 Aragonese infantrymen and knights, who had a reputation throughout Europe for their fighting skills. The marriage ceremony took place in the capital in September. The elite Aragon troops were part of the marriage contract and were expected to reinforce the Sicilian monarch's campaign to subdue the realm's rebel barons, but many of them died in Palermo from an epidemic shortly after the wedding.

The new queen was from a royal court known for its culture and elegance, while Frederick had grown up with little refinement and limited training in etiquette. Despite their difference in age, Constance and Frederick became close during their thirteen years of marriage and she bestowed considerable counsel and civility to her young husband. In 1210 the future Hohenstaufen succession of the Sicilian monarchy was ensured with the birth of a son, named Henry after the king's father. During his lifetime Frederick had many wives and mistresses, but

Constance remained his greatest love. At the queen's funeral in 1222, Frederick displayed genuine sorrow at her loss, placing his golden crown on her coffin.

Soon after the marriage ceremony, the young monarch began to exert his sovereignty over his recalcitrant warlords, who had expanded their territorial holdings during Frederick's minority and were reluctant to relinquish their newly acquired properties. He assembled a contingent of soldiers and forced the nobles to abandon the lands. When several of the barons refused to obey the edict, they were arrested and executed. As the monarch expanded his campaign against the rogue barons, many Sicilian lords withdrew their allegiance to the Hohenstaufen crown, joining Emperor Otto IV, who was attempting to reimpose German hegemony over southern Italy.

In the months following his coronation in Rome, Otto IV had imposed his authority over the imperial lands in northern and central Italy. He proceeded from city to city reclaiming the rights of the Holy Roman Empire, while in Sicily Frederick was regaining Hohenstaufen sovereignty over his inherited lands. After securing his Italian properties, Otto moved south, invading Frederick's Sicilian kingdom. When the emperor entered the southern regime, he was excommunicated by Innocent III and his imperial subjects were freed from their oaths of allegiance. Otto ignored the pope's decree and advanced against the towns of Apulia, which opened their gates to him without a fight. The Hohenstaufen king had not yet consolidated his rule over his Sicilian realm and was forced to withdraw his forces from the Italian mainland. The emperor continued his campaign and by mid-1211 much of Frederick's territory was in Otto's hands. Frederick managed to hold on to Palermo and a few other towns, but his chances of retaining his inherited monarchy looked bleak. He kept a ship moored in Palermo harbour ready to carry him to safety in North Africa, and attempted unsuccessfully to negotiate a settlement with the imperial regime but the advancing emperor had little interest.

As Otto IV solidified his hold on the southern Italian mainland, he began preparations for the crossing to Sicily. While the Sicilian king reinforced his defences for the anticipated imperial invasion, Pope Innocent III's envoys were active in Germany in support of the Hohenstaufen cause. The Archbishop of Mayence, Siegfried, and the

King of Bohemia raised a rebellion to advance the candidacy of Frederick to the German throne. As support for the emperor began to wane, Innocent III issued a manifesto to the princes of the empire exhorting them to dethrone Otto and elect Frederick monarch. Near the end of February 1211, the mutinous German princes assembled at Nuremberg, voting to depose Otto and elect Frederick as the new emperor of the Holy Roman Empire. Envoys were sent to Sicily to invite the Sicilian king to accept the imperial throne. Each of the German princes personally wrote a letter to Frederick assuring him of their loyalty.

While the Hohenstaufen king was enforcing his suzerainty over his rebellious lords, many northern Italians, who had earlier backed Henry VI, revolted against Otto IV, accepting Frederick as their new emperor. The outbreaks of armed rebellion in Germany and northern Italy compelled Otto to abandon his Sicilian campaign in November 1211 and move against the rebels in Germany. On his way north, he stopped at several cities to settle disputes and appoint officials to local governments that were loyal to him. The important cities of Milan and Pisa continued to endorse Otto, but the citizens of Genoa and many other towns threw their support behind Frederick.

In early 1212 representatives from the Nuremberg Diet arrived in Palermo, extending the offer of the German monarchy to Frederick. The king's hold on the Kingdom of Sicily was precarious and many of his mainland barons had retained their allegiance to Otto's rule. Frederick's advisors cautioned him about leaving his Sicilian realm while his support from the nobles was still questionable, urging him to remain in Italy and solidify his power. He had no ties to Germany and questioned whether this was the time to travel north and risk his overthrow in Sicily by rebels during his absence. Unable to reach a decision, in March Frederick set out for Rome to seek the advice of Innocent III.

The pontiff had consistently lobbied to keep the German and Italian kingdoms under separate rulers, but now approved Frederick's assumption of the imperial crown. Before giving his approval, the pope secured the king's pledge to repudiate the Sicilian monarchy in favour of his infant son and appoint his wife as regent. As part of his agreement with the Holy See, on 25 March 1212 Frederick knelt before the pontiff, pledging feudal homage to the Church in the name of his son for Sicily.

Before Frederick departed for Germany, the pope crowned Henry as King of Sicily, while Bishop Walter of Pelear was recalled to serve as advisor to Constance during Frederick's absence in the north.

Soon after receiving the blessings of the pontiff, Frederick proceeded to the west coast of Italy with a small entourage and sailed to Genoa. He remained in the port-city for three months, staying with Simone Doria, a Genoese consul and admiral. The king negotiated a commercial agreement with Doria's family during his stay and confirmed the merchants' trading privileges in Sicily. While in Genoa, Frederick borrowed money from the Dorias to supplement his small treasury. His journey was continued in late July, reaching Pavia overland without encountering the roving bands of Milanese militiamen who were searching for him. He left the city on 29 July with a contingent of Pavian horsemen serving as his bodyguards. When he reached the Lambro River, his party was attacked by the Milanese. Before departing from Pavia, the king had made arrangements to meet a force of soldiers at the river from the friendly city of Cremona. Hearing the sounds of the battle, the Cremonese rushed to Frederick's rescue, escorting him to their city.

After remaining in Cremona for a short period, Frederick continued north through Mantua and reached Verona at the foot of the Alps. Otto IV's forces were still lurking in the region searching for the king. The easiest route over the mountains was through the Brenner Pass, but troops friendly to the emperor stationed in the area forced Frederick to follow the Adige River through the Alps, descending into Switzerland on the shores of Lake Constance. Frederick and his soldiers moved from abbey to abbey receiving food and shelter as they made their way steadily toward the German border. While he proceeded through the countryside, the news of his arrival spread and troops rushed to his support. The king's men followed the course of the Rhine to the town of Basel, where they were welcomed by the Landgrave of Alsace and Rudolph II, Count of Habsburg. After resting and receiving pledges of allegiance from the rulers, the Sicilian sovereign turned north along the Rhine to the town of Haguenau in eastern France, which was his ancestral home. Entering the town, he received an enthusiastic reception from the residents and was escorted to the imperial palace, which had been built by his father.

While Frederick was making his triumphant passage into Germany, Emperor Otto IV was in France allied with King John of England against Philip II. John had formed an alliance with the German emperor to regain his lands in western France, and on 27 July 1214 their forces clashed with the French at Bouvines. The battle was a disaster for John and Otto, with the emperor barely escaping capture and his German army shattered. The imperial cause of Otto ended on the battlefield of Bouvines and he was never able to effectively resist Frederick's advance to the throne of the Holy Roman Empire.

When Frederick learned of Otto's defeat at Bouvines, he quickly marched his growing army deeper into Germany, systematically eliminating the remaining strongholds of the emperor. At the approach of Frederick's army, many towns surrendered and welcomed him, while those who retained their allegiance to Otto were attacked and forced to submit. Frederick pressed his campaign of conquest, and when the city of Aachen opened its gates to his army in July 1215 resistance was broken and Germany was now again under Hohenstaufen rule.

Following the capture of Aachen, plans were made for Frederick's second coronation. He had already been crowned king on 9 December 1213 at Frankfurt, but the ceremony was not held with all the representatives of Germany present and a new coronation was necessary to unite the entire kingdom under his rule. Aachen was chosen as the site for the imperial anointment, and on 15 July 1215 the ritual was performed at the city's historic cathedral, which had been originally constructed by the first Holy Roman Emperor, Charlemagne. A large crowd of princes attired in surcoats decorated with gold, silver and pearls, along with soldiers dressed in full armour and courtly ladies, gathered in the cathedral to witness Frederick's crowning. The Archbishop of Mayence performed the religious rites, while the Hohenstaufen sovereign lay prostrate before the great altar. He made a public confession of his faith and swore to deal justly with his subjects. When he sat on the throne of Charlemagne, the archbishop anointed him with holy oil and the silver crown of Germany was placed on his head.

During the ceremony Frederick took measures to closely associate himself with the first emperor of the Holy Roman Empire. He had the body of Charlemagne reinterred in a newly built reliquary of gold and silver in Aachen Cathedral and reconfirmed the rights originally granted by the first emperor to the city. Charlemagne was widely considered to have been an early crusader against pagan tribes in Eastern Europe, and following his coronation Frederick took the cross to follow in his path by opposing the Muslims in the Holy Land.

While Frederick was solidifying his rule over Germany, in Rome Pope Innocent III assembled the Fourth Lateran Council to approve the past acts of the Holy See and decide the future of the Church. As part of the agenda for the great assembly of over 1,500 prelates from the western and eastern Churches, the Council approved the deposition of Otto IV and acknowledged the election of Frederick as King of Germany. The Lateran Council endorsed the Fifth Crusade to recover the Holy Land from the Saracens, a decision that would greatly affect the future reign of King Frederick.

On 16 July 1216 Innocent III suddenly died at Perugia. Frederick was greatly saddened by the death of the pope, who had been his trusted mentor and advisor. Without his guidance, he was forced to depend on his own judgment and resources. Innocent had adopted a relentless campaign to expand the political power of the Church and his papacy had a significant effect on Frederick's past and future decisions. The pope's reign marked the apex of temporal power for the medieval Holy See, and his successors were unable to enforce his policies to advance the teachings of the Christian God. Two days after Innocent's death, the cardinals met at Perugia and elected Frederick's first tutor, Cencio Savelli, as the new pontiff, who took the name of Honorius III. The choice of the elderly and frail pope gave the twenty-two-year-old Frederick the opportunity to act without the control of the papacy. Honorius III assumed his papal reign with only a single agenda: to launch the new crusade as authorized by the Fourth Lateran Council. Frederick had earlier taken the cross of a crusader at Aachen, but now without the strong hand of Pope Innocent protecting his Sicilian and German kingdoms from usurpation during his absence in the Levant, he believed only his personal presence could protect his lands.

In late 1216 Constance travelled north with the young Henry to join Frederick in Germany after a separation of five years. After the years apart their earlier closeness had disappeared. Frederick had moved beyond the rule of the isolated Kingdom of Sicily and was now on the central stage of European politics. The queen stayed in Germany for only a short period before returning to Palermo and her rule of Sicily in the name of her husband. When she departed from the Hohenstaufen court, her son remained in the royal household to be raised by his father as successor to his dual monarchies. Frederick still had complete trust in his wife, and when he later travelled to Rome for his coronation as Holy Roman Emperor, arrangements were made for her to be crowned as empress in honor of her faithfulness to his cause.

Before his death, Innocent III had issued a decree for the knights of Europe to embark on a crusade to drive the infidels out of Outremer. Although he died before the Fifth Crusade was launched, Honorius III lost no time in pressing Frederick's participation in the expedition as one of the powerful rulers of Europe. The new German king was occupied securing his hegemony over his northern realm and had little interest in leaving Germany for a prolonged period. Yet despite his desire to remain at home, he needed the sponsorship and support of the papacy and continued to express his willingness to undertake the campaign. When the pope was forced out of Rome by its people for infringing on their perceived rights, Frederick came to his rescue, arranging a reconciliation between Honorius and the Romans. His successful intervention gave the king a weapon to continue his delays for the crusade.

In 1218 Otto IV died and the civil war that had raged for over twenty years in Germany finally ended. Over the last several years, Frederick had established his power and laws over his German princes and subjects. With Sicily under the peaceful regency of Constance and Germany pacified, Frederick's delays in answering the call for the crusade had lost their pretext. Despite the lack of a clear danger to his kingdoms, the king relentlessly pressed his delays, which were accepted by the pontiff.

By 1220 Frederick had secured his kingship in Germany and through his wife held unchallenged power over Sicily. He then undertook a political campaign to claim the crown of the Holy Roman Empire and attain the succession of his son to the title. In April he assembled a diet in Frankfurt, where the German princes elected Henry as King of the Romans: the first step for his son's future election as emperor. During his many correspondences with the pope concerning the crusade,

Frederick negotiated his coronation as emperor by the Church. He promised Honorius that with Henry's election as future king, the realms of Germany and Sicily would remain separate, fulfilling his earlier pledge to Innocent III.

The German king had been absent from Sicily for eight years, and in 1220 made preparations to return to his southern realm and receive the crown of the Holy Roman Emperor from Honorius in Rome. He left Henry to rule in Germany under the guidance of the Archbishop of Cologne, Englebert, and in August crossed the Alps into Italy. In the north he was joined by Constance, and they travelled from city to city, receiving a joyous reception on their way to Rome and his coronation. Many cities in Lombardy had been loyal friends of Otto IV and were suspicious of Frederick's future actions as emperor, but they kept the peace and sent emissaries to honour him.

In November 1220 Frederick and Constance reached Rome and began preparations for their coronations at St Peter's Basilica. On 22 November a brilliant assembly of princes, nobles and clergymen gathered for the service. The German and Sicilian king entered the church with his wife, advancing to Honorius III and kneeling before him. As Gregorian chants echoed through the basilica, Frederick made his confession of faith and, dressed in white robes, was taken to the altar to receive the symbols of his new office. After taking the Holy Lance and Golden Apple – signs of the spirit of the Church and the tasks awaiting the new emperor – Honorius III placed the golden crowns on the heads of Frederick II and Constance. At the conclusion of the service, the cross was brought forward and Frederick renewed his vows as a Christian warrior, swearing to sail to the Holy Land the following August. At the conclusion of the imperial ceremony there was a grand procession through the streets of the city. When the pope mounted his horse to ride in the parade, the emperor held his stirrups in a sign of the supremacy of the pontiff, and as Honorius rode forward Frederick followed on foot for a short distance before mounting his horse and joining the procession with Constance. A banquet ended the day, the emperor sitting on the right of the pontiff in a show of reverence. Frederick II's assumption of the imperial crown was widely acclaimed by the nobles, clergy and people throughout the Holy Roman Empire with only the barons and cities of Lombardy expressing little joy.

In the aftermath of his coronation, Frederick remained in Rome a few days distributing gifts and granting petitions before renewing his journey to the land he loved: Sicily. On his way south, he stopped in his Italian properties of Apulia and Calabria. During his long absence, the two mainland provinces had been taken over by recalcitrant princes and the emperor was resolved to reimpose his rule. He issued an edict voiding all titles granted after 1188, requiring the nobles to have their bestowments reviewed by a special court. Rebellious magnates were aggressively suppressed and their properties seized, while despite the protests of the pope, the special rights and privileges granted to the Holy See by Queen Constance were repealed. The emperor uncompromisingly banished dishonest clergymen and took back the sees issued by his mother, restoring them to his throne.

After imposing his reign on his mainland subjects, Frederick crossed the Strait of Messina to the island of Sicily. Upon his arrival in his beloved homeland, he received a triumphant welcome by his people. Shortly after reaching Sicily, Frederick held another court to verify the legitimacy of numerous privileges and titles granted during his eight-year absence. The emperor set to work voiding many titles given to the barons during the German occupation and those unlawfully seized while he was in Germany. Frederick was popular with the Sicilians, who took great pride in their native-born emperor, and he quickly regained control of the towns but still faced opposition from factions of rebellious Saracens and nobles. For his many accomplishments at such a young age, Frederick was considered the wonder of the world by his people.

While Frederick governed his German and Sicilian realms, in early September 1221 the Christian-held city of Damietta in Egypt was recaptured by the Saracens. The infidels had been willing to exchange Jerusalem for Damietta, but the leader of the Christian forces, Cardinal Pelagius of Albano, refused the offer. The cardinal had joined the crusade in 1218 as its papal legate but soon assumed command of the expedition against the Muslims. He issued laws governing the army and used his powers of excommunication and the granting of indulgences to hold the army together until the expected arrival of Emperor Frederick II. When prophecies spread through the ranks of the soldiers that a new King David and western emperor would capture Cairo, the cardinal urged the army to move forward. Following a long delay, he sent his crusaders, including German troops from Frederick, to attack the Muslims. The men advanced down the east bank of the Nile from Damietta but were forced to sue for peace after they were trapped by the Saracens and the flooding river. The failed offensive led to the fall of Damietta and the opportunity to regain Jerusalem. Pope Honorius III blamed the emperor for the catastrophe, claiming the defeat was the result of his continued delays in sailing to the Levant. The surrender of Damietta was greeted with widespread calls for vengeance against the 'infidels' and demands for Frederick to honour his crusader pledge. The pope wrote chastening letters to the emperor, threatening to excommunicate him. Despite Honorius' criticisms, Frederick remained in the empire, mollifying the pope with his promises to lead the crusade.

The fall of Damietta and the emperor's continued resistance to setting out on crusade resulted in his meeting with Honorius at Veroli in April 1222. At the conference Frederick again pledged to depart for the Latin East, but with rebellious princes still defying his rule in southern Italy he argued that his monarchy lacked the manpower and resources to mount a successful campaign. The pope was once again compelled to accept the emperor's delay.

As Frederick continued his campaign to enforce his rule over his Kingdom of Sicilian, on 18 June 1222 Constance died at Catina at the age of thirty-eight. Despite the emperor's long absences in Italy and Germany and his many relationships with other women, the queen remained loyal and devoted to her husband. Shortly after his coronation, Frederick had resumed his marital relationship with Constance, and while the many years in Germany had dampened what love he had for her, she performed her duties as queen faithfully. The queen was buried at Palermo in the royal chapel.

During the tenth century Muslims from North Africa had invaded Sicily and established their dominance, but were later overwhelmed by the arrival of the Christian Normans. Enclaves of Saracens remained in southern Italy and continued to defy the rule of the Christian government, while showing no willingness to agree to a negotiated reconciliation. During the rule of Frederick II, his regime was unable to suppress the rebellious Muslims and after his return from Germany he decided to transplant them to the southern Italian mainland. Over 20,000 'infidels' were moved to the plains of Apulia and settled in new cities built by the emperor. The transfer virtually ended the revolts in Sicily and eventually turned the Muslims into loyal subjects.

Frederick's status as an unmarried ruler quickly attracted the interest of the European courts with unmarried daughters. Still at a young age and widely considered the most powerful monarch on the continent, many offers of marriage reached the imperial court at Palermo. Before Frederick could accept a marital contract, the consent of the papacy was required. The emperor considered marriage an act of state in which love played no part, and wanted a second wife who would advance his power and wealth, while Honorius III sought to use his approval powers to gain advantages for the Holy See. In early 1223 a second meeting between the emperor and pontiff was held at Florentino in central Italy. Present at the conference was King John of the Christian Kingdom in the Holy Land, husband of the deceased Queen of Jerusalem, Marie. John was the youngest son of the Count of Brienne, and with the eldest son the legal heir to their father's countship he sought his personal land and titles by serving the counts of Champagne in France. He became a favourite of the French king, Philip II, and through the royal court's influence was chosen to marry Queen Marie of Jerusalem. From the marriage with Marie, a daughter named Isabella-Yolande was born around 1208. When Marie died in 1212, John assumed the kingship as regent for his daughter. The young queen was a descendent of the second King of Jerusalem, Baldwin II, and the hereditary ruler of the Christian Kingdom. Through the influence of the King of Jerusalem, Pope Honorius III proposed to Frederick his union with the fifteen-year-old heiress to more closely tie him to the recapture of Jerusalem. The Holy Roman Emperor, viewing the marital contract as a way to satisfy his crusading commitment, agreed to the marriage but with the stipulation of another delay before his departure to Outremer. At Florentino it was decided that Isabella-Yolande would travel to Italy and Frederick would succeed to the Kingdom of Jerusalem as king upon the death of John. The pontiff hoped to gain a monarch who would have the ability and will to organize and defend the Levant. Despite his desire to send an army to the Latin East, Honorius realized there was little enthusiasm in the courts of Europe for another crusade and was forced to grant a two-year delay to Frederick.

By 1224 Frederick II's relentless campaign against the Saracen rebels, along with their relocation, had enforced his rule and peace prevailed in the Holy Roman Empire and Sicily. Now freed from the demands of warfare, the emperor was involved in the administration of his many lands, while becoming occupied with his love for learning. He founded Naples University, which developed into a centre for the teaching of science and secular topics. Leading Jewish, Greek and Arab teachers were brought to the university and permitted to instruct their students in a wide range of scientific and liberal arts subjects. Scholars were welcomed at his court and encouraged to freely teach their subjects without reservations. Frederick was an avid collector of artworks and aggressively sought out new treasures for his many palaces. At his court he created an atmosphere for learning and eagerly engaged the scholars in discussions on varied topics, always seeking new knowledge. Through his attraction of noted poets and writers to his kingdom, the use of the Italian language, in lieu of Latin, came into greater usage.

In the wake of the Florentino Conference, Frederick intensified his preparations for the Sixth Crusade. The grand master of the Teutonic Knights, Herman von Salza, was sent to Germany to recruit troops and collect arms and supplies for the crusade, while King John travelled throughout Western Europe to encourage nobles, tradesmen and peasants to participate in the expeditionary force. In spite of the dedicated efforts of the two imperial envoys, little interest in crusading was aroused. At the Florentino meeting, July 1225 was set for the beginning of the Sixth Crusade, but with lack of men and finances and the imperialists still unenthusiastic, the emperor sought a further postponement.

To secure the pope's approval for the crusade's delay, Emperor Frederick II sent King John and the Patriarch of Jerusalem to convince him of the need for a postponement. After talking with the pontiff, a meeting was set for San Germano for further discussions between Honorius and the emperor. The aged pope had fallen ill and two trusted cardinals were sent to deal with Frederick. At San Germano the papal envoys agreed to the delay, but with the provision that the emperor forfeit a deposit of 100,000 gold ounces and face excommunication for his non-compliance. Frederick was forced to accept the treaty, despite the harsh terms.

In August 1225 Frederick ordered fourteen imperial galleys to sail to Acre, the last surviving enclave of the Christian Levant, to conduct Yolande to his Sicilian Kingdom. On board one of the vessels was the Bishop of Patti, who was sent to conduct the proxy marriage ceremony between the emperor and Yolande. In the late summer the bishop performed the wedding service, and after the ceremony Frederick's wife was crowned Queen of Jerusalem. Following the rites, the queen embarked on the voyage to Italy, landing at Brindisi on the Adriatic, where she was met by her new husband. A second marriage took place on 9 November in Brindisi Cathedral before a large assembly of nobles and churchmen. Soon after the wedding, Yolande was anointed Empress of the Holy Roman Empire.

On the day of the wedding ceremony, Frederick demanded King John abdicate the Jerusalem crown in his favour as the husband of the heiress. John resisted, claiming the emperor's envoys had promised his retention of the monarchy. The allegations were denied by the emperor, who now called himself King of Jerusalem.

Following his assumption of the Jerusalem throne, Frederick renewed his preparations for the Sixth Crusade, summoning a diet to Cremona to gain the support of the Lombardy barons and cities. He invited his imperial magnates to the diet and sent for his young son, Henry VII. As the emperor marched north with his Sicilian forces toward Cremona and King Henry VII travelled south from Germany with his army, northern Italy feared their enslavement by the imperialists. All of upper Italy rose up in arms against the Hohenstaufens, and when the Germans from the north neared the city of Verona they discovered their route blocked by the Italians. The emperor had no desire to attack the Lombards and ordered Henry's forces to return to Germany. While the northern imperial troops withdrew toward the Alps, Frederick advanced to Cremona, brushing aside the harassing sorties of the rebels. On the march north, he stopped at numerous towns, winning converts to his cause. Upon reaching Cremona, the emperor assembled the diet, but with nearly all of Lombardy rallied against him was forced to withdraw south. In response to the northern citie's refusal to participate in the crusade, Honorius III placed an interdiction on the citizens.

Honorius had dedicated his pontificate to the goal of recovering Jerusalem from the 'infidels', but on 18 March 1227 he died without fulfilling his quest. Shortly after the pontiff's death, the cardinals assembled and elected Cardinal Ugolino of Ostia as the next pope, who chose the name of Gregory IX. The new pontiff had strongly disapproved of his predecessor's reluctance to force Frederick's fulfilment of his crusading vows and now adopted a more confrontational policy toward him determined to force his obedience. On the day of his succession to the St Peter's throne, he called upon all Christians to carry out the crusade and demanded the emperor implement his pledge to free the Holy Land of Muslim occupation. The pope sent a letter to Frederick II, reminding him of the crusade and his expected participation at the head of the Christian army. Under increasing pressure from the papacy, in the summer of 1227 the emperor ordered the knights and foot soldiers of Europe to assemble at the disembarkation port of Brindisi. The troops from Germany formed the largest part of the army, while other kingdoms had little enthusiasm for the crusade, sending only a limited number of men. Gregory IX continued to press the emperor to begin the expedition, but the hot summer weather and the effects from an epidemic that swept through the camps greatly reduced the available soldiers. Despite his already failing health, Frederick rode to join the crusaders at Brindisi. His presence at the encampment sent a wave of enthusiasm through the troops, and with a new burst of determination the final preparations for departure were completed.

In the late summer of 1227 the fleet set sail, with Frederick commanding the Sixth Crusade from his flagship. Shortly after putting to sea, disease struck the emperor's vessel and he became seriously ill. Unable to lead the expeditionary force, he ordered part of the fleet to continue to Outremer under the command of Herman von Salza, while the remainder of the vessels returned to Italy after only three days at sea. After reaching the Holy Land, the crusaders proceeded down the coast to Caesarea and then Jaffa, restoring the demolished fortifications, while others occupied the town of Sidon.

Soon after landing back in Italy, the emperor traveled to Pozzuoli to rest and recover his health, dispatching envoys to explain the expedition's failure to Gregory IX. After receiving the ambassadors, the pope issued a communique listing his many grievances against the emperor, emphasizing his failure to launch the crusade, and on 29 September announcing his excommunication. In spite of the pope's bull of excommunication, Frederick renewed his plans for the crusade and set a date in the late spring of 1228 for his departure to the Holy Land.

After regaining his health, the Hohenstaufen overlord spent the following months preparing for the campaign, raising additional troops and acquiring arms and supplies. By spring 1228 the crusader army and naval forces were ready to launch the expedition to the Levant. Prior to leaving, the emperor sent emissaries to the pontiff notifying him that he had now fulfilled his crusader pledge. On 28 June the Christian fleet set out from Brindisi, carrying 1,500 mounted troops and over 10,000 foot-soldiers, including an infantry force of loyal Saracens. The ships moved down the Italian coast before sailing to Cyprus. After remaining on the island for over a month, recruiting local soldiers and making contact with the surviving crusader enclaves at Antioch and Tripoli, the crusaders sailed on to the Holy Land. On 7 September the army disembarked at Acre, where Frederick and his troops were welcomed by cheering townspeople and troops.

From Acre the emperor dispatched emissaries to negotiate with the Saracens. Prior to leaving on his crusade, II had contacted the sultan of Cairo, al-Kamil, who had offered Jerusalem in exchange for the crusaders' help in driving his brother, al-Muazzam, out of the city of Damascus. In the interim al-Muazzam had died, threatening to end the need for the Christian intervention, but fearing the loss of a potentially powerful ally against further rebellions from his relatives, the sultan resumed negotiations.

The Christian embassy met with the sultan at Nablus as he was attempting to seize Damascus and gain control of his brother's lands. While the discussions continued, the emperor paraded his army down the coast to Jaffa in a show of military might to intimidate the sultan. By the thirteenth century, Jerusalem had become an insignificant town, largely depopulated, and was now less important to the Saracens than the Christians. In February 1229 the terms of a treaty were settled. Frederick and al-Kamil agreed to honour a ten-year truce: Jerusalem was to be transferred to the Christians, with the holy sites at the Temple Mount and

Dome of the Rock remaining under Muslim control, while the Crusader Kingdom would be expanded from Beirut in the north to Bethlehem in the south, with corridors of land connecting the cities. The remaining countryside stayed in Saracen hands.

Frederick reached Jerusalem on Saturday, 17 March and accompanied by the Teutonic Knights and pilgrims that had followed him to the Levant made a ceremonious entry into the Holy City. Many of the churchmen refused to enter the city with the excommunicated emperor, obeying the orders of Pope Gregory. At the gates he was met by the representative of the sultan, who handed him the keys of the city. Frederick proceeded through empty streets to the former hospital, where he made his residence. The next day he made his way to the Church of the Holy Sepulchre with von Salza and his knights to attend Mass, but no priest was present for the service. In the midst of the gathered soldiers and Teutonic Knights, Frederick walked to the altar and picked up the golden crown, placing it on his head and declaring himself King of Jerusalem after failing to find a prelate to perform the ceremony. No Mass was heard and no ecclesiastic blessings were given by priests. He had now reclaimed the most holy site in Christendom but was denied recognition by the Church.

From the church the emperor returned to his residence and met with the Masters of the Military Orders, ordering them to begin repairs on the city's defences. Following his discussions with his military leaders, he toured Jerusalem, visiting the holy Christian and Muslim sites. During his youth at Palermo, Frederick had been exposed to Muslim architecture, philosophy, religion and literature, and was always interested in advancing his knowledge. Walking through the streets of Jerusalem, the emperor talked to Saracen clerics and civic leaders, questioning them about their culture and city. On 19 March the Archbishop of Caesarea arrived, carrying an interdiction against the city from the patriarch. Frederick was enraged at the affront and immediately began preparations to depart the city.

Frederick and his entourage set out for Italy, proceeding first to Jaffa and up the coast to Acre, arriving on 23 March to find the city plotting against him. The resident nobles were in an uproar over his self-enthronement and the signing of a treaty with the Muslims without their consent. Riots erupted in the streets between the emperor's troops and townspeople, compelling Frederick to send men from the Military Orders into the streets to restore order. As the emperor attempted to quell the violence, he received word that John of Brienne had invaded his Italian territory with papal troops. He was now needed in his kingdom, and to bring peace to the citizens of Acre appointed two moderates to rule in his name. On 1 May he sailed from the Crusader Kingdom, never to return.

During Frederick's nearly year-long absence in the Holy Land, Pope Gregory IX unleashed a propaganda campaign to discredit him and invaded his lands to force his dethronement. King John of Brienne was appointed to command the papal army and he led the troops into southern Italy. To regain his secular rule in Sicily, the pope summoned all of Europe to send aid and urged them to join his fight to win back the former papal lands from the emperor. Marching under the Church's insignia of the Keys of St Peter, the mostly mercenary soldiers of King John moved against Frederick's ally, Rainald of Spoleto, quickly overrunning his princedom. In early 1229 he resumed his campaign of conquest, invading the Kingdom of Sicily in March and defeating the royalist forces. After his initial successes, Gregory offered Naples and several other cities generous privileges to gain their submission. As the pope's troops advanced into Saracen territory on the mainland, they were met with harassing attacks, which slowed their offensive. While struggling against the Muslims, John led other papal forces into Apulia, slowly gaining control for the papacy. Nearly all of the mainland provinces of southern Italy had now fallen under the authority of Rome. While Gregory was occupying the south, in Germany his papal legate was attempting to raise rebellion and manoeuvring to convince the heirs of Henry VII to dethrone him.

On 10 June 1229 the imperial flag appeared off the Italian coast, to the wild acclaim of the people. Landing at the port of Brindisi, the emperor was greeted with jubilation and acclaim by the local residents. Proceeding from the harbour to the town of Brindisi, he issued an edict stating that he had recovered Jerusalem for the Christians. From all parts of his kingdom, Italian nobles made their way to join him, pledging their support and offering men and money for the recapture of his lands. Frederick spent the next three months raising an army largely of German crusaders and Saracens from Luceria, and in late September moved out to confront the

Holy See's troops. He advanced his troops against the town of Capua, and within a few weeks the papal forces had been routed. Despite the defeat of his army, the pope issued a second ban against Frederick in August 1229, hoping it would stir the renewal of rebellion against the emperor, but the people remained loyal and pressed on with their attacks. Under the unceasing assaults of Frederick's troops, King John was forced to flee for safety to San Germano and the remaining cities in revolt soon submitted. After three months of fighting, large regions of the Kingdom of Sicily were again under the emperor's hegemony.

Following the defeat of the papal army, Frederick urged Pope Gregory to make peace, pledging immunity for all who had opposed him. With his armed forces in disarray, the pontiff was compelled to end the war and in August 1230 rescinded the excommunication order against the emperor. His formal restoration to the Church took place on 1 September in the church at Anagni, where Frederick knelt before the pope to receive the kiss of peace before an assembly of churchmen and laymen.

In the aftermath of his reconciliation with the papacy, Frederick applied his energies to the establishment of a new administrative system for Sicily. He drew up the Constitution of Melfi in 1231, a revamping of the monarchy's government. The emperor decreed twice-yearly meetings in every province presided over by an imperial representative and open to all people. At the gatherings, the citizens were informed of Frederick's will and permitted to present their grievances. Under the edict, the sovereign's rights and obligations to the citizens were formalized. Peace in the Sicilian Kingdom was enforced by the imperial army and the emperor ruled his subjects as an absolute monarch, permitting the barons and cities little influence in the government. To administer the regime, he chose the advisors and officials known to him as the most capable, with a preference for those skilled in law. Frederick spent much of his reign in Apulia, frequently travelling with his court from town to town. He continued to patronize scholars, scientists, musicians and poets, inviting them to reside in his kingdom. During periods of peace, there were frequent jousting tournaments and carnivals sponsored by the emperor.

The southern kingdom of Italy had once been the richest in Europe and Frederick began measures to expand economic growth and wealth. The principal means of generating money in Sicily was agriculture, while trade was conducted largely by foreign merchants from Pisa living on the Sicilian Island and in Venice on the mainland. The growing of export grain was his main source of income, and different ways to increase output were aggressively sought. The emperor enacted new policies to encourage the growth of agricultural production, ceding lands in Apulia and Sicily to exiles from the north and aiding Muslim farmers in Luceria, while bringing in foreigners to grow new crops unknown in his kingdom, such as cotton, sugar-cane and indigo. He augmented the income of his treasury by creating monopolies in raw silk, copper, iron and salt.

The Holy Roman Emperor stayed in contact with the papacy and their peace accord continued. When he had departed for the Holy Land in 1227, the political discord with Lombardy's city-states had remained unresolved. The Lombards held their independence over their fealty to the imperial throne and closely guarded their freedom from outside interference. The emperor utilized his friendly relationship with Pope Gregory to encourage the papacy to intercede in his favour with the upper Italian cities. With its great cities and control of the passes through the Alps, the recognition of his crown by Lombardy was vital to the security of the empire. In late 1231 a diet was summoned by Frederick to meet at Ravenna, to determine his rights and those of the cities. Frederick's goal was to acquire the acknowledgement of his authority and acceptance as overlord.

Frederick had been absent from Germany since 1220 and wanted to meet with his son, Henry VII, to discuss his rule over Germany, ordering him to travel to the diet at Ravenna. Henry was now king of the realm, ruling with the advice of men considered incompetent by the emperor. Under the influence of his counsellors, Henry sought to establish his independent reign over Germany. As the date for the diet drew closer, the Lombard cities sent envoys to Bologna in October to renew the Lombard League as a guarantee to their continued liberty against a possible united German and Sicilian army. When the emperor reached Ravenna in November, the northern Italian cities united in the League refused to attend the diet. As a further safeguard against Henry merging his army with his father's, the passes through the Alps were blockaded. Henry had little desire or interest in meeting with the emperor, remaining in southern Germany, while Frederick was greatly displeased at the lack of attendance by the cities. From Ravenna he made arrangements with Pope Gregory to send representatives to the League members, encouraging them to attend the diet, and after the emperor made some concessions a meeting was finally held in late December, but no reconciliation was possible.

After the German king had failed to appear at the assembly in Ravenna, the emperor sent messages to him ordering him to attend another diet in April 1232 at Aquileia in north-eastern Italy. Frederick departed from Ravenna in March, travelling north to Venice and boarding a ship across the Adriatic to Aquileia. In Germany the young king had surrounded himself with anti-imperial advisors who were eager to drive a wedge between the father and son by urging Henry to rule autonomously. Through his agents in Germany, Frederick was kept well informed of his son's actions and had become increasingly concerned about his continued defiance. Under the increased demands of the imperial regime, the king met his father at Aquileia, quickly admitting his mistakes and swearing to adopt the emperor's policies and obey his commands. To ensure his son's compliance, Frederick acquired the promise of the German barons to guarantee their king's conduct.

Following his reconciliation with Henry, Frederick proceeded to Ravenna to renew his talks with the Lombard League. He attempted to negotiate their obedience, but after several weeks no settlement was reached. With talks at an impasse, Frederick asked the pope to broker an agreement and returned to Apulia in May. Gregory dispatched letters to the Lombard cities but could only secure a truce between the two belligerent factions.

With his empire outwardly at peace, the emperor resumed his efforts to improve the economy by issuing edicts to foster the growth of trade, which had benefitted from the renewed interest in the Levant as a result of the crusades. He encouraged his Sicilian merchants to aggressively participate in commercial actives with the Latin East, issuing them with special trading privileges. In Apulia he continued to invite scholars, scientists, musicians and intellectuals to his court. Frederick maintained a personal menagerie of animals from Africa, including elephants and lions, which became a favourite of his many visitors. The emperor was an avid supporter of education in his realm and continued to take a personal interest in learning. Men with a wide divergence of opinions were welcomed by the sovereign, who wrote to tell Bologna University: 'We have always loved knowledge from our youth, whatever time we can steal from state affairs were cheerfully dedicated to reading the many volumes in our library.'

Over the next few years Frederick's cordial relationship with Pope Gregory continued in an outward atmosphere of friendship. Despite their appearance of harmony, the emperor and pope remained distrustful of each other. While Frederick stayed in southern Italy, in Germany and increasingly in Lombardy there was a surge of religious persecutions against assumed heretics under orders from the pope. Large numbers of religious criminals were thrown into the fires of damnation, while Frederick remained silent. In Rome a revolt erupted against Gregory, who was forced to flee and appeal to the emperor for support. Frederick, involved in suppressing a local uprising, met with the pontiff at Rieta in the following year to discuss the growing violence. He agreed to dispatch aid for the recovery of Rome, while Gregory pledged to advocate the empire's interest in Lombardy and Germany. The emperor fulfilled his promise, sending troops to force the Romans' submission.

While Frederick II was subduing the Roman citizens, in Germany Henry VII had broken his pledges made at Aquileia and was again plotting to seize sole authority over Germany. In an attempt to force a reconciliation between father and son, the pope issued a bull of excommunication against Henry, but it had little effect. In September 1234 Henry sent a proclamation to his German princes declaring the emperor was planning to reduce his powers as king, despite his loyal service to the empire. He summoned his faithful followers to Boppard in central Germany, where the arrangements for his separation with the imperial state were finalized. To augment his independence from his father, the rebellious son negotiated an alliance with the Lombard League for their mutual support.

As Henry finalized the separation of Germany from his father's Italian lands, in April 1235 Emperor Frederick, with a small contingent of soldiers, proceeded over the mountains to Nuremberg. When the German king learned his father was in the city, he sent emissaries to appease him. Frederick ordered Henry to appear at Worms to defend his continued defiance. Meeting with the emperor, he refused to surrender unconditionally and after attempting to escape was taken prisoner, never to regain his freedom.

Empress Yolande had died in 1228 just prior to the beginning of the Sixth Crusade, and following her death Frederick displayed no interest in a third marriage, ignoring many offers from the courts of Europe. He continued to have numerous sexual encounters with women, but in 1231 fell in love with Bianca, from a minor noble family in the Piedmont region of Italy. She was described as a woman of great beauty, possessing a natural charm and elegance. He remained with Bianca for several years, but since she was a low-born princess a marriage to the emperor of the mighty Holy Roman Empire was impossible. In 1234, through the influence of Pope Gregory, the emperor agreed to marry the sister of King Henry III of England, Isabella. The union with the English crown gave Frederick the support of the Plantagenet king in his quest to dethrone his son, while also providing a sizeable dowry. While he was in Germany dealing with his son, the marriage with Isabella was celebrated at Worms in great splendour.

Remaining in Germany, Frederick summoned his barons and churchmen to a diet at Mayence (current-day Mainz). During the assembly the emperor announced a new constitution for the regime, regulations for the issuance of coins and tolls and the naming of a chief-justice for the empire, while all brigands were to be aggressively pursued and punished to end the growing wave of crimes. Existing laws were ordered codified in the German language for the first time. The final acts of the diet were to confirm the dethronement of Henry VII, the election of the emperor's son, Conrad IV, as German king and a declaration of war against the Lombard League.

When Pope Gregory was informed of the imperial announcement of war, he wrote to the German princes asking them to persuade Frederick to accept his mediation. Under pressure from his barons, the emperor agreed to delay his advance into northern Italy and give the pontiff the opportunity to negotiate a settlement. In spite of the appeals of Gregory, the League cities refused to enter into talks and the Hohenstaufen overlord ordered his troops to muster for the campaign. By the summer of 1236 over 3,000 knights had crossed the Alps led by Frederick, reaching Verona, which was an ideal base of operations to subdue the

Lombard League. As the army approached the city in August 1236, the governor, Ezzelino da Romano, opened the gates to welcome them. After assuring the loyalty of Verona, the emperor proceeded west to Cremona, but was soon summoned back by Ezzelino, who was under siege from the rival city of Vicenza under Azzo d' Este. Frederick moved toward Verona, driving Azzo away and besieging Vicenza. The city's defensive works were weak and the Germans and their Italian allies soon pierced the walls and sacked Vicenza leaving the buildings in ashes. The pillaging of Vicenza served as a warning to other towns not to defy the emperor's authority.

After appointing Ezzelino as his local commander, Frederick II was forced to leave Italy in November and after appointing Ezzelino as his local commander travelled north to quell a revolt by the Duke of Austria, Frederick. He proceeded to Vienna, where a great diet of warlords was assembled, while the duke retreated to Neustadt. Meeting with the nobles, the emperor received their pledges of fealty and granted them new privileges to gain their dependence on his continued support. The Duke of Austria remained at Neustadt for several months before negotiating a peace agreement with the emperor.

While Frederick II was in Austria, his envoys in Italy attempted to settle the Lombard League uprising peacefully but failed to win the obedience of the rebellious cities. The pope, increasingly concerned about a powerful imperial presence in both Germany and Sicily encroaching upon his papal lands, threw his support behind the Leaguers. With Austria again under his suzerainty, the emperor returned to Lombardy in September 1237 to renew his campaign of suppression against the Lombard League. Mantua was compelled to submit in early October, while the Milanese defenders in the city rushed back to reinforce their home city.

In November Frederick began moving his army of 15,000 men to Cremona for the winter, and with their withdrawal, the Leaguers set out for Milan. When informed by his scouts of the enemy's movement, the emperor changed direction and followed the Lombard forces, which were led by Pietro Tiepolo of Milan. As the Milanese and their allies began to cross the Oglio River at Cortenuova on 27 November, Frederick ordered a contingent of soldiers to rush forward and attack them, while the remainder of his army hastened forward. The advance guard struck the Leaguers and pushed them back. The emperor reached the ongoing battle and threw his army into the fray. Hard-pressed, the Lombards rallied around the Milanese Carroccio, an ox-cart containing religious relics and the city's standards. Under a hail of arrows from Muslim archers, the imperial cavalry charged into the defenders,inflicting heavy casualties. The Milanese and their allies held their lines until nightfall, when the two forces fell back. Before dawn the Lombards began retreating, attempting to bring the holy relics and Carroccio with them, but were overwhelmed by the emperor's forces. Tiepolo surrendered and thousands of his troops were killed or captured, while the highly treasured Carroccio was seized.

In the wake of his victory at Cortenuova, Frederick renewed his march to Cremona and went into winter quarters. While the imperialists spent the winter at Cremona, the rebellion by the Lombard League then lost momentum, with several cities transferring their loyalties to the emperor. The Lombards were willing to negotiate a settlement with the empire, offering to acknowledge Frederick as their overlord without the loss of their cities' rights and pledging to pay a monetary penalty for their revolt. When the emperor demanded the Milanese surrender their city unconditionally, the talks broke down without resolution.

With Milan and other Lombard cities still resisting imperial rule, in the spring of 1238 Frederick resumed his campaign of subjugation. During the winter he had reinforced his army with troops from his father-in-law in England and German barons, and he advanced to besiege the fortified city of Brescia in July, battering the walls with catapults and battering rams. With the assistance of a Spanish mercenary named Calamandrino, the Brescians built their own catapults, firing repeatedly on the enemy's siege towers. With their towers under attack, the besieging troops tied captured soldiers to their fronts to discourage the Brescians from shooting at them. The Leaguers countered by lowering captives from their walls in front of the imperial battering rams. The barbaric siege wore on into October before Frederick was compelled to withdraw his army to Cremona. As a result of the failed assault against Brescia, other cities felt emboldened to break away from the emperor and join the League.

Interactions between the emperor and Gregory IX had remained contentious, but this changed in the summer of 1238 when the pope appointed a clerical enemy of the imperial regime, Gregorio di Montelongo, as special legate to Lombardy, to the disapproval of Frederick. Hostilities escalated after the pope proposed the marriage of the widowed Queen of Sardinia, Adalasia, to an ally of the papacy, while the emperor advanced his illegitimate son, Enzio. The pontiff threatened to excommunicate Adalasia to secure her commitment, but she chose Enzio, expanding imperial influence into her realm of Sardinia and infuriating the pope.

Relations between Frederick and the papacy had steadily deteriorated in recent years, and in the spring of 1239 Gregory issued a bull of excommunication against the emperor, charging him with interfering in papal lands and the functions of the Church. The pope sent priests into the Holy Roman Empire to vilify the emperor, while in the Lombard cities the papal envoys attempted to convince the pro-imperialists to change their allegiance. Frederick responded by dispatching emissaries to the north to justify his policies and attack the pope. There were charges and counter-charges, as the imperialists and papists engaged in a war of words with little overall effect.

During the 1239 campaigning season, the Frederick remained in Lombardy attempting to gain new allies. He managed to win Como and a few other towns to his banner, but also lost Bologna and Treviso to the Holy See. In the course of the year, Pope Gregory finalized an alliance with Pisa and Genoa against the empire. As the Holy See raised troops under its standard, Frederick led his army down the western side of Italy, while Enzio marched through the eastern part of the peninsula, attacking papal forces in Ancona. The emperor drove the papists back and entered the lands of the Duke of Spoleto. The duke's troops were unable to stop the imperialists, and soon the duchy was occupied by Frederick's forces. He next took Ravenna, and after a long siege Faenza was occupied. As the emperor pressed his offensive, the papal army was sent to Sicily but with little success.

After consolidating his authority over the conquered territories, the emperor turned his army toward Rome, threatening Pope Gregory IX. The pope rallied the Romans to his cause and the gates were closed to the Germans and their Italian allies. Unwilling to attack the Holy City, the emperor withdrew to his Kingdom of Sicily to negotiate a settlement through his allies in the Church.

Waiting for his allies in the papacy to negotiate a settlement with the pontiff, in the spring of 1240 Frederick marched his army out of the Kingdom of Sicily into the Papal States to regain the allegiance of the local lords and towns. Ravenna was recaptured after earlier deserting the emperor, and several towns were besieged. As Frederick reimposed his rule in Tuscany, Gregory issued an invitation to his cardinals and the heads of state to meet in Rome in the spring of 1241 for the removal of the emperor. Frederick responded by voicing his objections and announced his intention to prevent anyone from attending the papal council. Despite his warnings, a large party of prelates set out for Rome from northern Europe, heading toward Genoa. To provide transportation for the cardinals, bishops and representatives from Lombardy, Gregory arranged for Genoese ships to transport them to Rome. The emperor, having no intention of permitting the envoys to travel by sea, set about enlarging his naval forces and appointed his son Enzio as commander of the imperial navy. Enzio was the eldest illegitimate son of Frederick, who appointed him king of Sardinia in 1238. In early May the two fleets clashed near the island of Montecristo, and Enzio, reinforced with Pisan warships, destroyed the papal flotilla. Several thousands died in the fighting and around 100 cardinals and deputies to the council were captured. When informed of the disaster, the pontiff wrote to the European kings, the Doge of Venice and cities of the League urging them to come to his aid against the oppressor of the Holy See. The European courts were horrified at the emperor's insolence against the papacy, ignoring his pleas that he was only at war with the pope and not the Church.

As Frederick continued his war against the papacy, on 21 August 1241, after a pontificate of over fourteen years, the aged Pope Gregory IX died in Rome from the strains of his conflict with Frederick and the summer heat. In a gesture of peace to the Holy See, the emperor ordered the suspension of military operations in papal territory, reiterating that he had only been battling the pontiff, not the Church. The cardinals gathered in Rome to elect the new pope, and following a long period of deliberations, they elected a friend of Frederick, who took the name of Celestine IV. The elation of the emperor was short-lived when the newly elected pontiff died just seventeen days later. The papal conclave was reassembled, but no candidate garnered the required majority, the cardinals' personal ambitions and jealousies preventing a compromise. The failure to quickly name another pope resulted in a rise in Frederick's prestige, many Italian city-states returning to their earlier allegiance with him.

While the papacy floundered without a leader, Frederick's rule was recognized in the southern and central regions of Italy, although he repeatedly failed to secure the allegiance of Lombardy. In Germany the reign of Conrad IV was challenged by the clergy, who sided with the papacy in the fight against the imperial crown. Frederick remained in Sicily awaiting the decision of the conclave of cardinals. In May 1243 he released the prelates captured near Montecristo. After a delay of one year and eight months, when the newly freed Cardinal James from France joined the council, Pope Innocent IV was quickly elected as pope. Frederick sent envoys to the papal court presenting his homage and expressing his desire for peace with the Holy See. He wrote a letter to Innocent IV, telling him: 'We have learned with extreme joy that our old friend had become our Father; we believe that your elevation to the papacy will put an end to all our discords.'

Pope Innocent IV took the throne of St Peter determined to follow in the path of his recent predecessors. The pope's position was strengthened by the people's faith in him as God's elected Earthly representative, while the power of Frederick was in decline. Innocent agreed to talks with the emperor, sending the Archbishop of Rouen and two other prelates to Melfi to meet with him. In return for peace, the new pope demanded the return of all overrun papal territory, resolution of the current conflict with the Lombard League and an understanding to settle their ongoing complaints by arbitration. Frederick countered the pope's demands by pledging to give up all seized lands, but with the stipulation that his regime received them back as a fief of the Holy See. At the intervention of the German princes and King Louis IX of France, both warring parties consented to the preparation of a preliminary reconciliation accord. A compromise was finalized and a peace treaty signed.

Despite their peace agreement and reconciliation, relations between the imperial crown and papacy became increasingly strained over the settlement of the emperor's rights in Lombardy and whether the banishment ban against him should be lifted. Innocent IV accused the emperor of breaking his oath and refusing to obey the orders of the Church. To settle Frederick's perceived rebellion, the pope summoned the kings, prelates and princes to Lyons. The assembly met in June 1245, with 150 representatives where the pontiff accused Frederick of multiple crimes against the Church. After three weeks of discussions, the council announced the deposing of Emperor Frederick II from the throne of the Holy Roman Empire. The pope declared the Hohenstaufen overlord the destroyer of the universe and demolisher of the Church's doctrine.

Frederick countered his deposition by writing to the princes and prelates of Europe telling them no law gave the Holy Father the right to overthrow empires or deprive princes of their secular dignities, while accusing the papacy of abusing its powers. He informed the royal courts that his regime would now defend its rule by military might, and hostilities quickly erupted across Italy. With the assistance of Enzio, the imperial armies marched against the supporters of the papacy and during 1246 enforced Frederick's rule over many rebel cities and barons. In the following year the tide of war turned against the emperor, when the pope's army outmaneuvered Enzio and overran the city of Parma in central Italy. The geographic location of the city with its access into Tuscany was vital to the imperial campaign, and in October Frederick ordered his men to besiege it. They constructed a small fortified town called Victoria, with houses, a church and palace, close to Parma, which the emperor planned to make the seat of his government. As the siege wore on without resolution, in February 1248, while the emperor was away with a hunting party, the Parma garrison and the citizen soldiers from the town unleashed a surprise sortie, rushing from the gates into the unsuspecting besiegers, quickly overwhelming them and sacking Victoria. During the fighting over 1,500 imperial troops were killed and 3,000 taken prisoner. Frederick's treasure and imperial crown were also seized by the pillaging troops. When the emperor returned from the hunt, he was forced to abandon the investment and retire his battered army to Cremona.

The battle at Parma was a major defeat for Frederick, compelling him to appeal to his vassal barons and towns for troops and levy new taxes to continue the war. The Parma disaster ended military operations for 1248, and during the next few months the emperor rebuilt his army. Innocent IV pressed his campaign against the imperial throne, sending his forces to retake lost territories in the Papal States and preparing to invade the Kingdom of Sicily, while the emperor remained in northern Italy holding his cities. In late 1249 he returned to Sicily. While he stayed in the south, his position in northern Italy improved after his armies in Lombardy and the central region of the peninsula regained control of the Ancona, Spoleto and Romagna areas. Despite the reverses and appeals by the European courts for peace, Innocent IV continued the war, refusing all negotiations for a settlement.

During 1250 Frederick II became ill and remained in Sicily to recover his health. By late December he felt well enough to prepare an advance against the papal forces. As the emperor rode in Capitanta, he fell ill again, this time with dysentery, dying on 13 December. The Archbishop of Palermo lifted the excommunication ban, allowing Frederick to be buried in the cathedral at Palermo, where his body remains. When the pope was notified of Frederick's death, he proclaimed: 'Let heaven and earth rejoice.'

In the aftermath of the emperor's death, his eldest surviving son, Conrad IV, assumed his father's crowns in Germany, Sicily and Italy and was recognized as successor to the Holy Roman Empire. During Conrad's four-year reign, the conflict with the Holy See continued unresolved. Conrad died in 1254 without a legitimate heir, and no ruler exhibited the power to regain control of the empire during the period known as the Interregnum until Rudolph of Habsburg was elected overlord in 1273.

Selected Sources:

Abulafia, David, *Frederick II – A Medieval Emperor.*
Allshorn, Lionel, *Stupor Mundi – The Life and Times of Frederick II, Emperor of the Romans, King of Sicily and Jerusalem, 1194–1250.*
Bressler, Richard, *Frederick II – The Wonder of the World.*
Bryce, James, *The Holy Roman Empire.*
Einstein, David G., *Emperor Frederick II.*
Ferguson, Wallace K., *A Survey of European History – Ancient Times to 1660.*
Heer, Friedrich, *The Holy Roman Empire.*
Henderson, Ernest F., *A History of Germany in the Middle Ages.*
Kantorowicz, Ernest, *Frederick the Second 1194–1250.*

Chapter Eight

Louis IX

Crusader King of France

In 1244 King Louis IX of France became severely ill with a malarial infection and was near death. When the king unexpectedly began to slowly regain his health, he was convinced it was only through the healing touch of God that his recovery was possible, pledging to recapture Jerusalem from the Muslims to demonstrate his piety. He spent the next three years preparing for the Seventh Crusade, and in late August 1248 set sail with 100 ships from southern France, first landing at Cyprus. On the island he met with his barons to finalize their plan of attack. The royal council agreed Jerusalem was too strong to capture by storm or siege, and instead the warlords decided to first occupy several key Egyptian towns and then negotiate their exchange for the city. Following a prolonged delay at Cyprus, on 4 June 1249 the crusader fleet arrived off the city of Damietta on the Egyptian coast. The next morning the crusaders landed, quickly encountering the waiting Muslims. The French knights and foot soldiers with their English and German allies charged into the enemy, with King Louis leading the assault. In the ensuing barbarous and fierce battle, the Egyptians were overpowered by the Christians, abandoning Damietta to Louis. On 6 June the French king made his formal entry into Damietta at the head of a great procession, giving thanks to God for the victory at the former Christian Church.

Louis was born a few miles west of Paris at Poissy on 25 April 1214 and was the second son of King Louis VIII and Blanche of Castile. As the younger son, Louis was not expected to ascend to the crown of the Capet monarchy, but in 1218 his elder brother Philip died and he was recognized as heir apparent. The young prince had little contact with his father, who was frequently away campaigning to secure his kingdom against rebellious barons. At a young age Louis developed a deep sense of piety and devotion to the Christian Church, which grew stronger as he matured. His dedication to his religion was manifested in his routine attendance of Mass and regular acts of charity to the sick and poor. During his reign, he was responsible for the construction of many cathedrals and abbeys, including Sainte Chapelle in Paris, which was built to house his collection of holy relics. As Louis grew older in the Capetian household, his mother became the strongest and most influential person in his life. Under the direction of Blanche, he attended church schools and was instructed by scholar monks. The future king was taught reading, writing and Latin. Around the age of eight, Louis began his training as a French knight. He spent many hours practicing with the sword, spear and cavalry javelin, while mastering the skills of an archer. When Louis later assumed the monarchy, he was energetically involved in encouraging the best scholars to reside at his court and remained a dedicated patron of learning throughout his reign.

In the summer of 1226 King Louis VIII embarked on a campaign to subdue the rebellious Cathars, who were members of a heretical sect active in southern France. After subjugating the region around Toulouse and leaving troops to enforce his authority, the king set out for his palace in Paris. When Louis reached Montpensier in central France, he fell ill with a high fever and dysentery brought on by the hardships of the campaign and unhealthy climate. As his health deteriorated, he summoned his prelates and barons, asking them to acknowledge his son Louis as his successor and pledge their allegiance to him. After they made their vows, King Louis VIII appointed his wife Blanche of Castile as guardian and regent for his son.

Under the reigns of Louis IX's grandfather and father, Philip II and Louis VIII, the independence of the French barons had been steadily reduced, but with the assumption of the twelve-year-old king they perceived an opportunity to regain their lost power. To assert the rights of her son to the French regime, Queen Blanche abandoned personal mourning for her husband and began making arrangements for young Louis' coronation. The ceremony of investiture with its oaths of fealty by the high magnates and churchmen bound them to the new king in the house of God, giving him the aura of divine approval. On 29 November 1226 Louis IX rode into the city of Rheims on a warhorse dressed in magnificent regalia, and entered the cathedral. The Bishop of Soissons presided over the ceremony, anointing the young sovereign with holy oil at the high altar. Many of the French warlords attended the coronation to pledge their allegiance to Louis IX, but the Count of Brittany, Peter Mauclerc, and Hugh, Count of La Marche, refused to appear, expressing disappointment at their loss of autonomy.

In the aftermath of her son's coronation, Blanche moved quickly to prevent an uprising of the barons, sending gifts of land and money to secure their loyalty. The Count of Boulogne, Philip Hurepel, was granted several castles and the County of Pol to maintain his friendship. Philip was signalled out for special favour as the half-brother of Louis VIII, who harboured ambitions to overthrow his young nephew and seize the crown. The queen also negotiated an agreement with the rebellious Count of Flanders, Ferrand, absolving him of his plot against Louis VIII for his oath of allegiance and pledge of peace.

While the regent's regime had secured royal power over northern France, to the west the counts of Brittany and La Marche began plotting against the new government, initiating contacts with the English monarchy for its intervention. Mauclerc, who ruled Brittany as regent count following the death of his wife, formed an alliance against the queen regent with Count Hugh of La Marche and Theobald of Champagne to reassert their independence. To quell the growing insurrection, Blanche ordered the royal army to assemble, and with reinforcements from Count Philip of Boulogne set out in the winter of 1227 toward the gathered rebels at Loudun in south-western France. Confronted by the massed forces of the king, and with the English reluctant to join their alliance, the conspirators soon agreed to end their rebellion and pledge homage. While the recalcitrant counts gave up their revolt, they continued to seek an opportunity to distance themselves from the rule of the French monarchy.

The barons soon resumed their struggle against the Capetian monarchy, devising a plot to kidnap Louis IX and take control of the kingdom. When the king heard of the plan to seize him, he was away from Paris and was compelled to ride to the security of the fortress at Monterey, twenty miles from Paris. The citizens of Paris quickly rallied to their popular sovereign, rushing to his rescue and allowing him to return to his capital in triumph. The failed conspiracy discouraged the rebel lords from mounting a serious threat for the next few years, but they remained determined to end the overlordship of the French king. To the north-west, Peter Mauclerc continued his defiance against the crown, while to the south the regime struggled to check the ongoing revolts of the Count of Toulouse, Raymond VII. When Count Philip of Boulogne defected to the conspirators, Louis' army lost a powerful ally, weakening its ability to maintain control over the rebellious nobles.

Queen Blanche had earlier negotiated a truce with the Plantagenet King of England, Henry III, but the three-year treaty was due to expire in July 1228. To end the revolts of the Count of Brittany and his allies before they received reinforcements from England, Peter was ordered to appear at court to pledge his fealty. When he failed to answer the summons, Blanche assembled the French army and invaded Brittany, with the fourteen-year-old Louis nominally leading the troops. In the cold weather of January 1229, the French set out for Brittany to subjugate Count Peter, laying siege to his formidable fortress at Belleme. After surrounding the castle with trenches, the king's men built catapults to batter the stronghold's walls, while miners dug tunnels under the foundation to open gaps in the defences. After the royalists breached the defensive works, the garrison surrendered, giving Louis a foothold in Peter's demesne.

In the wake of his loss of Belleme, Count Peter sailed across the Channel to England in the autumn of 1229, conferring with Henry III. During the meeting he pledged the fealty of Brittany to the king and convinced him that the French army could quickly be defeated. The English sovereign agreed to support the Bretons in their struggle against Queen Blanche, pledging to send soldiers to buttress the revolt. Following an unexpected delay, in early May 1230 the English sailed to St Malo in north-western France, where they were greeted by Peter and his rebel lords. As the united English and Bretons moved against the Capetian monarchy, Blanche assembled the royal army, with the vassals reluctantly sending only their required number of knights and troops. When the allies advanced into the crown's territory of Poitou, the local warlords remained loyal to King Louis and prepared to attack the invaders. Receiving little support for their rebellion, the insurgents withdrew to Brittany and Henry III soon returned to England, disappointed that the promised reinforcements never materialized from the local French lords.

The failure of the rogue league to attack the crown gave the queen regent the opportunity to forge a reconciliation with the dissident French bishops and barons, including Philip of Boulogne, who abandoned Peter and rejoined the royalists with his formidable military forces. In July 1231 the weakened coalition forces of Count Peter again attempted to occupy royal lands, but their attacks were repeatedly thwarted. As the conflict continued in western France, Pope Gregory IX sent envoys to the warring factions to resolve the periodic wars. Under the direction of the legates, both rivals agreed to terms, signing a three-year truce. The enemies of Louis IX had been checked but not yet defeated in their quest for independence.

While the campaign against the rebels in the west had suppressed the revolts of the local warlords, in the south of France at Toulouse a final settlement of the prolonged Albigensian Crusade had been finally negotiated. The Albigensians, also known as Cathars, were a heretical Christian sect, which denied the divinity of Christ and his physical incarnation. In 1209 Pope Innocent III declared a crusade against the religious faction after his legate was murdered by Albigensians. The conflict dragged on for twenty years in southern France until the heretic Count Raymond VII was defeated and compelled to sign the Treaty of Paris. Under the terms of the accord, Raymond was forced to return to the Roman Church and renounce the followers of the sect, while ceding the County of Trencavel to the French crown. The count further agreed to the marriage of his daughter and sole heir to a brother of the sovereign, and at his death for his territorial holdings to pass to their children. If there was no recognized heir, the count's lands would then be annexed to the French throne. The reconciliation contract created a wave of support for Louis IX, enhancing his popularity and prestige among French magnates, the Church and citizens.

In the aftermath of the settlement with the rebellious northern warlords and defeat of the Cathars, the regent queen and her son spent the next three years travelling throughout the realm consolidating the regime's authority and buttressing its military support among the magnates and bishops to quell a resumption of the barons' rebellion.

While the monarchy was strengthening its rule over its vassals, the marriage of King Louis to Margaret of Provence was arranged. She was the eldest daughter of Raymond Berenguer IV, Count of Provence, and was born in the spring of 1221. Margaret was described by her contemporaries as a lady of grace and beauty, renowned for her religious devotion and courtly manner. After the marital agreement was finalized, in May 1234 Margaret travelled to Lyon with her parents for the signing of the marriage contract. The wedding ceremony was held on 27 May 1234 at the cathedral in Sens, and on the following day she was crowned Queen of France. During their thirty-six years of marriage, Louis IX and Margaret became devoted to each other, developing a close supporting relationship. Together they enjoyed riding, reading and listening to the court musicians. The pious couple had eleven children, including the future King Philip III, born in 1245.

In 1234 Count Theobald of Champagne, who had earlier joined the rebel league against the French crown, succeeded to the throne of Navarre after the ruling king, Sancho VII, died without direct heirs. The monarchy of Louis IX had aggressively supported Theobald's rights to Navarre and was given control of the Champagne countship to govern in the name of the count. As part of his assumption of Navarre, Theobald was required to pay an indemnity to Alix, Queen of Cyprus, who had a counter-claim to the kingdom. King Louis agreed to pay the money for the count, receiving in exchange the suzerainty of the counties of Blois, Chartes and Sancerre and jurisdiction over Champagne. The acquisition of the three countships added strategic and wealthy lands to the king's demesne, while giving the crown a strong foothold in Champagne. After taking hegemony over Navarre, Theobald returned to Champagne, claiming he had not renounced his overlordship but only used it as security for the payment of the settlement fee to Queen Alix. To strengthen his position, he renewed his alliance with Brittany and La Marche, threatening to attack the French king. Provoked by Theobald, Louis summoned his soldiers and in April 1236 prepared to advance against Champagne. When Theobald learned the French were mustering their formidable army, he ended his revolt and submitted. Under the terms of a treaty, he pledged to stay away from France for seven years and surrender three of his castles to Louis, giving the king a secure hold on Champagne.

During his minority years King Louis slowly began to assume the powers of the monarchy, and after reaching the age of 21 in 1235 began to rule the French kingdom independently. His mother remained an important advisor and he continued to confer with her on many decisions. Queen Blanche had dominated Louis IX's early reign as regent, but after his assumption of the regime and marriage she resented her reduced authority. The new queen was intelligent and highly educated, and sought to replace the queen regent as the primary advisor to Louis. As the queen schemed to shape the monarchy, she had to counter the manoeuvrings of Blanche, who struggled to retain her influence. After the conclusion of the regency period, Louis increasingly asserted his control and was determined to govern autonomously, in spite of his wife's frequent attempts to sway his decisions. Despite her lack of political power, Margaret provided her husband with a happy family life and was actively involved with the Church.

After settling with the recalcitrant Count of Champagne, Louis moved against the rebellious Peter Mauclerc of Brittany. When the three-year truce between the French regime and the count's coalition expired in June 1234, Henry III of England failed to honour the terms of his agreement with Peter, sending only a token force to support the new campaign against the French kingdom. With the English now disinterested in pursuing the war against King Louis and many of the French rebel lords reconciled with the throne, in November Count Peter agreed to pledge his fealty, acknowledging the suzerainty of Louis IX over Brittany. Two years later, Peter's son and heir, John the Red, acquired the countship from his father after reaching the age of majority and also recognized the French king's overlordship. The ever-rebellious and restless Peter remained in western France until 1239, when he took the vows of a crusader and joined the crusade called by Pope Gregory IX against the heretic German emperor, Frederick II.

Throughout his reign, Louis IX remained a pious and devoted follower of the Church of Rome. He displayed his religious fervour with his acquisitions of a large collection of holy artifacts. In 1238 the king sent two Dominican monks to Constantinople to bring the 'Crown of

Thorns' to Paris after the emperor of the eastern empire, Baldwin II, gave it to him as a gift. When the two French priests reached Constantinople, they discovered the relic had been pledged as collateral for a large loan from Venetian bankers. One of the Dominicans hurried back to France, notifying the king of the amount of money required to pay off the Venetians. Louis agreed to provide the necessary funds, and in August 1239 the relic arrived in France in a gold and silver chest. The artefact was first taken to the cathedral at Sens and paraded through the streets in a grand procession, with King Louis and his brother, Robert of Artois, carrying the relic on their shoulders. Following religious services in Sens, the gold and silver box was transferred for safekeeping to the royal chapel at St Nicholas. The king continued to purchase additional religious items, including a piece of the 'True Cross'. To house the precious treasures, he ordered the construction of Sainte Chapelle in Paris. The structure was completed in 1246 and the holy relics were kept over the altar in gold and silver reliquaries in the upper chapel of the Gothic masterpiece.

During his last campaign, Louis VIII had reasserted his crown's suzerainty over the County of Toulouse and the ruling count, Raymond VII, pledged his fealty and peace. In 1240 fighting broke out between Raymond and the neighbouring Count of Provence, Ramon Berenguer IV, over control of the wealthy trading centre of Marseilles. Ramon was unpopular with the port's inhabitants and they turned to Raymond for support. The ruler of Toulouse advanced his army into Provence, pillaging the land and capturing three castles across the Rhone River. As the fighting in the south intensified, Louis IX sent 700 knights with a large military force to aid his father-in-law. With the royal reinforcements, Ramon drove off the enemy troops to secure control over the border.

With prospects for peace with his vassals restored, Louis directed his policy toward the resolution of his realm's internal problems. He promoted programmes to improve the economy and trade, while continuing to participate in the activities of the Church, nobles and towns. He endeavoured to retain the loyalty and support of his barons and allies, actively taking actions to prevent their desertion. The monarch personally mediated disputes between his vassals to thwart the outbreak of private wars. The French court presented a patriarchal appearance that was dominated by advisors and friends from the provinces of his kingdom. The court moved continually from monastery to monastery and one royal house to another in the environs of Paris. Ruling his expanding domain, Louis had neither a first minister nor court favourite. To protect his eastern borders, the king pursued friendly relations with the German emperor, Frederick II. The policy had given the French kingdom peace on its eastern frontier, but in 1239 cordial relations became threatened by the escalating conflict between Pope Gregory IX and the German emperor. Louis sent an embassy of his bishops to Rome to serve as intermediaries between the two hostile powers.

In 1241 the French king's brother, Alfonso, reached the age of majority and was knighted and invested with the Countship of Poitou by the monarchy. He travelled with Louis to his countship, receiving oaths of fealty from the local lords. The neighbouring Count of La Marche, Hugh X of Lusignan, felt threatened by the nearby presence of the new count with his close relationship to King Louis and the resulting spread of French dominance into his demesne. As his hostilities against Count Alfonso grew, Hugh X formed a league with regional French barons, Raymond VII of Toulouse and Henry III of England. When the La Marche count withdrew his homage to Alfonso, the French court declared his lands forfeited to the royal crown. In the spring of 1242, Louis assembled his army and advanced against the rebels. In early May the formidable host marched into Poitou from Chinon. The size and strength of the French forces convinced many of the barons to withdraw from the coalition and submit to the king. The royalists then moved against Hugh X of Lusignan, capturing several of his castles.

As the French continued to press their offensive against the rebel league, in mid-May Henry III crossed the Channel and landed his small army in France, hastening north to attack King Louis. When the royalists learned of the English presence, Louis turned his forces south, meeting King Henry at the strategic stone bridge at Taillebourg. On 19 July the French knights charged from the Taillebourg fortress, compelling their opponents to withdraw to the village of Saintes. As the French slowly moved forward, on 21 July their foraging party skirmished with the soldiers of the Count of La Marche near Saintes. The sounds of the encounter quickly reached both armies, and they advanced forward, clashing in the vineyards and narrow lanes around Saintes. The heavy infantrymen and horsemen crashed into each other, in a fury of fighting with the noise of the mêlée echoing across the battlefield. Following a massed cavalry charge by Louis' knights, the rebels were beaten back in bloody and brutal fighting, abandoning hundreds of dead and captured.

In the aftermath of his defeat at Saintes, Henry III withdrew his battered forces, while the French moved to Tours. While the English remained at Bordeaux, Hugh X abandoned the coalition, again submitting to the king. With his wife and children beside him, the count pleaded for the king's mercy after his betrayal. He pledged his fealty and was compelled to recognize the crown's possession of his captured castles and lands. While the king was in the north defending his monarchy against the rebels and English, to the south Raymond VII of Toulouse had broken his pledge of fealty, moving against the royal fortress at Penne l'Agenais. The royal garrison led by Humbert of Beaujeu withstood the attacks of the rebel count, forcing him to abandon his siege. After the Count of Toulouse retreated, Humbert sent his men to harass Raymond 's lands and castles, forcing him to submit to the regime. In October the count pledged his allegiance and surrendered additional fortresses, further weakening his control over Toulouse.

By October 1242 Louis IX had received the homage of his rebellious French barons and next advanced against Henry III of England. An earlier attempt by the English to blockade the port of La Rochelle had ended in failure, and now with the desertion of his French allies Henry III became more willing to negotiate a settlement with Louis. In April 1243 the two kings agreed to a five-year truce, while the French were ceded all their recent conquests. Following the signing of the treaty with the English, a contemporary wrote: 'From this time the barons of France undertook nothing against their anointed Lord, seeing that God was with him.' The revolt of the warlords had been crushed by the power of King Louis, and the Capetian throne reigned superior over the magnates. Louis was firmly established in his domain, which had been enlarged by the victories over the barons and English. The once–great feudal warlords of Brittany, Toulouse and Champagne had been broken, while the English king had been repelled in his attempt to regain his former French lands lost during the wars with Philip II.

Louis IX had maintained friendly relations with the Germans along his eastern frontier, but in 1242 was drawn into the ongoing struggle between Emperor Frederick II and Pope Gregory IX. The pope had excommunicated the emperor for his attempt to impose imperial rule over all of Italy, including Rome (see previous chapter). As the imperialists escalated their aggression, the pontiff responded by convening an ecclesiastical council to depose Frederick. The emperor countered by invading northern Italy and advancing against Rome, while threatening to seize all prelates travelling to the papal conclave. When several French bishops and abbots on their way to the assembly were arrested and ill-treated by the Germans, Louis corresponded with the emperor demanding the immediate release of his churchmen and warning of military confrontations. Frederick agreed to return the priests, but before peace was restored between the two rulers Pope Gregory died. He was first replaced by Pope Celestine IV but after after a short pontificate he died and Innocent IV was elected to the papal throne. The new pope aggressively continued Gregory's campaign against Frederick. The emperor moved against Rome with his army, forcing the pontiff to flee to southern France. Innocent IV petitioned Louis for refuge, but knowing his barons were strongly anti-papal, the king refused to grant the request without their approval. By his manoeuvring the king avoided his involvement in the dispute between the emperor and Rome. Failing to secure French support, Pope Innocent travelled to Lyon and called another church council. In 1245 the pontiff's assembly excommunicated and deposed Frederick, while announcing a new crusade to regain the holy city of Jerusalem from the control of the Muslims. Louis was later asked by the emperor to act as arbitrator between the two warring factions, but never responded to the proposal. The bitter conflict between Innocent IV and Frederick II continued until the emperor's death in 1250.

During the first phase of his war against the recalcitrant French barons and English, Louis had become seriously ill from the constant hardships of campaigning and the demands of his reign. In 1244 his health seriously deteriorated and he was near death, suffering from high fever and dysentery. Prelates and lords gathered around his bed at Pontoise, while religious processions and prayers were made in the Paris churches. From his sickbed the king summoned his advisors, thanking them for their services to his regime and encouraging them to live godly lives. After reports of his imminent death spread through France, the people filled the churches offering prayers for his recovery. When he lost consciousness, sacred relics were brought to his bedside and placed on his motionless body by his mother. As Blanche prayed before her son, she vowed that if God granted his recuperation, he would visit Jerusalem to offer thanks at the Church of the Holy Sepulchre. As his wife Margaret, the dowager queen, high magnates and bishops remained around the bed, Louis slowly opened his eyes and moved his arms. In a weak and faint voice he said: 'The dayspring from on high hath visited me and hath lifted me up out of the shadow of death.' In December 1244, after the king regained some strength, he summoned the Bishop of Paris to place the cross of a crusader on his shoulder.

By the beginning of Louis IX's reign, the Western Christians had attempted five times to seize permanent control of Jerusalem. In 1229 the Sixth Crusade, led by Emperor Frederick II, had won back Jerusalem by diplomacy, but within fifteen years the city was again under Muslim control. Most European monarchs were now disinterested in answering the papal summons for a new crusade, but in the aftermath of his near-death illness Louis was anxious to lead the warriors of Christ in the Seventh Crusade.

After taking the vows of a crusader, King Louis began preparations for his expedition to Outremer. He was determined to assemble a large and well-equipped army, aware that recent crusades had suffered from acute shortages of men and supplies. To recruit soldiers for his expeditionary force, the king sent priests and friars throughout his kingdom to preach the cause of the crusade. Meetings were held in churches and public assemblies, with hymns, prayers and a sermon exhorting the Christian virtues of the campaign. During the homily, the clergymen compared men who were afraid to take the cross to tranquil cows in a pleasant field and emphasized that going on crusade assured their passage to Heaven. The monarch also ordered poets and minstrels to travel through the kingdom promoting the crusade with poems and songs. The pope sent a special legate to preach the Christian cause to the magnates, whose participation was vital to the success of the expedition. The call for the crusade was answered mainly by French knights and soldiers, who responded to the appeal of their popular and beloved sovereign. Prior appeals for a crusade were met by troops from many regions of Europe, but in 1245 the eastern warlords were pressed to hold their frontier against the attacks of the Mongols, while the Germans and Italians were tied down by the ongoing conflict between the pope and emperor. King Henry III of England had no interest in sending his knights and soldiers to fight for the French king, but a small contingent of Englishmen did participate in the campaign, led by Lord William Longespee of Salisbury.

While the French regime was recruiting men for the Levant, Louis was raising money to finance the crusade. Pope Innocent IV's Council of Lyons granted an ecclesiastical levy on church income, which became the primary source of funds for the crusade. The French towns also made sizeable contributions and many nobles paid their own expenses, pledging large parts of their lands to equip and sustain themselves, while the king distributed large sums of money from the royal treasury to fund the campaign and borrowed heavily from Italian bankers.

As preparations for the Seventh Crusade continued, Louis chose the port of Aigues-Mortes in southern France to assemble his great military force. The monarch had earlier purchased the small town from the Psalmod Abbey, giving him a foothold on the Mediterranean coastline. Louis began negotiations with the Venetians to acquire a flotilla of transports and escort vessels for the campaign, but finding them too costly agreed to purchase and lease his fleet from the shipbuilders of Genoa and Marseilles. He appointed two experienced admirals for the voyage, making them responsible for overseeing construction of the ships and acquiring naval supplies. By the summer of 1249, the shipbuilders had delivered thirty-eight vessels. While Louis made arrangements for acquiring the royal fleet, the great barons negotiated their own transport to the East. Large quantities of provisions and supplies were required for the crusade and the French regime spent significant sums for the purchase of ships, food, wine, horses and equipment. The provisions and supplies were delivered to Cyprus, which served as the final assembly point. Approximately two-thirds of the cost of the crusade was paid by the Church, with the remaining amounts coming from the towns, nobles and king.

Louis expected to be away from France for several years, and before his departure took measures to ensure peace in the kingdom. The five-year truce negotiated with Henry III after the conclusion of the campaign in Poitou was due to expire in April 1248, and the king was concerned that the English would take advantage of his absence to renew their quest for land in western France. Louis persuaded Pope Innocent IV to issue a decree forbidding the English monarch from attacking French territory during the crusade. Louis intervened in the ongoing quarrel between Frederick II and the pope to find a reconciliation, but their differences were too great and bitter to resolve. The Countship of Flanders in northern France was in turmoil over the succession of the next ruler. To bring peace to his vassal state, the king divided the county between the two contenders, ending their confrontation, while the once-rebellious counts of Brittany, La Marche, Champagne and Toulouse pledged to remain loyal to the throne. Before leaving for the Holy Land, Louis summoned the barons to Paris, where they swore allegiance to his heir, Louis, if he did not return.

Once preparations were finalized, Louis named Queen Blanche to rule the kingdom as his regent during his absence, with the assistance of his brother, Alphonse of Poitiers. Before departing for the invasion fleet, the king, along with his wife, mother and brothers rode to St Denis on 12 June in a grand procession to pray for the success of the crusade. In the basilica the king received the staff of a pilgrim and the sacred banner of St Denis, known as the oriflamme of France, from the papal legate. Following the service at the church, the monarch went to Notre Dame to hear Mass with his family and courtiers.

In the late spring, Louis left his mother in Paris and, wearing the garments of a pilgrim, led the crusaders through the French countryside in great expectation of the coming expedition. On the journey south, he frequently stopped at monasteries and convents to offer prayers for God's help in subduing the Muslims. When the French crusaders reached Lyons, the monarch met with Pope Innocent, requesting his continued intervention against the aggression of Henry III and imploring him to resolve his differences with Frederick II, while asking for the papacy's prayers for the reconquest of Jerusalem.

In mid-August the crusader army reached Aigues-Mortes and the waiting fleet. Most of the men and supplies had already been loaded, and on 25 August Louis and Margaret boarded their ship. The flotilla was forced to wait two days for the winds to change direction before sailing

across the Mediterranean to the assembly point on Cyprus. Following
a three-week voyage, the French vessels reached the port of Limasol in
southern Cyprus. In the fading light of 17 September, the king's ship
dropped anchor and he went ashore the next morning. Louis was ready
to continue to the Levant but was compelled to wait until his great army
gathered on the island. The arrival of his knights, soldiers and supplies
took longer than expected, and following the advice of his barons, Louis
was forced to delay the campaign until spring.

Over the following weeks, the crusaders continued to arrive in their
ships from France and other parts of Europe. As the expeditionary force
remained on the island, the sovereign of Cyprus took the cross, joining
the crusade with many of his magnates. The northern European men soon
discovered the change in climate, food and living conditions caused a
great sickness among them, which killed and incapacitated many soldiers.
Louis was endlessly occupied resolving old feuds between the warlords,
while settling dissension between the Greek and Latin archbishops over
the proper religious rites. Contingents of knights from the Military
Orders, which had been organized following the First Crusade for the
care of pilgrims and defence of the Holy Land, had joined the campaign,
and when discord erupted between them the French sovereign reconciled
their differences through his personal intervention. When hostilities
broke out between the rival Genoese and Pisans, who were under contract
to provide ships and seamen for the voyage to the Holy Land, Louis sent
envoys to settle their differences. While the king continued to reconcile
ongoing disagreements, he monitored his troops, keeping them battle-
ready to engage the enemy.

While still in Cyprus, the king summoned his council to decide where
to first attack the Muslims. Realizing that Jerusalem was too strongly
protected by the Egyptian army and formidable defensive works, the
king ordered his army to advance against the port city of Damietta in
northern Egypt and then move against Cairo. Following the occupation
of Egypt, the monarch planned to exchange his conquests with the
sultan for Jerusalem. After spending over eight months in Cyprus, the
crusaders, reinforced with troops from Latin Greece, were ready to
board their ships for the Holy Land. In excess of 120 transport and escort
vessels were assembled in the port, and the 2,700 knights, 5,000 archers
and crossbowmen and 7,300 foot soldiers with tons of equipment and

supplies were transferred to the waiting navy. On 13 May 1249 Louis and Queen Margaret boarded their ship and on the following morning set sail for the Levant. The Christian naval force was soon dispersed by a violent storm that drove many of the crusader vessels to the coast of Syria. The sovereign and about a quarter of his navy sailed back to Cyprus to await the return of the scattered flotilla. After a week's delay, the crusaders put to sea again with most of their fleet in a calm favourable wind, setting a course for the fortified city of Damietta at the mouth of the western Nile. As his flagship, *Montjoie*, neared the coastline of Egypt on 4 June Louis exclaimed to his men: 'Either we shall conquer and increase God's glory and the honour of France, or we shall fall as martyrs.'

As the fleet of the crusaders approached the shoreline, the Sultan of Egypt was occupied in the north and appointed Fakhr ad-Din as his vizier for Damietta. When the Christians neared the city, the vizier led his mounted horsemen out to repulse their landing. From the beach ad-Din attempted to intimidate the Europeans by ordering his men to create loud noises with their horns and cymbals. After reaching the harbour at Damietta, the crusaders could see the Saracen horsemen dressed in armour aligned along the shore in a show of military power, challenging the Christians to attack. Louis gathered his advisors and decided not to wait for the remainder of his army to arrive, ordering his men to attack the Saracens in the early morning. After attending Mass, the following day Louis, dressed in full armour, issued orders for his troops to board their landing barges and advance against the shore. The banner from St Denis was placed in the lead craft, as the landing forces led by Louis set out for the shoreline under a cloudless blue sky. When the knights and infantrymen approached the beach, they could see the Saracens deployed in battle formation. Many soldiers jumped into the sea, wading ashore to attack the Egyptians. When the king witnessed his men fighting the Muslim troops, he immediately leaped into water up to his chest, struggling to reach the beach. Reaching the shore, Louis placed his spear under his arm and hastened toward the Saracens, eager to attack them. Witnessing their sovereign charging against the Muslims alone, his men chased after him to restrain him.

When the remainder of the barges grounded in the sand, the men climbed over the sides to engage the Egyptians. On the beach the French crusaders formed into a line with their shields locked together and spears ready to strike. The Saracen cavalrymen unleashed a fierce charge against the first wave of Christians, but were driven back, unable to penetrate their defences. As additional boats reached the beach in the midst of the fighting, the infantrymen charged into the Egyptian horsemen under a barrage of enemy arrows. Driven back, the Saracens reformed and charged again into the European forces with renewed energy. The king's troops held their line, repulsing the Muslim horsemen. Dispirited by their failure to repulse the Christians, the Saracens began to withdraw. When the horses were brought up from the ships, the knights mounted and galloped after the fleeing Egyptians. The Saracens managed to escape, crossing the river into Damietta. The city was strongly fortified with walls and towers, but when royal scouts reached Damietta they found it deserted by the Muslim garrison troops and inhabitants. Informed that the city had been abandoned, Louis ordered his soldiers to sing a *Te Deum* in praise of God's intervention.

On 6 June the French king, dressed as a pilgrim, entered Damietta in a grand procession with his wife, brothers and papal legate. He went to a mosque, which had earlier served as a Christian church, and with the legate, barons and crusaders heard Mass, ending the service with the singing of a *Te Deum*. After his capture of Damietta, the monarch wanted to press on to Cairo, but after meeting with his counselors was persuaded to wait until the seasonal flooding of the Nile was over. With only minor losses, the crusaders had seized the second-strongest fortification on the Egyptian coast, gaining control of a formidable fortified city.

After the decision was made to wait until the late autumn to resume the expedition, Queen Margaret and her ladies were brought ashore and installed in the sultan's palace. The legate and each baron were assigned separate residences, while the king and the army made camp outside the walls. While at the encampment, the crusaders had to contend against frequent raids by Bedouin horsemen, who had been encouraged by the sultan to harass the Christians. During the summer, the soldiers suffered from the oppressive heat and deadly diseases. The unplanned delays in Cyprus and now Damietta created shortages of provisions and critical war supplies.

By early October the flooding Nile slowly began to recede. On 24 October Alphonse of Poitiers arrived from Paris with reinforcements, and the crusaders could proceed against the Egyptians. After a council meeting, Louis ordered his army to move against Cairo in the next phase of the conquest of Egypt. In late November the soldiers set out for the town of El Mansura, forty-five miles to the south-west, with the Knights Templar leading the vanguard. Following the course of the Nile, the ships sailed up the waterway in support of the army, while the troops marched overland. During the advance, the crusaders were slowed by many deep inland waterways, which were difficult to ford, and frequent attacks by Muslim cavalrymen.

As the Saracens continued to harass the Christian column, the heavily armoured Templar Knights in the vanguard rushed forward into the Egyptians, quickly breaking through their defensive line and slaughtering hundreds. The crusaders took nearly a month to reach the bank of the eastern Nile opposite the fortress-town of El Mansura, but were separated from the town by a large canal. The men tried to build a causeway across the waterway but were thwarted by the deep water and harassing Saracen attacks. Several other attempts were made to pass over the channel, but they ended in failure. Finally, in early February 1250, a rogue Bedouin came to the Christian camp to advise the king of a passageway farther downstream. Leaving a strong guard under Count Peter of Brittany to protect the encampment, the crusaders set off with the Bedouin leading them to the channel. After reaching the inland waterway, the king's brother, Count Robert of Artois, led the first contingent of knights and foot soldiers across with orders to wait for the remainder of the army. Robert and his men crossed the canal with the Knights Templar and a company of English troops led by William of Salisbury, but upon reaching the far bank they disregarded the king's instructions, setting out up the canal to the Muslim outpost on the Nile. Reaching the fortified camp, the Frenchmen with their English allies charged into the Saracens, catching them by surprise and quickly overrunning them. Count Robert rushed toward El Mansura, breaking through the fortified gate into the narrow streets of the town. The Muslim garrison and local inhabitants unleashed furious counter-attacks, clashing with the crusaders in hand-to-hand combat. At the approach of the European troops, the Muslims in the city had assembled two regiments of elite Mameluke guards, who launched a devastating attack against the Christians, forcing the survivors to withdraw under a storm of arrows. During the fighting, Robert of Artois and Lord William of Salisbury were killed, along with most of the Knights Templar. Meanwhile, Louis' forces were under attack as they continued to cross the waterway to link up with Robert's contingent. On the banks of the river a savage battle was raging as the European knights and infantry pushed the infidels back with their swords, spears and flights of arrows. The king led his men into the melee on his horse, striking down several Muslim warriors with his sword. As more crusaders reached the far bank, they joined the fight, compelling the Egyptians to withdraw, leaving hundreds of dead and wounded on the battlefield.

As the battered survivors from the battle at El Mansura retreated upriver, they met Louis and the main army. After uniting their forces, the crusaders, led by the king, rushed down river slamming into the Egyptians. In the ensuing battle, the Frenchmen fought valiantly. When the crusader archers and crossbowmen crossed the river, firing volleys of arrows at the Muslims, the knights and foot soldiers forced the Egyptians to withdraw into the town. The crusaders occupied the outpost on the canal and during the day reinforced the defences in anticipation of a Saracen counter-attack. Early on 11 February the Saracens unleashed their assault under a cloud of arrows. As the sultan's troops crashed into the Christians line, the king held his cavalry in the rear. When the centre of his line began to falter, the king led his horsemen into the opposing infantrymen in a series of charges. As a wave of carnage swept through the Muslims' ranks, their attack wavered and the survivors retreated to El Mansura, abandoning their dead and wounded.

The French crusaders and their allies lacked the military strength to force their way into El Mansura, and during the next two months maintained their position along the canal, keeping watch on the enemy. Despite the oppressive heat and an outbreak of plague, which caused havoc among the ranks of the soldiers, Louis refused to abandon his campaign against the Muslims, praying for God's intervention. While the Christian army grew weaker, the Egyptians at El Mansura were reinforced with the arrival from the east of the new sultan, Turanshah. Under orders from the sultan, small boats were disassembled and sent by camel caravan upstream above the French encampment. The crafts were rebuilt and began launching harrying attacks against the Christian supply ships. With their communication lines from Damietta partially cut, the crusaders suffered from critical shortages of provisions. As the stalemate continued, Turanshah's horsemen repeatedly assaulted the French encampment, threating to overpower the defenders.

Unable to counter the sultan's blockade against his resupply ships in the Nile and cavalry sorties against his encampment, Louis was finally compelled to abandon the attack against El Mansura and withdraw. In early April the wounded and sick were loaded onto ships, and with the flotilla providing protection, the shattered army set out for the safety of Damietta. The Muslim scouts quickly reported the crusaders' retreat and the sultan ordered his men to pursue and attack them. The Egyptians pressed their assaults, capturing the ships and slaughtering many of the sick and wounded soldiers, while surrounding Louis' army. The king took refuge in a village but was soon captured and held for ransom.

In the aftermath of his capture, Louis was taken in chains to El Mansura. He was now ill with dysentery and cared for by doctors provided by Turanshah. When the crusader monarch began to recover, he started negotiations for the release of the Christian prisoners. While he continued his talks with the sultan's envoys, many of the great barons tried to arrange their own release. After Louis learned of the private discussions, instructions were sent to the magnates telling them that only he could set the terms with the sultan. A treaty was finally negotiated, which secured the release of all Christian captives for the payment of a large ransom, the return of Damietta and the king's pledge to free his Muslim prisoners. After the terms of the agreement were finalized, the sultan's bodyguards, the Mamelukes, rebelled and murdered him, threatening the provisions of the settlement. The crusaders feared for their lives, but the Mamelukes honoured the treaty and on the evening of 6 May, following the partial payment of the ransom, the agreed number of captives was freed. On the following day the king, with the remnants of the army, boarded their ships leaving the shores of Egypt behind, and sailed to the Christian enclave at Acre. After landing at St Jean d'Acre, Louis was reunited with Queen Margaret, who had travelled there with their new son John Tristan.

The battered crusaders were welcomed by the inhabitants of Acre at the seashore and escorted into the town. Following his safe arrival at Acre after a six-day voyage, Louis had to quickly decide whether to return to France or remain in Outremer and reinforce the remnants of the Crusader Kingdom. In 1250 the Christians controlled most of the eastern Mediterranean coastline, from Gaza in the south to Cilician Armenia in the north, while Acre served as the perforce capital of the Kingdom of Jerusalem. King Louis discussed his decision with his advisors, and near the end of June announced to his barons and soldiers that he would stay in the Holy Land. He sent his two brothers back to France to aid Blanche with the administration of the kingdom and to raise more troops and money for the campaign to regain possession of Jerusalem. In early August Alphonse of Poitiers and Charles of Anjou, along with many French barons, sailed for home.

Louis remained determined to renew his crusade for Jerusalem, and in the summer his quest was aided by the arrival of envoys from An-Nasir, Sultan of Aleppo and great-grandson of Saladin. The sultan greatly disdained the murder of his cousin Turanshah by the Mamelukes, offering the return of Jerusalem to the king for his military intervention against the new ruler of Egypt, Aybak. While Louis continued to negotiate with An-Nasir, he sent an embassy to Cairo to press for the release of the remaining Christian prisoners. Aybak pledged to return all of the captives if the French would join his fight against An-Nasir. In a display of good faith, in October over 700 crusaders, including Hospitallers and Templars, were freed.

As Louis pressed his efforts for the release of all prisoners held by the Egyptians, war erupted between Cairo and Aleppo. An-Nasir invaded Egypt in February 1251, but was defeated near Cairo and forced to retire to Damascus. After his withdrawal he sent messengers to the Acre court asking for military aid against the Mamelukes. Louis was still negotiating with the Egyptians, and for his support against Aleppo demanded the delivery of all captives and the remission of the remaining ransom. The Mamelukes agreed to the terms, and the crusader knights and foot soldiers were soon released to the king.

While the sultans of Egypt and Aleppo continued their conflict, in March 1251 Louis travelled from Acre to Nazareth on a pilgrimage to the Church of the Annunciation, where the angel Gabriel appeared before Mary announcing she would bear the son of God. As the crusader king neared the town dressed in the hair shirt of a pilgrim, he dismounted from his horse and fell to his knees in prayer before walking into Nazareth on foot. He visited the church and offered prayers to Mary before hearing Mass and receiving communion in the morning from the legate. During his stay in the Latin East, Louis IX was offered safe passage to the holy sites of Jerusalem for a pilgrimage by the Sultan of Damascus, but he was prepared to visit the shrines only as the conqueror by force of arms.

From Nazareth the French king and his escort of knights and churchmen travelled further south to Caesarea and began his programme to reinforce the Christian presence in the Holy Land by repairing and strengthening the damaged fortifications. Under his direction craftsmen and workmen constructed a high thick wall with strategically placed towers surrounding the town. He remained in Caesarea for a year monitoring the fighting between the sultans of Cairo and Aleppo, while guarding the Christian-occupied towns, settling disputes between his barons and keeping his army ready to fight against the Muslims. The Christian towns along the Mediterranean coast were protected by their fleet, but the fortifications inland were more susceptible to attack and too difficult to defend. After meeting with his advisors, the king decided to order the abandonment of all fortified towns away from the coastline.

After the defensive works of Caesarea were restored, the king travelled to the Christian-held enclave at Jaffa. As the Frenchmen approached the town, Louis was greeted by the Count of Jaffa, John of Ibelin. The count had earlier joined the Seventh Crusade in Egypt, participating in the attacks against the Saracens at Damietta. He welcomed the king to his town and escorted the crusaders into Jaffa. Louis quickly set his men to work repairing and reinforcing Jaffa's defences, rebuilding the walls and towers and enlarging them to encircle the town. While in the fortified town, the crusaders fought sporadic skirmishes with the forces of Al-Nasir, who were probing the Christian defences for weak spots.

In April 1253 the Caliph of Bagdad mediated the ongoing war between the Egyptians and the Sultan of Aleppo. As the army of An-Nasir withdrew north from Egypt, the Muslim troops passed within several miles of Jaffa. Louis, still in Jaffa with his 1,400 knights and infantry, closely monitored the advance of the Saracens. In early May the Christian crossbowmen began harassing the Muslims' flanking guard, and a few days later they were attacked by a contingent of enemy soldiers. The crusaders were hard pressed to hold off the sultan's men and Louis was compelled to send a force of cavalry to rescue them.

After the clash with the crossbowmen, the Saracens resumed their march north, attacking the Christian-occupied town of Sidon. The defenses of the town had not yet been restored by the French crusaders and the Saracens overran the fortification, massacring over 2,000 Christians and looting the town. After hearing of the Muslim assault, in June 1253 the king set out for Sidon with his army. When the French reached the town, they began reconstructing the walls and ditches. While at Sidon, Louis received the news that his mother had died in November 1252. Overcome with grief, he withdrew from the encampment in solitude. Queen Margaret shortly joined her husband from Jaffa following the birth of a daughter, consoling and comforting him.

Without the experienced and capable rule of Blanche in France, Louis was greatly concerned for the future of his realm. The regency of France passed to his youngest brother, Charles of Anjou, who lacked maturity and experience to govern effectively. With an untested and fragmented government, open rebellion was threatened in Flanders and Henry III of England began reinforcing his army in his French fiefdom of Gascony. Louis IX was pressed by his vassals and prelates to return home, while the Levant barons encouraged him to sail to France and serve as an advocate for continued European support of the endangered Christian kingdom. By early 1254 the Capetian king was satisfied that he had accomplished everything possible to safeguard the crusader-held enclaves, and preparations were made for the voyage back to France.

The Christian fleet of eighteen ships set sail from Acre on 24 April 1254, first heading for Cyprus. As the king's vessel approached the island in dense fog, it hit a partially submerged sandbank. Believing the ship was going to sink, Louis prostrated himself and prayed for God's intervention. Lodged in the sand, the craft was finally freed by the crew manning the oars and with favourable winds. The journey to Cyprus was resumed and the damaged boat put into the harbour for repairs. The voyage was renewed, and after ten weeks Louis' ship sailed into the port of Hyeres in Provence. After reaching land the royal party had to wait several days before horses could be purchased and travel arrangements made. In Hyeres Louis heard stories about a shrine in the town of Aix where it was said the body of Mary Magdalen was buried. He travelled to the holy site to pray at the tomb before starting out for Paris. The royal entourage rode north, reaching the French capital in September. Before entering the city, Louis went to St Denis to thank God for the safe return of his family and the surviving crusaders. The Seventh Crusade had lasted six years and resulted in little appreciable gains for the Crusader Kingdom. The monarch took full responsibility for the failed expedition, which he believed was God's punishment for his sins. He returned to his French kingdom broken and defeated, saying: 'If I alone bore the shame and the calamity, I could suffer it, but all Christendom has been brought to confusion through me.' The ordeal in the Levant made him more pious and determined to rule his realm with gratitude by taking the role of European peacemaker.

While Louis was in the Levant, France had remained at peace under the firm reign of Queen Blanche and her three prelate advisors. The once-rebellious barons had learned the futility of defying the overlordship of the king's regime, remaining loyal to the throne. The king's two brothers had returned home from the Holy Land in August 1250, but were mainly occupied governing their extensive countships and regent queen continued to rule with her counsellors. Soon after the death of the regent queen, the monarchy was assumed by Charles of Anjou, who governed effectively with the assistance of the capable and experienced royal council. After arriving in Paris, Louis was anxious to re-establish his personal administration and reinstate his authority over his magnates, bishops and towns.

Over the past fifty years the Capetian and Plantagenet monarchies had negotiated a series of temporary truces to their ongoing dispute over the English claims to lands in western France. In his new role as European peacekeeper, Louis was determined to settle the conflict. The opportunity to meet with the English occurred in November, when Henry III petitioned the French regime for permission to bury his mother at the former Plantagenet Abbey of Fontevrault near the city of Chinon. Louis permitted the English party to cross his territory, and after the burial ceremony rode to Chartres to meet with Henry. They travelled together to Paris, passing through towns where they were greeted by large cheering crowds and colourful decorations. In Paris the Plantagenet king was lavishly entertained with state banquets, tours of the city and a visit to the recently completed Sainte Chapelle. The two monarchs exchanged valuable gifts and created a feeling of friendship during the visit. Before departing from Paris, Henry agreed to send an embassy to resolve his hereditary rights to the French territories of Maine, Anjou, Poitou and Normandy.

During 1257 the English regime sent several delegations to meet with Louis in Paris, but the rightful possession of the French lands remained unresolved. The discussions were renewed the next year, but the French demand for the renunciation of any claims by the English king's brother, Robert of Cornwall, and sister, Eleanor of Leicester, prevented a resolution. Pope Alexander IV intervened, encouraging the two kingdoms to find a compromise. In early May 1258 Henry III sent a new embassy to resume the treaty talks. They met with their French counterparts in late May, and after negotiating for just over a week signed a preliminary agreement.

At the beginning of February 1259, the French regime sent its envoys to England to receive the renunciation of King Henry, his brothers and Eleanor for their claims to their Capetian lands. While his brothers took the oath, Henry's sister refused to renounce her rights, putting peace between England and France in jeopardy. Before Eleanor agreed to relinquish her claims, she demanded a large financial compensation. Despite several attempts to negotiate with Eleanor, the final treaty was signed by the envoys of the two kings in late October 1259 without her agreement. A month later the English monarch travelled to Paris and was welcomed by Louis with a solemn procession to Notre Dame to offer prayers for peace. Following some last-minute modifications, the Treaty of Paris was signed in early December. Under the terms of agreement, the English pledged to abandon all their claims to Normandy, Anjou, Touraine, Poitou and Anjou, while the French ceded Henry some minor additions to his Gascony lands. The Plantagenet king, his heirs and relatives promised to pay liege homage for their French territories as a vassal to the Capetian kingdom and become one of its peers.

While the French crown was dealing with the English over their hereditary claims to French lands, Louis was negotiating with the King of Aragon, James I, over the countship of Languedoc in south-eastern France. King James I held possession of the city of Montpellier in the county and used it as a pretext to intervene in local affairs. He had earlier supported Count Raymond VII during the conflict in Toulouse and encouraged the Albigensians in their quest for religious freedom. After his return from the Seventh Crusade, Louis was anxious to preserve peace in the southern countship and opened negotiations with the Aragonese regime to end its political intrigues and seizures of land. Under the resulting Treaty of Corbeil, James gave up his hereditary rights to the territories in southern France, while Louis abandoned his claims to the region bordering the Pyrenees. Included in the settlement was the marriage between Louis' second son and future successor Philip to Isabella of Aragon. Similar border disputes were settled with Flanders and lesser neighbouring fiefdoms. As a result of his quest for peace through arbitration, Louis' reputation for justice and fairmindedness enhanced his renown as the peacekeeper of Europe. The King of the French continued to follow the Capetian policy of avoiding involvement in foreign affairs, directing his initiatives toward expanding his rule within the natural boundaries of France.

The Holy See and the Hohenstaufen heirs of Emperor Frederick II had been engaged in a struggle for control of Italy, and Louis had avoided involvement to maintain peace on his eastern border with Germany. In 1265 Guy Fulcod succeeded to the papal throne as Clement IV. He had previously been a minister at the French court and was a close advisor and friend of King Louis. Following his election, Clement IV renewed his predecessors' conflict with the King of Sicily, Manfred, of the Hohenstaufen family. The pope excommunicated Manfred, but undeterred by the Holy See's decree, he expanded his presence into northern Italy. Threated by the expansion of Manfred, the Holy See ceded the Kingdom of Sicily to Louis' brother, Charles of Anjou, to secure the involvement of the French in his conflict with the Germans. In 1265, with financial and military support from his brother, Charles crossed the Alps and advanced into Italy with his 30,000 soldiers. He moved through Lombardy, entering Rome unopposed by the troops of Manfred. In St Peter's Basilica on 6 January 1266, Charles was anointed King of Sicily by five cardinals empowered by Pope Clement. In late January the newly crowned monarch marched his forces south into the Sicilian kingdom and shattered Manfred's army at the Battle of Benevento. This decisive victory solidified Charles' rule over the Kingdom of Sicily, while the succession of his brother to the Sicilian throne greatly increased Louis' presence and influence in southern Italy.

During Louis' reign following his return from the Levant, his government was primarily guided by the quest for justice and maintenance of peace. He was greatly interested in the enforcement of neutrality and order in his courts and tried to secure equal justice for rich and poor. He frequently acted as judge, hearing each case with impartiality. The regime expanded the judicial function of the Paris Parliament and named the assembly as the Supreme Court of Justice for France, empowered to hear all appeals from the king's vassals. The parliament approved Louis' abolishment of private wars and settlement of disputes by individual combat, which were now to be resolved through court hearings. The king energetically participated in the debates of his parliament and held public audiences where all claimants had access to his personal justice. To promote the honesty of his appointed royal officials, directives were enacted to ensure their faithful performance of their duties; special representatives were sent each year to review the operation of his administrators. By actively pursuing these measures, the prestige and authority of the monarchy were increased over its vassals, towns and churchmen.

While the Christian states in the Outremer had been temporarily reinforced by the presence of Louis and his strengthening of their fortifications, within four years of his departure they were confronted by the resurgent Muslims of Egypt and a powerful new force from the east, the Mongols of Asia. The Mongols swept south from their lands in Asia, capturing Baghdad and moving down the Mediterranean coastline to overrun the Christian enclave at Aleppo in current-day Syria. Under increasing danger of destruction by the Muslims and Asians, the crusaders at Antioch were forced to negotiate an alliance with the Mongols to preserve their independence. The surviving crusader princedoms pleaded with the sovereigns of Europe for their intervention but there was little enthusiasm for another expeditionary force to the Levant.

In early September 1260 the Egyptian army, led by Sultan Baibars, advanced into eastern Galilea and decisively overwhelmed the Mongols at the Battle of Ain Jalud. With their victory the Muslims again became the dominant power in the Near East, while the Christians' quest for independence through their alliance with the Mongols was destroyed. In the aftermath of his defeat of the Mongols, Baibars moved against the crusaders. In 1266 he laid siege to Acre, the capital of the remnants of the Kingdom of Jerusalem, but his attacks were thwarted in bloody fighting. After failing to occupy Acre, the Muslims attacked Nazareth, overrunning the defensive works and sacking the town. Two years later Baibars marched his anti-Christian forces against Caesarea, battering the walls with catapults and breaking into the town, massacring the garrison and inhabitants. The Egyptians next attacked the walled town of Arsuf. After a siege of forty days, the Saracens smashed through the defences and stormed the town. Baibars offered the Knight Hospitallers, who were defending the citadel, safe passage if they surrendered. When the knights agreed and marched out of the fortress, they were enslaved and sold into bondage. The Muslims renewed their campaign of conquest against the Christian-held towns, capturing Acre in 1267. The next year the crusader fortress at Antioch fell to Baibars, who sold the entire population into slavery and burned the town to the ground.

While the Egyptians continued to widen their threat against the remaining crusader states, Louis grew increasingly determined to return to the Holy Land with an army to recapture Jerusalem and defend the Christian fiefdoms. In the early spring of 1267 he summoned his barons and prelates to discuss a papal bull calling for aid for the Levant. The king's vassals had little desire for another crusade and could only agree to order more prayers and holy processions, while forbidding martial tournaments to encourage knights to serve in the Holy Land. While the anti-crusading sentiment remained strong in France, Louis was compelled to delay his desired expedition to Outremer.

By early 1267 the few surviving crusader states in the Near East were hard pressed to survive under the constant pressure of the Egyptians. At the end of March, King Louis summoned his knights and bishops to announce his decision to again take the cross of a crusader. The original eagerness for holy war against the Saracens had greatly moderated over the years since the First Crusade in 1096, and the monarch's proclamation was not popular with his vassals and bishops.

Despite the opposition of his barons and his increasingly frail health, Louis pressed on with preparations for his second crusade to the Latin East. He sent messengers to King Charles I in Sicily encouraging him to take the cross. The Sicilian king had little interest in participating in the crusade, delaying his response to his brother. Pope Clement IV answered the French king's request for assistance by authorizing a levy against the Church's wealth in France. The Christian cause was preached throughout France and the surrounding princedoms by special legates from the pope. Members of the royal family joined the expedition, including Philip, now heir to the throne following the death of his older brother Louis in 1260. King Louis dispatched two envoys to contract for ships from the cities of Genoa and Marseilles. In April 1269 he ordered his agents back to Genoa to buy or lease additional vessels. Royal representatives were sent to acquire vast quantities of provisions, supplies and military equipment. In January 1270 Louis prepared his will and announced his regents to rule during his absence. In his will he made large donations to various charities and religious houses, while leaving lesser amounts to his wife and children. The king named two trusted advisors and friends as regents: Baron Simon of Nesle and Matthew of Vendome, Abbot of St Denis. Louis relentlessly supported the crusade, and largely through his efforts by early 1270 an army of knights and foot soldiers was organized.

By mid-March 1270 preparations were completed, and after attending religious services at St Denis, Louis and his sons set out for the Holy Land with the crusader army. Queen Margaret followed her husband to Vincennes, where they parted. The royal procession travelled slowly south, stopping briefly at various holy sites for the king to pray for God's support. The army did not reach the port of Aigues Mortes in southern France until late June, and on 1 July Louis embarked on his ship with his sons. On the following day the fleet set sail for the assembly port at Cagliari on the southern coastline of Sardinia, and on 3 July a second expedition led by the King of Navarre, Theobald II, put to sea from Marseille.

While the French were preparing for the Eighth Crusade, King James I of Aragon took the crusader cross and agreed to participate in the French campaign to the Levant. He assembled his army and set sail for the rendezvous point in Sardinia. As the Aragonese flotilla voyaged across the Mediterranean, it was caught in a terrible storm, with many of the transport vessels sunk and the survivors returning to Spain. Only a small contingent of James I's soldiers was able to join King Louis' army in North Africa.

During the voyage to the Latin East, Louis' crusader fleet was also struck by a great storm and the vessels were pounded for hours by large white capped waves. Despite the violent weather, the expeditionary force pushed on, reaching Sardinia on 8 July. The flotilla moored in the harbour for four days awaiting the arrival of the ships, which had been scattered during the squall. On 12 July Louis met with his great barons aboard his flagship to decide the location for the first attack of the army. Considering the chaotic state of the Crusader Kingdom, the logical choice was a campaign against the Egyptian forces in the region, but the North African Caliphate of Tunisia was chosen as the objective of the Eighth Crusade. The Islamic state was judged by the king's advisors to be lightly defended and would allow an easy conquest. The region held close ties to the powerful Egyptian sultan, and its seizure would eliminate a source of aid to the Muslim war effort against the Christians. The King of Sicily had a personal dispute with the Caliph of Tunisia, Muhammad I al-Mustansir, who had supported the Germans in the recent Italian wars. Charles of Anjou claimed rights against the caliph and was seeking an avenue to intervene to enforce them. However, the most important reason for selecting Tunis was the large army of the Sicilian king, which was needed to offset the tepid response in France and other parts of Europe to Louis' summons for crusader volunteers.

On 15 July 1270 Louis' crusader army sailed south from Cagliari, and with favourable winds driving the fleet the crossing to Tunis was made in just two days. The French landed on the coast unopposed, and the soldiers were sent to capture the harbour. The king established his encampment several miles from the city of Tunis and waited for the arrival of his brother Charles with his Sicilian troops, which were badly needed to reinforce his 10,000 men. When no safe water was found in the area, the crusaders were forced to move close to the ruins of the ancient city of Carthage. The Muslin caliph, Muhammad I, was not intimidated by the size of the Christian army, sending his skirmishers to attack the defences of the king. The French engineers were ordered to construct a wide trench around the fortified camp to deter further assaults by Muhammad I.

The crusader army had arrived in Tunisia at the height of the summer heat, making campaigning difficult. With soaring temperatures frequently reaching over 100 degrees, the crusaders laid siege to Tunis. Unable to find relief from the intense African heat and dressed in heavy wool tunics and chain mail, many French soldiers and their allies became ill with fever and dysentery. Numerous great barons died; the king's youngest son, John Tristan, was among the first victims, along with the papal legate.

As the siege against Tunis continued, Louis, who was in frail health at the beginning of the crusade, fell ill from the effects of the heat and contaminated food. As the monarch's health steadily grew worse and his life hung in the balance, the pestilence swept through the crusader ranks. The king's son and heir, Philip, also became ill. Father and son shared the same tent, and Louis frequently discussed with his son the rightful duties of being king. He admonished his son to always be the guardian of the Christian faith and defender of his subjects. The successor-designate was to exercise justice and promote peace in his kingdom. He warned his son not to undertake a war against any Christian state without great cause and deliberation.

With death approaching, Louis summoned his priests to his tent. He received the sacraments and called upon the patron saints of France, St Denis and St Genevieve, to intercede on his behalf with God. Despite his deteriorating health, the monarch remained conscious, even though at times he was unable to speak. On 25 August Louis had his body placed on ashes arranged in the shape of a cross on the floor, dying in the afternoon after uttering his final word: 'Jerusalem'.

Philip III was now acknowledged as successor to the Capetian throne, but he was still weak from fever and command of the army was assumed by King Charles I of Sicily, who had arrived shortly after the death of John Tristan. Philip ordered the corpse of his father prepared for the return to Paris and burial at St Denis. The body was boiled in water, separating the bones from their flesh, and carefully placed in chests.

The Christian army had been decimated by the epidemic of dysentery and high fever, and there was little enthusiasm for the continuance of the war against Caliph Muhammad I. Despite their apathy, under the leadership of Charles I the crusaders moved against the Muslims' fortifications, capturing the Tunisian outposts and winning two minor skirmishes. When the caliph sent messengers offering to discuss peace terms, Philip III agreed to meet the Tunisian envoys on the advice of his uncle. Under the resulting treaty signed in October 1270, the crusaders agreed to withdraw from Tunisia, while Muhammad I pledged to pay a large sum in gold to offset the expenses of the expedition, permit the Christians free trade in Tunis, allow monks and priests to reside in the caliphate and exchange prisoners. After the treaty was finalized and signed on 1 November 1270, Philip III and the crusaders embarked on their ships, sailing to Trapini on the southern coast of Sicily. After landing in Italy, Philip led the army overland back to France, travelling slowly up the peninsula.

While the French crusader army advanced north to France in 1271, a force of knights and foot soldiers attempted to continue the Eighth Crusade against the Muslims in current-day Syria. As the small Christian flotilla sailed toward the Holy Land, its ships were hit by a fierce storm and the soldiers were forced to return to France, concluding the campaign to recapture Jerusalem for the Christian world. The Eighth Crusade had lasted for fifteen months and ended with the Egyptian Muslims still in control of the Holy Land, with the exception of the city of Acre and a few small fortified enclaves. Acre remained the sole remaining princedom until it fell to the Saracens in 1291.

King Philip III arrived in Paris in May 1271, and after establishing his rule led the funeral procession to St Denis for the burial of his father. King Louis IX had reigned over France for forty-three years and died at the age of fifty-six. In the years following his death, his tomb became a holy shrine for pilgrimages, where many miracles were said to have occurred. In 1297 the Holy See ordered an investigation of the reported acts of divine intervention, and based on the results and the ongoing prestige and reputation of Louis, Pope Boniface VIII consecrated him to sainthood.

Selected Sources:

Bartlett, W.B., *The Last Crusade – The Seventh Crusade & the Final Battle for the Holy Land*.

Bradbury, Jim, *The Capetians – Kings of France 987–1318*.

Castries, Rene de la Croix, *The Lives of the Kings and Queens of France*.

Fawtier, Robert, *The Capetian Kings of France*.

Ferguson, Wallace K. & Bruun, Geoffrey, *A Survey of European Civilization*.

Hallman, Elizabeth M., *Capetian France 987–1318*.

Joinville, Jean de, *Saint Louis, King of France*.

Law, Joy, *Fleur de Lys – The Kings and Queens of France*.

Masson, Gustave, *Medieval France*.

Matthews, Rupert, *The Popes*.

Perry, Frederick, *Saint Louis – The Most Christian King*.

Rendina, Claudio, *The Popes*.

Riley-Smith, Jonathan, *The Crusades*.

Runciman, Steven, *The Sicilian Vespers – A History of the Mediterranean World in the Thirteenth Century*.

Chapter Nine

Robert I the Bruce

Defender of Scottish Independence

By the beginning of the fourteenth century much of Scotland had been occupied by the English regime, but under Robert the Bruce's unrelenting irregular warfare campaign of ambushes, marauding raids and attacks against the enemy's lines of communications, the occupation forces had been largely driven out of the kingdom, with only two enclaves remaining at Stirling Castle and the fortress at Berwick. The reigning Plantagenet king, Edward II, was determined to reimpose his sovereignty over the rebellious Scots, and at Berwick Castle in May 1314 assembled a formidable army from all parts of his realm. As the English marched toward their garrison at Stirling Castle, King Robert I summoned the soldiers of Scotland to muster in defence of their land. By June over 9,000 men from every region of the land answered the call to repel the invaders. The Scottish troops were organized into four large mobile formations of pikemen, called schiltrons. Bruce deployed his forces in a wooded area at New Park, which straddled the road from Falkirk near the crossing of the Bannockburn, and awaited the arrival of the invading army of approximately 20,000 troops. In the morning of 23 June, after attending Mass, the Scots took up their defensive positions. As the Plantagenet vanguard approached on the old Roman road and emerged from the woods, their multi-coloured banners and armour glistening in the bright summer sun were clearly visible to Bruce's men. When the English knight Sir Henry de Bohun saw the mounted Scottish king in the distance inspecting his battle line, he seized the opportunity for personal glory, charging across the green pasture land to challenge him with his lance positioned for battle. King Robert answered the taunt of his adversary, galloping toward him armed with an axe. As Bruce reached de Bohun, he swerved away from his lowered lance and, rising in his stirrups, brought his axe down on the helmet of his opponent, piercing his skull, to the thunderous roars of the Scots. The battle was renewed the following day, and despite their repeated attacks, the English cavalry could not break the determined Scots' schiltrons, as the pikemen held their ground. King Robert's great victory at Bannockburn consolidated his reign over Scotland and later led to the full recognition of Scottish independence by the English throne.

The future King Robert I the Bruce was born at Turnberry Castle on the Ayrshire coast of Scotland, overlooking the Firth of Clyde, on 11 July 1274, the first of five sons and six daughters born to Robert VI of Annandale and Marjorie, heiress to the Earldom of Carrick. Through his father, Robert was the seventh Earl of Bruce and the direct descendent of Adam the Bruce, who had sailed from Normandy to England with the invasion army of William I in 1066. Adam was granted titles and properties in the northern region of the realm for his martial exploits during the conquest of England. Succeeding generations acquired wealth, privileges, titles and lands through marriages and military services to the Scottish and English regimes. By the time of the seventh Earl of Bruce's birth, his family commanded a large following among both the Plantagenet and Scottish warlords and churchmen, while acquiring prestige and respect.

Soon after his birth, Robert VII of Bruce was placed with foster parents, spending his first twelve years in their household. He acquired their language of Gaelic, which was widely spoken throughout western Scotland, the central Highlands and Western Isles. Under the guidance of monks, he was taught reading and writing and was exposed to the French, Lowland Scottish and English languages. While Robert was acquiring a basic education, he began training as a feudal warlord under the tutelage of renowned masters of arms and was instructed in the weapons of a knight, mastering the use of the lance, sword and axe, while learning to fight from a charging warhorse. To practice his martial skills, Robert took part in numerous jousting tournaments in England and Scotland, gaining a reputation for his fighting abilities and acts of chivalry, while spending long hours hunting wild boar and deer in the forests, sharpening his prowess in preparation for battle. It was customary for the sons of high-ranking noblemen to spend their late boyhood years in the household of an ally of their fathers, performing the duties of a page and later squire, and Robert served his apprenticeship learning the proper etiquette and fighting skills of a knight.

In 1286 the reigning Scottish king, Alexander III, died, leaving only his Norwegian-born granddaughter Margaret I as his successor to the throne. In April the great earls, barons and prelates assembled at Scone to pledge their fealty to Margaret I, swearing to protect and defend the peace in Scotland. To rule in the name of the minor queen, a regency council was organized with six guardians. Three of the appointed guardians were supporters of Robert of Annandale, the sixth Earl of Bruce, while the remaining three safeguarded the interest of John Balliol. While the queen stayed at the Norwegian court, the guardians governed Scotland for the next three years, maintaining the peace among the warlords.

During the summer of 1289, King Edward I of England exercised his hereditary rights as the great-uncle of the young queen and brother-in-law of Alexander III, petitioning the Scottish regency and Norwegian king to send representatives to England to discuss the future of Queen Margaret. Meeting at Salisbury in October, they agreed to bring the queen to Scotland and delay negotiations for her marriage until receiving the endorsement of the King of Norway and Edward I. Soon after the agreement was accepted by the Scottish nobles and churchmen, the English monarch proposed the marriage of his young son, Edward, to the queen. The union between the two crowns promised to strengthen Scottish independence, and with assurances of the continued individual sovereignties of each kingdom the proposal was approved by the magnates and prelates. The arrangements for the marriage were finalized and in September 1290 the seven-year-old Queen Margaret embarked on a ship in Norway, sailing first to the Orkney Islands. However, during the voyage she became ill and died soon after landing in Orkney. Margaret was the last surviving member of the Canmore House and her death thrust Scotland into a succession crisis that was only resolved by the bloody wars of independence and the emergence of Robert I as king.

In the aftermath of the end of the Canmore dynasty, the right of succession to the Scottish crown was pursued by numerous claimants. The Bruce faction, led by the eighty-year-old Robert V the Competitor, presented a strong challenge as the direct descendent of David, the younger brother of two former Canmore monarchs, Malcolm IV and William I. The family began to mobilise for the coming conflict and the young Robert, now sixteen, actively took part in the preparations, while their vassals and allies gathered to protect their interests. While the Bruces mustered their forces, in southern Scotland John Balliol rallied his supporters and laid claim to the monarchy, while other groups armed to take the throne by force-of-arms. As the kingdom rapidly moved toward civil war, the Scottish Parliament intervened, offering Edward I of England the right to arbitrate the rising crisis. The Plantagenet king accepted the petition, but with the provision that each pretender must acknowledge him as overlord of Scotland. With the threat of open warfare escalating, the terms were accepted by the parliament.

In May 1291 the English king invited the Scottish representatives and claimants to meet at Norham Castle in northern England to hear his decision. Meeting with the Scots, Edward forced the guardians and magnates to publicly recognize him as overlord for Scotland. On 13 June he received the fealty of the Scottish lords and later in the month travelled from castle to castle in the kingdom, establishing his supremacy over the abbots, bishops, barons, knights and freemen, who knelt before him to swear their loyalty.

After securing suzerainty over Scotland, in June 1291 Edward I convened a great court at Berwick Castle to name the next King of Scotland. Over 100 auditors were chosen, with forty nominated by John Balliol, forty from the Bruce party and the final twenty-four selected by the English realm. The court was reconvened the next year and the auditors began debating the pleas of Bruce and Balliol. The Scottish auditors were unable to make a decision, referring the choice to the king's delegates. On 17 November 1292, in the great hall of Berwick Castle, the auditors announced their decision, declaring John Balliol as the rightful successor to the Scottish throne. After hearing the proclamation, the Bruce faction withdrew from the castle without offering homage to John of Balliol. Thirteen days later Balliol was crowned monarch on the Stone of Destiny at Scone, and on 26 December rendered fealty to Edward I as his lord superior.

While the Bruce family remained away from court on their properties in Scotland and England, John Balliol was confronted with a series of demeaning edicts from Edward, making it clear that he was now considered a puppet king of the English regime. Edward voided his prior agreements with the Scots, which guaranteed their courts and laws, and imposed his authority over the legal rights and independence of King John. During the reign of the Canmore dynasty, the monarch was regarded as the source of legal justice and expected to punish criminals and judge equitably. When Edward allowed appeals from Balliol's justice to be heard in English courts, the role of Scottish kingship was reduced to provincial governor. In November 1293 King John appeared before the Plantagenet parliament to defend his judgement in a legal challenge, and was treated with discourtesy and contempt by the representatives. While the English increased their pressure on the Scots, the Bruce faction stayed away from the Scottish court, still refusing to offer fealty to King John. Robert VII of Bruce had been granted the Scottish Earldom of Carrick by his father, and the young lord continued to administer his lands in the north, while Balliol struggled to maintain his independence from England. Earl Robert travelled extensively through the region, expanding his powerbase and imposing his authority over the Bruce family's vassals and allies, while gaining a loyal following of non-partisan warlords.

As Robert VII expanded his powerbase, in 1295 the twenty-one-year-old lord was married to Isabella, daughter of the Earl of Mar. The Bruce family had longstanding political ties to the Earldom of Mar, and the marriage strengthened its relationship. The marriage to Isabella was brief, ending two years later with her unexpected death. Robert and his wife had one child, Marjorie, whose descendants later established the Stuart dynasty, beginning with King Robert II in 1371. Robert of Carrick did not marry again until 1302, when he married Elizabeth of Burgh, the daughter of the powerful and influential English Earl of Ulster. The politically arranged union gave the Bruce faction increased access to new allies and friends in northern Ireland and resulted in the births of four children, including the future King David II, who was born in March 1324 and succeeded to the Scottish throne in 1329.

As Balliol endured the relentless humiliations of the English crown, in 1295 the Scots were forced by Edward to participate in his campaign of suppression against the rebellious Welsh. The Scottish earls considered the demand an infringement on the realm's rights to declare war and sent envoys to France to negotiate a military alliance without the approval of King John. At the same time, they formed a new advisory board of four earls, four bishops and four barons to serve as a policy-making body. Under the direction of the council, a military alliance was signed with the French in February 1296. As part of the treaty, the Scottish council pledged to invade England in support of the French in their ongoing conflict with the English.

As events were rapidly unfolding in Scotland, Robert VII of Bruce was on his English lands, while his father had gone to Norway to negotiate an alliance with the Norwegian king, Eric, against John of Balliol. Following the death of Robert the Competitor, his son Robert VI of Bruce travelled back to England to assume leadership of the family. Shortly after his return, the English regime named Robert VI to the governorship of Carlisle, promising him the Scottish crown when Balliol was deposed. Meanwhile in Scotland, Balliol finally countered the relentless interventions of King Edward in Scottish affairs, summoning the earls to assemble for war against the Plantagenets. The Bruce faction had not given homage to King John and ignored the petition to mobilize. In retaliation, the Scottish monarch ordered the seizure of the Bruce family's properties in Scotland.

The Scottish host was ordered by John Balliol to assemble at Caldenly on 18 March 1296. The bulk of Balliol's forces were militiamen, who were farmers and craftsmen required to perform military service in times of danger. The men served as the infantry of the army and were armed with spears, axes and swords, while the magnates and knights performed the duties of the light cavalry. Edward I mustered a large army of well-trained and experienced soldiers, and in March advanced against the English Lord of Wark, who had sided with the Scots in defiance of his sovereign. The English king hastened to Northumberland and seized control of Wark Castle to ignite the Scottish War of Independence.

In the wake of the encounter at Wark Castle, the Scots, led by John Comyn, Lord of Badenoch, swept through Northumberland, putting to sword and flame the scattered villages in support of John Balliol's independence from England. After ravaging the area, Comyn led his men in an attack against the Bruce stronghold at Carlisle. Under the command of Robert VI of Bruce and his eldest son, the Earl of Carrick, his forces manned the walls to repel the attacks of the Scots. Repulsed from Carlisle, the Scottish army hastened southeast, laying waste through Northumberland. While the Scots were ravaging the region, King Edward advanced his powerful army against the castle at Berwick in the Borders. The town served as an important trading seaport for commerce with the Flemish and German merchants, and was only lightly defended with earthen works and timber stockades. Edward ordered his navy to launch the initial attack, attempting to take the city from the seaward side. When four vessels from the English fleet ran aground, Scottish troops launched a sortie from the fortress to burn them, while the defenders on the walls yelled insults at the English calling them, 'Tailed dogs.' After the failure of his initial assault, Edward sent his soldiers against the weak defences, breaking into the town and massacring the men, women and children. Following the slaughter of hundreds, the English king ordered a halt to the plundering and murder.

With Berwick now under English control, Edward sent a large contingent of troops under the command of the Earl of Surrey to seize the fortress at Dunbar at the mouth of the Firth of Forth, which had been recently occupied by the Scots. As the English knights and foot-soldiers proceeded north, their scouts reported the presence of a large Scottish force on the heights surrounding the town. On 27 April 1296 the Earl of Surrey led his men forward, deploying them into the valley below the enemy. When the English disappeared into a wooded area, the Scottish soldiers believed they were retreating and charged down the hillside in great disorder. At the approach of the Scots, Surrey formed his veteran cavalry into battle formation, ploughing into the enemy forces to steadily drive them back, massacring the militiamen and capturing many of the knights for ransom. The next day Edward arrived at the battlefield and accepted the surrender of Dunbar Castle. The defeat at Dunbar ended John Balliol's hopes of gaining independence.

Following the battle, Edward demanded King John renounce his throne and accept unconditional surrender. With the suppression of his rebellion, the Scottish king was forced to submit to the Plantagenet crown and agree to the English terms. John Balliol was taken prisoner and sent to the Tower of London, where he remained for three years.

Edward stayed at Berwick Castle for three weeks organizing his new Scottish government before making a triumphant march through Scotland, receiving the homage of the prelates, nobles and towns. During the tour Robert VI and the Earl of Carrick, Robert VII, issued letters patent declaring fealty to the Plantagenet monarch as their overlord. In the aftermath of John Balliol's surrender of his monarchy, Robert VI of Bruce reminded King Edward of his earlier promise to name him King of Scotland, but Edward cunningly replied: 'Have we nothing else to do than win kingdoms for you?' Following the king's terse response, the Bruce faction left court and returned to their lands in England.

In early September 1296, King Edward I returned to England to pursue his ongoing war with France, leaving the conquered Scottish kingdom under the rule of four English magnates. The Scottish castles were garrisoned with English troops and the government of the realm was administered by the king's bureaucrats from Berwick Castle, which was being rebuilt into a formidable fortress. Edward, in need of money to fight the French, pressed his Scottish lieutenants to collect additional taxes from the Scots. As the Plantagenet officials demanded more money, a growing band of dispossessed and oppressed men gathered and, under the leadership of Andrew Moray and William Wallace, revolt erupted throughout Scotland by the late spring of 1297. Operating in small groups, the Scots ambushed and harried the English occupiers. As the rebellion gained momentum, more fighters joined with Wallace in the south and Moray in the north, the attacks against Edward's forces intensifying.

Robert VII of Bruce, Earl of Carrick, was at Carlisle when the Scottish revolt erupted and became increasingly distraught at the humiliations suffered by his native land. He had earlier sworn fealty to the English king, but at the price of the subjugation of Scotland. While the earl remained at Carlisle, Sir William Douglas of Douglasdale broke his allegiance to the throne and joined the rebellion. When informed of Sir William's revolt, King Edward ordered Robert of Carrick to take an armed force and seize his castle. The twenty-two-year-old Bruce retained aspirations for the Scottish crown that had earlier been promised to his father, but resented the English usurpation of his homeland. He gathered his father's retainers in Annandale and hastened toward Douglasdale. During the journey he decided to disavow his allegiance to the English and fight to secure his inheritance to Scotland's monarchy. The earl summoned his knights, telling them: 'No man holds his own flesh and blood in hatred and I am no exception. I must join my own people and the nation in which I was born.'

Shortly after abandoning the English regime, Robert united his forces with the men of James Stewart at Irvine in southwestern Scotland. As the Scots were assembling their forces, Edward ordered his northern barons, Sir Henry Percy and Robert Clifford, to crush the uprising. The two English warlords mustered a formidable army of knights and militiamen, advancing against the rebels at Irvine. Confronted by the large royal host and with dissension among the ranks rampant, the Scots were compelled to surrender without a fight, agreeing to give hostages to guarantee their good faith. While the Scots in the southwest had been neutralized, in other parts of the kingdom the insurgents led by Wallace and Moray continued the fight against the English. They gained control of castles in the northeast, and in the summer of 1297 Moray and Wallace joined forces, striking the invaders repeatedly and expanding the territory under their control.

When King Edward was notified of the loss of Scottish towns and castles, he appointed John Warenne, sixth Earl of Surrey, to crush the Scottish uprising and left for France to renew his war with King Philip IV. While Surrey was assembling his army, Wallace and Moray proceeded south to Stirling and deployed their 5,800 troops to defend the crossing of the Forth River by occupying the high ground overlooking Stirling Bridge. On 9 September Warenne encamped near the river, where he made two attempts to find a peaceful settlement, but Wallace and Moray refused to talk, using the interlude to gather more men and reinforce their positions. On the morning of 11 September, Surrey ordered his 2,000 cavalry, led by Hugh of Cressingham, to advance over Stirling Bridge and attack the rebels. When about half of the English horsemen had crossed the narrow wooden bridge, riding two abreast, Wallace and Moray gave the order for their foot-soldiers to move forward. The Scottish pikemen rushed down the hillside into the long column of knights before advancing to attack the English infantry in a savage onslaught. During the melee Cressingham charged the massed Scottish pikemen but was pulled from his horse and butchered. The Scotsmen gained control of the bridge, cutting off any chance of relief forces reaching the battlefield or escape for the king's soldiers. With his army on the north side of Stirling Bridge virtually destroyed, Warenne ordered his men to retreat toward Berwick Castle, abandoning the Lowlands to the Scots. As the English army fell back in disarray, the rebels continued to harass their supply trains and slaughter stragglers. Moray and Wallace declared their kingdom's freedom from English occupation.

During October and November Wallace advanced his forces into northern England, razing towns and causing havoc. As he continued his triumphant campaign, additional Scottish magnates with their vassals joined the fight. In March 1298 the Scottish earls and churchmen met at the Forest Parliament in the Selkirk woodlands and elected William Wallace as sole guardian of Scotland. Robert of Bruce was one of the four earls present at the parliament and supported Wallace's election.

While the Scots were proclaiming their independence, Edward I returned from France after arranging a truce with Philip IV. He moved his seat of government from London to York and mustered his army, determined to reimpose his power over the Scottish realm. The king assembled a force of 2,500 cavalrymen, archers from Wales and French Gascon crossbowmen, while amassing over 12,000 infantrymen. The royal host passed into Scotland on 1 July. When Edward received news that the Scots were encamped near Falkirk in the central Lowlands, northwest of Edinburgh, he advanced to attack them, riding at the front of his army. While the English hastened toward Falkirk, Wallace established his defensive position on a hillside and surrounded it with a barrier of wooden stakes. The Scottish pikemen were drawn up into four large schiltrons, with groups of archers stationed between the infantrymen. The battle began with Edward sending his heavy cavalry crashing into the flanks of the schiltrons, as the English archers fired volleys into the ranks of the Scots, decimating the pikemen. After their initial charge, the horsemen re-formed and attacked again, cutting down the Scots in a great slaughter. Wallace and the survivors fled, leaving thousands of wounded and dead on the battlefield.

Following his defeat at Falkirk, William Wallace resigned his guardianship and was replaced by Robert of Bruce and John III Comyn of Badenoch. The Comyn alliance ardently supported John Balliol's kingship and was suspicious of Robert's ambitions for the throne. As a means of maintaining peace, Bishop William Lamberton of St Andrews was added to the guardianship council. In November 1299 the three guradians mustered the army and proceeded to the English garrison at Stirling Castle. The Scotsmen besieged the stronghold, and the garrison surrendered when Edward failed to mount a relief.

Edward, resolved to regain hegemony over Scotland, amassed a large army at Carlisle in late 1300. When friction between Bruce and Comyn intensified over how to defend the kingdom against the impending English attack, Robert was replaced by Sir Ingram of Umfraville, an ally of John Balliol. In midsummer the English host marched into Scotland, led by the king and his son, Edward of Caernarvon, and made for Galloway in the southwest. While the king's troops were moving deeper into Scotland, Robert of Bruce launched a series of independent raids against the English occupation forces in his home region, overrunning them and freeing his lands of foreign occupation.

Meanwhile, after advancing as far as Wigtown without encountering the Scots, Edward returned to his base at Kirkcudbright. At his encampment he was met by the papal representative of Pope Boniface VIII, who had been sent to petition the king to end his conflict with Scotland. Edward refused to comply with the request, but was faced with the growing dissension of his vassals and the desertion of his militiamen. As internal and external pressures mounted against renewing the campaign, in late October 1301 he agreed to a seven-month truce arranged by the French monarch.

During the truce the Scottish magnates reorganized their government, replacing the three guardians with sympathizers of the deposed King John of Balliol. As the Scots continued to plan for Balliol's restoration, Edward used the armistice to prepare a new invasion of the northern kingdom. In 1301 the Plantagenet king named his son successor-designate and gave him command of half of the invasion army, under the guidance of the veteran soldier Henry of Lacy, Earl of Lincoln. Edward prepared a two-pronged attack into Scotland, sending the newly named Prince of Wales with half of the forces to the southwest to break local resistance, while the remaining troops advanced to Bothwell Castle under his command, ravaging the Scots during the march north. By 24 September Edward had captured Bothwell, while his son seized the Bruce fortress at Turnberry. After abandoning Turnberry, Robert of Bruce refused to engage the English in a pitched battle but constantly harassed their flanks and lines of communication, compelling Prince Edward to pull back south. While Edward of Wales had been thwarted in his campaign, King Edward was forced to retire from Bothwell to Linlithgow, where he was joined by his son. The king's initiative in 1301 had failed to achieve any favourable results and a new truce was negotiated with the Scottish regime, agreeing to place the towns and castles recently captured under French custody until a permanent peace was arranged.

During the course of the English campaign, John Balliol was released from papal custody and sent to his castle in Picardy by the French king. Soon a rumour spread in Scotland that Philip IV of France was sending Balliol to his kingdom with a great army to impose his rule. If Balliol returned to Scotland, Robert Bruce's expectations of becoming monarch would end and his properties would be seized. He refused to make peace with John Balliol and chose to secure his English properties by submitting to King Edward. In January 1302 he surrendered to the Plantagenet monarchy, negotiating a settlement that guaranteed the rightful possession of his lands in England and Scotland.

In 1302 the English kingdom's relations with Europe improved dramatically with its reconciliation with the French and Pope Boniface VIII. Following years of war with Philip for possession of his French lands, Edward could now devote his full energies and resources to the destruction of the Scottish rebellion. In a prelude to his invasion of Scotland, he aggressively raised new revenue and recruited a formidable army. In May 1303 the troops were assembled around Roxburgh in southeastn Scotland. The host was divided into two wings, with the Prince of Wales nominally leading the western arm and Edward taking the remaining soldiers up the eastern route.

Edward, Prince of Wales, reached western Scotland in mid-May accompanied by Robert of Bruce. The prince's men marched virtually unopposed into the realm, capturing castles and towns as they moved north. Meanwhile, in eastern Scotland, Edward advanced north, bypassing the great stronghold at Stirling and encountering little opposition. In September he reached Kinloss Abbey near Elgin, receiving the submissions of the local warlords and people. The army turned south for Dunfermline Abbey, where they spent the winter. While the king remained at his winter quarters, many Scots came to offer their submission. John Comyn, Lord of Badenoch, had earlier assumed the guardianship from John Soules, and on 9 February 1304 negotiated a settlement with the English at Strathord near Perth. Acting under the advice of Robert Bruce during the discussions, Edward offered generous terms to the Scots, allowing them to retain their properties and agreeing to protect their laws and customs. As part of the agreement, the Scottish rebels were required to hunt down and capture William Wallace. Robert Bruce was ordered by the king to participate in an attack against Wallace and his men at Selkirk Forest. The English raiding party charged into the forest, scattering the rebels, while Wallace fled to safety. Edward suspected Robert had warned the insurgents, and gave him a stern rebuke. On 3 August 1305 William Wallace was seized in Glasgow, then brutally tortured and decapitated in London on orders from King Edward.

Following his rejection of John Balliol's kingship and submission to the English crown, Bruce had maintained cordial relations with the Plantagenet government. He had been summoned several times to perform martial service, but his participation was continually delayed and muted. In April 1304 he was ordered to supply soldiers for the ongoing siege against the garrison at Stirling Castle, which had refused to surrender without receiving permission from King John Balliol. Robert sent a message to the king, notifying him he was having difficulty collecting men and horses for the campaign. In May Bruce arrived at Stirling to render fealty to the monarch for his English estates. While at Stirling, in June, Bruce held a secret meeting with Bishop Lamberton to discuss his succession to the Scottish throne as the rightful heir. Lamberton became committed to Robert's assumption of the crown, and with his support the allegiance of the Scottish Church was transferred to him from John Balliol.

While Robert and Bishop Lamberton made secret preparations to recover their homeland, in May 1305 a Scottish Parliament was assembled at Perth with the approval of Edward I to elect ten advisors to meet with the English regime to recommend a future government for their land. Under the resulting Ordinance for Government, an English viceroy was named for Scotland, while a chamberlain and chancellor were chosen from the Plantagenet court. To give the appearance of Scottish participation in the new administration, a council of twenty magnates and prelates, including Robert of Bruce, Bishop Lamberton and John Comyn, was appointed to assist the viceroy. To ensure peace, English soldiers were garrisoned in the principal castles. Despite the presence of the advisory board, Scotland continued to be ruled by foreign officials.

Through Bruce's association with Bishop Lamberton of Glasgow, many Scottish warlords were attracted to his banner of rebellion, but to unite northern Scotland to his cause the rebels needed the endorsement of the Comyn alliance led by John III Comyn of Badenoch, also known as the Red Comyn. Bruce met with him and negotiated a settlement to secure his allegiance. The Red Comyn agreed to Robert's assumption of the Scottish crown, while receiving the ownership of the Bruce properties. Shortly after his meeting with Robert, John III Comyn sent messages to King Edward informing him of their arrangement. During the winter Robert Bruce was summoned to the royal court and confronted by the king. Robert made light of the accusations but was forced to remain at court. Several days later the king announced to his inner circle of advisors his intention to order the death of Bruce. Among the sovereign's confidants was a friend of the Scottish earl, who sent a message informing him of Edward's plans. During the night Robert quietly slipped away from the palace making his way back to Scotland.

In the wake of his escape to Scotland, Bruce quickly made arrangements to meet the Red Comyn at the church in Gray Friars in Dumfries, near the mouth of the River Nith. The two warlords met at the church on 10 February 1306, with Bruce confronting Sir John with his treachery. A fight erupted near the alter and during the struggle Red Comyn was killed, when Bruce stabbed him with his dagger. Bruce was now in danger of an attack by the Comyn alliance in revenge for his involvement in the death of their leader and excommunication from the Church for killing Sir John on religious property. To prepare for a possible confrontation with the Comyns, the Earl Robert assembled his retainers and allies and ordered his men to reinforce his castles. While strengthening his fortifications, he sent troops to seize several enemy strongholds. As news of Robert's attacks against Sir John spread across Scotland, many warlords, primarily from the southwest, rallied to his cause for the kingship. As Robert's quest for the monarchy gained momentum, he made his way to Glasgow to make his confession to Bishop George Wishart. After securing forgiveness from the Church, the bishop gave him the royal standard and coronation robes. He now rode to Scone, near Perth, with a growing retinue of supporters for his inauguration as Scottish monarch.

On 25 March 1306 at the time-honoured site for the enthronement of Scottish kings at Scone, the lords and prelates assembled for the crowning of Robert I of Bruce. It was the traditional right of the Earl of Fife to lead the new king to the throne, but he was now in London as a ward of King Edward, so his aunt, Isabella of Fife, performed the function. She led Robert to the throne and placed a golden crown on his head. Two days later Bishop Lamberton arrived at Scone and celebrated High Mass for the newly crowned King Robert I of Scotland.

The hurried coronation signalled the outbreak of civil war in Scotland. When Edward I received reports of the Scottish revolt, he began preparations to invade. To turn the Scots against their new king by separating him from the Church, he wrote to Pope Clement V informing him of Bruce's act of murder against John Comyn in a religious site and petitioned his excommunication. The pope quickly granted his request and the announcement was made on 5 June by the Archbishop of Canterbury.

While the English king was preparing for the Scottish invasion, King Robert was raising an army in his base of support in the southwest, with most of his men coming from his own properties and allies. He rode north to recruit additional soldiers but found few volunteers in the lands of the Comyn faction. Meanwhile, Edward sent an army led by Aymer de Valence, Earl of Pembroke, north to reimpose his sovereignty. The earl advanced into Scotland, encountering little opposition, and soon captured Perth. To defend his newly claimed monarchy, Bruce moved south to confront Pembroke at Perth. The Scots lacked engines and towers to besiege the city, forcing Robert to challenge the English to abandon their defensive works and fight in the open. Under the influence of his Comyn warlords, who wanted to mount a surprise attack on the Scots that night, Pembroke agreed to the battle on the following day. The

Scotsmen drew back and built an encampment at Methven Wood, six miles away, believing they were secure for the night. The English and their Comyn allies waited until dusk before charging into the Scottish camp, catching Robert's men unprepared. The Scottish king rallied his forces as his knights and infantrymen rushed into the fray. They were quickly overwhelmed by the larger army and compelled to retreat, leaving hundreds of dead on the battlefield. King Robert escaped accompanied by his wife Elizabeth, daughter Marjorie and a contingent of knights and pikemen. Less than four months after his coronation he was a fugitive pursued by the English.

Following his devastating defeat at the Methven Wood, Robert and his small band of survivors withdrew to the foothills of the Atholl Mountains, waiting for stragglers to join him from the battle. After several weeks he made his way to Perthshire. As the Scots travelled through the lands of the Macdougalls of Lorne, who were ardent supporters of the murdered John Comyn, they were ambushed at Dalry on 11 August. Led by John Macdougall, brother-in-law of the Red Comyn, the Highlanders swarmed down the steep hillsides armed with axes crashing into the king's soldiers. Robert quickly reformed his battered men and began to retreat, fighting off the enemy forces as he fell back. He took charge of the rearguard when it was attacked by the Highlanders, and during a fierce melee killed three men before leading his troops to safety after the loss of many soldiers and horses.

Robert was pursued by the English and their Comyn allies and forced to flee to the west. He sent Elizabeth and his young daughter to the care of the Earl of Atholl at Kildrummy Castle. In early September King Edward's forces renewed their campaign of subjugation against the rebel lords, capturing the Earl of Atholl's fortress. The king's family had escaped at the approach of the English, but as they travelled to join Robert's sister Isabella in Norway, they were intercepted at Tain by a Comyn supporter, who handed them over to Edward's men. The Scottish monarch's lieutenants were brutally tortured and executed by Pembroke, while Marjorie was sent to a nunnery and Elizabeth placed in a royal manor house under close guard.

In the aftermath of the battle at Dalry, King Robert and his small band of soldiers made their way toward Dunaverty Castle in the Western Isles.

During the journey they had to avoid roving bands of Comyn supporters, while enduring the cold and hunger and surviving on berries, roots and small wild game. When they reached the eastern shore of Loch Lomond, they rowed across the waterway to the western coast. They established an encampment and set out to search for food in the lands of the friendly Malcolm, Earl of Lennox. As the Scots struggled through the dense underbrush, they encountered Earl Malcolm. Robert embraced his friend, who took him and his companions to his camp. While the Scots ate together, Neil Campbell was sent ahead to find several boats for the crossing to the Kintyre Peninsula. Robert's followers soon departed from the encampment, heading to the coast to rejoin Campbell, who had collected the ships. They put to sea, passing down the Firth of Clyde, rounding the island of Arran and crossing the open sea to the Kintyre Peninsula.

On the peninsula the Scottish band of loyalists made their way to Dunaverty Castle, where they were welcomed by Angus MacDonald of Islay. While staying with the MacDonalds, the king was informed there were numerous English patrols in the area searching for him. Robert also received a warning that an enemy fleet was fast approaching, compelling him to set out for northern Ireland with his companions. After briefly staying on the island of Rothlin, the small flotilla continued on to Ireland across the North Channel, where Robert spent the winter. Robert the Bruce owned properties in Ireland and his father-in-law was a powerful Irish warlord, who provided him with weapons and troops. Remaining in Ireland, he recruited soldiers from his lands and enlisted local mercenaries to renew his quest for the Scottish throne. From his secure base of operations, the Bruce dispatched envoys to his homeland to collect tax money and troops, while sending his brothers into Ireland to raise volunteers. By early 1307 a small fleet of ships and a military force of several hundred men had been mobilized, enabling Robert to begin the reconquest of his kingdom.

In February1307 King Robert divided his small army, sending his brothers Thomas and Alexander with a contingent of volunteers from Ireland in eighteen ships to Galloway to harass English supply lines in the western Scottish mainland, in preparation for his invasion. Robert's brothers were soon attacked by local troops loyal to Edward I, led by

Dougal Macdowall. The Scottish king's forces were quickly overwhelmed, with Thomas and Alexander captured. The brothers were taken under guard to Carlisle, where they were hanged and beheaded on orders from King Edward. As a warning to other rebels, their heads were placed on spikes above the town's gate.

While his brothers' force was being destroyed in Galloway, Robert was on Arran preparing for his invasion of Scotland at Carrick. He boarded his small army on his ships and crossed the Firth of Clyde. Upon landing he was told by his spies that nearby Turnberry Castle was occupied by Sir Henry Percy with over 100 troops, while several hundred more were patrolling the approaches to the stronghold. Robert decided to attack the village of Turnberry, which was only lightly guarded. At night they quietly surrounded the village and fell upon the English, quickly killing many of them and compelling the survivors to flee. The Scots encircled the castle but made no attempt to storm it. After three days on the outskirts of the fortress, Bruce and his soldiers disappeared into the countryside with their plunder from the village, including Sir Henry's horses.

When King Edward learned that Bruce had returned to Scotland, he poured additional troops into Galloway under the command of Aymer de Valence of Pembroke, with over 2,000 royal soldiers and auxiliaries from the Comyn faction. Confronted by the large army, Robert was compelled to remain in the mountains, launching small harrying raids against the English lines of communications, isolated outposts and small patrols of enemy troops. As reports of the Scots' successful forays spread, many knights and pikemen rushed to the Bruce banner.

While Robert stayed in the Carrick Mountains with his small band of soldiers, his scouts reported that the Macdowalls of Galloway were approaching his camp with a force of over 200 cavalry. He abandoned his encampment and deployed his men along the bank of a nearby river. When the rebels were spotted, the Galloway cavalry leaped into the river on their horses and swam across to attack Bruce's troops. As the Macdowalls reached the opposite bank, they were attacked by the waiting Scots and routed. Meanwhile, Robert's supporter James Douglas, known as the Black Douglas, outmaneuvered the English at Douglas Castle and set it ablaze.

The aged King Edward I had grown increasingly frail and ill in recent years, but when informed of the Bruce victories against the Macdowalls and at Douglas Castle, he rose from his sickbed and dispatched an angry letter to the Earl of Pembroke, ordering him to destroy Bruce. Pembroke met with John of Lorne and decided to entrap King Robert by feinting a frontal assault, while Sir John with his Highlanders attacked the rebels from the rear. As Robert watched Pembroke ride by from the seclusion of the mountains, his scouts informed him of John of Lorne's approach from the rear. Bruce divided his forces into three divisions, ordering them to flee in different directions and reassemble later at a designated location. As his men separated, the soldiers of Lorne followed Bruce and his men. After several brief skirmishes, Robert escaped the pursuing English and rejoined his troops.

Following the first contacts with the rebel Scots, Pembroke re-formed his army and returned to his base at Carlisle, but left enough men in the mountains to monitor Bruce's movements. As the English withdrew, Robert moved his troops south and established a fortified camp at Glen Trool. English spies soon learned of the loyalists new location, informing the earl. He assembled a force of 1,500 knights to attack the Scots, travelling toward their camp at night to avoid detection. While the earl's cavalry manoeuvred to attack the rebels on open ground, Bruce was informed of their presence by a woman from a nearby farm and quickly mustered his troops. They were barely armed when the English horsemen came rushing toward their encampment. The king grabbed his flag and shouted to his men, 'Upon them now.' The mounted Scots charged forward and drove back the English in confusion. Losing the advantage of surprise, Pembroke retired to Carlisle.

Although Pembroke sustained few casualties at Glen Trool, the enforced retreat of his superior forces by a small ragged group of men lifted the spirits and resolve of the Scots, and new volunteers flocked to the Bruce king's growing army. During the summer Robert continued to raid and harass the English garrisons and patrols from the security of the mountains as the strength of his forces grew stronger daily.

With his army reinforced, Bruce left the mountains and established a new encampment at Galston in southwestern Scotland, while acquiring the allegiance of the local towns. As more Scotsmen rallied to Robert's banner, King Edward again urged Pembroke to take the field. Under increasing pressure from Edward, in May 1307 Pembroke moved against

Bruce at Galston. At the approach of the English, Robert's men withdrew to Loudoun Hill and built a fortified camp. In the early morning of 10 May, Robert deployed his 300 soldiers across a narrow front, with his pikemen's spears forming a strong barrier. Pembroke ordered his men to charge, but his first squadron of cavalry was thrown back in disarray. The Scottish pikemen advanced to rout their opponents, and Pembroke hastily withdrew his defeated troops to Bothwell Castle.

In the wake of his lieutenants' continued failure to defeat Robert, Edward left his sickbed and summoned his warlords to meet at Carlisle on 8 July with their militia. The king, too weak to ride a horse, was carried in a litter to the assembly point. After four days of travel, the strain of the journey became too much and on 7 July 1307 King Edward I died almost within sight of the Scottish border. The throne of England was now taken by his son Edward II, who made arrangements for his father's burial at Westminster Abbey, while taking command of the advancing expeditionary force. When the English reached the border, the new monarch halted his march and remained there until August before returning to London without engaging the rebels. He reappointed Aymer de Valence of Pembroke as his viceroy for Scotland before leaving.

Edward II did not share his father's determination or desire to conquer Scotland, resulting in the diminishment of the English war effort against the rebels. As the English king remained in England, Robert now had the opportunity to enforce his kingship over the recalcitrant Scottish warlords. With Edward II occupied with the opposition of his barons and prelates, the King of the Scots moved to destroy the Comyn alliance. He first swept into the lands of Dougal Macdowall, forcing the supporters of the Comyns to submit. The king followed up his victories by marching his small army into the western Highlands and forcing John of Lorne to accept a truce. With the Lorne troops now immobilized, Robert's forces hastened up the Great Glen to seize the Comyn strongholds at Inverlochy and Urquhart on the shore of Loch Ness. Near the lake Bruce joined his forces with Bishop David of Moray, who had been clearing the region in the north of English partisans. With his reinforcements the sovereign seized and burned Inverness and Nairn. All the recently captured fortresses were razed to the ground, rendering them useless to the Comyn men. He then advanced to eliminate the threat of Sir William

II, Earl of Ross. The king offered the earl a truce to last until June 1308, which William readily accepted as it gave him the opportunity to wait and ascertain if the English would respond to Bruce's new uprising. After securing the agreement with the Earl of Ross, Robert had acquired the submission of virtually all of northern Scotland, albeit for only the next year.

In the wake of Bruce's exploits in the north, his men could move against the leader of the English supporters, John Comyn, Earl of Buchan and cousin of the murdered John III of Badenoch. The King of the Scots hastened forward with 700 knights and pikemen to attack the Comyns. As they travelled in the Garioch region, Robert became violently ill, compelling his troops to carry him on a litter to avoid enemy patrols. On Christmas Day 1307 the Earl of Buchan discovered and attacked the king's hiding place. In thick snow King Robert's forces withdrew, the rearguard holding back the earl's forces. While John of Buchan waited for reinforcements, Bruce's soldiers carried him to safety in the mountains of Strathbogie in northern Scotland.

Robert slowly regained his strength and in January 1308 was well enough to resume his campaign against John Comyn. His troops moved to the outskirts of Inverurie and set up camp. After Buchan's scouts discovered the still weak king's location, Robert mounted his horse and led his army forward to assail the enemy cavalry and infantry. When the earl's horsemen saw the approaching loyalists, they turned and fled, the foot soldiers following in their wake. The king's cavalry pursued and caught them at Old Deer, where there was a fierce clash. John of Buchan fled and escaped to England, where he soon died. The fiefdom of Buchan was now undefended and Robert's brother Edward was sent with troops to raze it. Edward's men advanced into Buchan virtually unopposed, pillaging farms, burning villages and slaying Comyn's supporters.

In the spring of 1308, Robert resumed his campaign against the rebellious warlords in the northeast of his kingdom. During the following months, he captured and destroyed the remaining strongholds of the Comyns and the Plantagenet regime's local deputies. In July the residents of Aberdeen revolted against the English garrison, giving homage to the King of the Scots. With possession of the port town, Bruce gained an important trading centre with continental Europe, giving him access to the markets of Germany and Flanders.

In July 1308, with the truce with John Macdougall of Lorne near expiration, Robert prepared to move against him. He summoned his loyal ally James Douglas from southwest Scotland and united his troops with the royal army. In early August the combined force proceeded west to campaign against Macdougall. As the army marched into enemy territory, the Macdougalls and their allies occupied the mountain Pass of Brander along their route. Macdougall planned to roll large boulders down the mountain into the royalists as they passed below before charging down the hillside. From his scouts Robert learned the position of Lorne's troops and sent James Douglas with a contingent of archers to occupy the area above the waiting foe. As the king advanced along the mountain road, Sir John's soldiers sent large rocks thundering down the slopes. Robert's men warned of the Macdougalls' presence, avoided the boulders. They charged up the hillside, while the Black Douglas' archers unleashed volleys of arrows before storming down the mountain. Caught between the two advancing forces, the men of Lorne were crushed and compelled to retreat.

Bruce's men pursued the fleeing Lorne soldiers across the Awe River to Dunstaffnage Castle. The king besieged the castle, and with little possibility of relief the garrison surrendered. The defeat of the Macdougalls of Lorne at Dunstaffnage ended their resistance, and the local lords and subjects offered their fealty to King Robert. He garrisoned the fortress with his men and left an occupying force to maintain his authority in the region.

While Robert was enforcing his rule against John of Lorne, his brother Edward of Bruce was in Galloway, where the previous year's truce with the Macdowall faction had expired. He advanced his army against Dougal Macdowall, defeating him and his English allies at a crossing of the Dee River. Following his victory Edward launched a brutal campaign of fire and sword across the region. Parts of Galloway still were not firmly under the rule of the Bruce monarchy, and the last of the English occupation troops were not defeated until 1313.

In the autumn of 1308 the Scottish king returned to the northeast to reach a settlement with the Earl of Ross, William II. Robert's subjugation of large parts of Scotland and the failure of Edward II to support his Scottish allies convinced William of Ross to offer his homage. On 3

October 1308 he submitted unconditionally to the Bruce regime and had his properties restored to him by the monarchy. To solidify their relationship, the king's sister Matilda was later married to the heir of Ross, Hugh.

In the aftermath of his assumption of the Scottish throne, Robert I had steadily expanded the territory under his regime's control, while Edward II remained in England involved with internal disputes. In early 1309 Pope Clement V intervened in the unresolved conflict, arranging a truce lasting until 1 November. At the cessation of hostilities, the King of the Scots summoned his first parliament to assemble at St Andrews in March. Eight of the kingdom's earls sent representatives, and numerous lords and prelates were present at the assembly. The parliament at St Andrews demonstrated to the courts of Europe that Robert was the rightful King of Scotland with his recognition by the nobility, Church and commoners. Robert spent the summer and autumn of 1309 solidifying his rule, travelling down the western coast in a display of power and royal authority to his subjects. During the truce he began the creation of a government, setting in place royal officials to enforce his justice and will.

When the armistice between England and Scotland expired in early 1310, Edward II began preparations to renew the war with the Scots, advancing to his Scottish stronghold at Berwick. He had been warned by anti-Bruce Scotsmen that all of Scotland would be lost to him if no Plantagenet army was brought into the kingdom. In September he moved his army to the castle at Roxburgh and launched his campaign to reimpose English rule over the rebels. As his troops marched to attack the Scots, Bruce refused to fight, withdrawing his men and harassing Edward's long exposed lines of communications and unprotected flanks. He continued to harry the English patrols and attack isolated forces, frustrating efforts to bring him to battle. As Edward's men pursued the Scottish raiders, they were forced to march through abandoned and burnt lands, finding little food or shelter. The campaign lasted until late October, when Edward retired to Berwick Castle with the approach of winter.

During the spring of 1311 Robert resumed his campaign of harassment, while Edward was increasingly pressed by the opposition of his warlords in parliament and their refusal to grant new revenue for the Scottish war. In July the English king returned to London to settle the discontent of his parliament. After Edward left Berwick, King Robert unleashed numerous pillaging raids into northern England, burning villages and farms while collecting large amounts of booty. As the Scots continued to harry and destroy Edward's northern towns, Robert forced the local population to pay large indemnities to prevent new attacks.

Edward II was beset with civil war in 1312, when his magnates openly defied the return of his favorite, Piers Gaveston, to court. As the king prepared to defend his monarchy against the dissident nobles, Robert took advantage of the uprising and led a large invasion force into northern England. He advanced across the border into northeastern England, devastating the area and burning the towns of Hexham and Corbridge east of the great English fortress at Carlisle. From his encampment near Corbridge, Robert sent Edward of Bruce with part of the army to attack the county of Durham. They fell upon the town of Durham, setting it ablaze. The civil officials of Durham offered the Scots 2,000 pounds for a ten-month truce, which was accepted by Robert. After learning of the armistice with Durham, the lords of Northumbria met with the king and proposed similar terms for a temporary peace. Meanwhile, James Douglas hastened to Hartlepod on the coast, sacking the town and returning with many prisoners to be held for ransom. In September 1312 the Bruce army returned to Scotland with a large supply of war spoils and many valuable hostages.

While Bruce was ravaging northern England, his envoys began negotiations with King Hakon V of Norway to re-establish relations between the two courts and reinstate peace on the borders with the Norwegian-occupied Shetland Isles. At the parliament held at Inverness, Robert signed the final treaty with Hakon V's ambassadors, restoring friendship between the two kingdoms. The formal recognition of Bruce's regime by a European power added to the credibility and prestige of his monarchy.

Despite the Scots' recent capture of numerous castles held by the English and the razing of their towns and lands, Edward II retained a formidable line of strongholds, which remained a constant threat to the security of the Bruce monarchy and gave the English troops a base of operations to mount new attacks. Unable to negotiate a resolution with his rebellious magnates, Edward remained in London, giving the Scots the opportunity to reclaim Plantagenet-occupied castles. In November 1312 Robert moved against the formidable fortress at Perth. The castle was well defended by a deep moat and strong walls and could not be taken by storm, compelling the Scots to begin siege operations. The investment dragged on for over six weeks, with the English garrison showing little willingness to surrender. Unable to break into the fortification, the king was forced to revert to deception, sending men under the cover of darkness to search the depths of the moat looking for the shallowest location. In the morning, he feinted a retreat and withdrew his army, to the insults and jeers of the garrison. When the Scots reached a concealed location several miles from Perth, they were put to work making rope ladders to reach the top of the walls. On 7 January 1313 the Scots set out at night back to Perth, and with Robert leading his knights and foot-soldiers they crept silently to the moat and waded across to the walls, throwing their ladders over the ramparts. They climbed up the ropes and stormed into the town. The defenders were surprised by the onrushing Scots, and by sunrise the fortress was in the king's possession. The castle and town of Perth were burnt to the ground. Following the destruction of Perth, Robert resumed his marauding raid, demolishing the English fortifications at Dumfries, Caerlaverock and Buittle. He then united his army with Angus Macdonald of the Isles in June, and together they sailed to the Isle of Man, overrunning the English garrison at Rushen to take control of the island.

While the regime of Edward II remained occupied with the barons' war, Robert and his men pressed on with their campaign of conquest, clearing the invaders from the region north of Edinburgh, with the exception of the great fortification at Stirling, which was besieged by Edward of Bruce. While the siege continued at Stirling, the formidable strongholds at Roxburgh and Edinburgh were captured by the king's lieutenants, James Douglas and Thomas Randolph, in daring night attacks. By the end of spring 1314 the Scottish had reconquered the majority of their kingdom, apart from Stirling and Berwick and several massive fortifications to the south.

During Edward II's prolonged absence in England, the Scots had recovered most of their realm from English occupation. In danger of losing control of his father's conquest, the king arranged a reconciliation with his barons and began preparations to reimpose his rule over his rebellious northern neighbour. In the spring of 1314 he amassed a large host at Berwick Castle, recruiting cavalrymen and infantry from all parts of his kingdom and hiring mercenary troops from France. In early May he set out with 20,000 men to relieve the ongoing siege at Stirling Castle. King Robert had joined his brother at Sterling and as the English began their march, summoned the men of Scotland to defend their land.

Scotsmen from all parts of the kingdom gathered during June at Torwood near Stirling Castle. Near the end of the month, Bruce's army had grown to over 8,000 men, with 7,000 pikemen, 500 cavalrymen and a contingent of archers. Lacking a strong cavalry force, Robert was compelled to choose a battlefield site that restricted the movements of the enemy's horse soldiers. He deployed his men at Bannockburn in the woods of New Park, where the English were hampered by marshes, a large ravine and dense woodlands. While his scouts monitored the movements of the English, the Scottish king organized his men into four large schiltrons of pikemen. On 23 June the advance guard of the English cavalry was spotted, and the scouts rushed back to the king at New Park notifying him of the advancing enemy. While the Scots prepared for battle, in the late afternoon the English vanguard approached. As the English horsemen came over a slope in the old Roman Road, Sir Henry de Bohun rode ahead of the other knights after identifying Robert in the distance inspecting his troops. Seizing the opportunity for personal glory by killing the king, he charged alone toward the king. Alerted by the sounds of the thundering warhorse, Robert swung his steed around to face the attacker and galloped toward the English knight armed with an axe. As Sir Henry neared, with lowered lance, Bruce swerved away and, rising in his stirrups, brought his axe down on his opponent's helmet, crushing his skull. The deafening roar of the kingsmen echoed across the battlefield, as they surged forward to assail the English advance guard, driving it back in disarray. Following the clash, Robert ordered his men back to their positions.

While Robert was clashing with de Bohun, a contingent of Plantagenet cavalry attempted to attack the Scots from the north. The area was defended by Sir Thomas Randolph, Earl of Moray, with a schiltron of pikemen. The English knights charged against the schiltron repeatedly but were unable to break the ring of spears. When Robert sent reinforcements to support Randolph's infantrymen, the English broke off their attack and retreated.

In the evening Bruce met with his lieutenants to decide whether to withdraw or renew the fighting in the morning. Without hesitation his commanders proclaimed their preference for battle. During their first encounters with the Scots, the English cavalry had been forced to fight on unsuitable ground and King Edward now moved his army and took up a new position to give his horsemen open fields to attack the Scottish infantry. Early in the morning of 24 June, the Scottish pikemen emerged from the woods to confront the English horsemen. As they drew closer, the Scots paused while Abbot Maurice of Inchaffrey held Mass. As the troops knelt in prayer, the abbot blessed them with the holy relics of St Fillan and St Columba. The Scottish pikemen then advanced, led by Edward of Bruce, as arrows from King Edward's Welsh archers flew across the morning sky. The Earl of Gloucester led the English attack, smashing into the schiltron, but was killed and his men were driven back. On Edward Bruce's left flank, the schiltron of Thomas Randolph charged into the horsemen, catching the English knights between two forces of pikemen. While the Scots on his right were pushing Edward II's army back, Robert led his schiltron, which included soldiers from the Highlands and Galloway, into the fray. With the impetus of Robert's new assault, the English began to fall back, driven by the wall of spears as Bruce's men shouted, 'On them they fail.' The Welsh archers were then called forward, firing flights of arrows into Bruce's pikemen and causing heavy casualties. As the Welshmen intensified their attack, Robert sent his light cavalry to attack them, driving them from the field. The Scottish bowmen were ordered into the fight, and fired volley after volley into the English cavalry, causing heavy casualties.

As the Scots pressed their assault, the English front broke and the men-at-arms fled across the Bannockburn in retreat. With his army in flight, King Edward, accompanied by his bodyguard of 500 knights, made his way to safety at Berwick Castle. The English infantry, who had played little role in the battle, fled to Stirling Castle. Many prominent knights were captured by the Scots and held for ransom. King Robert exchanged the Earl of Hereford for Queen Elizabeth, his daughter, Marjorie, and sister, Mary. In the wake of the Bannockburn victory, many pro-English magnates from Scotland gave their oaths of allegiance to the Bruce throne and by the end of the year all of Scotland, with the exception of Berwick, was under the rule of King Robert.

Despite the loss of his presence in Scotland, Edward II refused to recognize Robert I as the rightful king. The Scottish regime offered to negotiate a settlement but their overtures were ignored. To force the English to the peace talks, the King Robert was compelled to resume his marauding raids into northern England. The pillaging Scots destroyed villages, burnt farms and crops, attacked English patrols and captured many prominent Englishmen for ransom, but the Plantagenet court still would not acknowledge the Bruce king.

As the Scottish crown continued its raids, the English earls rose up against King Edward, demanding a resolution to the ongoing war. The Plantagenet king's military might had been destroyed at Bannockburn, and without the intimidation of his army he was in no position to defy the demands of his lords. He met his rebel warlords at York and was forced to agree to begin peace negotiations with the Scots. The talks were held at Durham in October, but ended in failure due to Edward's refusal to recognize the independence of Scotland. At the conclusion of the negotiations, Robert renewed his attacks into Northumbria, sacking towns and carrying off plunder and captives for ransom.

In the wake of the failed peace negotiations, Robert expanded the area of the war against the Plantagenet crown in 1315 by invading English-held Ireland. The acceptance and strength of England's control over the Irish had steadily eroded over recent years due to heavy taxes and relentless demands for troops and war supplies. Bruce envoys were dispatched to Ulster to negotiate an alliance with the growing rebellious Irish faction. The rebels pledged to acknowledge Edward of Bruce as their new monarch providing the Scottish regime agreed to drive the English from their lands. King Robert summoned his parliament in April, and the proposal was accepted by the representatives. With the approval of his brother's government, Edward began preparations for his expedition to Ireland. In May 1315 he sailed to Ireland with Sir Thomas Randolph and 6,000 troops on galleys provided by the insurgent warlords. After landing at Larne on the east coast of Ireland, the Scots with their

Irish confederates moved against the English, capturing many towns and forcing the occupation troops to withdraw. By the spring of 1316 the Scots and their allies had gained control of northern Ireland and Edward of Bruce was crowned king on 2 May at Dundalk. Shortly after landing in Ireland, Edward had besieged the great fortress at Carrickfergus to gain dominance over the Ulster region, and in 1316 the castle garrison finally surrendered to solidify the Scots' hold on northern Ireland. As Edward continued his campaign of conquest, his brother arrived from Scotland with reinforcements. The united Bruce army pushed on, devastating the Anglo-Irish lands toward Dublin. The farther the Scots and their local followers advanced into southern Ireland, the weaker the support they received from the inhabitants. When Robert and Edward learned that new English troops had landed on the southeastern coast of Ireland at Youghal, and with their provisions and supplies nearly exhausted, they were forced to order a withdrawal to Ulster. On 22 May 1317 King Robert sailed back to Scotland, leaving part of his army with Edward to continue the fight against the English. Edward of Bruce resumed his campaign against the Anglo-Irish, but was killed the following year in battle.

Following his return to Scotland, Robert intensified his attacks in northern England to force Edward II to recognize him as the Scottish king. He led his men across the border, harassing the English counties with little resistance. In April 1318 Thomas Randolph and James Douglas led a daring night attack against the defenders of Berwick Castle, finally gaining control of the great fortification after several failed attempts. Following the fall of Berwick, no area in northern England was safe from attack by the Scots. In 1319 the Bruce regime launched a large marauding raid into England, advancing as far south as York, while King Edward remained in London occupied with the unrelenting insurgence of his earls.

With Robert sending raiding parties deeper into England to force Edward II to recognize him as Scottish king, in the autumn of 1317 Pope John XXII ordered two papal negotiators to broker peace between the Scots and English in order to find support and volunteers for his new crusade to the Levant. The envoys carried a letter from the pope addressed to the governor of Scotland, disregarding Robert's assumption of the crown. The Bruce king refused to accept the correspondence. Pope John replied to the affront by extending Robert's excommunication and placing his realm under interdiction. In response, Robert assembled his parliament at Newbattle in March 1320 to draft a reply to the papacy. The 'Declaration of Arbroath', which resulted from the assembly, was sent to the pope, asking for his intervention in the war with England and defiantly defending Scotland's right to independence. Motivated by the document, the pope agreed to encourage the Plantagenet government to make peace, but Edward II refused to abandon his claim to Scotland.

While the war with England continued, Robert was involved with the administration of his kingdom. He summoned parliaments routinely, enacted laws to encourage the expansion of the realm's economy, promoted trade with Europe and restructured the army. Robert the Bruce was still childless, and to provide a successor for the crown, the assembly appointed the king's grandson, Robert Stewart, as the next in line to the throne.

After the loss of his great castle at Berwick and the continuing Scottish plundering raids into his kingdom, King Edward II was compelled to reach a settlement with his earls and barons to gain support for a new attack against Scotland. In September 1319, after ending the uprising of his warlords, he assembled a formidable army of over 12,000 knights and foot-soldiers at Newcastle, advancing to recover Berwick. The fortification was besieged by land forces and an English fleet anchored in the bay. On 7 September the first assault against the defensive works was unleashed. The defenders, led by Walter Stewart, repelled repeated attacks, throwing scaling ladders to the ground and firing large rocks from their catapults at the massed enemy, while English archers fired rounds of arrows and sappers attempted to mine under the walls. The fighting continued throughout the day without the English breaching the defenses. The Plantagenet soldiers launched their second attack on 13 September, wheeling a huge siege tower toward the walls under a hail of Scottish arrows, while infantry moved forward with scaling ladders. The Scots concentrated on the tower, destroying it with huge boulders from their catapults.

Despite the loss of the siege tower, the English continued their attack. They stormed the outer works of the main gate, threatening to break into the town. Walter Stewart gathered a force of men and ran to defend the entrance. Upon reaching the gate, he threw it open and charged into the English troops, beating them back with his surprise attack. After securing the area, Stewart withdrew into the fortress and closed the entrance. Following the failure to penetrate the defenses, the English withdrew, leaving Bruce troops still in control of the castle.

The Scottish king lacked the military might to drive the large English army from the siege at Berwick and decided to force them to abandon their attack by seizing Edward II's queen, Isabella of France, at her residence in York and exchange her for the fortress. With the English host massed at Berwick, northern England was bare of troops, and Thomas Randolph and James Douglas were sent with a contingent of knights and pikemen to seize the queen at York. The Archbishop of York, William Melton, was informed of the planned kidnapping of Isabella by a spy in the Scottish camp, and she was taken to safety at Nottingham. The spy also told the archbishop the raiding party was made up of only a small force and was camped at Milton. Melton assembled a large group of citizens, clerks, monks and priests and set out to attack the Scots. The scouts of the Black Douglas and Randolph spotted the approaching Englishmen on 12 October and deployed into a schiltron formation to move against their attackers. At the sight of the advancing Scots, the English turned and ran. The Bruce men charged after the fleeing English, cutting them down. They continued their raid through Yorkshire, leaving a wide trail of destruction. When King Edward was informed of the raid, he was compelled to abandon his siege at Berwick and return to northern England to protect his lands. On 1 November Douglas returned to England, pillaging Westmorland and Cumberland. Edward had rejected all previous overtures of peace from the Scottish king, but after the recent raids agreed to meet at Berwick to negotiate a settlement. Envoys from both kingdoms gathered in late December and approved a two-year truce lasting until the end of 1321.

During the next two years the English and Scottish realms respected the Berwick agreement and northern England had a short period of peace. At Berwick the English had refused to acknowledge Scottish independence, and after the expiration of the truce King Robert resumed his cross-border plundering. While the Scots pillaged English lands, war erupted again between the Plantagenet king and his barons. Determined to force the obedience of his nobles, Edward II assembled his loyal knights and retainers, marching against the rebellious lords. While the king was proceeding to Burton-on-Trent, his lieutenant, Sir Andrew de Harclay, intercepted the rebel English lords at Boroughbridge and destroyed their army as they crossed the bridge. Without fear of attack from his barons, Edward then moved against the Scots to force their acceptance of his sovereignty. He assembled a formidable army at Newcastle in August 1322, including allies and mercenaries from France. After the defeat of his rogue lords, Edward wrote to Pope John XXII telling him he intended to impose peace on Scotland by force of arms.

As the Plantagenet crown finalized its invasion preparations, Robert led a plundering raid down the coast of Cumberland and Lancashire, harrying the towns and farmlands as far south as Preston, while leaving orders for the inhabitants in southeastern Scotland to evacuate the area and leave nothing for the advancing invasion force of Edward II. By late July the king was back in his homeland with a large cache of plunder. In early August, King Edward invaded Scotland with 20,000 men. King Robert made no attempt to intercept the English, withdrawing and laying waste to the region. Entering the desolate area, the English were dependent on their own provisions for survival. Foraging parties sent to search for food found only a scorched land. By the end of August, the English army, depleted by desertions and sickness, was forced to return to England. Following the defeat of the invasion, Robert hastened back into England, ravaging the district around Carlisle.

Northern England had endured over ten years of unrelenting Scottish raiding, while the local barons' appeals to their king for relief were largely ignored. Under increasing pressure from his lords for peace and a personal appeal from Pope John, in early 1322 King Edward authorized a meeting between Sir Henry de Sully and the Scottish king. When Robert met with Sir Henry, they soon came to terms. Under the treaty signed near York on 7 June, the two kingdoms approved a thirteen-year truce; Robert ratified the agreement as King of Scotland, but Edward still refused to recognize him as Scottish monarch.

After the end of hostilities with England, Robert returned to the governing of his kingdom. Parliament was again summoned regularly and an advisory council appointed, with a chamberlain for royal household affairs and chancellor for judicial matters. The system of sheriffs and bailiffs employed during the reign of Alexander III was reintroduced, with loyal

Bruce representatives named to the offices. The Bruce parliament passed new laws favouring trading centres with grants of privileges and exceptions to encourage economic growth. The royal court routinely patronized the Scottish Church and its abbeys and monasteries with special favours and financial offerings. Aside from domestic issues, the regime sent envoys to Paris to negotiate a mutual defence treaty with the French court of Charles IV, which ensured military assistance against any English invasion.

In spite of his denial of official recognition by the Plantagenet court, Robert ruled Scotland unchallenged, while Edward was continually pressed by his barons and growing discord with France. The sister of the French king was the wife of Edward II, and his rumoured abuse of her created hostilities between the regimes. In 1326 Queen Isabella was sent to her brother's court with her young son and English successor-designate, Edward, to give homage to the French for the Plantagenet region of Gascony. While in Paris, the queen became romantically involved with the English exile, Lord Roger Mortimer, and refused to return to England. Mortimer was the sworn enemy of King Edward, and together with Isabella he gathered a force of English dissidents and recruited a mercenary army. In September the queen and Mortimer crossed the Channel, landing in England and marching against London. When the city officials declared their allegiance to Isabella, all support for Edward collapsed. The king attempted to escape, but was captured in Wales and deposed on 20 January 1327. On 1 February the fifteen-year-old Edward III was anointed King of England, but Queen Isabella and Lord Mortimer were the power behind the throne. Despite the change in kings, relations between Scotland and England remained hostile. Soon after the coronation, King Robert sent raiding parties to pillage deep into England. During the summer, Edward III advanced north with a large army but Robert refused to fight a pitched battle, drawing the enemy deeper into an abandoned and barren land using time and space as his greatest ally. The Scots attacked the English lines of communications and reconnaissance patrols, moving freely about northern England. Finally, in frustration, King Edward abandoned his campaign. After the retreat of the Plantagenet troops, the Scots unleashed a large plundering sortie into the northern counties, ravaging the strongholds at Alnwick and Norham.

In the autumn of 1327 Edward II died while a prisoner of the queen and Mortimer. Rumours spread quickly through the kingdom that he had been tortured to death. When they attempted to assemble the forces for a new Scottish invasion, parliament refused to provide the money. Facing the revolt of parliament, Isabella and Mortimer sent envoys to Scotland proposing negotiations for a permanent peace. The Bruce regime agreed to meet with the English representatives at Newcastle-on-Tyne. On 17 March 1328 the talks ended with the signing of the treaty at the Abbey of Holyrood in Edinburgh, and the ratification by Edward at Northampton on 3 May. By the terms of the accord, England renounced its claims to Scotland and acknowledged Robert I of Bruce as king. The agreement was sealed with the contract for the marriage of the Scottish heir, David, to Joan, the seven-year-old sister of the English king.

The Treaty of Edinburgh ended over twenty-two years of war for King Robert but left him exhausted and frail. During the following year the king's health deteriorated further. He spent more time away from court, becoming confined to his bed. On 7 June 1329 Robert died at Cardross at the age of fifty-five, after a reign of twenty-three years. His body was carried in a funeral procession to Dunfermline Abbey and buried among the former kings and queens of Scotland. Following the death of Robert, his five-year-old son, David II, was recognized as successor to the throne under a regency government headed by Sir Thomas Randolph, first Earl of Moray. Two years later he was formally invested with the crown of Scotland and ruled for the next forty-one years.

Selected Sources:

Barrell, A.D.M., *Medieval Scotland.*
Barrow, G.W.S., *Kingship and Unity – Scotland 1000–1306.*
Barrow, G.W.S., *Robert Bruce.*
Bingham, Caroline, *Robert the Bruce.*
Donaldson, Gordon. *Scottish Kings.*
Lynch, Michael, *Scotland – A New History.*
Mackie, J.D., *A History of Scotland.*
Magnusson, Magnus, *Scotland – The Story of a Nation.*
Oram, Richard, *The Kings and Queens of Scotland.*
Penman, Michael, *Robert the Bruce – King of the Scots.*
Scott, Ronald McNair, *Robert the Bruce – King of the Scots.*

Postscript

During the centuries following the Early Middle Ages, the monarchies of Europe continued to utilize their martial might, defending their rule and expanding their territorial holdings that were made possible by the military victories of their warrior kings. In the final years of the thirteenth century, the royal realms entered a period of gradual evolution that changed them from medieval to modern states. Early in the Late Middle Ages, national kingdoms began to form as the sovereigns subdued the power of their feudal barons and the Church. Strong regimes developed first in England, Scotland, France and the Holy Roman Empire, which ended internal dissent and restrained the ambitions of the nobles. The final stages of the transition from a feudal-based government to the national state occurred during the reigns of Henry VII in England, James I in Scotland, Louis XI in France and Albert II, who began over 300 years of Habsburg rule in the Holy Roman Empire.

During the kings' ascent to prominence in the Late Middle Ages, they continued the practice of their predecessors by personally leading their soldiers into battle, seeking power, land and wealth. The quest for supremacy in England was renewed in 1415 by Henry V, who crossed the English Channel with his army and faced the French at the Battle of Agincourt, defeating their vastly superior forces by skilfully deploying his men to minimize the charge of the French heavy cavalry and employing his archers to their maximum effect. In the culmination of the Wars of the Roses, Henry Tudor led his troops into battle at Bosworth Field in August 1485, dethroning the last Yorkish king, Richard III, to rule as Henry VII. In Scotland the reigning Stewart family maintained its ongoing campaign of harassment against the English castles and towns along the border, keeping its enemy distracted. In 1513 King James IV led his army across the Tweed River, moving against the English strongholds at Norham and Ford. As the Scottish forces advanced farther south, they encountered the English at Flodden Hill. Under a devastating cannon barrage from the English, James IV was killed leading his pikemen down the hill in a charge.

Meanwhile in France, the kingdom was finally united by King Louis XI, who had relentlessly suppressed the rebellions of his barons, his military forces breaking their feudal power by 1480. With their reigns now secured, the French monarchs began their quest for domination over a fragmented Italy. King Charles VIII marched his army south over the Alps into the Kingdom of Naples, defeating the Neapolitans at Ovo in late February 1495, and on 12 May was crowned King of Naples. In 1500 King Louis XII renewed the French quest for Italy, leading his forces over the border and seizing the Duchy of Milan. Following Louis XII's defeat twelve years later, Francis I resumed the struggle for Milan, returning to northern Italy and leading his army to victory at the Battle of Marignano in September 1515.

In the Holy Roman Empire, the power of the reigning imperial governments had deteriorated under the inept rule of the emperors, but after Maximilian I ascended the throne in 1493, his regime regained its lost authority and began to expand the Habsburg Empire into the Netherlands and Spain. In 1519 Maximilian I was succeeded by his grandson, Charles V, who enlarged the Habsburg's sovereignty into northern Italy, confronting the French for control of the region, while protecting his eastern lands against the invasion of the Ottoman Turks.

Over the following years the era of the warrior kings slowly ceased, and by the seventeenth century few battles were fought with the royal monarch leading his soldiers into the fight.

Bibliography

Abulafia, David, *Frederick II – A Medieval Emperor* (New York and Oxford: Oxford University Press, 1988).

Allshorn, Lionel, *Stupor Mundi – The Life and Times of Frederick II, Emperor of the Romans, King of Sicily and Jerusalem, 1194 – 1250* (Miami, Florida: HardPress Publishing, 1912).

Ashley, Mike, *British Kings & Queens* (New York: Carroll & Gray Publishers, 2004).

Ault, Warren O., *Europe in the Middle Ages* (Boston, New York and Chicago: D.C. Heath and Company, 1937).

Barber, Richard, *The Devil's Crown – A History of Henry II and his Sons* (London: British Broadcasting Company, 1978).

Barnes, Thomas G., Blum, Jerome and Cameron, Rodo, *The Emergence of the European World* (Boston and Toronto: Brown and Company, 1966).

Barrell, A.D., *Medieval Scotland* (Cambridge: Cambridge University Press, 2000).

Barrow, G.W.S., *Kingship and Unity – Scotland 1000–1306* (London: Edward Arnold Publishers, 1981).

Barrow, G.W.S., *Robert Bruce* (Berkeley and Los Angeles: University of California Press, 1965).

Bartlett, W.B., *King Cnut and the Viking Conquest of England 1016* (Gloucestershire: Amberley Publishing, 2016).

Bartlett, W.B., *The Last Crusade* (Stroud, Gloucestershire: Tempus Publishing Ltd, 2007).

Bates, David, *William The Conqueror* (Stroud, Gloucestershire: Tempus Publishing Ltd, 2001).

Becher, Matthias, *Charlemagne* (New Haven and London: Yale University Press, 2003).

Bingham, Caroline, *Robert The Bruce* (London: Constable and Company, 1998).

Bingham, Caroline, *The Crowned Lions – The Early Plantagenet Kings* (North Vancouver, British Columbia: Douglas David & Charles Limited, 1978).

Bradbury, Jim, *The Capetians – Kings of France 987–1328* (London: Hambledon Continuum, 2007).

Bressler, Richard, *Frederick II – The Wonder of the World* (Yardley, Pennsylvania: Westholme LLC, 2010).

Bridge, Antony, *Richard the Lionheart* (New York: M. Evans & Company, Inc., 1989).

Brook, Christopher, *The Saxon and Norman Kings* (Glasgow: Fontana and Collins, 1982).

Brundage, James A., *Richard Lion Heart* (New York: Charles Scribner's Sons, 1974).

Bryce, James, *The Holy Roman Empire* (New York: Schocken Books, Inc, 1961).

Cannon, John and Hargreaves, Anne, *The Kings and Queens of Britain* (Oxford and New York: Oxford University Press, 2001).

Castries, Rene de la Croix, *The Lives of the Kings and Queens of France* (New York: Alfred A. Knopf, 1979).

Chamberlin, Russell, *The Emperor Charlemagne* (New York: Franklin Watts, 1986).

Chambers, James, *The Norman Kings* (London: Weidenfeld and Nicolson, 1981).

Donaldson, Gordon, *Scottish Kings* (New York: Barnes & Noble, 1967).

Douglas, David C., *William The Conqueror* (Berkeley and Los Angles: University of California Press, 1964).

Duckett, Eleanor Shipley, *Alfred The Great – The King and His England* (Chicago and London: The University of Chicago Press, 1956).

Einstein, David G., *Emperor Frederick II* (New York: Philosophical Library, 1949).

Fawtier, Robert, *The Capetian Kings of France* (New York: St Martin's Press, 1968).

Ferguson, Wallace K. and Bruun, Geoffrey, *A Survey of European Civilization* (Boston, New York and Chicago: Houghton Mifflin Company, 1952).

Fraser, Antonia, *The Lives of the Kings & Queens of England* (New York: Alfred A. Knopf, 1975).

Freed, John B., *Frederick Barbarossa – The Prince and the Myth* (New Haven and London: Yale University Press, 2016).

Gillingham, John, *Richard I* (New Haven and London: Yale University Press, 1999).

Gioia, Francesco, *The Popes – Twenty Centuries of History* (Patriarchal Basilica of St Paul, Rome: Pontifical Administration, 2005).

Grabsky, Phil, *The Great Military Commanders* (New York: TV Books, Inc., 1993).

Hallam, Elizabeth M., *Capetian France 987–1328* (London and New York: Longman Group Limited, 1980).

Harvey, John, *The Plantagenets* (London and Glasgow: B.T. Batsford Limited, 1959).

Heer, Friedrich, *The Holy Roman Empire* (New York and Washington: Frederick A. Praeger, 1968).

Henderson, Ernest F., *A History of Germany in the Middle Ages* (New York: Haskell House Publishers, 1968).

Henry of Huntingdon, *The History of the English People 1000–1154* (Oxford: Oxford University Press, 2002).

Horspool, David, *Alfred the Great* (Gloucestershire: Amberley Publishers, 2014).

Humble, Richard, *The Saxon Kings* (London: George Weidenfeld and Nicolson, 1980).

James, Edward, *The Origins of France* (Houndmills, Hampshire, and London: Macmillan Press Limited, 1982).

Joinville, de Jean, *Saint Louis – King of France* (London: FB & C Ltd., 2015).

Kantorowicz, Ernst, *Frederick the Second* (New York: Frederick Ungar Publishing Company, 1957).

King, Edmund, *Medieval England* (Oxford: Phaidon Press Limited, 1988).

Komroff, Manuel, *Charlemagne* (New York: Julian Messner, Inc., 1964).

Labarge, Margaret Wade, *Saint Louis – Louis IX, Most Christian King of France* (Boston and Toronto: Little, Brown and Company, 1968).

Larson, Laurence, *Canute the Great* (Lexington, Kentucky: Jovian Press, 2017).

Lasko, Peter, *The Kingdom of the Franks* (New York: McGraw-Hill Book Company, 1971).

Law, Joy, *Fleur de Lys – The Kings and Queens of France* (New York, St. Louis, San Francisco, Dusseldorf, Mexico & Toronto: McGraw-Hill Book Company, 1976).

Lawson, M.K., *Cnut – The Danes in England in the Early Eleventh Century*) London and New York: Longman Group, 1993).

Linton, Barry, *History's Greatest Military Commanders* (Make Profits Easy, 2015).

Lynch, Michael, *Scotland – A New History* (London: Pimlico, 2003).

Mackie, J.D., *A History of Scotland* (New York: Dorset Press, 1985).

Magnusson, Magnus, *Scotland – The Story of a Nation* (New York: Grove Press, 2000).

Masson, Gustave, *Mediaeval France* (New York: G.P. Putnam's Sons, 1901).

Matthews, John and Stewart, Bob, *Warriors of Christendom* (Poole, Dorset: Firebird Books, Limited, 1988).

Matthews, Rupert, *The Popes* (New York: Metro Books, 2013).

McKitterick, Rosamond, *The Frankish Kingdoms Under the Carolingians* (London and New York: Longman Group Limited, 1983).

Miller, David, *Richard the Lionheart* (London: Orion Publishing Group, 2003).

Munz, Peter, *Frederick Barbarossa – A Study in Medieval Politics* (London: Eyre & Spottiswoode, 1969).

Norwich, John Julius, *A History of Venice* (New York: Vintage Books, 1989).

Norwich, John Julius, *Absolute Monarchs – A History of the Papacy* (New York: Random House, 2011).

Oman, Charles, *The Dark Ages – 476–918* (London, Rivingtons, 1901).

Oman, Richard, *The Kings and Queens of Scotland* (Stroud, Gloucestershire: Tempus Publishing, 2001).

Otto of Freising, *The Deeds of Frederick Barbarossa* (New York: Columbia University Press, 1953).

Pacaut, Marcel, *Frederick Barbarossa* (New York: Charles Scribner's Sons, 1970).

Peddie, John, *Alfred – Warrior King* (Stroud, Gloucestershire: Sutton Publishing, 2005).

Penman, Michael, *Robert the Bruce – King of the Scots* (New Haven and London: Yale University Press, 2014).

Perry, Frederick, *Saint Louis – The Most Christian King* (New York and London: G.P. Putnam's Sons, 1902).

Pollard, Justin, *Alfred the Great* (London: John Murray Publishers, 2005).

Rendina, Claudio, *The Popes – Histories and Secrets* (Santa Ana, California: Seven Locks Press, 2002).

Rex, Peter, *Harold II – The Doomed Saxon King* (Stroud, Gloucestershire: Tempus Publishing Limited, 2005).

Rex, Peter, *William the Conqueror – The Bastard of Normandy* (Stroud, Gloucestershire: Amberley Publishing, 2011).

Riche, Pierre, *The Carolingians – A Family Who Forged Europe* (Philadelphia, Pennsylvania: University of Pennsylvania Press, 1993).

Riley-Smith, Jonathan, *The Crusades* (New Haven and London: Yale University Press, 1987).

Roberts, Andrew, *Great Commanders of the Medieval World 454–1582* (London: Quercus, 2011).

Roberts, Clayton and Roberts, David, *A History of England – Prehistory to 1714* (New Jersey: Prentice Hall, 1991).

Rodes, John E., *Germany: A History* (New York, Chicago and London: Holt, Rinehart and Winston, 1964).

Romier, Lucien, *A History of France* (New York: St Martin's Press, 1953).

Runciman, Steven, *A History of the Crusades Volume II* (London: Penguin Books, 1990).

Runciman, Steven, *A History of the Crusades Volume III* (Cambridge, New York and New Rochelle: Cambridge University Press, 1951).

Runciman, Steven, *The Sicilian Vespers – A History of the Mediterranean World in the Later Thirteenth Century* (Cambridge and New York: Cambridge University Press, 1992).

Saul, Nigel, *The Three Richards* (London and New York: Hambledon and London, 2005).

Scherman, Katharine, *The Birth of France – Warriors, Bishops and Long-Haired Kings* (New York: Random House, 1987).

Scott, Ronald McNair, *Robert the Bruce – King of the Scots* (New York: Peter Bedrick Books, 1989).

Slocombe, George, *William the Conqueror* (New York: G.P. Putnam's Sons, 1961).

Smith, Goldwin, *A History of England* (New York: Charles Scribner's Sons, 1957).

Smyth, Alfred P., *King Alfred the Great* (Oxford: Oxford University Press, 1995).

Trow, M.J., *Cnut – Emperor of the North* (Stroud, Gloucestershire: Sutton Publishing Limited, 2005).

Whitlock, Ralph, *The Warrior Kings of Saxon England* (New York: Barnes and Noble Books, 1993).

Williams, Hywel, *Emperor of the West – Charlemagne and the Carolingian Empire* (London: Quercus, 2011).

Wilson, Derek, *Charlemagne* (New York, London and Toronto: Doubleday, 2006).

Index